BEST PRACTICES SERIES

# Healthcare Information Systems

## Second Edition

# THE AUERBACH
## BEST PRACTICES SERIES

## AUERBACH PUBLICATIONS

www.auerbach-publications.com
**TO ORDER:** Call: 1-800-272-7737 • Fax: 1-800-374-3401
E-mail: orders@crcpress.com

BEST PRACTICES SERIES

# Healthcare Information Systems

## Second Edition

*Editor*

# Kevin Beaver

CRC Press

Taylor & Francis Group

Boca Raton  London  New York

CRC Press is an imprint of the
Taylor & Francis Group, an **informa** business
AN AUERBACH BOOK

CRC Press
Taylor & Francis Group
6000 Broken Sound Parkway NW, Suite 300
Boca Raton, FL 33487-2742

First issued in paperback 2019

© 2003 by Taylor & Francis Group, LLC
CRC Press is an imprint of Taylor & Francis Group, an Informa business

No claim to original U.S. Government works

ISBN-13: 978-0-8493-1498-8 (hbk)
ISBN-13: 978-0-367-39558-2 (pbk)

Library of Congress Card Number 2002035646

## Library of Congress Cataloging-in-Publication Data

Healthcare information systems / editor, Kevin Beaver.-- 2nd ed.
     p.  cm. -- (Best practices series)
    Includes bibliographical references and index.
    ISBN 0-8493-1498-4 (alk. paper)
    1. Information storage and retrieval systems--Medical care. 2. Medical informatics. I. Beaver, Kevin.

R858 .H384 2002
362.1'0285--dc21                                  2002035646

**Visit the Taylor & Francis Web site at**
**http://www.taylorandfrancis.com**

**and the CRC Press Web site at**
**http://www.crcpress.com**

# Contributors

KEVIN BEAVER, CISSP, *President, Principle Logic LLC, Kennesaw, Georgia*

PATRICIA S. COLLINS, *President, Collins Technology, Inc., Sedalia, Colorado*

DAVID COOK, *Assistant Director, Telemedicine Services, University of Kansas Medical Center, Kansas City, Kansas*

PHILLIP L. DAVIDSON, PH.D., *President and Director, CedarCreek Values Research Center; Dallas, Georgia*

RHONDA DELMATER, *Program Manager, Health Care Programs, Computer Science Innovations, Inc., Melbourne, Florida*

GARY C. DOOLITTLE, M.D., *Associate Professor of Medicine and Director, Telemedicine Services, University of Kansas Medical Center, Kansas City, Kansas*

VICTOR S. DORODNY, M.D., PH.D., *Patient Advocate, Formerly of Superior Consultant Company, Inc., Southfield, Michigan*

STEVE ENDOW, *HIPAA Practice Manager, Ballantyne Inc., Irvine, California*

ROBERT G. GEHLING, *Director of Financial Information Systems, Auburn University, Auburn, Alabama*

MICHAEL L. GIBSON, *Assistant Professor of Management Information Systems, Auburn University, Auburn, Alabama*

GILBERT HELD, *Director, 4-Degree Consulting, Macon, Georgia*

CYNTHIA M. HEMSOTH, *Director of Customer Service, Information Services, Fairview and Lutheran Hospitals, Cleveland Health System, Cleveland, Ohio*

REBECCA HEROLD, CISSP, CISA, FLMI, *Senior Security Consultant, North Central Region, Netigy Corporation, Van Meter, Iowa*

PHILIP J. HOLT, *President, Altis, Inc., Warrenton, Virginia*

DONALD M. JACOBS, M.S., C.P.A., C.D.P., *Inteck, Inc., Denver, Colorado*

ROBERT A. JENDERS, M.D., *Assistant Professor, Department of Medical Informatics, Columbia University, New York, New York*

MERIDA L. JOHNS, PH.D., R.R.A., *Vice President, Education and Certification, American Health Information Management Association, Chicago, Illinois*

CHRIS KAVANAUGH, *President and Chief Executive Officer, Health Card Technologies, Inc. (HCT), Oklahoma City, Oklahoma*

ROSE ANN LAURETO-WARD, *Corporate Vice President, Superior Consultant Company, Inc., Southfield, Michigan*

MARK LEAVITT, M.D., PH.D., *President and Chief Executive Officer, MedicaLogic, Inc., Hillsboro, Oregon*

MICHELE LETTIERE, *Manager, Clinical Data Management, KnowMed Systems, Berkeley, California*

RICHARD J. LINDERMAN, *Manager/Associate, Clinical and Operations Consulting, Premier, Inc., Tampa, Florida*

ANDRES LLANA, JR., *Consultant, Vermont Studies Group, Inc., King of Prussia, Pennsylvania*

YVES A. LUSSIER, M.D., *Assistant Professor, Departments of Medical Informatics and Medicine, Columbia University, New York, New York*

PATRICK MCNEES, PH.D., *Chief Executive Officer, Applied Health Science, Inc., Seattle, Washington*

ENEIDA A. MENDONCA, M.D., PH.D., *Assistant Professor, Department of Medical Informatics, Columbia University, New York, New York*

STEWART S. MILLER, *President and Owner, Executive Information Services, Carlsbad, California*

MARIANNE F. MIRAGIA, R.N., B.S., SNA, *Independent Consultant, Glen Ellyn, Illinois*

J. MARC OVERHAGE, M.D., PH.D., *Senior Investigator, Regenstrief Institute for Health Care and Associate Professor of Medicine, Indiana University School of Medicine, Indianapolis, Indiana*

JIM PETERSON, *Director, Managed Care System Support, Inteck, Inc., Denver, Colorado*

GREGORY W. PIERCE, *Founder, HealthCare Technology Associates, Danville, Pennsylvania*

RAYMOND J. POSCH, *Manager, Education Services, Covia Technologies, Englewood, Colorado*

WULLIANALLUR RAGHUPATHI, PH.D., *Visiting Professor of Information Systems, Communication and Information Systems GBA, Fordham University, New York, New York*

RUSSELL H. SACHS, M.D., *Corporate Regional Vice President, Superior Consultant Company, Southfield, Michigan*

DUANE E. SHARP, *President, SharpTech Associates, Mississauga, Ontario, Canada*

RICK SKINNER, *Chief Information Officer, Providence Health System, Tigard, Oregon*

SCOTT STUEWE, *Managing Director, Clinical Commerce Business Unit, Cerner Corporation, Concord, California*

MICHAEL E. WHITMAN, *Assistant Professor of Management Information Systems, Auburn University, Auburn, Alabama*

# Contents

Contents

*Contents*

# Preface

In the years since this book was originally published in 1999, a great deal has changed with regard to healthcare information systems. Issues such as the impending deadlines of the HIPAA regulations and the demand for improved healthcare have given organizations many things to consider and implement. Other changes, such as the increased reliance on PDAs, electronic medical records, and decision support systems, have allowed, and will allow in the future, greater ease in providing quality healthcare. As much as healthcare organizations depend on information technology to offer services, it must remain a core competency of the organization. Healthcare organizations must now, more than ever, embrace information technology as a standard part of doing business and regularly educate themselves on how to best implement new initiatives. When integrated properly, information technology can provide solutions to the increased demands for quality, efficiency, and improved workflow to help streamline healthcare operations. This book presents insight into the myriad of healthcare information technologies and associated regulatory controls that can be leveraged to assist with administrative processes, clinical decision making, and other complexities that the healthcare industry will face moving forward.

# Section I
# Introduction and Overview

# Chapter 1
# Introduction

*Phillip L. Davidson*

**INFORMATION TECHNOLOGY (IT) IS A VERY COMPLEX TOPIC**

Healthcare is a very complex topic. Put the two topics together into health-care information systems, and it seems that you have irreconcilable differences that are so complicated as to defy resolution.

IT has progressed at fantastic rates over the past 40 years: smaller packages with greater power and more versatility at a lower cost. Healthcare, it might be argued, has not progressed quite as well. While the technical aspect of medicine seems alive and well, the move to manage medicine from the financial perspective (i.e., "managed care") has added huge layers of bureaucratic and administrative functions that beg for IT solutions.

While many in the healthcare community might argue that managed care is the worst thing to happen to medicine since smallpox, the patient may ultimately be the victor here. The need to be able to track patient data for utilization statistics (an absolute must for managed care) is pushing the development of data warehouses and electronic patient medical records. Along with government legislation, such as the Health Plan Employer Data and Information Set (HEDIS) and the Health Insurance Portability and Accountability Act (HIPAA), the move to a "universal" medical record and absolute patient portability seems a reasonable possibility in the not too distant future.

This text does not spend a lot of time on history, but is focused largely on the challenges of the future. The contributors are experts from many fields. Each, whether practicing in healthcare or IT, or working as a consultant or vendor, is acknowledged as a leader in what he or she does. Each has taken a piece of this complex puzzle and brings the reader up to date not only on the technology involved, but also on how that technology interrelates with and affects the healthcare arena.

**LAYOUT OF THE BOOK**

The chapter immediately following this introduction is a survey by Wullianallur Raghupathi of the state of the art of information technology in healthcare. Raghupathi presents a rich and detailed overview of the complexity of the many areas in which we find ourselves involved.

0-8493-1498-4/03/$0.00+$1.50

## INTRODUCTION AND OVERVIEW

After the introduction and overview, the remainder of the text is divided into eight sections. While there is considerable overlap in some areas, the intent is to try and combine closely related topics.

### Section II: Healthcare Systems

Section II deals with the complexity of systems in healthcare. Interface engines are a relatively recent tool that have had a significant impact on simplifying the interconnections between disparate systems. While there are always issues in such an alliance, Scott Stuewe presents in Chapter 3 a clear and understandable picture of this powerful tool. Next, the discussion moves to wireless networks. While this discussion could easily be included in the section on emerging technologies, it is an application currently being widely installed in medical institutions. Gilbert Held's discussion of both wireless application directions in Chapter 4 and how to overcome wireless LAN security vulnerabilities in Chapter 5 provides excellent insight into wireless network technologies.

Chapter 6 focuses on middleware, that elusive group of products that actually allows all of the pieces to talk to each other within an information system. Raymond Posch helps bring definition to this complex topic. However, for those of us who may be running on multiple platforms with more than a hundred separate applications, an understanding of the role of middleware is absolutely essential. Even smaller healthcare organizations might be surprised at the large role played by middleware in their own institutions.

The last chapter in this section presents the perspective on large enterprisewide healthcare groups that try to share resources and the tools they use to do so. The issue of maximizing resources is directed at lowering overall costs while — hopefully — also providing additional services to the patient.

### Section III: Disaster Planning and System Security

The issues of disaster planning and security are some of the most complex and expensive issues that must be dealt with in healthcare systems. Chapter 8 by Merida Johns begins with a discussion of building the infrastructure for business continuity planning. This type of planning is essential in laying out a disaster recovery plan.

Chapter 9 by Cynthia Hemsoth focuses on security policies within healthcare, looking at both the needs to protect patient privacy as well as access to patient information. At the same time, she also covers the wide variety of regulations that impact the area of security within healthcare.

The final chapter of this section discusses a topic that could easily also be placed in the emerging technologies section. The subject of biometrics is addressed in Chapter 10 by Philip Holt. The implications for security applications and the tremendous variety of information presented make this a most intriguing chapter.

## Section IV: Standards and the Regulatory Environment

While it would be impossible in a book of this type to include all the various mandatory standards involved with healthcare, four chapters are included that discuss issues of major impact on healthcare and healthcare systems. Chapter 11 by Marianne Miragia presents the role of the information management standards in the Joint Commission on Accreditation of Healthcare Organizations (JCAHO) accreditation program. This is a complex and multilayered topic that needs to be understood by everyone in our field.

Chapter 12 by Rebecca Herold provides an overview and implementation guidelines for the HIPAA privacy rule. In Chapter 13, Kevin Beaver presents insight into the HIPAA security rule, along with the steps healthcare organizations and other covered entities can take to get started on compliance efforts. Chapter 14 by Steve Endow provides in-depth coverage of the HIPAA transactions and code sets rule, including anticipated issues and practical implementation steps.

## Section V: Quality, Risks, and Costs

Chapter 15, the first in this section, is written by Donald Jacobs and Jim Peterson. They focus on the Health Plan Employer Data and Information Set (HEDIS). HEDIS is discussed here as an important healthcare tool from a quality perspective. This chapter also discusses the National Committee of Quality Assurance (NCQA) and the important role it plays.

The next two chapters cover topics that could just as well fit into the emerging technologies section. Chapter 16 by Marc Overhage provides excellent insight into understanding and implementing computerized physician order entry. Chapter 17 by Eneida Mendonça, Robert Jenders, and Yves Lussier provides an overview of clinical decision support systems as well as an in-depth analysis of the knowledge engineering process.

Risk management is always lurking in the background. In Chapter 18, Patricia Collins addresses this issue. She discusses how risk management is rarely part of the project plan and the belief that risk is not really controllable. She also discusses the implications of such thinking.

Richard Linderman, in Chapter 19, addresses a topic close to all of our hearts — how much does it really cost? Healthcare information systems are notorious for ignoring true costs, frequently only including the costs of hardware, software, and the installation team. Linderman's chapter goes deeper.

### Section VI: EMR and the Data Warehouse

Fewer topics have captured as much of our collective attention as the subject of an electronic medical record (EMR). Known by numerous other initials, having an easily accessible EMR has proven financially rewarding for those institutions that have already put them in place.

In Chapter 20, Mark Leavitt drills down into the details of the EMR. He brings us some of its history and the forces driving its development. Leavitt discusses stakeholders, potential capabilities involved with EMR, and system architecture issues.

Chapter 21 correctly follows and discusses the costs associated with the EMR. Nothing is for free, and Russell Sachs presents a realistic picture of the costs associated with EMR. The information is not anecdotal but focuses on quantitative information from five different organizations.

Closely allied with the issue of the EMR is the issue of the data warehouse. Institutional, regional, and national healthcare data warehouses are widely discussed in today's press and are a significant challenge for healthcare informaticians. In Chapter 22, Michele Lettiere takes us through the steps necessary to build a healthcare data warehouse, including the key players needed to make it a success. The final chapter in this section, Chapter 23 by Duane Sharp, addresses the critical factors involved in constructing a data warehouse. He discusses how to select the right partners, as well as offers insight into the return on investment of such a project.

### Section VII: The Changing Organization

The discussion of information systems within healthcare is not all about hardware and software. People play an increasingly important role even while organizations continue to trim the workforce. Chapter 24 begins with a real-life system implementation and the difficulties in getting the two opposing parties together for a successful implementation. It was not easy, but it is possible.

In Chapter 25, Rick Skinner regales us with a "chicken and egg" story. Seriously, Skinner addresses the issue of whether healthcare information systems ever considered the necessity of being able to change during their early development. He goes on to discuss how the mindset may or may not have changed.

One of the most important recent developments in the changing healthcare informatics field is the increasing presence of the physician informatician. Historically relegated to being the recipient of whatever systems were devised by IT, physicians (in some cases) are stepping up to take charge of the tools that allow them to do their work. An expert in this topic area was asked to address the issue of the chief medical information officer. In Chapter 26, Victor Dorodny shares the breadth of this complex role.

Dorodny discusses in detail the role of the CMIO, both as a people leader and as the director of healthcare information systems. Dorodny also introduces the new term "INFOgration."

Chapter 27 brings us back to reality as Rose Ann Laureto-Ward attacks the difficult issue of outsourcing in healthcare. Healthcare has always been heavily weighted as regards staff ratio to health plan members. Staff is the biggest expense we must deal with. Like many industries, one solution is to contract out services to others who may do it for less and allow you to reduce staff as well. Laureto-Ward covers outsourcing in detail.

In the final chapter in this section (Chapter 28), Patrick McNees brings an international flavor, and he does so while writing from an island in French Polynesia. McNees discusses international systems and how these can incrementally improve the practice of healthcare at the international level.

## Section VIII: Telemedicine and the Internet

Telemedicine is very glamorous in concept. I watched a presentation of a physician teleconferencing with a midwife through a difficult delivery while the physician was several thousand miles away from the patient and midwife. The topic, however, is very complex, but one of those challenges IT loves to tackle.

In Chapter 29, Gary Doolittle and David Cook tackle head-on the issues involved with telemedicine. They discuss the technological and infrastructure issues necessary to make the system work and provide numerous examples of working systems. They also address less mechanistic issues, such as the cost to us as humans when medicine is practiced in this fashion.

Chapter 30, written by Stewart Miller, changes the focus a bit to the Internet. Miller's emphasis is on using the Internet to do business. While not focused specifically on healthcare, Miller does mention that it is a tool healthcare will be considering. This editor's own experience has shown that healthcare institutions are already beginning to use the Internet (or extranet) for communicating with vendors as well as using the Internet for establishing a Web presence for would-be health plan members.

## Section IX: Emerging Technologies

The final section of this text refers to technologies that are making inroads into healthcare. There are other chapters that could easily fit within this section, but the five included here focus on handhelds, voice technology, smart cards, messaging, and imaging.

Chapter 31, by Andres Llana, Jr., covers the latest handheld technologies being used in the healthcare industry. Details on both hardware and emerging applications that the medical practitioner can benefit from are presented, along with real-world examples of how these technologies are being used.

In Chapter 32, Gregory Pierce, an expert in voice recognition technology, provides insight into what is currently available and what is to come. Pierce defines the issues for us and talks in realistic terms about hardware, software, and other technological issues that may or may not make voice technology practical in healthcare.

Chapter 33, by Chris Kavanaugh, considers barcoding, smart cards, and automated patient identification. It is difficult to exactly estimate the costs to healthcare systems created due to incorrect or inaccurate patient identification. Kavanaugh discusses these products, their criticisms, and other possibilities for healthcare.

In Chapter 34, we return to our friend e-mail. Rhonda Delmater presents some unique information on how e-mail is being used in the healthcare industry and she uses a great case study to make her point.

The final chapter, written by Robert Gehling with Michael Whitman, and Michael Gibson, deals with imaging and information management. In this case, imaging is not radiological, but document imaging. Anyone familiar with healthcare knows that document storage is a horrific problem. Document imaging offers a realistic solution.

# Chapter 2

# Information Technology in Healthcare: A Review of Key Applications

*Wullianallur Raghupathi*

The general perception that the use of information technology (IT) in healthcare is ten to fifteen years behind that of other industrial sectors such as banking, manufacturing, and the airline industry is rapidly changing. Healthcare providers, faced with an unprecedented era of competition and managed care, are now exploring the opportunities of IT in improving the quality, while simultaneously reducing the cost, of healthcare.

## INTRODUCTION

From a provider perspective, health maintenance organizations (HMOs), which added millions of members in the past couple of years, need information to analyze the outcomes and costs of different treatment plans. The ease with which this information can be accessed and integrated is, however, contingent upon how IT is used in healthcare. Potential use ranges from routine, stand-alone information systems (IS) to integrated hospital information systems (HIS) to sophisticated artificial intelligence-based clinical decision support systems (CDSS). Today, hospitals and HMOs are demanding a move from stand-alone, fragmented information systems to integrated HIS and CDSS. Modules within an integrated HIS may include an admission/discharge/transfer (ADT) system, scheduling and registration, the electronic patient record (EPR), a laboratory information system (LIS), a pharmacy system, a financial management system for reporting and billing, and even an embedded CDSS or a connecting digital teleradiology system.[1]

As well, in today's information-intensive society, consumers of healthcare need and want to be better informed of their health options and are therefore demanding easy access to relevant health information.[2] In this context, the Internet is playing a crucial role in bridging the gap between providers and consumers of healthcare and in making available the required health information. Even so, the challenge lies in using various forms of IT in a strategic and intelligent manner for supporting effective health-related decision making. In other words, all related parties, including profit and nonprofit healthcare stakeholders, providers (e.g., hospitals), payers (e.g., insurance companies), employers, practitioners, public health officials, educators, and others (e.g., consumers) must meet the challenge of addressing these new expectations.

The healthcare professional as well as the computer professional, then, must be concerned with the twin issues of how these changes would affect them as facilitators of IT applications development and as consumers of healthcare. In the former case, issues of concern include the design and development of applications to capture, organize, store, rationalize, and present health information, the integration of existing and emerging technology, acceptance testing, and others (e.g., issues on standards); while in the latter these include confidentiality, ethics, privacy, security, and user-friendly interfaces.

Accordingly, a revolution is taking place in the healthcare industry, with IT playing an increasingly significant role in its delivery, as shown in Exhibit 1. In 1996, healthcare spending on IT alone was estimated to be between $10 billion and $12 billion.[3] Further exponential growth is thus expected as the industry implements large-scale electronic medical record, provides remote diagnostics via telemedicine, upgrades hospital information systems, sets up intranets and extranets for sharing information among key stakeholders, and uses public networks such as the Internet for distributing health-related information. Along with these drastic changes and the new approach to healthcare, the field of health/medical informatics and telematics has also experienced significant growth in recent years. This chapter identifies and surveys the critical information technologies that are being adopted to provide strategic benefits to the various healthcare constituencies, including hospitals and health maintenance organizations (HMOs).

## THE INTERNET, INTRANETS, AND EXTRANETS

The Internet may be conceived as a complex web of networks.[4] Briefly, Internet services include electronic mailing (e-mail), newsgroups, file transfer protocols (FTP), and other information transfer and exchange

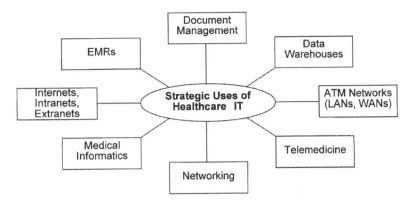

**Exhibit 1. Strategic Uses of IT in Healthcare**

services such as Telnet and World Wide Web (WWW) access using browser software (e.g., Mosaic, Netscape Navigator, and Microsoft Internet Explorer). Presently, this technology has become an important interactive research and communication tool for aiding both medical professionals and health consumers in search of health-related information and knowledge.

Conceivably, there are many more examples of the use of the Internet to provide relevant health information and services. A notable objective here is to provide users such as patients, doctors, hospitals, and others with access to online insurance service data. The benefits of electronic filing of insurance benefits and claims include cutting costs for the company and its network of hospitals, doctors, and corporate clients, as well as improving access and usability for members. It is also believed to cut agency and other labor costs while providing insights to healthcare trends and medical practices.

In one case, Blue Cross/Blue Shield of Massachusetts facilitates access to online insurance services via an Internet WWW server as well as on-site multimedia kiosks equipped with modem connections to the insurance carriers' customer service operations. The Internet services provide users with access to information about particular Blue Cross services as well as healthcare and medical data. The Web site also provides a front end for medical information available at other points on the Internet, such as OncoNet, a repository for data on treatment for cancer patients. The kiosks let users search and print physician and hospital database information as well as peruse information about drugs, treatment alternatives, and Blue Cross services. The kiosks also provide telephony links to customer service representatives and member services. Corporate customers have claimed that being able to provide services and information to users directly, over the Internet and via kiosks, can significantly reduce the cost of in-house insurance support and education.[5,6]

Fundamentally, the intranets and extranets are extensions of the Internet concept in that these technologies take advantage of the same hardware and software used to build, manage, and view Web sites. Unlike the Internet, however, these virtual private networks are protected by security software known as "firewalls" to keep unauthorized users from gaining access. In essence, an intranet is a private computer network built for the purpose of providing Internet-based services only to inside organizational members. Similar to the intranet concept, the extranet extends network access privileges to certain partners, giving them access to selected areas inside the virtual private network, thereby creating a secure customer or vendor network.

To date, both the intranet and extranet technologies have been tapped by a growing number of hospitals for in-house and external sharing of medical information and collaboration. For example, Omni Healthcare was engaged in an intranet development to create a few core general-purpose Web programs that can serve many roles ranging from project management to training. Future efforts planned include an extranet so that the organization's subscribing physicians can check information on patients' insurance eligibility.[7] Other examples of intranet and extranet applications in healthcare organizations are discussed below.

Aetna/U.S. Healthcare of Hartford, Connecticut, uses an Internet-based service that lets members change their primary care providers online.[8] The EZenroll application handles the critical process of adding, dropping, or changing between health plans. Members get access, often through their intranet, with a user name and password supplied by their employer, and the employer also approves the transactions online. Implementation of computerized patient records via this technology has been shown to be generally reliable and secure. Moreover, Web-based transactions provide the potential to cut out some of the inherent inefficiencies of paper forms and provide the needed integration and interoperability among different vendors' biomedical and IT systems.[9]

Promina Health Systems of Atlanta[10] implemented an intranet to facilitate access to human resource (HR) policies, procedure manuals, workflow software, travel vouchers, and phone book calendar of events. The intranet also supports home pages for physician profiles, for continuing education courses, and for policy manuals. The main objective was to streamline departments at nine hospitals and cut down on paper-related costs. In another case, Boston's Beth Israel Deaconess Medical Center has planned to implement an intranet offering doctors easy access to medical records (MR). It is called CareWeb[11] and provides a consolidated view of the legacy systems.

Kaiser Permanente, northwest region,[12] developed an intranet site to communicate with its geographically dispersed customer base. This intranet includes clinical practice guidelines for physicians, scheduling, and important links to medical sites. Group Health, another northwest HMO (GHNW), decided to Web-enable the company's patient accounts data so that users at outlying physician offices would be able to query the data.[13] GHNW has been among the first to recognize the potential of intranet technology to aid in sharing information in a cost-effective, user-friendly manner. The systems were based on a client/server architecture where PC clients accessed data from a database. Previously, the information had been disseminated in paper form. The new intranet was not expected to improve patients' health in any way but it provided a better solution than a costly closed network (i.e., in favor of Web technology).

PacifiCare Health Systems developed COMPASS, an intranet.[14] The system provides easy access to proprietary records such as sales figures and budgets. Executives can then view reports in various formats and import these into spreadsheet applications. Embedded in COMPASS is also a knowledge base created by its HR staff using the *Health Care Encyclopedia* published by HealthWise in Boise, Idaho. This added capability allows users to search healthcare topics for preventative information, referrals, and other sources.

Geisinger Health Care System of Danville, Pennsylvania, the largest rural HMO in the United States, is believed to be rapidly emerging as an industry leader by leveraging IT networks and intranets to reinvent healthcare.[15] Its system concept includes the extension of intranets for use by patients. The company replaced disparate legacy systems with a universal workstation concept that resulted in an Ethernet backbone. The network allows Geisinger to offer innovative services such as Tel-a-Nurse, a system that permits users to call in with medical questions that are answered by nurses who have access to relevant information and expert knowledge through the intranet. A clinical management system was also installed in the network. Geisinger's doctors can then use digital cameras to take pictures of patients' injuries and make these pictures accessible via the intranet. Geisinger's intranet is also being used to support patient education. In this regard, the radiology department, which performs diagnostic procedures such as X-rays, mammograms, and magnetic resonance images (MRIs), has a kiosk placed in its waiting room where patients can click onto the radiology home page and get a list of the various procedures performed in the department.

## ELECTRONIC MEDICAL AND PATIENT RECORD (EMR/EPR)

One of the important trends is the move toward a universal electronic patient record (EPR). It could be defined as electronically stored health information about one individual uniquely identified by an identifier.[16] Essentially, EPR technology entails capturing, storing, retrieving, transmitting, and manipulating patient-specific, healthcare-related data singly and comprehensively, including clinical, administrative, and biographical data. It would eliminate the need for data duplication and reduce the costs of maintaining duplicated databases. The goal, therefore, is to control costs by controlling the quality of care. Its adoption is slow because of practical issues such as complexity, cost, privacy and security, confidentiality, and lack of standards (e.g., for a data dictionary).

As a typical EPR example, Cabarrus Family Medicine in Concord, North Carolina, a practice that has 26,000 patients across four clinics, installed an intranet-enabled EPR.[17] The system frees up time for the patients, residents, physicians, and their secretaries. Until recently, Cabarrus' doctors spent about 40 percent of their time sifting through paper-based patient records. With the intranet, however, physicians and residents will be able to access records quickly using standard browser technologies. In the future, however, we will expect to see healthcare providers implement some aspects of this technology on a wider scale using "smart cards." Some researchers have already advocated access to online information from home or at remote locations via the use of a smart card.[18] The patient could carry this "repository of information" wherever he or she went to receive healthcare.

Intermountain Health Care's (IHC) nine hospitals have an EMR that includes every drug prescribed, symptom observed, and medical test given in a patient's history. Further, it has built a health decision support system (HDSS) that helps physicians deliver the highest quality care at the most effective cost.[19] Also, the 260-bed Health Care International (HCI) Limited medical center at Clydebank, Scotland, has implemented a paperless MR state-of-the-art IS.[20] With this system, patient files are always accessible to doctors at any terminal in the building. HCI's next project is to integrate the doctors' dictation systems with the EMR.

In the case of West Palm Beach Veteran's Administration Medical Center, all MR and associated paperwork have been distilled down to about 200 clinical and 1000 administrative electronic forms which can be accessed from PCs in each screening room and nursing station.[21] These forms let doctors point and click to enter results of any type of examination and issue a prescription. To ensure secured recording of transactions, all entries require an electronic signature. While the employees did require training, the paperless system is believed to have resulted in a physical storage cost saving of about $500,000.

Finally, the Methodist Hospital in Indianapolis set up an EPR system that would store all patient records in a central database.[22] The system would significantly reduce the use of paper and would eventually give departments access to all patient information instead of requiring each department to collect its own. Further, it would allow remote sites to access the patient data. It was estimated that the system would require the hospital to physically hold 25 percent fewer charts than it had in previous years.

## DOCUMENT MANAGEMENT SYSTEM (DMS)

As managed care pressures hospitals and pharmaceutical companies to operate on a tighter budget, healthcare is turning more to technologies such as document management (DM), including document imaging, workflow, electronic forms processing, mass storage, and computer output to laser disk (COLD) to put clinical and financial data online.[23] Hospital CEOs now realize that the only way to survive and grow in a managed care market is to gain significant expertise in managing information, knowledge, and documentation.

Many hospitals need DM to handle the paper-intensive process of collecting and filing patient information. For example, the sheer volume of patient care documentation convinced the IS department at Florida Hospital to choose a combination of document imaging and optical storage technology to image-enable more than 2000 business processes encountered routinely in admissions, laboratory tests, insurance claims, general ledger, and accounting. This data is to be logged in to a central repository. The overall purpose of the project was to achieve two goals: (1) to provide better customer service, and (2) to augment the existing HIS. Thus, in addition to character-based data, the upgraded HIS will be able to capture, store, and manipulate documents and other data types such as video and photos. Each individual record would then contain the patient's clinical and financial information as well as a historical account of each of the patient's encounters at the hospital.

The San Jose Medical Center, California, faced a similar challenge; that is, how it could access MR speedily and make record management more efficient. The solution was to use DM software, a relational database, and imaging equipment on a local area network (LAN). The results have been strategic and dramatic: overall staff has been reduced and the hospital was able to collect additional revenues by handling external record requests.[24]

In another example, St. Vincent's Hospital, Birmingham, Alabama, was able to reduce patient registration time, reduce insurance verification time, eliminate some business office staff, increase registrations, sort all patients' records and insurance information online, and reduce delayed payments into accounts receivable via the installation of an image-based client/server system.[25] Essentially, the system converted paper-based records into electronic images. This data, in turn, was merged with data from a mainframe-based HIS and other departmental laboratory and pharmacy systems to form a comprehensive EPR.

Finally, the field nurses at St. Mary's Medical Center, a home healthcare provider in Long Beach, California, no longer spend hours at company headquarters managing large numbers of patient records.[26] The project goal was to cut down the overwhelming paper load. The use of notebook computers and a customized application has freed these nurses from attending to routine administrative chores to visiting more patients. Further, the strategic use of these technologies has also increased revenues by streamlining the healthcare provider's documentation process. By employing notebooks and customizable form templates in DocPlus application, these nurses can update all patient and insurance information electronically, eliminating the need to hand-write several new forms with each visit. This eventually led to faster filing of insurance documents, which in turn translated into quicker payments. Nurses were thus enabled to visit about 600 additional patients per month and revenues have also increased.

## DATA WAREHOUSES

Data warehousing refers to "setting up large stores of data for strategic decision-support analysis."[27] The growth of managed healthcare has hospitals and other medical organizations searching for quick and affordable ways to tap into their information banks of detailed patient records. Data warehouses are becoming crucial as the industry moves from a revenue-based business model to one focused on cost-outcomes information management.

Johnson Medical Center in Johnson City, Tennessee, needed a data warehouse for studying historical records of patient treatments and spotting trends or anomalies.[28] Its aim was to help create report cards about physicians, thereby measuring the cost of each doctor's services at the hospital in terms of the types of treatments they use, the time they spend with their patient, and other factors. Also, the data gathered could be used to analyze the cost of each treatment *vis-à-vis* the amount of money paid for by health insurers. This technology, then, permits the comparison of information among the various departments to show which operations are less or more profitable.

Aetna U.S. Healthcare is building a data warehouse.[29] It is envisaged that the data warehouse will collect data such as medical claims, laboratory test results, hospital discharge data, and demographic information from three of Aetna's insurance lines. As noted previously, managed care is about managing data and information well so as to determine what works in improving health outcomes without correspondingly increasing the cost of healthcare. In this sense, analysts can use the data warehouse to extract information to study trends related to the cost and use of medical services. Also, one could use it to build a medical history of enrollees by linking records of medical claims across its insurance products. In fact, users can request to look at standard reports or build their own. Another data warehouse project supported by Aetna identifies members who have any of 65 chronic diseases and assigns them to a risk category based on the severity of their illness. Based on this information, Aetna can encourage affected enrollees to get ongoing outpatient healthcare to keep their illnesses in check.

More recently, HIC, the Australian federal agency that processes all medical claims, uses data mining software to sift through seemingly unrelated data to discover subtle patterns that can be used to make strategic business decisions.[30] Given the breadth of its transactions, HIC is a classic example of a company that could benefit from the data warehouse technology. The staff traditionally relied on paper reports to ensure medical services were appropriately prescribed and billed. But with HIC conducting more than 300 million transactions and paying out $8 billion to physicians and hospitals each year, the ability to keep tabs on everything was almost impossible. By using various data mining tools, HIC's staff can now track areas never before possible. For example, the different ordering habits of doctors in similar clinical situations can be analyzed in order to establish best practices for various treatments. However, the key challenge in these data mining projects is often to decide what information to tap and to make sure that the information tapped is reliable and valid.

Last but not the least, the U.S. Department of Defense plans to deploy what officials say is the largest known medical data warehouse.[31] Since 1995, it began converting its fixed-cost healthcare system to a managed care model to lower costs and increase patient care for active military personnel, retirees, and their dependents. The managed care model is currently supported by a $450 million medical data warehouse project called Computerized Executive Information System (CEIS). The project has eliminated 14 redundant systems at an estimated saving of $50 million per year.

## NETWORKING AND ATM NETWORKS

The impact of all of the technologies surveyed so far can be augmented strategically through electronic and digital networking. This is the logical next step for health services to be delivered in the coming years. Understanding and maturing this technology will therefore be critical, especially from the perspective of managed care as multi-provider organizations vie to provide integrated delivery of quality health services along the entire continuum of care.

Orlando Regional Healthcare System has begun to build an integrated delivery network (IDN), a form of one-stop shopping for all types of healthcare.[32] This is one response to an industry that has become cost and marketing conscious. The other notion is that of virtual healthcare;

that is, the formation of networks of coordinating partners where each provider does what it does best. As the information needs are often similar in many cases, providers are investing heavily in distributed, client/server networks and object-oriented technology to deliver the necessary links. Within a health organizational perspective, the closest thing to a health network is the electronic data interchange (EDI) that hospitals conduct internally among admissions, clinical, and accounting departments, as well as externally with insurers. In some cases, hospitals have provided admitting physicians with online terminal-based access to patient records. Another alternative, according to Steven Mortimer of HIP Health Plan of New Jersey, is to build a system that follows patients through each encounter with a medical professional.

From a community-based health services perspective, a few independent healthcare organizations have grouped together to build a Community Health Information Network (CHIN).[32] In Dayton, Ohio, for example, the Greater Dayton Area Hospital Association (GDAHA) is building links to all 20 hospitals and approximately 2400 independent physicians within a nine-county region, covering a population of about 1.4 million people. Anthem, the Southwest Ohio Blue Cross plan, the dominant insurer, will also be connected to the CHIN. A demonstration project involving a patient encounter record system shared among seven competing hospitals was positively supported. Initially, the goal was to provide patient demographics, claims eligibility, a provider directory, and clinical results. By the year 2000 the system was expected to track encounters, imaging services, and patient status by physician, and to have full capabilities to link to pharmacies and long-term care facilities. In this sense, the network will resemble an intranet in that it will use a common Web browser front end to access a master patient index.

Shands Hospital at the University of Florida built patient care systems on the backbone of a large database.[33] This helped streamline large amounts of information without having to replace its paper-based MR. The hospital is building core patient systems and an HDSS component on top of a single Oracle relational database management system (RDBMS). In a single production instance of Oracle, it is expected that everything from clinical data, patient data, and cost accounting data to records of how patients move throughout the hospital and its multitude of clinics will be integrated. Client/server prototypes will be in place for the three most critical applications: patient registration and tracking, clinic appointment scheduling, and the online outpatient MR. A patient management system will also be included to capture data about referring physicians inside and outside the health center and to track multiple caregivers in multiple roles. Coordination of services will thus translate into money saved. The clinic appointment system will address staff downtime by coordinating separate calendars for several clinics and services. The online EPR will provide doctors with the most up-to-date information without having to keep separate charts on their patients.

More recently, a network-based clinical information system (CIS) installed at the Lutheran Hospital, La Crosse, Wisconsin, has also produced evidence of productivity gains among key intensive care unit (ICU) staff.[34] Not only did the patients receive better care in that the new system has enabled ICU nurses to spend considerably more time caring for patients, but it has also improved the accuracy of data collected, reduced overtime wages, and trimmed one full-time position from ICU nursing staff.

At this point, we refocus the discussion to an associated network technology designed for handling multimedia applications without degradation, the asynchronous transfer mode (ATM) technology. ATM technology offers a vision of the ultimate integrated-services network. Potentially, the technology is characterized by (1) the provision of unlimited bandwidth on demand (currently up to 2.5 Gbps); (2) the integration of data, voice, and video over one cost-effective infrastructure; and (3) the seamless interconnectivity of data systems between the local area and the wide area.[35] Increasingly, ATM is being deployed in networks supporting bandwidth-intensive applications with well-defined quality of service. It is an ideal service for integrated telemedicine because of: (1) the transmission speeds it can support, and (2) its ability to integrate multiple traffic streams. In this sense, radiology and teleradiology are among the applications that can benefit greatly from the broad bandwidth of ATM technology. Chicago's Rush-Presbyterian/St. Luke's Medical Center, for example, is developing an ATM backbone network for its radiology department.[36] St. Paul's Hospital, a teaching hospital at the University of British Columbia, Vancouver, is also using an ATM-backbone network to connect its pulmonary research laboratory with doctors outside the hospital.[37] The network allows the two groups to compare test results and diagnose patients quicker. For example, its application speeds up the process of diagnosing patients suffering from lung disease. In the future, it is envisaged that researchers in the pulmonary research laboratory and doctors can view slides and x-rays, trade data, and compare findings online.

Currently, doctors at Duke University Medical Center can sit down in front of their computers and call up 10-MB x-ray images in 1.5 seconds. As well, Hershey Medical Center in Hershey, Pennsylvania, has developed a medical conferencing application that integrates physician-to-physician videoconferencing, patient charts, laboratory results, and radiology images on a single computer screen. For Pro Medica Health Systems, Inc., an ATM network is expected to help the Toledo Hospital integrate voice, data, and imaging traffic over clinical workstations. Also, this network supports a repository storing more than 700,000 patient records to give 2200 physicians, nurses, and other staff access to patient data.[38]

An equally important emerging technology is Gigabit Ethernet. Its benefits can be tied to its Ethernet legacy. Gigabit Ethernet's high bandwidth capabilities will alleviate traffic congestion on large, fast Ethernet networks as well as enable ultra-high-speed data transfers. Lowell General Hospital's move to Gigabit Ethernet could mark a trend in the way the healthcare industry views advanced LAN technologies. While there still is a lot of old technology being used in hospitals, the push for newer and more strategic network applications is inevitable as these institutions deploy some of the healthcare industry's most bandwidth-intensive applications (e.g., medical imaging, teleradiology, and desktop video). Indeed, for hospitals to extend computer systems to the bedside effectively, a robust network infrastructure must be in place. Lowell General's WWW site includes interactive heart tests; electronic mail links to doctors for medical queries; and SurgeryCam, an application providing a surgeon's eye view of a surgical procedure.[39]

## HEALTH/MEDICAL INFORMATICS AND TELEMATICS

Health informatics (including medical telematics) is the field that concerns itself with "the cognitive, information processing, and communication tasks of medical practice, education, and research, including the information science and technology to support those tasks."[40] More broadly speaking, its emphasis is on clinical and biomedical applications of the various technologies we have surveyed with the added possibility of integrating these clinical components either among themselves or to more administrative-type HIS. In this regard, the field of health/medical informatics and telematics has evolved very rapidly over the past several years.

At the clinical level, applications utilizing artificial intelligence (AI), neural network (NN), and fuzzy logic techniques are being developed to provide clinical decision support to physicians. It deals primarily with information used in medical decision making. The primary objective in this category of IT is to assist physicians and other medical experts in diagnosis and treatment. Tan with Sheps[41] use the "term health decision support systems" (HDSS) (more specifically, clinical decision support systems and expert systems — CDSS/ES) to characterize many of these applications. Accordingly, our review on health/medical informatics will focus first on general HDSS and CDSS applications, followed by more specific ES applications and more integrated HDSS-ES applications. As for health telematics, we will focus chiefly on one of its key application; that is, telemedicine.

An example of a CDSS is an interactive videodisk system that helps enter personal health data to weigh the pros and cons, for example, of surgery. Researchers say that such software promotes shared decision making and holds the promise of improved quality of care without increasing costs. Dr. Richard Foster, medical director of a 40,000-member HMO operated by

South Carolina Blue Cross/Blue Shield, is buying the equipment. Patients and doctors who tried it found that it enhanced the physician–patient relationship. Others trying similar programs include Massachusetts General Hospital in Boston; Dartmouth Hitchcock Medical Center in Hanover, New Hampshire; Veterans Administration; as well as several regional Kaiser Permanente HMOs and others.[42] In yet another example, Tufts Associated Health Plan, Inc., Waltham, Massachusetts, installed a homegrown PC-based HDSS to access data more efficiently.[43]

The Lahey Clinic, Burlington, Massachusetts, faced several problems. Hospital statistics were maintained as hard copies and it was difficult to disseminate this information to department heads and managed care organizations. As a result, managed care organizations were reluctant to refer their patients and physicians to Lahey because of its lack of current information on cost and clinical performance. The clinic also risked losing patients to larger hospitals. To overcome these problems, Lahey installed HealthShare One, an HDSS. Not only did the HDSS help Lahey improve on-line access to key operational data while cutting costs, but it also enables Lahey to tell potential patients how well it is performing on certain medical procedures compared with its competitors. The data warehouse embedded in the HDSS further permitted Lahey's management to do queries and perform complex comparative cost analysis. Also, it was used to improve internal efficiencies by supplying information to specific departments. In summary, the HDSS was able to cut costs, attract new business, and help improve Lahey's quality of service.[44] At Boston-based Faulkner Hospital, users also rely on HealthShare One to compare the strengths of their hospital with others in the area. The HDSS aids the users in better understanding the competitive strengths for the individual services they provide, such as acute medical and surgical procedures, addiction recovery, and psychiatric care. One comparative function, for example, involves analyzing the length of patient stays at other hospitals.[45]

In the area of ES applications, the development of a computerized system for more accurate monitoring of the fetal heart rate during the human birthing process was reported.[46] The data is fed into a rule-based ES and an NN to classify the situation as normal, stressed, indeterminate, or ominous. In another ES example, a computerized voice response system provides medical advice for 100 common ailments. The advice, available via telephone 24 hours per day, is based on a caller's self-reported symptoms, consultation history, and the latest medical research. The system also tracks the improvement or deterioration of the patient's condition during follow-up calls.[47]

In St. Paul, Minneapolis, an ES that spots irregularities in doctors' bills is saving Fort's Benefits Insurance Company/Woodbury an estimated $540,000 a year.[48] In the case of LDS Hospital at Salt Lake City, an automated patient information system is used to detect adverse drug events such as allergies, unpredicted drug interactions, and dosage problems. The ES alerts the staff to such possible occurrences and is purported to identify adverse drug events 60 times better than did practitioners.

Patient care management and patient education is increasing the demand for integrated HDSS and ES among hospitals, HMOs, and other agencies. A new strategy against escalating healthcare costs is disease management. The Henry Ford Health System in Detroit and Sentara Health system in Norfolk, Virginia, keep patients with chronic illnesses such as asthma or diabetes out of the hospital and the emergency room by teaching them how to prevent these attacks. Both health systems are developing real-time client/server ES to prompt caregivers to follow standard guidelines as they enter orders for care, such as prescriptions or lab tests, into a clinical system. The prompts will be based on standard practice guidelines that are developed through ongoing analysis of medical outcome and cost data. Healthcare providers need online advice about the best treatment; hospitals need to track and analyze the results of each course of treatment to come up with these guidelines.[49]

We now turn to telemedicine, a key area of health telematics. Here, the basic concept is to geographically connect dispersed healthcare facilities via video and telecommunication. More simply, telemedicine is the use of digital networks to perform long-distance diagnoses of diseases and disorders. One current use of this technology is to access tele-imaging patient records or films (e.g., MRI) to perform remote clinical diagnoses and surgeries. Lower healthcare costs and online access to top medical experts are the two major benefits of this technology. Further possibilities include medical education and intercontinental healthcare.

Pittsburgh's Allegheny Health Education and Research Foundations is in the middle of a five-year pilot program to develop high-speed, digital multimedia networks that link major healthcare and teaching institutions throughout Pennsylvania. NeuroLink, the first phase of the project, has been in operation for more than a year. Dr. Julian Bailes, a hospital neurosurgeon, has used NeuroLink to diagnose more than 100 patients remotely and saved more than $500,000 in transportation costs. Institutions share CAT scans, MRI, x-rays, and other medical data. Brain surgeons in Pittsburgh will be able to interact with medical students in Philadelphia while conducting brain surgery. The network was further extended to the Medical Consultation Center in Cairo, a clinic operated by an Egyptian neurosurgeon Dr. Amr Mansy.[50]

The telemedicine system at Pathway Health Network, Massachusetts, uses videoconferencing systems for urban medicine. This has enabled linking the network of hospitals. In the short term, this has helped built strong physician-to-physician relationships across the hospitals. In the longer term, it is anticipated that the network system will improve patient care delivery. The system is used primarily for consultations among physicians.[51] In another example, the Texas Department of Information Resources expects to save 50 percent annually by running a two-way, statewide video network to deliver medical help and educational programming to all corners of the state. One purpose of the video network, called Vidnet, is to eliminate the high cost of transporting prison inmates hundreds of miles to state health centers for medical care. With Vidnet, a physician's assistant at a prison can transmit images to, and confer with, a doctor at the University of Texas medical branch, thereby speeding postoperation follow-up. Through easy and inexpensive remote access capabilities, Vidnet is believed to have extended telemedicine to a large population.[52]

Finally, Indian River Memorial Hospital in Vero Beach, Florida, needed high bandwidth capacity for telemedicine applications.[53] It opted for an ATM backbone with switched Ethernet. ATM packages voice, video, and data traffic into 53-byte cells switchable at very high speeds. It also enables diverse traffic to travel over the same network infrastructure so that it provided Indian River the high-volume, heterogeneous networks needed to support telemedicine activities. The scalability also makes ATM an attractive technology for hospitals expecting mixed high-bandwidth traffic and requiring meshed connectivity. These features would be typical of hospital wide area networks (WAN) carrying large medical record files, telemedicine video, and radiological image traffic. Indian River's clinicians and administrative staff can now access a surgical scheduling system, physician billing software, and the Internet.

## CONCLUSION

The healthcare industry is finally viewing IT as a fundamental asset in providing efficient health-related information services and cost-effective decision support on demand, in managing rising cost and rapid change in organizational needs, in improving the quality of health services and patient care, and in fighting illness while promoting wellness. Instead of relying on handwritten notes buried in poorly organized paper files, doctors, nurses, and other healthcare providers are now turning to different forms of advanced IT such as EMR, DM, and data warehouses; point-of-care HDSS applications; distributed networks; and telematics to provide them with current and useful information needed for quality patient care.

More generally, this growth in IT innovations is fueled by drastic changes in the healthcare industry and its approach to healthcare. The various strategic IT applications we have surveyed so far, including electronic systems for claims processing,[54] imaging systems to scan documents as part of the move toward a paperless environment,[55] multimedia technology incorporating data, voices, and images for the education and training of physicians, nurses, and patients,[5] speech recognition in transcription,[56] robots in surgery,[57] kiosks for presenting health information to consumers and employees,[5] and other integrated IT applications, have indicated how far we have progressed in the last few years in the applied field of healthcare computing.

We believe that the next breakthroughs will be in areas of integrated systems, intelligent networks, and robotics. Indeed, the ability to integrate clinical and administrative information about patients means that doctors can provide better care at lower costs. For example, integrated HDSS can provide health professionals in a distributed clinical setting with an online, real-time history of patients included in a master patient index database. These systems will also let physicians and hospital management track and analyze patient care history, test results, and cost information. Typically, such applications combine data warehouse, electronic data entry, messaging, and graphic user interface (GUI) tools.[58] Brigham and Women's, an integrated HDSS pioneer, implemented the Eclipsys Sunrise application, a Web-based suite of rules-oriented applications. The hospital estimates it saves $5 million to $10 million annually. Vendors include Eclipsys, Pharmaceutical Care Network, and ThinkMed.

Again, the strategic uses of intelligent networks to automate patient record-keeping, provide integrated patient care, timely decision support, and remote consultation, as well as expert knowledge in specific domain areas together promise not only to lower the high costs of treating complex case-mix groupings but also improve the quality of care delivered. Thus, the most enlightened healthcare organizations are now discovering that higher quality care can in fact lead to lower costs.[59] Beth Israel Medical Center, for example, realized that if it were to succeed in the highly competitive deregulated healthcare industry, it must network intelligently its radiology system by building an ATM-based medical imaging system and connecting it to a laboratory in which robots process tests. The ATM-based network will then let the hospital extend its services to St. Luke's-Roosevelt Hospital Center. The network was key to the merger, especially in speeding bandwidth-intensive processes such as the new radiology system.

In the area of robotics and as a further example of the promise of robots, Automated Healthcare, Inc., a task automation technology provider to the healthcare industry, has developed a robot designed to distribute patient medications within hospitals. The robot is called the Automated Pharmacy Station (APS), a three-axis robot with a gripper arm that picks up patients' medications from storage cells and delivers them to bar-coded patient bins. Hospital technicians then bring the bins to the nursing floors where nurses administer the medications to the patients. The robots will help hospitals substantially reduce, if not completely eliminate, the human error rate of medication distribution. The robot keeps track of dispensed drugs through an intelligent inventory control system. In addition, APS calculates the shortest paths for medication pickup and delivery. APS has been in use at Pittsburgh's St. Claire's Hospital, a 350-bed acute care facility.[60]

Altogether, while various strategic uses of IT can facilitate easy and rapid access to critical health information and knowledge for providers and consumers alike to support all kinds of administrative and clinical decisions, it also opens up vulnerabilities. The overall prospect of storing health information in electronic form, for example, raises concerns about standards, ethics, patient privacy, data confidentiality, and security. Unless proper controls, procedures, and policies are in place, these IT innovations will also invite the acquisition of data by unauthorized users and even the misuse of information by authorized users. In fact, if the concerns are not sufficiently addressed, they can discourage the healthcare industry from exploiting IT and make healthcare consumers hesitate to share information. Hence, IT application development and use must be done in the midst of maintaining confidentiality, privacy, and security. Furthermore, medical information standards for the nomenclature, coding, and structure must be developed. These must be universally accepted to accomplish uniformity of definition and meaning of terminology. Standards for electronic signatures, especially for the validation of physicians' prescriptions, in the era of the Internet must be discussed. These are exciting times for the healthcare industry and IT. The strategic integration of the two will revolutionize healthcare delivery in the decades ahead while opening up new areas for applications and research.

**REFERENCES**

1. Raghupathi, W. 1997. "Health care information system," *Communications of the ACM,* 40(8): 81–82.
2. Ferguson, T. 1996. "Consumer health informatics," *Healthcare Forum Journal,* 38(1): 28–32.
3. Alter, A. E. 1993. "CIOs brace for health care reform," *Computerworld,* October 25: 28.
4. Stull, A. T. 1997. *On the Internet: A Student's Guide.* Upper Saddle River, NJ: Prentice Hall.
5. Schroeder, E. 1995. "Health-care industry gets the multimedia treatment," *PCWeek,* May 15: 114.
6. Ouellette, T. 1995. "Health-care at your fingertips: Blue Cross/Blue Shield of Massachusetts unveils health care ATMs," *Computerworld,* May 29: 42.
7. Gallaway, E. 1997. "Making intranets a one-person job," *PCWeek,* October 20: 29–36.
8. Carr, D. F. 1997. "Aetna brings health forms to customers via intranets," *WebWeek,* December 8: 29.
9. Girishankar, S. 1998. "IT Rx: trim costs, move medicine to Internet," *InternetWeek,* March 2: 9.
10. Rice, V. 1996. "Health group gets intranet treatment," *PCWeek,* May 6: 51–54.
11. Waltner, C. 1997. "Private web," *Information Week,* June 23: 65–70.
12. Mullich, J. 1996. "An obvious prescription," *PCWeek,* July 1: 42.
13. Paul, L. G. 1997. "Closing the door on proprietary nets," *PCWeek,* August 4: 27–34.
14. Watt, P. 1998. "PacifiCare takes the plunge," *Network World,* August: 9–12.
15. Mullich, J. 1997. "Intranet gives HMO a shot in the arm," *PCWeek,* February 3: 27–34.

16. Raghupathi, W. 1997. "Towards a global healthcare system," *Siliconindia,* October: 28–30.
17. Hoffman, T. 1997. "Health care groups struggle with the web," *Computerworld,* February 24: 17.
18. Pickover, C. A. (Ed.). 1995. *Future Health: Computers and Medicine in the Twenty-First Century.* New York: St. Matin's Press.
19. Garner, R. 1995. "A medical moonshot?" *Computerworld,* April 10: 78–80.
20. Betts, M. 1994. "Scottish hospital unwraps paperless system," *Computerworld,* July 18.
21. Ouellette, T. 1995. "Hospital takes paperless route," *Computerworld,* September 4.
22. Mohan, S. 1994. "Hospital goes paperless," *Computerworld,* August 22: 62.
23. Hoffman, T. 1996. "Document management helps medicine go down," *Computerworld,* June 10: 24.
24. Nash, J. 1992. "Imaging heals hospital's sick file system," *Computerworld,* March 2: 43.
25. King, J. 1995. "Image systems cures hospital records ills," *Computerworld,* August 7: 59.
26. Dicarlo, L. 1995. "Notebook PCs solve health-care providers document ills," *PCWeek,* August 7: 37.
27. Goldberg, M. 1996. "Data warehouse fills CVS prescription," *Computerworld,* April 1: 77.
28. Waltner, C. 1997. "Specialized warehouses cut medical center costs," *Information Week,* November 3: 104.
29. Wilson, L. 1998. "Warehouse care: keep costs healthy," *Computerworld,* April 6: 65–68.
30. Crowley, A. 1996. "Pattern matching," *PCWeek,* June 3: E1–E14.
31. Hamblen, M. 1998. "Pentagon to deploy huge medical data warehouse," *Computerworld,* August 3: 25.
32. Baer, T. 1996. "Tales from the network," *Computerworld Healthcare Journal,* October: H8–H16.
33. Johnson, M. 1993. "Hospital admits RDBMS," *Computerworld,* March 22: 52.
34. Molloy, M. 1991. "Hospital network reduces paperwork for ICU nurses," *Network World,* December 23: 15.
35. Wigand, R., Picot, A., and Reichwald, R. 1997. *Information, Organization and Management: Expanding Markets and Corporate Boundaries.* Chichester: John Wiley & Sons.
36. Wienberg, N. 1995. "Hospitals call ATM good medicine," *Computerworld,* December 4: 20.
37. Network World Canada. 1995. "ATM speeds Vancouver hospital's diagnoses," *Computerworld,* June 12: 68.
38. Hoffman, T. 1996. "Managed care undergoes networking transfusion," *Computerworld,* March 11: 28.
39. Wallace, B. 1997. "Hospital goes for gigabit," *Computerworld,* April 7: 55.
40. Greenes, R. A. and Shortliffe, E. H. 1990. "Medical Informatics — An emerging academic discipline and institutional priority," *JAMA,* 263(8): 1114.
41. Tan, J. K. with Sheps, S. 1998. *Health Decision Support Systems,* Gaithersburg, MD: Aspen Publishers, Inc.
42. Freudenheim, M. 1992. "Software helps patients make crucial choices," *New York Times,* October 14: C8.
43. Nash, K. S. 1994. "Tufts implants decision support system — Red Brickís databases improve data access for the HMO," *Computerworld,* August 1: 60.
44. Neil, S. 1998. "Clinic prognosis: IS on mend," *PCWeek,* July 13: 49–57.
45. Dash, J. 1998. "Decision support practices," *Software Magazine,* March: 24.
46. "Patent watch," *Computerworld,* February 24 (1997): 110.
47. "Patent watch," *Computerworld,* February 9 (1998): 102.
48. Margolis, N. and Booker, E. 1992. "Taming the health care cost monster," *Computerworld,* August 3: 14.
49. Wilson, L. 1995. "Disease management comes to IS," *Computerworld,* November 27: 92.
50. Baer, T. 1996. "The info highway to Wellville," *Computerworld,* February 5: 73.
51. Garner, R. 1996. "Prescription for urban ills," *Computerworld,* October: H6.
52. Wallace, B. 1996. "Savings in focus," *Computerworld,* May 27: 57.
53. Watson, S. 1996. "ATM revs up hospital network," *Computerworld Healthcare Journal,* October: H5.
54. Hoffman, T. 1995. "HMO cures service, claims processing ills," *Computerworld,* September 9: 75–76.
55. Ouellette, T. 1995. "Imaging software follows doctors' orders," *Computerworld,* June 26: 24.
56. http://voicerecognition.com/physicians/article_697.html.
57. Koprowski, G. 1998. "Robots set to invade operating rooms," *Wired News,* January 5.

58. Fryer, B. 1998. "Decision support aiding health care," *Information Week*, June 15: 159–64.
59. Wallace, B. 1997. "Spinal tap heals hospital — backbone technology delivers competitive edge," *Computerworld*, May 5: 51, 57.
60. Hoffman, T. 1993. "Hospital robots have the RX for efficiency," *Computerworld,* January 11: 69–72.

# Section II
# Healthcare Systems

# Chapter 3
# Interface Tools for Healthcare Information Technology

*Scott Stuewe*

Through the 1980s and 1990s, healthcare information technology (HIT) systems moved from stand-alone implementations focused on the needs of a single hospital unit or department to complex inter-networked solutions. Most health systems acquired these systems over many years, and as a result, integration was often achieved through a hodge-podge of poorly understood custom interfaces between systems maintained by the hospital's information technology organization. Some trends in the HIT business are listed in Exhibit 1.

Closely examine the trend toward integrated healthcare information systems. This timeline progresses from the beginning of healthcare computing through the emergence of the interface engine as a product.

The late 1960s and 1970s → computer time-share and remote computing option (RCO) for financial applications begins healthcare automation → those applications that are in place on-site are built by the information systems department of the large hospital → only a few suppliers of systems

The early 1980s → applications integration begins by pulling financials together with the hospital intake process → the "hospital information system" (HIS) emerges → some large health systems choose to build their own "home-grown" systems → these organizations gain interface competency

The mid-1980s → process automation within departments gains favor → niche suppliers provide applications for clinical laboratory, blood-banking, radiology, pharmacy, dietary, and other depart-

0-8493-1498-4/03/$0.00+$1.50
© 2003 by CRC Press LLC

## Exhibit 1. Healthcare IT Business Trends

Leading to the need for specialized tools for connecting systems:

| | | |
|---|---|---|
| •Stand-alone departmental systems | Æ | •The need for integrated solutions |
| •Systems focused on financial process | Æ | •Systems focused on clinical process |
| •The age of the community hospital, cost-based reimbursement, and stand-alone systems — slow pace of consolidation | Æ | •The rise of the "integrated delivery network" — capitation and falling government reimbursement causes rapid consolidation of hospitals with existing legacy systems |

Key enablers, making the new tools possible:

| | | |
|---|---|---|
| •Most interfacing done in custom, mutually agreed upon formats | Æ | •Standards for message format become more complete and ubiquitous |
| •No universally accepted communication protocol | Æ | •TCP/IP becomes the standard for network communication |

mental systems → these are interfaced to the legacy HIS and "home-grown" systems → information systems suppliers gain interface competency

The late 1980s → the rise of the clinical information system vision → orders are added to the HIS, home-grown systems get clinical components, and new players emerge with one-architecture integration as a strategy

The early 1990s → The availability of integrated systems for clinical process "off-the-shelf" improves the clarity of integration mission → "best of breed" emerges as a strategy for health systems that are seeking to preserve their investments in legacy systems while automating processes a department at a time

The mid 1990s → the interface engine emerges as a product to support the integration of applications built and bought; best-of-breed departmental systems become harder to manage with the rapid consolidation of health systems

The late 1990s → COBOL and C programmers are in short supply as the healthcare industry struggles to cope with the Year 2000 issue

The move toward integrated information systems ironically has driven more, not less interfacing. The desire to "simulate" an integrated system through interfaces was born in the "best-of-breed" strategy. "Best-of-breed" began to wane as a strategy when health system consolidation made it impossible to achieve. Strategic plans for moving the business of healthcare forward looked like messy spider webs. The interface engine was to play a role in making pictures like the one displayed in Exhibit 2 somewhat simpler.

By the middle of the 1990s, the time required to specify, design, code, and test an interface between two systems frequently exceeds the period that interface would be in production in its original form. At the same time,

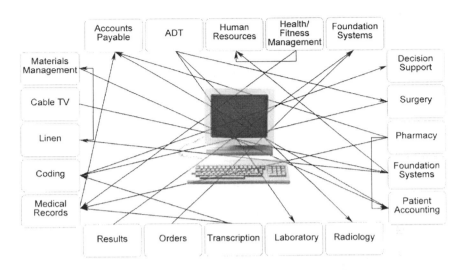

**Exhibit 2. Complex System with Complex Interfaces**

resources required to do traditional, custom interface work are increasingly hard to find. Projects stall behind missed interfacing milestones. New tools are needed.

## INTERFACING BASICS: COMMON VOCABULARY

Before embarking on a technical review of interface engine technology, a review of some basic terminology is wise.

*Listener*: computer program awaiting a connection from an outside source across a network

*Initiator*: computer program that creates a connection with another across a network

*Message*: data organized in a format agreed upon by the sender and receiver and communicated over the network

*Transport*: the protocol or standard of communication that carries the message

*Feed*: source of information in the form of messages

*Trigger-event*: business or workflow activity within a computer system that results in a message being sent

*Format*: organization of message, including order and length of fields, meaning or use of data within fields, and special characters (delimiters) used to separate fields

*Envelope*: special characters that define the beginning and ending of (or otherwise encapsulate) messages; the envelope may also include information about the source and destination of the message

33

*Check-digit*: a series of bytes used by the listener/receiver to validate that the message is complete and as accurate as it was when it was sent; usually sent as a part of the envelope

*Acknowledgment* or *ACK*: a message sent by the listener/receiver in response to a message; the ACK notifies the sender that the message was received and appears to be correct

*Non-acknowledgment* or *NACK*: a message sent by the listener/receiver in response to a message; the NACK notifies the sender that the message or envelope is incorrect in some way, and frequently includes a reason for the non-acknowledgment

*Store-and-forward*: the primary mission of most interface engines, to accept messages, store them as received, and forward them to their destination in a new format or protocol

## DEFINING AN INTERFACE ENGINE

Interface engines, like most products, are marketed with a mind toward differentiation, even in cases where products are not fundamentally very different. The marketing language used to describe interface engine products frequently includes proprietary names for generically available commodity services. Any good definition includes attributes — in this case, the generic services that the product can provide. The *services* provided by any good interface engine include the following:

- Communications protocol harmonization: accepting a message in one transport protocol (TCP/IP) and forwarding it to a destination that requires communication by another (LU6.2).
- Transactions formatting or translation: accepting a message in one format (fields of fixed length, proprietary structure) and forwarding it to a destination in a different format (HL7).
- Object definition libraries: providing a message structure object that simplifies the process of scripting and perhaps allows inbound messages to be automatically associated with the object definition.
- Scripting language: a third-generation language (3gl) based on Structured Query Language (SQL), or SQL itself, is a minimum requirement and is present in the vast majority of products.
- Transactions routing features
  - "Store-and-forward" routing (utilizing queues): this kind of routing is the simplest; it involves first placing the original message in disk storage, then placing it on one of many logical or physical queues to be handled by an outbound process.
  - Guaranteed delivery routing: supports the basic function above, but provides additional retry and escalation mechanisms.
  - Replication of messages to multiple destinations (one-to-many) is supported by almost all.
  - Routing based on message content is broadly supported.

- Transactions queuing: provision for storage of messages that have been received but which cannot be sent to destinations for some period of time.
- Transactions logging, rollback, and replay: this ability is essential to the role of the interface engine in enterprises today. Frequently, issues on the receiving system cause a range of records to be lost. Being able to re-send a range of records easily and effectively is for the most part a commodity service among interface engine suppliers. However the ability to be somewhat selective, (i.e., all orders on the queue, but not all admissions, discharges, and transfers [ADTs]) is not available with all products.
- Data normalization: simple tables for translating data values from one set to another and facilities for accessing them in scripting are widely available. Access to foreign databases for this purpose are available in most products.
- Basic error handling and reporting and notifications: all products support some level of error handling and reporting and most provide notification by pager or fax.
- Monitor and control functions: all products available provide tools for monitoring and control, that are designed for use by nontechnical staff. The control functions start and stop interfaces and configure interface processes. Also, control functions associate processes with scripts and other steps that provide an interface process with custom behavior. Monitoring provides a view of interface status as well as thresholds of performance, which can be used to trigger notifications.

There are other key attributes of some interface engines that outline the differentiation of those products from others. Some of these features include:

- *Scalability.* Some interface engines are architected of modular components, which can be replicated on a single machine or distributed to more than one processor to improve overall throughput in enterprise-wide application.
- *Controlling many environments centrally.* Some of the products available (or in development) today offer the ability to manage multiple instances of interface engines in a consolidated manner.
- *Multiple control consoles.* Some products available today need to be controlled by a single console. Others can be controlled by many client machines by virtue of a client/server architecture.
- *Handling synchronous messages.* Solicit or query interfaces are not handled equally well by all products and are not handled beautifully by any currently available product.
- *Access to a relational database.* Many products have access to relational databases and many have the capacity to query external databases to support data normalization. Some products are

"connected" to suites of other products from the supplier to do a broad range of functions.

- *Aggregation of messages.* Many-to-one messages are not supported in a systematic way by all suppliers. Most fully functional engines can be made to do this, but not simply.
- *Auto-mapping from object to object.* Tools that define ways in which two object libraries interact (HL7 and ASTM, for example) are not available from all suppliers. Most products provide a mechanism for associated fields in two different libraries, but most do not provide tools to create these scripts.
- *XML parsing, validation, and mapping.* Some products are beginning to accept XML documents and auto-map them to objects defined by document type definitions (DTDs) held in the library.
- *HTML interfaces.* Few (if any) products provide easy to use interfaces incorporating HTML. The predominance of web applications and the interface engine's current architecture makes it likely that we will see major improvements in this area which may cause significant changes in the architecture of some products.
- *Incorporating low-level message broker functions.* Most products in use today have as part of the architecture, a message broker, either proprietary to the supplier or a third-party product. Some of the features that have been traditionally hidden from the view of interface engine users are now of interest, for example processing that involves interaction with foreign objects (CORBA, COM) are being provided as new services.

## ARCHITECTURE SEMANTICS

There are many products available today to improve the interface development process. Metaphors from information technology are used to describe their function — gateway, message broker, hub. Each of these terms has specific IT meaning and does not serve as an acceptable definition for an interface engine. In fact, if we define each of these terms generically, they make a common-sense way of thinking about the components of interface engine architecture.

*Message broker* describes a "middleware" product that is traditionally a part of most interface engine products. The message broker provides a traffic cop for an application's internal interprocess communication. Some interface engines are built on top of a proprietary application framework including such middleware which is used for a broader set of applications, while others will embed commercially available middleware products and proclaim that the choice of a third-party product makes their product more "open." In most cases, this component of interface engine architecture is hidden from users. One supplier is using this term to describe the entire product.

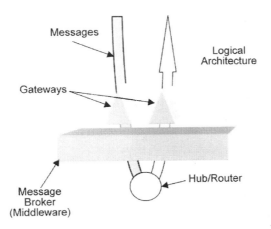

**Exhibit 3. A Simple Interface Model**

*Gateway* is a popular term that is used generically in the industry and by some suppliers in a more proprietary usage. A gateway is a hardware device that provides connectivity from one proprietary environment to another. This provides a convenient generic metaphor for in and out doors in the interface engine architecture.

*Hub* is used by some suppliers as part of the product name or description. A networking hub is a hardware device that multiplexes connectivity to more than one network user. This provides a convenient way of thinking about the routing process generically.

## ARCHITECTURE

The logical architecture of the interface engine is supported by these metaphors. Exhibit 3 shows the simple gateway, hub, and message broker configuration. In this simple picture, messages resulting from trigger events in one system flow through an inbound gateway, across message broker and the hub (from a logical perspective), and routes to an outbound gateway.

## CLIENT/SERVER INTERFACE ENGINES: ACCESS TO SERVICES

In a client/server model, the gateway processes are clients needing access to services. Those services may be provided by other servers connected to the middleware, or they may be endowed with the ability to access shared configuration facilities and perform those services on their own. The various interface engine suppliers have implemented this in different ways, but most products are built on a client/server model. Exhibit 4 provides a view of this architecture. It shows a client application running

37

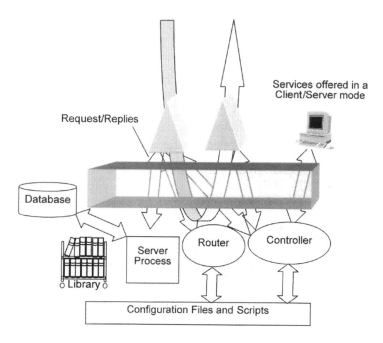

**Exhibit 4. Client Application Monitoring System**

on a desktop machine that operates on the files that define configuration. In addition, this application can be used to monitor the status of interfaces by requesting service from the controller process that polls across the middleware to other processes.

At start-up, the gateway process reads its configuration from files through a server process. When the messages flow into the gateway, the process gets attention from a server process for database access and for-matting according to configuration files, object libraries, or scripts. Routing services can be provided by the hub, which provides an address for the outbound gateway process. Additional formatting is usually available in the outbound process as well. Queuing is sometimes supported in memory or disk or both, but in most cases the queue is a part of the middleware features. Note that all interprocess communication passes through and is con-trolled by the middleware.

The primary advantage of this model includes the ability to scale by cre-ating more server processes to support gateway processes or to distribute gateway processes or servers on to dedicated CPUs for higher through-put. It is possible for the router process to become a bottleneck in this model, so some suppliers prefer to endow the gateway process with more functionality — formatting or routing — or to provide multiple routers.

## INTERFACE ENGINE PACKAGING

Here are some of the ways the interface engine is packaged:

- *Stand-alone applications.* Most suppliers will provide stand-alone packaging for interface engines and sell them without other applications. Few vendors of interface engines offer only an interface engine as a product. Most suppliers are healthcare information technology companies, while a very few have created generic applications for use outside of healthcare and focus on a broad array of products for systems integration.
- *Included with application at additional cost (but required for interfacing).* A few of the HIT vendors in the market will only sell their information systems products including an interface engine (at additional cost). This makes sense because the interface engine tools are the only tools available for interfacing to the product and few if any implementations of HIT products will be done without interfaces.
- *Included with healthcare information systems application.* Some interface engines are fundamentally part of the architecture of the application. In this case, the middleware and the queuing model used for the engine are used by all applications in the architecture. This is true even if no interfaces are needed.

## IMPLEMENTING AN INTERFACE ENGINE

### Roles and Tasks in Interface Engine Implementation

The introduction of an interface engine at a health system will require a number of tasks, not all of which require technical knowledge of the interface engine itself. While it is common that analysts are expected to be able to be effective in this entire range of tasks from the most political to the most technical, this rarely works very well.

Roles that must be fulfilled are as follows:

- *Executive sponsor.* This person provides goals for the group assembled. It is ideal if only one of these is in place for the entire project. it is common that one exists for each domain involved. It is essential that a clear hierarchy exists for all other roles in relation to the executive sponsor. Gross inefficiency results when analysts serve more than one executive sponsor.
- *Project manager.* This person tracks project milestones from start to finish. It is best for this to be a single person as with the executive sponsor. At a minimum, however, one project manager will be required for each business entity (departmental domain, hospital system, vendor, or consultant) that is involved.
- *Technical analyst.* This person evaluates the current state on the technical level. There may be one of these individuals for each feed in the beginning of a project during the documentation of current state.

- *Network analyst.* Each network involved will provide a network analyst to support connectivity between systems.
- *Business analyst.* It is essential that business acumen be available to the team. This may not be a separate person, but this skill set should be available.
- *Domain expert.* This is the most frequently omitted essential role in an interface engine implementation. It is often assumed that the presence of an interface engine trivializes the process of connecting two systems so that this person's advice is not required. Nothing could be further from the truth.
- *Programmer.* This person actually performs the scripting and configuration process.

The ideal project is able to consolidate some roles into the following core positions:

- *Executive sponsor* — single point of contact for escalated issues.
- *Project manager* — one (ideal) or more.
- *Architect* — (one) creates a bridge between the requirements definition and execution phases.

Teams that support the core include:

- *Domain expert team.* A group assembled to describe the current behavior and the desired future state of the connected systems.
- *Programmer/technical team.* A team assembled as resources for the core group; not decision makers.

### Task/Skill-Set Inventory Matrix

Exhibit 5 shows the tasks required, the skills needed to complete those tasks, and a proposal for the responsible person from the above set of roles. Such a task/skills inventory is a good first step in the implementation of an interface engine.

### Strategic Considerations

While interface engines frequently are key elements of HIT strategy, implementing an interface engine is not a panacea that solves all systems integration woes. Here are a few things interface engines *cannot* do:

1. *Interface engines do not replace point-to-point interfaces.* Interface engines in effect produce two interfaces where one existed. It is not wise to insert interface engines in extremely simple environments where the net effect is to double the work.
2. *Interface engines alone cannot fix bad data.* If a complex interface in place today suffers from poor identification of persons or other entities, no scripting process will fix this. While the insertion of an MPI

**Exhibit 5. Tasks/Skills Inventory**

| Task | Description | Skill | Role |
|---|---|---|---|
| Evaluating and selecting an interface engine product | This process will require significant technical and business skill as many products exist and many variables operate in the choice of an appropriate product for an implementation. | Business acumen, technical knowledge, needs understanding | Executive sponsor, architect |
| Installation of an interface engine product | This may have multiple components. There are hardware, network and software implications for this effort. In a stand-alone product, the introduction of a new hardware platform and operating system may pose challenges for the support organization of a health system. | Technical expertise in the component | Technical analyst or supplier analyst |
| Analysis and documentation of the business requirements of the interface environment | Each feeder system must be examined to determine what data must be replicated and how trigger events must be propagated from system to system. Frequently, contracts for interface work will not have taken into account this first step and resources for this activity are overlooked. This is fundamental to determining the complexity of the task at hand and to a successful implementation. | Business acumen, domain expertise, technical knowledge | Architect |
| Due diligence to bureaucracy and politics | In the consolidating health system, this can be a full-time task. No interface implementation is without political considerations, and some projects never progress to completion because of the barriers to efficiency inherent in the new mega-organizations created by mergers and affiliations. | Political skills, communications skills, administration skills | Project manager |
| Analysis of the current technical state | Existing feeds and specifications (if they exist) need to be analyzed. Coherent, consolidated documentation that captures all aspects of the technical (transport, formats, socket numbers) business rules (trigger events passed, range of data sets) and the political (contact names and numbers, executive sponsors) environment is required. | Technical skills | Architect, technical analysts |

41

**Exhibit 5. Tasks/Skills Inventory** *(Continued)*

| Task | Description | Skill | Role |
|---|---|---|---|
| Specification of future state interface environment | High-level expectations of the implementation must be established. The future state of the entire technical environment must be captured at the same level of detail as the current state documentation. | Communications skills, technical skills, domain expertise | Architect |
| Specifications for interface process behavior | This task takes into account all aspects of the current and future states and defines the behavior for each individual interface process. Each trigger event will need separate treatment. This task will scope the effort required in configuration and scripting of the interfaces as well as collection and organization of data required for normalization services. | Communications skills, technical skills, domain expertise | Architect |
| Coding and configuration | After the behavior of each process is specified, interfaces can be built to these specifications. | Technical skills | Programmer |
| Unit testing | Basic validation task. | Technical skills, knowledge of specifications | Programmer |
| System testing | Ensure that interfaces behave as specified in an environment which simulates productions. | Domain expertise, knowledge of specifications and of testing plan | Domain team |

or complex logic may help, in the end, only clean-up of the source environment will solve this problem.

3. *Interface engines cannot be operated by dummies.* Despite the hype, good analyst skills (at a minimum) and programming skills are required to do engine work. Good users will be more productive using an engine and most products do not require that you know C++, so it is easier to find analysts with adequate programming skills and good domain expertise. That is usually the best combination.

4. *Interface engines cannot replace strategy.* While interface engine deployments can be essential components of the strategic mission of an institution, they and their operators do not replace a "big-picture" thinker calling the shots.

5. *Interface engines do not set standards.* While it is possible that an institution may wish to settle on a single protocol and format for messages into and out of the engine, the decision to do this is not to be taken lightly. This involves significant rework on the part of others and the engine is well suited to harmonizing these differences without asking those others to change.

6. *Interface engine work cannot be done in a vacuum.* The interface organization cannot be independent of the analysts who work on the various systems; A fundamental understanding of the systems to be interfaced is required for success.

Now that we know the things that an interface engine implementation cannot do, here is the chief information officer's valid value proposition for the implementation of an interface engine:

1. *Provide a transition strategy.* Interface engines are terrific tools for moving through dynamic times. A health system moving from legacy systems to more integration may wish to place an interface engine between the HIS and all the ancillaries so that as ancillaries are retired or replaced, the interfaces in place can be upgraded efficiently with a common interface specification if possible.

2. *Provide a mechanism for distributing a feed of broad interest, reducing interface support cost.* Admits, transfers, and discharges from the HIS can be replicated to the ancillaries in a complex health system. Results from ancillaries can be sent to the HIS and to the clinical data repository.

3. *Provide a way to cope with new alliances.* This is a big one. The pace of consolidation may force nonstrategic interfaces that have short useful lives — in the case of a laboratory system consolidation where all the legacy HIS systems will be consolidated over time, for example.

## TACTICAL ANALYSIS OF INTERFACE ENVIRONMENTS

### Creating Interfaces with an Interface Engine

Each interface engine product has its own implementation, but in general, these are the steps required to create interface processes.

**Configuration.** This is the process of defining attributes for interfaces. In the configuration process, transport protocol is chosen, ports for communication or file and directory designations are elicited by an application designed to modify configuration files. Also, we may use the configuration tools to define what sort of standard message format and trigger event will be coming or going on the new interface. If special error handling is required for the interface, this is usually where it is configured, though some products require scripting calls to support this feature. ACK/NACK processing is usually defined here, as well as the association of scripts. Some products require that you build outbound interfaces first (since the configuration of inbound processes requires the outbound route).

Frequently, these configuration applications are graphical user interface (GUI) applications with point-and-click features. Some are "wizard"-style applications that collect all the pertinent information form by form. In practice, some aspects of configuration are done in simple character cell applications rather than by GUI applications, but these relate to the more arcane features of configuration. The purpose of most of the GUI tools is to simplify the process of creating a shell for an interface, and consequently, most interfaces cannot be entirely completed in the GUI configuration process alone.

**Routing.** Some interface products treat routing as a separate feature entirely with graphical tools to facilitate the process. Others include routing as a part of configuration with options to modify route based on branching logic in scripts.

**Script Editing.** To the extent that messages are received in the format in which they need to be forwarded, scripting may not be necessary. In most cases, however, scripts must be provided that either do string manipulation, shuffle or modify fields, or map a fixed-length message to a library object (like HL7). All products provide a script editor, but features differ widely. Some products provide code-generation tools that make the creation of scripts a "drag-and-drop" affair, but these tools rarely are self-contained or complete. Usually, the tools create stubs of code, which need further manipulation to support the necessary business logic. There are a few products that use an object-oriented model for defining relationships between objects. Some users prefer that model, whereas others prefer the freedom and power of scripting for making such relationships.

**Compiling/Validation.** Most products require that the text of a script be compiled into some executable or interpreted form. At the least, all products will conduct some validation step to ensure that the script will run at all. Most products do not reinterpret the text of the script at interface start-up, just at compile time.

**Modification of Object Libraries.** A new interface for a new format, which is not in the object library, need not necessarily require that a new object be built by most systems. Others treat all messages as objects and as a result, considerable pre-work may be required if the messages are not to be treated as strings. Another reason for modifying the object library would be to adjust to a local implementation of a not terribly rigorous standard — HL7 2.1, for example — which the health system wishes to define as a local standard. Once object definitions for message structures are complete and match incoming messages, most products will autoassociate fields by position with those built in the library. Some products come with many libraries — HL7 (2.1, 2.2, 2.3, 3.0[1]) ASTM, X.12, NCPDP — while others come with few to none and expect users to build the library. If an interface is HL7 2.2 or 2.3, most products will accept the message, making this step optional.

**Unit Testing/Debugging.** This step is required for all implementations and products. Some products have tools to facilitate the cycling of a dummy message through the system artificially, while others require a small amount of work to set up a "loop-back" test in which interfaces can be iteratively tested. Focus here is on passing messages without error and apparent correctness of the interface configuration and scripts based on outputs.

**System Testing.** In this process the interface is hooked up with live feeds inbound and outbound and system-to-system validation is done. Focus is placed on the database state of the two connected systems — debugging system testing issues requires a focus on message content and may send a user back to the unit testing stage with a transaction that caused the errant condition.

## CREATIVE IMPLEMENTATION

Significant integrative tasks can be achieved with interface engines with access to the database of an effective healthcare application. Projects of the following types have been observed:

- Creation of a complex multiplexor feeding orders placed in three environments and 37XX sites to a robotic device for accessioning, aliquotting, and sorting of specimens
- Creation of an aggregation mechanism for reference laboratory orders enabling a single connection from multiple sites

- Facilitation of 60 feeds into a data repository
- Use as an adjunct product with an MPI to facilitate affiliation with an outside entity — the MPI was a part of an integrated product and as a consequence, implementation was rapid

## FUTURE DIRECTIONS

Several trends today will change the focus of interface engines and the companies that produce them including:

- Competition with middleware suppliers. Many of the middleware products for sale today begin to approach some of the basic functions that interface engines provide
- XML, HTML, and the Web. New interface requirements will emerge based on the new technologies for the World Wide Web.
- E-commerce requirements. As the field of clinical commerce becomes more mature, interfacing will need to take into account new levels of confidentiality and openness, two conflicting goals.

**Notes**

1. HL7 3.0 requires the ability to parse and validate XML.

# Chapter 4
# Wireless Application Directions

*Gilbert Held*

While most readers are very familiar with the use of cell phones, what may not be as familiar is the large number of applications that either are now available for use or are on the horizon. This chapter focuses on a wireless application that can provide the ability to not only use a cell phone to directly surf the Web and send and receive e-mail, but in addition, integrate a phone with a PDA. This chapter also addresses a new type of wireless technology referred to as fixed wireless, which can provide subscribers with an alternative to such broadband access methods as digital subscriber lines (DSLs) and cable modems. This chapter concludes with an examination of the use of IEEE 802.11 wireless LANs and how the a and b extensions to the standards not only permit high data rates but, in addition, allow hospital administrators to select operations within a frequency band that minimizes interference with existing equipment. Thus, the purpose of this chapter is to make the reader aware of the spectrum of relatively new and emerging wireless applications that one can consider for use.

## OVERVIEW

Recently, several new wireless products emerged from the drawing board and conceptual stage into commercial products. One such product is referred to as Bluetooth, which represents a limited distance transmission scheme originally developed to provide handheld devices with the ability to communicate with one another. As Bluetooth development progressed, a number of potential applications emerged for the technology that considerably expands its potential use.

Another emerging technology expected to begin realizing its potential is the HomeRF standard and equipment developed that operates according to this standard. HomeRF can be considered to represent a low-cost and limited transmission capability alternative to an IEEE 802.11 wireless LAN. Unfortunately for many persons and organizations that like to employ multiple technologies, as we will note in more detail later in this article, the frequency used by Bluetooth, HomeRF, and one version of IEEE 802.11 LANs, and even the friendly office microwave overlap.

While Bluetooth, Home RF, and IEEE 802.11 LANs are relatively short-distance transmission technologies, there are also several longer distance wireless technologies that are expected to obtain a significant base of additional subscribers. Those wireless technologies include Local Multipoint Distribution Service (LMDS) and Multipoint Multichannel Distribution Service (MMDS). Both LMDS and MMDS are fixed wireless technologies that are being used to provide broadband Internet access — providing competition to such fixed landline technologies as digital subscriber lines (DSLs) and cable modems. In the hospital and clinical laboratory environment where many electronic devices can be adversely affected by wireless devices, extensions to the basic IEEE 802.11 standard now provide hospital administrators with the ability to minimize potential interference while obtaining the advantage of wireless networking. Given a general appreciation for what is on the horizon, take a more detailed look at each of the technologies.

## BLUETOOTH

Named for Harald Bluetooth, a 10th century Viking king, this relatively new technology provides the ability to transfer information at data rates up to 1 Mbps at distances up to 100 meters. Bluetooth uses the 2.45 GHz unlicensed Industrial, Scientific and Medical (ISM) band for transmission on a worldwide basis, providing the potential for compatible products to obtain an interoperability capability on a global basis.

The origins of Bluetooth date to 1998 when a group of computer industry leaders (to include IBM, Toshiba, Ericsson, and Nokia) began developing a way for users to easily connect a wide range of mobile devices. Those vendors formed a special interest group to develop a royalty-free, open specification technology that was given the code name Bluetooth.

As a result of the Bluetooth development effort, tiny, inexpensive, short-range transceivers are beginning to be installed in laptops, notebooks, PDAs, and other devices. In addition to supporting a data transfer rate up to 1 Mbps, Bluetooth also supports three 64-kbps voice channels, making it possible to talk, send a fax, transfer data, and even perform another operation.

The key benefit of Bluetooth is its expected minimal cost. While a few Bluetooth transceivers produced during 2001 probably cost more than $30, by mid-2002 economies of scale should bring unit production to below $5 per transceiver. At that cost it will be relatively inexpensive to add the technology to fax machines, computers, PDAs, and even cell phones.

As this occurs, the only limitations on the use of Bluetooth technology will be developers attempting to tailor software to the technology and the imagination of developers and consumers. For example, during 2002 or perhaps by 2003, one may well walk into one's office and type a report on the computer; but instead of printing the report and walking with it to the fax room, one might point a PDA at the computer, press a button, and download it into the PDA. Upon walking into the fax room, one might point the PDA at the fax machine, press another key to download a relevant fax number, and another key to transfer the previously stored document into the fax. Thus, the paperless office might move further along toward reality due to Bluetooth.

As a second example concerning the potential of Bluetooth, consider the electric meter reader who, on a monthly or perhaps bimonthly schedule, walks the neighborhood, checking the reading of each meter. Because the primary cost associated with meter reading is the salary of the people traversing different neighborhoods, anything that can be done to enhance their productivity will reduce the overall cost associated with meter reading. With this in mind, assume that over the next few years meters are upgraded to support Bluetooth. Then, instead of having to physically visit each meter, it could be possible for the person to drive down a street and take meter readings. As the vehicle proceeds down the street, a Bluetooth-compatible transceiver with appropriate software polls each meter and records its current setting. Now, instead of walking to the side of each home, the meter reader can drive through the neighborhood, significantly boosting his or her level of productivity. With an appreciation for the potential of Bluetooth, one can now focus attention on another emerging wireless technology that also has a limited transmission distance capability. That technology is the HomeRF standard.

## THE HOMERF STANDARD

The HomeRF standard represents the effort of leading companies from the personal computing, consumer electronics, peripheral products, communications, software, and electronics industries. Those vendors formed the HomeRF Working Group (HRFWG), which developed a specification for wireless communications in a home environment referred to as the Shared Wireless Access Protocol (SWAP). Thus, SWAP actually represents the HomeRF standard although many people and most trade literature refer to both terms synonymously.

SWAP is designed to transport both voice and data, providing a mechanism to interface with the public switched telephone network (PSTN) and the Internet. SWAP technology was derived from extensions to the existing cordless telephone standard, referred to as Digital Enhanced Cordless Telephone (DECT) and IEEE wireless LAN standards. It supports both Time

Division Multiple Access (TDMA), which enables six full-duplex conversations, and Carrier Sense Multiple Access with Collision Avoidance (CSMA/CA) for the transfer of high-speed data.

SWAP uses frequency-hopping technology at a rate of 50 hops per second. Frequency hopping occurs in the 2400 MHz ISM band, which is the same general band used by Bluetooth. Thus, the HomeRF standard and Bluetooth-compatible devices have the potential of causing a degree of interference with one another. However, because of the frequency-hopping nature of HomeRF, the interference can be expected to be intermittent and, as a worst-case scenario, either slightly delay data transfer or result in very short periods of static when a voice conversation is in progress and a Bluetooth device operation causes interference.

When used for data transfer, SWAP supports two data rates. A data transfer rate of 1 Mbps is obtained when frequency shift keying (FSK) modulation is employed using a pair of frequencies. When four FSK frequencies are used, a 2-Mbps data transfer rate becomes obtainable. Up to 127 devices can be supported on a HomeRF network with a transmission range of approximately 100 feet, which should be sufficient to cover most homes and even a portion of a yard surrounding that home.

## NETWORK TOPOLOGY

The HomeRF standard supports two network topologies. As an ad hoc network, stations are limited to data transmission and all stations are considered equal. In this networking environment, control of the network resides in all stations through the use of the CSMA/CA access protocol.

A second network topology results when voice and time-critical applications are supported. When this occurs, the network is managed under the control of a Connection Point. The Connection Point provides a gateway to the PSTN and is connected to one PC via a standard interface to support voice and data access to the PSTN. In addition, SWAP can also use the Connection Point to support power management operations for battery-operated devices by scheduling device wakeup and polling operations.

## SWAP EVOLUTION

During August 2000, the Federal Communications Commission (FCC) agreed to allow SWAP a fivefold increase in power in the 2.4-GHz band. This action resulted in the HomeRF Working Group focusing its attention on a revision to SWAP, referred to as SWAP 2.0, which was expected to be completed during 2001. Under SWAP 2.0, the data transfer rate of SWAP will be increased to 10 Mbps, which should make it more suitable for providing multiple accesses to DSL or a cable modem router installed in a home. Under this networking scenario, it is envisioned that one of the primary uses of SWAP will be to enable a person with multiple PCs in a home and one high-speed Internet connection to obtain shared access to the Internet without having to rewire their home.

## LMDS

Local Multipoint Distribution Services (LMDS) represents a broadband wireless technology that operates primarily in the 25-GHz spectrum, with its actual frequency based upon license issued by the FCC in the United States and other regulatory bodies in other countries.

### Operation

LMDS can be considered to represent a fixed cellular-like network architecture, with a base station used to service subscribers within an approximate 10-km radius. The frequency assigned to LMDS in the United States covers several areas ranging from 27.5 GHz through 31.3 GHz, presently the highest frequency range licensed for wireless communications. Due to this high frequency, LMDS represents a point-to-point or point-to-multipoint, line-of-sight transmission method.

In the United States, 1.3 MHz of bandwidth is allocated to LMDS, which represents the largest amount of bandwidth allocated to any wireless transmission method. This permits a data transmission rate up to approximately 1 Gbps to be supported between the LMDS base station and all subscribers within the LMDS cell.

### The Base Station

Each LMDS base station can support a data transfer capacity ranging from approximately 375 Mbps to approximately 1 Gbps. The exact capacity of a base station depends on several factors. Those factors primarily include the modulation method used and the number of directional antennas mounted on the base station.

LMDS supports both Time Division Multiple Access (TDMA) and Frequency Division Multiple Access (FDMA), using either 4, 16, or 64 constellation pattern Quadrature Amplitude Modulation (QAM). In general, the higher the level of QAM the greater the transmission rate, although higher levels of QAM result in closer modulation points that become more susceptible to impairments that result in retransmission and lower actual obtainable throughput. Thus, a complex site survey to include an examination of potential interference is normally required prior to selecting a modulation method.

The number of directional antennas used on a base station reflects its sectors of coverage. In most operating environments, a base station will use a single directional antenna for 90 degrees of coverage, resulting in four antennas providing 360 degrees of coverage. Then, each antenna's operating rate is multiplied by four to obtain the system capacity of the base station.

### Utilization

LMDS is being used as a mechanism to provide both business and residential customers with high-speed Internet access without wiring. The only cable a subscriber requires is from an antenna mounted on the side or roof of an office building or home to an access point within the home or office that converts digital data to radio frequency (RF) modulation for transmission via the antenna and reverses the process. At the time this chapter was written, several communications carriers had collectively purchased a large number of licenses and were expected to begin offering service during 2001. Otherwise, several small Internet Service providers (ISPs) were offering LMDS service primarily in urban areas in California. However, as more equipment is manufactured and economies of scale translate into lower cost of antennas and access points, it is expected that the deployment of this technology will provide a valuable alternative to DSL and cable modem usage. Given an appreciation for LMDS, this chapter concludes with a discussion of a second type of fixed wireless transmission referred to as Multichannel Multipoint Distribution Service (MMDS).

### MMDS

Multichannel Multipoint Distribution Service represents a fixed wireless broadband access technology that operates in the 2.5- to 2.7-GHz frequency spectrum. This frequency spectrum is significantly below the 27- to 31-GHz frequency used by LMDS.

In actuality, MMDS predates LMDS, as the former was originally licensed by the FCC during the 1980s as a mechanism to provide instructional television fixed programming (ITFP). Initially, the FCC allocated a number of GMHz channels within the 2.5- to 2.7-GHz spectrum for TV broadcasting. Although the use of MMDS achieved a degree of popularity on college campuses, the growth in the use of cable TV resulted in most licensed spectrums becoming unused as campus TV systems converted from "on the air" to cable.

In the United States, the FCC allocated a total of 33 GMHz TV channels for MMDS within different areas of the country. As different operators failed to use their allocated spectrum, the FCC regained the spectrum, resulting in the FCC auctioning MMDS spectrum for different regional licenses during the early 1990s.

The original intention of companies purchasing MMDS licenses was as a mechanism for providing wireless television in competition with cable TV operators. However, a surprise changed events. That surprise was a small network called the Internet, which gained significant popularity and made the licenses more valuable for use in providing high-speed wireless Internet access.

## MULTIPATH COMMUNICATIONS

Both MMDS and LMDS are similar in that they represent fixed wireless transmission methods now being used or expected to shortly provide high-speed Internet access. Unlike LMDS, which represents a point-to-point, line-of-sight transmission method, MMDS is a multipath transmission method. Because MMDS operates at a much lower frequency than LMDS, signals will be reflected off different objects located in the path between transmitter and receiver. Such objects can be buildings, trees, and even moving vehicles.

The addition of duplicate or reflected signals to the composition of the primary signal occurs by the bouncing of the microwave signals off previously mentioned objects. As portions of the reflected signals reach the receiver, it is similar to having echoes bounce back from a canyon wall. Thus, the reflections can make it difficult to separate the primary signal from the reflected signals.

The previously described echoes or reflected signals can be considered similar to observing ghosts on a TV receiver. By adjusting the antenna, one may be able to minimize the effect of the reflected signals. Another method used to control reflections is to focus the beam width into a narrower point. A second method being experimented with to reduce reflections is the use of dual antennas that are separated from each other by approximately 12 meters. The use of multiple antennas permits a different set of multipath signals to be received by each antenna. Because the signal received on each antenna will have a different set of multipath signals, it is often possible to dynamically switch a receiver's use of antennas to obtain a better signal at each point in time.

Although MMDS is evolving as a mechanism to obtain a wireless-based broadband transmission method, it is important to note that it is not presently universally available. Even if it is available within the geographic area where a subscriber resides, it is still important to note that the ability to use the technology depends on several factors. Those factors include the distance between the transmitter and receiver, the curvature of the Earth if the primary path exceeds 7 km, the antenna height at each end of the path, the transmitter power, and the antenna gain. Thus, a site survey is normally performed to determine the suitability of a subscriber's location for MMDS service.

### IEEE 802.11 a and b Extensions

The basic IEEE 802.11 wireless LAN standard provided support for data rates of 1 and 2 Mbps using one of three physical layer technologies: frequency hopping spread spectrum (FHSS), direct sequence spread spectrum (DSSS), or infrared (IR). FHSS and DSSS represent radio frequency (RF) technology and use the 2.4-GHz frequency band. This band represents an unlicensed frequency band where microwave ovens and cordless telephones as well as HomeRF network equipment operate.

The use of wireless LANs literally began to explode during 2001 when equipment compatible with the recently defined IEEE 802.11b standard reached the market. The 'b' extension extended the data rate of wireless LANs from 1 and 2 Mbps to 5.5 and 11 Mbps using DSSS in the unlicensed 2.4-GHz frequency band. While many organizations were able to take advantage of the higher data rate afforded by the 'b' extension to the 802.11 standard, its use of the 2.4-GHz frequency band represented a problem for other organizations. The problem associated with the 2.4-GHz frequency band results from the fact that it is known as the Industrial, Scientific and Medical (ISM) band for good reason. As an unlicensed frequency band, many equipment vendors previously manufactured industrial, scientific, and medical equipment for operation in that band prior to the development of the wireless LAN standard. As a result of this action, wireless LANs can cause radio frequency interference (RFI) when installed within several hundred feet of ISM equipment operating in the 2.4-GHz frequency band. Thus, while equipment compatible with the IEEE 802.11b standard found a viable market in the normal office environment, such equipment could be unsuitable for use in hospitals, factories, and other locations where equipment was in operation that used transmission in the 2.4-GHz band.

One potential solution to frequency interference from IEEE 802.11b equipment occurred when communications vendors developed devices compatible with the 802.11a extension. The IEEE 802.11a extension not only defines a new modulation method referred to as orthogonal frequency division multiplexing (OFDM) that supports data rates up to 54 Mbps, but in addition, specifies the use of frequency in the 5-GHz band. The 5-GHz frequency band, referred to as the National Infrastructure (NI) band, represents a relatively new unlicensed band. This means that the probability that an organization already has existing equipment that could be adversely affected by wireless LAN operations occurring from equipment complying with the 802.11a standard is minimal. Thus, hospitals, industrial plants, and other facilities operating electronic equipment that need to minimize RF interference can do so while obtaining the benefits of wireless LAN operations by using IEEE 802.11a-compatible equipment.

**Recommended Course of Action**

As indicated, there are several limited and long-distance wireless transmission technologies that can increase our communications capability. In a local area networking environment, it is important to note that the difference between equipment compatible with the 'a' and 'b' extensions to the IEEE 802.11 standard is more than just the obtainable data rate. The two extensions represent transmission in different frequency bands, which can be important considerations for organizations with a base of installed equipment that uses wireless technology. By understanding how these technologies operate and their capabilities and limitations, we will be better prepared to use the technologies as they become available for use.

# Chapter 5
# Overcoming Wireless LAN Security Vulnerabilities

*Gilbert Held*

The IEEE 802.11b specification represents one of three wireless LAN standards developed by the Institute of Electrical and Electronics Engineers. The original standard, which was the 802.11 specification, defined wireless LANs using infrared, Frequency Hopping Spread Spectrum (FHSS), and Direct Sequence Spread Spectrum (DSSS) communications at data rates of 1 and 2 Mbps. The relatively low operating rate associated with the original IEEE 802.11 standard precluded its widespread adoption.

The IEEE 802.11b standard is actually an annex to the 802.11 standard. This annex specifies the use of DSSS communications to provide operating rates of 1, 2, 5.5, and 11 Mbps.

A third IEEE wireless LAN standard, IEEE 802.11a, represents another annex to the original standard. Although 802.11- and 802.11b-compatible equipment operates in the 2.4-GHz unlicensed frequency band, to obtain additional bandwidth to support higher data rates resulted in the 802.11a standard using the 5-GHz frequency band. Although 802.11a equipment can transfer data at rates up to 54 Mbps, because higher frequencies attenuate more rapidly than lower frequencies, approximately four times the number of access points are required to service a given geographic area than if 802.11b equipment is used. Due to this, as well as the fact that 802.11b equipment reached the market prior to 802.11a devices, the vast majority of wireless LANs are based on the use of 802.11b-compatible equipment.

## SECURITY

Under all three IEEE 802.11 specifications, security is handled in a similar manner. The three mechanisms that affect wireless LAN security under the troika of 802.11 specifications include the specification of the network name, authentication, and encryption.

0-8493-1498-4/03/$0.00+$1.50
© 2003 by CRC Press LLC

## Network Name

To understand the role of the network name requires a small diversion to discuss a few wireless LAN network terms. Each device in a wireless LAN is referred to as a *station,* to include both clients and access points. Client stations can communicate directly with one another, referred to as ad hoc networking. Client stations can also communicate with other clients, both wireless and wired, through the services of an access point. The latter type of networking is referred to as infrastructure networking.

In an infrastructure networking environment, the group of wireless stations to include the access point forms what is referred to as a basic service set (BSS). The basic service set is identified by a name. That name, which is formally referred to as the service set identifier (SSID), is also referred to as the network name.

One can view the network name as a password. Each access point normally is manufactured with a set network name that can be changed. To be able to access an access point, a client station must be configured with the same network name as that configured on the access point. Unfortunately, there are three key reasons why the network name is almost as valueless as a password. First, most vendors use a well-known default setting that can be easily learned by surfing to the vendor's Web site and accessing the online manual for their access point. For example, Netgear uses the network name "Wireless." Second, access points periodically transmit beacon frames that define their presence and operational characteristics to include their network name. Thus, the use of a wireless protocol analyzer, such as the Wild-Packets' Airopeek or Sniffer Technologies' Wireless Sniffer could be used to record beacon frames as a mechanism to learn the network name.

A third problem associated with the use of the network name as a password for access to an access point is the fact that there are two client settings that can be used to override most access point network name settings. The configuration of a client station to a network name of "ANY" or its setting to a blank can normally override the setting of a network name or an access point.

Exhibit 1 illustrates an example of the use of the SMC Networks' EZ Connect Wireless LAN Configuration Utility program to set the SSID to a value of "ANY." Once this action was accomplished, this author was able to access a Netgear wireless router/access point whose SSID was by default set to a value of "Wireless." Thus, the use of the SSID or network name as a password to control access to a wireless LAN needs to be considered as a facility easily compromised, as well as one that offers very limited potential.

## Authentication

A second security mechanism included within all three IEEE wireless LAN specifications is authentication. Authentication represents the process

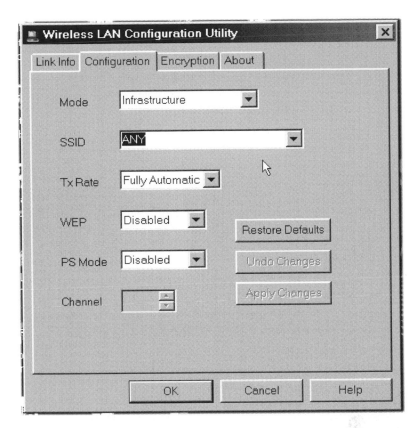

**Exhibit 1. Setting the Value of the SSID or Network Name to "ANY"**

of verifying the identity of a wireless station. Under the IEEE 802.11 standard to include the two addenda, authentication can be either open or shared key. Open authentication in effect means that the identity of a station is not checked. The second method of authentication, which is referred to as shared key, assumes that when encryption is used, each station that has the correct key and is operating in a secure mode represents a valid user. Unfortunately, as soon noted, shared key authentication is vulnerable because the WEP key can be learned by snooping on the radio frequency.

**Encryption**

The third security mechanism associated with IEEE 802.11 networks is encryption. The encryption used under the 802.11 series of specifications is referred to as Wired Equivalent Privacy (WEP). The initial goal of WEP is reflected by its name. That is, its use is designed to provide a level of privacy equivalent to that occurring when a person uses a wired LAN. Thus, some of the vulnerabilities uncovered concerning WEP should not be shocking because the goal of WEP is not to bulletproof a network. Instead, it is to simply make over the air transmission difficult for a third party to understand. However, as we will note, there are several problems associated with the use of WEP that make it relatively easy for a third party to determine the composition of network traffic flowing on a network.

Exhibit 2 illustrates the pull-down menu of the WEP settings from the SMC Networks' wireless LAN Configuration Utility program. Note in the exhibit of the WEP pull-down menu that the highlighted entry of "Disabled" represents the default setting. This means that, by default, WEP is disabled; and unless you alter the configuration on your client stations and access points, any third party within transmission range could use a wireless LAN protocol analyzer to easily record all network activity. In fact, during the year 2001, several articles appeared in *The New York Times* and *The Wall Street Journal* concerning the travel of two men in a van from one park-

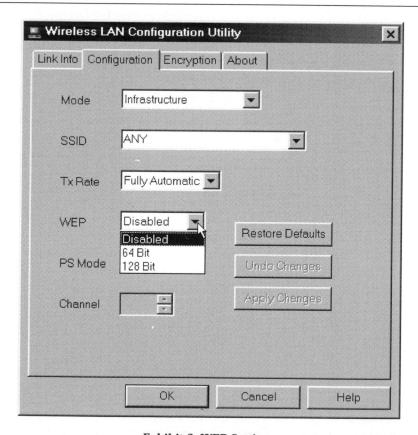

**Exhibit 2. WEP Settings**

ing lot to another in Silicon Valley. Using a directional antenna focused at each building from a parking lot and a notebook computer running a wireless protocol analyzer program, these men were able to easily read most network traffic because most networks were set up using WEP disabled.

Although enabling WEP makes it more difficult to decipher traffic, the manner by which WEP encryption occurs has several shortcomings. Returning to Exhibit 2, note that the two WEP settings are shown as "64 Bit" and "128 Bit." Although the use of 64- and 128-bit encryption keys may appear to represent a significant barrier to decryption, the manner by which WEP encryption occurs creates several vulnerabilities. An explanation follows.

WEP encryption occurs via the creation of a key that is used to generate a pseudo-random binary string that is modulo-2 added to plaintext to create ciphertext. The algorithm that uses the WEP key is a stream cipher, meaning it uses the key to create an infinite pseudo-random binary string.

Exhibit 3 illustrates the use of SMC Networks' Wireless LAN Configuration Utility program to create a WEP key. SMC Networks simplifies the entry of a WEP key by allowing the user to enter a passphrase. Other vendors may allow the entry of hex characters or alphanumeric characters. Regardless of the manner by which a WEP key is entered, the total key length consists of two elements: an initialization vector (IV) that is 24 bits in length and the entered WEP key. Because the IV is part of the key, this means that a user constructing a 64-bit WEP key actually specifies 40 bits in the form of a passphrase or ten hex digits, or 104 bits in the form of a passphrase or 26 hex digits for a 128-bit WEP key.

Because wireless LAN transmissions can easily be reflected off surfaces and moving objects, multiple signals can flow to a receiver. Referred to as multipath transmission, the receiver needs to select the best transmission and ignore the other signals. As one might expect, this can be a difficult task, resulting in a transmission error rate considerably higher than that encountered on wired LANs. Due to this higher error rate, it would not be practical to use a WEP key by itself to create a stream cipher that continues for infinity. This is because a single bit received in error would adversely affect the decryption of subsequent data.

Recognizing this fact, the IV is used along with the digits of the WEP key to produce a new WEP key on a frame-by-frame basis. While this is a technically sound action, unfortunately the 24-bit length of the IV used in conjunction with a 40- or 104-bit fixed-length WEP key causes several vulnerabilities. First, the IV is transmitted in the clear, allowing anyone with appropriate equipment to record its composition along with the encrypted frame data. Because the IV is only 24 bits in length, it will periodically repeat. Thus, capturing two or more of the same IVs and the encrypted text makes it possible to perform a frequency analysis of the en-

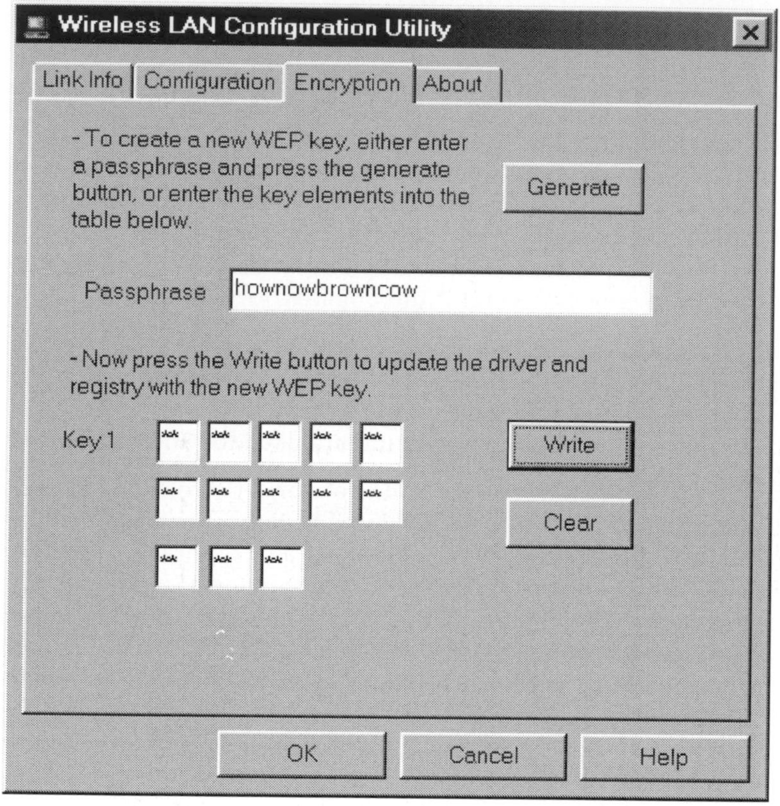

**Exhibit 3. Creating a WEP Encryption Key**

crypted text that can be used as a mechanism to decipher the captured data. For example, assume one has captured several frames that had the same IV. Because "e" is the most common letter used in the English language, followed by the letter "t," one would begin a frequency analysis by searching for the most common letter in the encrypted frames. If the letter "x" was found to be the most frequent, there would be a high probability that the plaintext letter "e" was encrypted as the letter "x." Thus, the IV represents a serious weakness that compromises encryption.

During mid-2001, researchers at Rice University and AT&T Laboratories discovered that by monitoring approximately five hours of wireless LAN traffic, it became possible to determine the WEP key through a series of mathematical manipulations, regardless of whether a 64-bit or 128-bit key was used. This research was used by several software developers to produce programs such as Airsnort, whose use enables a person to determine the WEP key in use and to become a participant on a wireless LAN. Thus, the weakness of the WEP key results in shared key authentication being compromised as a mechanism to validate the identity of wireless station operators. Given an appreciation for the vulnerabilities associated with wireless LAN security, one can now focus on the tools and techniques that can be used to minimize or eliminate such vulnerabilities.

## MAC ADDRESS CHECKING

One of the first methods used to overcome the vulnerabilities associated with the use of the network name or SSID, as well as shared key authentication, was MAC address checking. Under MAC address checking, the LAN manager programs the MAC address of each client station into an access point. The access point only allows authorized MAC addresses occurring in the source address field of frames to use its facilities.

Although the use of MAC address checking provides a significant degree of improvement over the use of a network name for accessing the facilities of an access point, by itself it does nothing to alter the previously mentioned WEP vulnerabilities. To attack the vulnerability of WEP, several wireless LAN equipment vendors introduced the use of dynamic WEP keys.

### Dynamic WEP Keys

Because WEP becomes vulnerable by a third party accumulating a significant amount of traffic that flows over the air using the same key, it becomes possible to enhance security by dynamically changing the WEP key. Several vendors have recently introduced dynamic WEP key capabilities as a mechanism to enhance wireless security. Under a dynamic key capability, a LAN administrator, depending on the product used, may be able to configure equipment to either exchange WEP keys on a frame-by-fame basis or at predefined intervals. The end result of this action is to limit the capability of a third party to monitor a sufficient amount of traffic that can be used to either perform a frequency analysis of encrypted data or to determine the WEP key in use. While dynamic WEP keys eliminate the vulnerability of continued WEP key utilization, readers should note that each vendor supporting this technology does so on a proprietary basis. This means that if one anticipates using products from multiple vendors, one may have to forego the use of dynamic WEP keys unless the vendors selected have cross-licensed their technology to provide compatibility between products. Having an appreciation for the manner by which dynamic WEP keys can enhance encryption security, this discussion of methods to minimize wireless security vulnerabilities concludes with a brief discussion of the emerging IEEE 802.1x standard.

## THE IEEE 802.1X STANDARD

The IEEE 802.1x standard is being developed to control access to both wired and wireless LANs. Although the standard was not officially completed during early 2002, Microsoft added support for the technology in its Windows XP operating system released in October 2001.

Under the 802.1x standard, a wireless client station attempting to access a wired infrastructure via an access point will be challenged by the access point to identify itself. The client will then transmit its identification to the access point. The access point will forward the challenge response to an authentication server located on the wired network. Upon authentication, the server will inform the access point that the wireless client can access the network, resulting in the access point allowing frames generated by the client to flow onto the wired network.

While the 802.1x standard can be used to enhance authentication, by itself it does not enhance encryption. Thus, one must consider the use of dynamic WEP keys as well as proprietary MAC address checking or an 802.1x authentication method to fully address wireless LAN security vulnerabilities.

**Additional Reading**

Held, G., "Wireless Application Directions," *Data Communications Management*, 53-10-36 (April/May 2002).

Lee, D.S., "Wireless Internet Security," *Data Communications Management*, 53-10-36 (April/May 2002).

# Chapter 6
# Using Middleware for Interoperable Systems

*Raymond J. Posch*

The increasingly distributed nature of business locations and operations has led to a concomitant expansion of client/server computing from the department level to the enterprise level. Yet the successful implementation of client/server, or distributed, business applications depends on interoperability — the ability of applications to work together across a network to perform business functions. Systems integrators need to know exactly how a client application will talk with a server application before either application can be designed or written. If they do not, unrealistic assumptions about applications-level connectivity can be project killers.

Because enterprises typically have many and diverse systems to meet their business needs, interoperability problems are almost always encountered as soon as applications on desktops, mainframes, midrange systems, and servers need to interact with each other. No products have emerged as clear-cut, widely supported standards, *de facto* or otherwise, for distributed enterprise applications. Systems integrators are tested to the utmost by the fact that these client/server applications must be developed with wide-ranging assortments of platforms, networks, databases, and tools.

The need for applications to be able to directly exchange information in real-time in a distributed heterogeneous environment has led to the development of middleware — software that bridges the gap between business applications and systems-level services such as databases, network protocols, and operating systems. This chapter discusses the business issues in enterprise computing and the myriad interoperability problems associated with achieving distributed business applications. It then reviews how middleware is being used to solve these problems.

## DISTRIBUTED APPLICATIONS DEFINED

A distributed application is an automated business activity broken down into multiple processing functions running on different computers and performed in a coordinated fashion by sending information across a network. Depending on the relationship of the components, such applications are also referred to as client/server or peer-to-peer applications. Because the application components must work together across the network, the applications are more generally referred to as cooperative processing applications.

The so-called two-tier client/server model divides the processing into a client portion, which interfaces with the user, and a server portion, which interfaces with the database. Execution of business rules is divided between the client or server components.

The three-tier model divides the work into presentation on the client platform, business rules on one or more application platforms, and database access on one or more database platforms. This model attempts (at least conceptually) to isolate the business rules to the middle tier so that client applications and database server applications are less affected by the frequent changes that occur in business rules. It is believed that this approach can lead to applications that are easier to maintain and that scale better as the volume of business transactions grows.

## BUSINESS ISSUES IN ENTERPRISE COMPUTING

### IT Infrastructure, Legacy Systems, and Changing Technology

Organizations invest in the IT infrastructure necessary for conducting business. This IT infrastructure comprises computers, software, and networks. An organization that has been in business for any period of time is likely to have legacy systems (i.e., hardware, software, and networks) that may not be easily replaced as newer capabilities become available. Such an organization is also likely to replace its computers or networks to increase speed and capacity, for example.

Because technology, especially information technology, changes continuously, organizations face at least two major challenges to their ability to manage their investments in IT infrastructure:

- Ensuring that business-critical applications can easily adapt and remain in operation when computers, operating systems, and networks are changed or replaced for reasons of capacity, price/performance, or functional fit. This is very much an issue of managing assets and operating costs.
- Choosing infrastructure components that allow for the quick use of new technologies. This relates particularly to applications software, because the cost efficiencies of operating the business are often directly

related to the applications. New technologies often have steep learning curves and existing applications may not be easily adaptable. Although this is an issue of managing assets and costs, it is also one of business adaptability and responsiveness. It is especially important for a rapidly growing business.

## Integration in a Distributed Business World

The challenges of managing an IT infrastructure are complicated further by the increasingly distributed nature of business organization and operations. Employees and business functions that were centralized in a single headquarters ten years ago are now likely to be scattered in dozens or hundreds of locations around the globe. Departments that previously consisted of employees performing the same or similar functions are now likely to be organized as distributed teams with team members in many different locations. This increasing physical distribution of people, functions, and supporting systems engenders at least three major challenges.

**Integrating the Business (Internally) in a Distributed Environment.** This issue actually breaks down into a series of related issues, such as:

- Ensuring that employees located in remote or branch offices have the information they need to do their work.
- Ensuring that employees across different locations can communicate effectively and work together as teams.
- Ensuring that employees across all locations understand critical objectives, are working together toward common goals, and receive the information feedback they need to evaluate and fine-tune their work. This is a huge problem and the reason why the concept of enterprise-wide information systems is becoming more important.

**Integrating Externally with Other Entities.** Companies that previously carried out business transactions with suppliers or customers primarily by phone or mail are now interacting through such electronic communications methods as Electronic Data Interchange, electronic mail (e-mail), and the World Wide Web. The question here is how to establish effective communication yet ensure that information is not shared inappropriately.

**Providing a Consistent — if Not Common or at Least Unified — Supporting Infrastructure.** Such an infrastructure comprises voice communications, fax, networked computers, and information access and exchange across all locations.

## INTEROPERABILITY: THE TECHNICAL CHALLENGE

Because organizations depend on the enabling tools of information technology, their business objectives for enterprise computing are accompanied by a host of technical issues. Interoperability, however, is most often the stumbling block to mission-critical client/server systems.

Large-scale client/server applications involve complex networks, usually with many local area networks (LANs) interconnected through a wide area network. More often, such applications involve multiple wide area network (WAN) and multiple network protocols, such as the IBM System Network Architecture (SNA), NetBIOS, Transmission Control Protocol/Internet Protocol (TCP/IP), and Frame Relay. They typically involve several different computing platforms, or different types of computers running different operating systems, such as PCs running Microsoft Corp.'s Windows; servers running Hewlett-Packard's HP-UX; and mainframes running IBM Corp.'s MVS and Canadian Independent Computing Services Association. They often involve multiple databases, perhaps based on different database management system (DBMS) platforms, such as Oracle Corp.'s ORACLE and the IBM DB/2 and Internet Multicasting Service. And, they will certainly involve business applications on distributed platforms tied together in a number of different ways, such as by transaction monitors, message-oriented middleware, data access middleware, Web services, and remote procedure calls (RPCs), or sometimes by clumsier mechanisms like file transfers or sequential batch processing jobs.

Systems integration at the enterprise level entails getting many different information systems components to work together across the enterprise network. Because these myriad components must interoperate effectively, interoperability is the first key to success. But, interoperability is not simply a problem of network protocol compatibility — it exists at many different levels, such as:

- Network interoperability
- Platform interoperability
- Database or data access interoperability
- Object or software component interoperability
- Presentation interoperability — graphical user interfaces (GUIs) and multimedia user interface (MUIs)
- Workgroup/workflow/e-mail interoperability
- Applications interoperability

**Network Interoperability**

Today, many companies running very large networks use multiple network protocols. If they are or were large IBM shops, they typically have 3270 terminal protocol, plus one or more SNA protocols on their wide area network (WAN), NetBIOS on their LANs, TCP/IP on their UNIX-based engineering networks, and perhaps even some Novell Internetwork Packet eXchange. Multiple Network Operating Systems may be a management issue, but at the application-to-application level, differing protocols and spanning across networks of varying types are usually the biggest problems. For example, on an System Network Architecture Logical Unit 6.2-only network, a client application can be written to invoke the APPC application programming interface (API) to establish a session and exchange information with a server application that also uses the APPC API. However, when one application is on a System Network Architecture network and the partner application is on a TCP/IP network, a major interoperability problem arises.

## Platform Interoperability

Organizations striving to implement mission-critical distributed applications face the difficult challenge of interoperability among platforms of completely different types, such as IMS on IBM mainframes and UNIX platforms. Much of what has been done to date under the client/server classification involves decision support applications. Most mission-critical functions are performed primarily with the assistance of mainframe applications; yet, getting IMS or CICS to talk to non-IBM platforms, and especially non-mainframe platforms, is proving to be difficult.

## Database Interoperability

This category of interoperability has to do with applications accessing information in databases located on multiple systems, in databases on different platform types, or — the most difficult of all — in databases of completely different types (such as Oracle and IMS). The interoperability problem is somewhat lessened if all databases are relational databases using Structured Query Language (SQL), although not all structured query languages are the same. It is definitely easier if all databases use the same DBMS product, but even then there may be difficulties between certain platforms or with certain network protocols. In any of these cases, database interoperability is a major consideration, especially when legacy systems are involved and are expected to work with newer systems.

## Object/Software Component Interoperability

The advent of object-oriented systems in which data is encapsulated in objects allows information to be exchanged between applications as objects. The exchange is handled by an Object-Request-Broker, originally defined by the Object Management Group. Object request brokers (ORBs) are now available from multiple software companies.

Issues are surfacing, however, with ORB dependence on remote procedure calls when operating across enterprise networks, and with ORB-to-ORB interoperability — that is, getting different ORB products from different vendors, usually also involving different platforms, to work together. Applications built using other types of component-based software are also becoming more commonplace — with Microsoft's VBX (Visual Basic

69

Custom Controls) being the most frequently cited type. The major issues are how such reusable components exchange information with other components and how they can work consistently and compatibly on different platforms.

### GUI/MUI Interoperability

Another issue concerns how applications using a graphical user interface or multimedia user interfaces can be written to work on different platforms. This is, in part, a portability problem rather than an interoperability problem.

The real interoperability problem with multimedia user interface applications, which are expected to proliferate in the future, is twofold. It concerns interoperation of graphical user interface (GUI) functions as part of client/server exchanges when different types of GUIs are involved, such as Windows, Presentation Manager, and Motif, and how to make Full-Motion Video or interactive compound media information exchanges work across heterogeneous platforms and heterogeneous networks.

### Workgroup/Workflow/E-Mail Interoperability

As groupware connectivity becomes more common, one workgroup using one groupware product will increasingly need to interoperate with other workgroups using different groupware products. This is especially true with intercompany connectivity. Workflow interoperability, therefore, is a problem of:

- Integrating different groupware, workflow, and e-mail products
- Supporting these types of applications across heterogeneous platforms and networks
- Integrating groupware, workflow, and e-mail applications with other types of applications
- Resolving differences in document formats such that, wherever possible, format conversion takes place automatically under the covers

### Applications Interoperability

Distributed computing usually refers to distributing the processing among applications located on different systems. Enterprise computing extends distributed computing to a larger scale — across an enterprise network of LANs, wide area network (WAN), and multiple kinds of platforms — but it may also go much farther by integrating applications in different business disciplines, such as the employee skills database and corporate directory services. In both cases, at the level where things must happen based on business events, one application somewhere on the network must exchange data with another application somewhere else on the network. Interoperability in terms of client/server computing always comes

| Business Applications |
| --- |
| Middleware<br>(Common Application Services) |
| System Services<br>(i.e., Database, Network, Operating System) |

**Exhibit 1. Layered Software Architecture**

down to application-to-application interoperability regardless of how many other kinds of interoperability issues are actually involved.

## MIDDLEWARE SOLUTIONS

Nearly all cases of successful large-scale distributed computing applications involve the use of middleware to solve interoperability problems. Middleware, as the name is meant to imply, is software that sits between business applications and the systems-level services, or so-called platforms that are the source of compatibility problems. Software layering, from which the middleware idea derives, is illustrated in Exhibit 1.

Because middleware is based on layering, with a new layer of software being inserted as a higher-level platform on which business applications will reside, it provides a degree of encapsulation or abstraction of the lower-level services. In fact, middleware typically introduces new APIs that are used to invoke the higher-level services. That is why it is common for applications designers and programmers to talk in terms of the new APIs — for example, Microsoft's Open Database Connectivity or MAPI, or the IBM DRDA — when describing how applications will be interconnected and how one or more of the interoperability problems will be solved.

Because of the layering effect, middleware helps insulate business applications from changes in platforms, networks, or other systems services. IT executives can therefore change the underlying technologies, using more effective and efficient ones, without changing the applications. The abstraction of services through the higher-level APIs also simplifies applications programming, enabling programmers to create or modify applications more quickly in response to business changes. By providing the means for linking applications together across a network, middleware provides a mechanism for applications interoperability and information access.

There are several types of middleware, including:

- X.400, MAPI, Simple Mail Transfer Protocol (SMTP)
- X.500, Streettalk
- ODBC, Distributed Relational Database Architecture, distributed DBMS

- DCE, ONC
- CORBA/ORB, OLE2/COM, OpenDoc, Enterprise JavaBeans
- Gateways (such as Structured Query Language Server and Omni-Connect)
- RPCs
- Message passing and queuing
- Transaction monitors

Most of these types of middleware are ultimately aimed at the application-to-application connectivity problem. Some are specific to e-mail interoperability (X.400, MAPI, SMTP); some are specific to database interoperability (ODBC, DRDA, distributed DBMS, database gateways); some are specific to object-oriented interoperability (ORB, OLE2, Open-Doc); and some are more generalized (DCE, Remote Procedure Call, message passing and queuing).

All these types of middleware let one application exchange information with another application. The exceptions are X.500 and Streettalk, which are directory services (i.e., middleware that addresses the problem of how applications are identified and actually found in large enterprise networks).

There are other interoperability solutions as well, such as protocol converters, bridges, gateways, data format translators, and other special-purpose hardware and software, but often these work at a system or network level and do not facilitate the application-to-application dialogues that are fundamental to client/server and other forms of distributed computing. The need for the direct exchange of information between applications in a heterogeneous environment has caused middleware to come into existence and to now play a dominant role in the IT architectures of progressive enterprises.

### Message-Oriented Middleware

One particular type of middleware — message-oriented middleware — allows an application to send messages (i.e., data) to other applications and to receive messages in return. It encompasses message passing, message queuing, and transaction monitors. Messages in this context are any type of transaction or other exchange that might occur between distributed applications. The meaning and the format of the messages are defined by the structure and contents of the data to meet the requirements of each particular distributed application.

One example of commercial message-oriented middleware, and probably the earliest to be used in a mission-critical production environment, is the Communications Integrator (CI) of Covia Technologies (Englewood Central Office). The Communications Integrator, first used in the computerized airline reservations system industry, was initially developed by

United Airlines for its Apollo reservations network. CI originated in the mid-1980s to allow applications to become independent of network protocols, which in turn would facilitate moving applications to new servers/hosts within the network, allow new hardware and software platforms to be added to the network more readily, and simplify the complexities of programming for application-to-application communication.

The Apollo network was already a very large network with database server applications running on mainframes, new services being added regularly, and transaction volumes growing rapidly. Because plans were being made for PCs and LANs at customer sites, LAN servers, and PC-based LAN-to-WAN gateways to be added to the reservations network, a much more dynamic and adaptable approach was needed for dealing with distributed applications in a changing network environment. It is also interesting to note that between 1985 and the early 1990s when commercial message-oriented middleware was not yet available, many other companies with large networks in industries other than airline reservations were going through similar transitions and developing their own in-house message middleware.

The approach used in the CI, which was sold for the first time in industries other than the airlines industry beginning in late 1991, was to architect an API having consistent functions, verb set, and options (i.e., parameters) across all platforms regardless of operating system, language used for the product implementation, or network protocols supported. The Communications Integrator API allows applications to register with the message service and then call a send routine to send messages or a receive routine to receive messages. Applications do not have to deal with the problems of network sessions because the Communications Integrator, running on each node, takes care of all session management under the covers.

When sending a message, applications take advantage of the CI directory services to simply specify the name of the application to receive the message; select a message type (i.e., asynchronous or one-way, or synchronous or query with correlated reply); select other options such as priority, assurance level, and whether notification is requested; and then issue the send. When receiving a message, applications select the mode (i.e., blocking or non-blocking), select whether looking for a reply to a specific query or simply the next one available, and then issue the receive command.

### An Example of Middleware Use

Healthcare Data Exchange (HDX), headquartered in Malvern, Pennsylvania, near Philadelphia, provides one example of how middleware is used in a large distributed application. Using the Communications Integrator, Half-DupleX channel has implemented a patient insurance eligibility and claims system for its multi-state network of healthcare providers. Client applications resident in PCs at the admission desks of providers initiate requests for patient records, eligibility, and admissions based on information supplied by the patient. These requests are sent to appropriate server applications running on local servers or on mainframes at HDX data centers. Switching applications at intermediate servers may trigger multiple requests to systems both inside the HDX network (e.g., HDX claims processing on an IBM mainframe or HDX accounting systems on Digital Equipment Corporation mainframes) and outside (e.g., eligibility with Medicare or commercial insurance companies). Responses containing screen displays, printed patient records, admissions paperwork, or billing statements are sent back to the admission clerk's PC or to a print server application located nearby. Response times must, of course, be kept as short as possible.

The networked healthcare information business places great demands on client/server applications. In the HDX case, middleware provided flexibility and adaptability to deal with several different platforms, the possibility of future network changes such as from System Network Architecture to TCP/IP, and rapid growth, while at the same time simplifying programming through a higher-level message API.

Although the Communications Integrator is no longer being sold, other middleware products are now available. Some examples include MQSeries from IBM, and PIPES from PeerLogic. In addition, distributed transaction monitors, such as Tuxedo from BEA and Microsoft Transaction Server, are now also positioned as message-oriented middleware products.

## TRENDS IN MIDDLEWARE DEVELOPMENT

Given the multi-platform, multi-protocol world in which most modern enterprises operate, middleware has come into existence in the past ten years as a necessary means of providing applications with a degree of insulation from the differences across platforms and protocols. As such, middleware allows the applications to be less affected by changes in those platforms and protocols, while simultaneously providing interoperability across a heterogeneous IT environment.

There has been a great explosion in products within each niche or type of middleware, and new types of middleware products are being developed to meet new needs and to solve new interoperability problems. The rapid growth of the Internet, for example, has generated new products for Internet-based applications, and middleware that allows applications on corporate desktops and servers to interact in real-time with applications on Internet servers should now be available. Middleware development is still in its growth stage, and the middleware marketplace has not yet seen much consolidation.

Ultimately, the market will determine which are the preferred middleware solutions. Such solutions will likely be strongly influenced by other IT trends, such as the development of object-oriented and multimedia technologies. In the end, the preferred middleware solutions must not only be embraced by end users, they must also be integrated by software vendors into the application and tool products that must interface with the end users' custom applications.

Critical issues to customers will be whether the middleware supports the customer's particular platforms and network protocols, is relatively easy to use, and is relatively easy to manage — that is, whether and how easily the middleware can be installed, configured, and tuned in a distributed manner. The market must also contend with issues relating to the degree of integration and compatibility with other middleware products and with common applications, especially those used by each customer to conduct day-to-day business.

Although applications developers would like it to be otherwise, evolution of middleware products, along with other client/server tools, will take time — maybe five to ten years. In the meantime, businesses must be able to solve their interoperability problems so that they can implement distributed computing solutions that meet business needs. In some cases, these systems might be characterized as enterprisewide information systems that are used throughout the enterprise and allow the enterprise to act in a more integrated way in serving customers. There may also be smaller enterprise client/server applications that improve some business process, such as customer support, by automating and facilitating customer interaction in a consistent way across many different functions of the enterprise.

In any case, distributed systems today, and for at least the next several years, will likely use point solutions — middleware tools selected according to the unique requirements of the particular system being implemented — rather than integrated solution sets that are suitable for use in all distributed applications of the enterprise.

Given time, however, client/server software and middleware tools will inevitably achieve greater maturity, and integrated solution sets will be offered by the major software companies. Many software vendors, just like end users, are struggling to deal with diverse platforms and protocols and the related interoperability problems. Some vendors specialize only in selected software markets and systems, such as PCs or UNIX, but the most complete solutions will likely come from the software vendors who are now established players in enterprise networking, such as IBM or Computer Associates, or those who may be able to expand to that level, such as Microsoft.

## RECOMMENDED COURSE OF ACTION

Because most situations in which organizations are striving to implement client/server applications are unique, IT staffs should research middleware options themselves or hire specialist consultants to find the best solutions to meet their specific requirements. In some cases, for example, a distributed DBMS such as Oracle may fit the particular situation; in others, message-oriented middleware may provide the right interoperability solution.

Assessing and managing the risks involved in proposed solutions cannot be taken lightly, however. Proof of concept should be considered a necessary phase of any first-time undertaking or sizable project to ensure that the software and the hidden complexities that are part of large-scale and mission-critical client/server applications are fully understood. System requirements must address the adaptability and probable life of the middleware as part of the adaptability and probable life of the overall client/server application. These strategies can be used to manage middleware decisions and distributed application projects.

Many successful mission-critical applications have been implemented in recent years, and middleware tools supporting such applications should continue to evolve to meet the needs of the market. As the market matures, middleware products will have added functions and features, improve in performance, and become more proven in real business conditions. These are the attributes that enterprise-level client/server computing demands.

# Chapter 7

# A Complex Multi-Location Enterprise: Issues and Possible Solutions

*Phillip L. Davidson*

The complexity of today's healthcare enterprises seems to grow exponentially, requiring new tools and new solutions to very complicated issues. The issues involve large databases that must coordinate active and inactive patient members, physician databases, benefits and eligibility databases, plus huge databases for pharmacy and laboratory, including inventory and tests performed. Size of the databases is certainly an issue, but at least as important is the ability to keep data current and in sync with other related databases.

The following discussion focuses on a large multi-facility healthcare enterprise that has connectivity to other medical centers from another organization. The solution must also consider connectivity to outside reference resources such as reference laboratories.

## INTERENTERPRISE CONNECTIVITY

Exhibit 1 reflects a generalized overview of an enterprisewide healthcare information system. This is a generic model commonly found in many large healthcare systems, and the difficulties of maintaining such a system are numerous: maintenance of patient demographics; maintenance of benefits and eligibility; timely admissions, discharges, and transfers; and maintenance of a provider database.

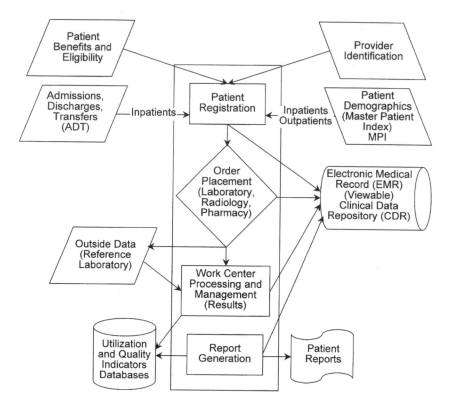

**Exhibit 1. Generic Inter-enterprise Healthcare Solution**

## Maintenance of Patient Demographics

Accurate patient information [name, social security number, home address and phone number, medical record number (MRN), etc.] are all critical for efficiency and efficacy of patient care and for billing and benefits issues. Many larger healthcare organizations now maintain active and inactive lists of over a million patients. Estimates of inaccuracies in these databases range as high as 20 percent, leading to increased inefficiencies, potential delays to the delivery of patient care, and higher administrative costs.

One solution to the difficulties in dealing with these problems is a truly relational database or master patient index (MPI) that allows the information system to reference multiple checkpoints and make match/no match decisions based on key criteria. This will be discussed in greater detail later, but such a solution brings its own problems.

An MPI should reduce overall administrative overhead. However, these types of products utilize very elaborate and resource-hungry database software such as Oracle or Sybase. While these are not the only tools available, they are the most commonly used. Both require significant hardware upgrades and dedicated staff for maintenance. However, the return on investment (ROI) is usually significant once the system is operational.

### Maintenance of Benefits and Eligibility

Being aware of what benefits accrue to each patient is a complex and incredibly important issue in today's very competitive healthcare environment. Patients hate long waits while clerks search to discover appropriate co-pays or services covered. In addition, employers must be able to offer a larger variety of health plan benefits to employee groups (this is frequently legislated at the state level). Therefore, a system that can keep track of benefits not only at the employer level, but also down to the specific contract level are essential in today's healthcare marketplace. Paper tracking in large healthcare enterprises with millions of patients is virtually useless, extremely expensive in the cost of personnel for tracking, and involves unnecessarily high administrative expenses. Several large healthcare organizations now have large, single-platform systems for tracking individuals down to the individual contracts and which are updated in near-real-time through a centralized benefits department.

This last sentence needs to be emphasized. Having a benefits system in place that tracks down to the contract level is worth its weight in gold. However, if benefit updates take weeks and months to happen, the value is questionable. A centralized, well-staffed benefits department with fast on-line access to the benefits and eligibility database is absolutely essential for the success of this aspect.

### Timely Admissions, Discharges, and Transfers

Administrative overhead is the single largest expense in managed care today. Timely admissions, discharges, and transfers (ADT) are essential for keeping administrative costs low. The frustration at not being able to track patient movement is both expensive and potentially dangerous to patient care. This seems like an obvious comment, but the issues are rarely dealt with at an enterprisewide level.

ADT is frequently not under the control and coordination of one group of people. In large enterprises, I have seen ADT managed by floor support staff, local business office personnel, and — in at least one case — by volunteers staffing the front information desk. Visual recognition of a patient coming into or leaving the hospital should clearly not be an acceptable method of admission or discharge, but it does happen.

Lack of formal protocols makes this process administratively expensive. Physicians frequently give transfer or discharge information verbally to support staff with the expectation that information will be acted upon.

However, physician providers rarely have the time or opportunity to follow up on this information, and support staff might have conflicting tasks, which delay or allow such information to go unacted upon for a significant time. Centralized, protocol-explicit ADT is essential in reducing administrative overhead.

### Maintenance of a Provider Database

Maintenance of the physician provider database for a one-hospital enterprise is not that difficult, even with paper. However, there are very few one-hospital organizations left. Most healthcare organizations have providers who work and practice at multiple locations. Being able to track the physician, and his or her payroll identification and specialty or service, is important in keeping efficiencies at their highest. Being able to track doctor office locations for the timely and accurate dispersal of reports is also a key aspect of such a database.

### PATIENT REGISTRATION

There have been many (not so funny) cartoons and editorials about patient registration in large healthcare enterprises. The "cattle-call" approach is, unfortunately, still alive and well. This is surprising considering that the process is relatively easy to automate with tools available to healthcare systems today. However, sometimes the initial costs are a bit daunting, yet the ROI is almost always quite sufficient.

Magnetic stripe health plan cards seem to offer a key advantage to those organizations that use them. Human error in manual registration is significant, regardless of the carefulness of the staff. Large organizations frequently have patients with the same first and last names, sometimes with the same date of birth. Being able to catch these is difficult with human-only intervention.

Magstripe cards offer significant advantages, especially if the databases above are current and reliable. The magstripe card only needs to contain the medical record number (or whatever key indicator the organization chooses). When passed through the magstripe reader, patient identification and benefits should automatically be presented to the registration clerk. The process should be quick and efficient.

One difficulty that arises in many larger organizations is that there is an apparent need for multiple registration areas. Patients who are being admitted must first present themselves in the admissions department. The laboratory, pharmacy, and radiology might have registration areas in addition, each requiring the patient to go through the same process (and frequently pay new co-pays each time) at each station. Such a process makes no sense from either the patient or the health plan perspective. While there are arguments against single entry and exit registration areas, those arguments do not stand up well against the savings in both administrative costs and increased patient satisfaction.

## ELECTRONIC MEDICAL RECORD

There are two chapters in this text on the electronic medical record (EMR). See Chapter 20 by Mark Leavitt on EMR and Chapter 21 by Russell Sachs on EMR costs for greater detail.

There is probably no other healthcare issue that has received the level of attention and that has caused more grief and utilized more IT money than the EMR. This is especially true in the attempt to come up with a national medical record.

From the standpoint of a healthcare organization that has control within its own boundaries, however, there is little excuse not to be using an EMR. The EMR provides the ability to display up-to-the-minute data to physician providers regarding all aspects of medical care. This might not have been as important 20 years ago when the difference of staying two or three days in the hospital did not seem to be a major event. However, in today's managed care environment (for better or for worse), utilization staff track inpatient time down to the hour. Patients can frequently be held unnecessarily for an additional day because of a delay in receiving essential discharge information such as laboratory tests.

## CLINICAL DATA REPOSITORY

One of the most surprising areas is that few healthcare organizations actually maintain a robust clinical data repository (CDR). They are becoming more common, but there are still a majority of organizations that have not yet implemented such an essential program.

The ability to retrieve archived patient data has numerous benefits. First, it is virtually impossible in today's healthcare environment to retrieve complete medical records after even a few months. In many cases, the chart might be fragmented, pieces being kept in multiple locations or departments. The CDR (which is essential in supporting the EMR) allows for quick retrieval of the complete record. With new storage media such as CD-ROM being available, retrieval can be quick and efficient.

In addition to the ability to track and retrieve complete medical records quickly, a robust CDR also allows the healthcare organization to do studies on utilization. The ability to study what works and what does not, and who is overutilizing, and to be able to present that data objectively, is incredibly important in maintaining costs in today's healthcare world.

## ELECTRONIC CHARTS

Related to the EMR and CDR is the idea of electronic charts. If one has a complete EMR, then there should be no need for paper charts. Paper charts are the bane of modern healthcare. They are rarely complete in one location. Interpretation of handwritten notes is difficult at best. Timely delivery to the proper location in a multi-site healthcare organization is unlikely at best, which only encourages the department or provider to start yet another chart.

Current areas of improvement in interfaces with radiology and laboratory systems allow not only notes but also actual images to be included in an electronic chart. Voice recognition technology (see Chapter 32 by Greg Pierce) now makes note transcription easier and faster and inputs data directly to the electronic chart.

The electronic chart also offers the advantage of accessibility. Through local intranets or even secure extranets, providers are no longer forced to be in any particular location to view this information. In addition, in large health plans with multiple sites, it is irrelevant as to where the patient presents as far as keeping the chart complete is concerned.

Problems with the electronic chart are primarily based on historical precedence. Providers have grown attached to the physical chart, even with its incompleteness. It seems illogical that it would be more cost efficient and more timely for the patient to have the physician thumbing through hundreds of patients to find specific test results or comments left by another physician. An electronic chart would have all this data available at a keystroke.

Another problem with electronic charts has to do with legislative and regulatory authorities that also have a hard time accepting the reality of our plugged-in world. Many times there is a demand for hardcopy, even when the electronic results are easily available. This last issue will eventually go away with time, but it seems slow in happening.

## THE NEXT STEP: PARTNERSHIPS

The competitive healthcare marketplace has forced healthcare organizations to be more cognizant of wasted resources. This includes both staff and facilities. A wide variety of permutations of shared partnerships have developed where staff and facilities are shared between organizations that have nothing more in common than the desire to save money and stay competitive. Such arrangements offer significant political and economic challenges. They also offer serious challenges to maintaining a coherent patient EMR. The remainder of this section deals with that issue.

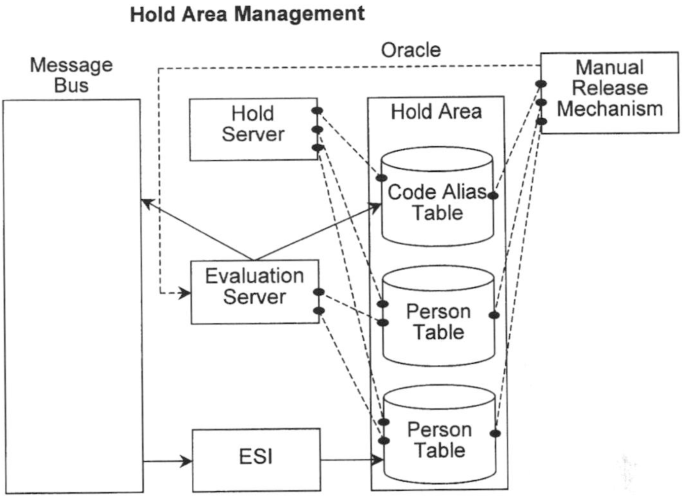

**Hold Area Management**

**Exhibit 2. Patient Identification, Evaluation, and Hold**

## Reaching a Common Ground

When interfacing to another healthcare program, it suddenly becomes very clear how dissimilar we really can be. The first point of contention concerns the issue of patient identification. Some health plans create their own MRN while many use social security number (SSN) as the patient identifier. The question is "how do disparate systems agree as to the identify of the patient?"

From your own perspective, you naturally choose your own patient identifier as "the gold standard." However, there needs to be some way of collating the other group's identifier as well, and that identifier can be used as a good check in future encounters. For these reasons, a robust relational database is necessary.

Such a database tool can allow the comparison of patient name, MRN, SSN, age, residence, and gender — or any other items in the patient demographic database — as points of comparison. Exhibit 2 shows what such a process might look like. The process involves receiving an HL7 (see below) message from the sending facility. The message goes into an evaluation server, where points you have chosen for comparison are evaluated. You weight the points of comparison, some being primary. If the evaluation server finds a clear match between patients in the demographic database, then the results attached to that HL7 message are passed along to the data repository and are available for viewing by the physician providers.

The evaluation server has access to a variety of information, including other names (aliases) that a person might use. This is especially important in names changed by marriage.

If the evaluation server cannot make a match on the patient data, the information string is passed to the hold server. At periodic intervals, the information in the hold server is compared against new data coming in, and might make a match as the patient demographic information is updated.

The last avenue of release is the manual release mechanism. A human can intervene for data in the hold server and make a determination that there is a match or not. If approved, the newly released data is entered into the database, and is then available for comparison to additional incoming data.

## HL7

A key to this process is being able to have message strings that mean the same to both the transmitting systems as well as the receiving system. This is done by changing inbound and outbound messages to HL7, a commonly agreed-upon standard.

HL7 stands for Health Level 7. It is a standard that allows disparate systems in the medical enterprise to intercommunicate freely. HL7 is a specification for electronic data exchange between healthcare institutions, particularly hospitals, and between different computer systems within hospitals. HL7 is oriented toward the clinical and administrative aspects of the medical enterprise. It defines standard message types (for example, admit a patient, report a lab result) with required and optional data for each. Messages are defined to be independent of computer system and communications protocol, and they are constructed so that later versions of the HL7 standard can add data elements without "breaking" systems using older versions of HL7.

HL7 began as a bottom-up movement by system vendors and hospitals to replace custom-built system interfaces with a shared standard. Systems using the HL7 standard can interact with other HL7 systems to:

- Inform other systems of information that it has created, destroyed, or modified
- Receive information about new, deleted, or changed information
- Ask other systems for information
- Be asked for information by other systems

HL7 systems can communicate the following types of information:

- Patient medical history and demographics
- Encounter and visit history
- ADT and patient tracking information

- Scheduling and referrals
- Orders and results (measurements, observations, impressions, reports)
- Pharmacy and diet information
- Census information

More detailed information about HL7 and message formatting can be located on the Internet at http://www.mcis.duke.edu/standards/HL7/faq/HL7FAQ10.HTM.

Having HL7 message formatting in place allows significant cost savings from older methods that tried to translate messages or parts of messages. And now, with new tools such as interface engines (see Chapter 3 on interface engines), we have a way of easily creating translation tools and converting non-HL7 messages into transmissible HL7 code.

### Connectivity to Another Health Plan

Exhibit 3 shows a diagram of one health plan connecting to another. It involves a foreign hospital information system (HIS) connecting via an interface engine to the local interface engine and then into the local HIS.

In this diagram, patient information is entered into the foreign HIS. That information is passed to the foreign interface engine, which performs multiple functions. One function is to retransmit the patient data and ordered

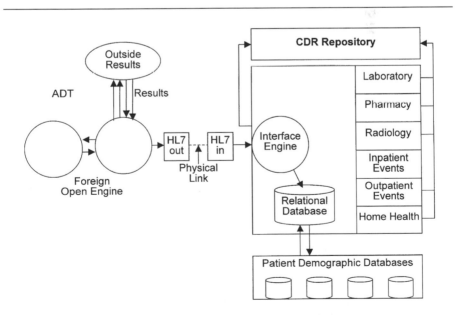

**Exhibit 7-3. Connectivity to a Foreign System**

procedures to the respective departments (laboratory, pharmacy, x-ray, etc.). The second function is to reformat the message into HL7 where it can be transmitted to the local HIS via the local interface engine.

The local interface engine receives the incoming HL7 message and "unpacks" it. Patient identity is established as mentioned before. If orders for work to be done at the local site are included in the HL7 message, those messages are passed along to the various performing departments.

Patient data and results data from the foreign HIS can be stored in the local CDR and made available for electronic display both locally as well as in the foreign HIS if necessary.

## Concerns and Issues

The use of HL7 has made life much easier than when we used to try and get very disparate systems to talk to each other. However, there are still issues. One issue is that the HL7 message is looking for specific information. If one system or the other does not used specific fields within the message string, it may not be possible to ignore that field. Second, both sides might populate a certain field with a completely different set of information. This is particularly true with patient IDs. If one HIS uses SSN as the gold standard for identifying a patient but the other HIS uses its own MRN, both fields will have to be seen by both systems and an agreement reached as to which fields those might be. Incoming databases will have to understand which of these fields is the local gold standard for patient ID.

Another issue has to do with databases. A good example is the clinical laboratory. Tests that are called the same thing in both systems may, in fact, not be the same. For example, a complete blood count (CBC) is a very common and routine procedure performed by virtually all clinical laboratories. However, a CBC will vary significantly between clinical laboratories, depending primarily upon the type of instrumentation utilized to perform the test. Therefore, you cannot assume that tests with the same name are identical. Chances are better that the opposite is true.

Therefore, in building an interface between disparate health plans, there is a lot of work required to compare data elements that will be shared. In many cases, unique data elements will need to be created for the other health plan. This is true for both sides.

One issue that occurs is identifying which health plan a patient belongs to. There are a variety of tools available for indicating that individuals belong to another group, but this must frequently be a manual intervention at the registration process. Anytime a manual intervention is required, you increase the likelihood of errors. The ideal situation would be that patients from the foreign system have magstripe health plan cards that are also recognizable by the local HIS.

There is also the inevitable question of ownership of responsibility of the correctness of data. If patient data entered in my hand at the foreign HIS contains a mistake, the local HIS hold management server will probably not be able to match the incoming data with the correct patient identification. Perhaps manual intervention will resolve the local issue and a message will be stored in the local MPI that tells us that this error did occur and — if we see it again — we can recognize it as the same error and then make the same match. However, the erroneous data are in two databases — the foreign database as well as the local database. You can make manual corrections at both locations, but it would be preferable to initiate a correction routine from the originating source that would make corrections on both sides.

Another smaller issue is actually connectivity. How expeditious does this interface have to be? Can results be "traded" once a day, or does the work need to be real time? The answer to that question will affect how you build the outgoing network. Will it be a modem or a direct connect? For real time, a direct connection is logical, but then the question becomes one of who owns the connection and who maintains it. Typically a leased line is the best solution for real-time connections and this avoids ownership issues.

**IN SUMMARY**

Over the past ten years, I have been involved with more than a dozen networks between health plans that were conglomerates of different groups and that were trying to maximize their resources. The work used to be brutal and was rarely successful. The advent of tools such as interface engines and protocols such as HL7 have significantly enhanced the likelihood of success. However, there are many versions of interface engines and several versions of HL7, so success is certainly not guaranteed.

In today's world, one common event is large managed care organizations buying groups of hospitals. Many of these hospitals already have HIS installed and the likelihood that they all have the same HIS is probably zero. It is therefore a common problem for large managed care companies to try and consolidate patient data much in the manner described above. There are disparate HIS software, running on disparate hardware (DEC, IBM, Tandem, UNIX), and somehow the data all needs to look the same.

The work is tedious and requires a significant focus on quality for it to maintain its value. However, my work experience tells me that these are not the biggest obstacles to success. The biggest obstacles come from people who want to be in control. Large healthcare organizations may be able to mandate ownership. They might even be able to consolidate their information systems groups into a single group under a single CIO or CMIO (see Chapter 26 relating to the CMIO). But creating a common database (especially test database) for laboratory, pharmacy, and radiology is very, very difficult. And the question about who will intercede when there is conflict must also be addressed.

Despite all of the issues and concerns raised, I have seen this process succeed and the results are very rewarding for the patient and the physician provider. The patient is able to experience a quick and efficient registration into the system and usually has increased mobility as to where he or she can be seen. The provider is also able to disregard location, and can view and access data from virtually anywhere. In addition, data is current and complete, which is a benefit for all sides, providing a higher quality of healthcare for less money.

# Section III
# Disaster Planning
# and System Security

# Chapter 8
# Building a Culture for Business Continuity Planning

*Merida L. Johns*

The "to do" list is at least arm's length — developing the repository, integrating the ancillary systems, updating the architecture, expanding the training program, bringing up the intranet, and implementing the document imaging system. An A+ for the information systems team as it adds up accomplishment after accomplishment! Until, that is, a disaster strikes, and accomplishments fall like a domino effect. Who remembers the accomplishments when the basket holding all the eggs falls apart? Or who cares about past accomplishments or who accomplished them when the effects of a disaster impair, impede, interrupt, or halt a company's ability to deliver its goods and services.

We plan for disasters in our everyday lives. A significant part of our personal disaster planning is taking preventative measures to minimize the likelihood that a disaster will befall us. We make sure that our automobile does not run out of fuel; we install smoke detectors in our homes; we pay our utility bills; and we do a host of other things that reduce the chance of a personal disaster.

We also put effort into developing an organized response if disaster does strike. We have candles and matches in the drawer and batteries in the flashlight should the electricity go off. We have a store of fuses in our closet should a fuse be blown. We have battery cables in our trunk should our battery die. We carry a spare tire in case we have a flat. Our lives are full of contingency plans should those "just-in-case" events occur.

In addition to preventing personal disasters and developing organized responses, we also ensure that we can carry out our response plans. We know how to replace fuses, we know how to operate the flashlight, and we know how to put on a spare tire. In other words, we are usually very good risk managers.

0-8493-1498-4/03/$0.00+$1.50
© 2003 by CRC Press LLC

The proclivity for self-protection is powerful when it comes to ensuring our personal well-being. The propensity for protection is also powerful when it comes to public safety. Many of the measures in place today to reduce the likelihood of disasters in the workplace and community are the result of experience with the effects of disasters or because we recognize the potentially disastrous effects that may result from an untoward event. While we try to minimize the likelihood of disasters and develop contingencies should they occur in our personal lives and in the community, why is it that too few organizations have contingency plans for information systems? Among the reasons cited for not committing to disaster planning is the perception that it is a process which is too costly, time-consuming, and tedious. The terminology "disaster planning" itself has propagated, to a great degree, misunderstandings about the true nature of the process and its intended outcomes. "Disaster planning" has been interpreted by some as planning for an event that has a very low likelihood of occurring. Is it any wonder that, when approached from this viewpoint, cost-conscious executives put disaster planning on the back burner? Why allocate resources for an endeavor that is not believed to have a good return on investment?

## THE PHILOSOPHY OF BUSINESS CONTINUITY PLANNING

It has been recognized that planning for a disaster is not an answer for ensuring that information systems, which support business processes, are not impaired, adversely impacted, halted, or interrupted by untoward events. The primary goal of any organization is to deliver its goods and services without interruption. Thus, the concept of planning for a disaster falls short of this intended goal. Instead, what is required is a broader view of keeping the organization in business by maintaining its processes so that goods and services can be delivered without interruption. Thus, the foundation for a successful business continuity planning (BCP) process is understanding that the primary goal and outcome is to save the business, not the computer. A critical component of saving the business includes setting up procedures that prevent an organization "from being placed at-risk or in jeopardy, and, if such unavoidably occurs, to provide the organization with the flexibility and elasticity to be able to bounce back with minimal effect on operational continuity" (p. 5).[1] Thus, like the personal preparedness scenarios cited above, experts agree that BCP has at least four components.[2-3] These include:

1. Identifying potential disasters and their effects
2. Taking preventive measures to minimize the likelihood of disasters occurring
3. Developing an organized response should a disaster strike
4. Ensuring that business processes continue during the disaster recovery period

Essentially, then, BCP is based on the theory of managing risk as opposed to preparing for a disaster. As Levitt[1] notes,

> The approach, the underlying philosophy, and the operational activities and functions are based on the premise that the organization (1) faces a finite number of definable risks; (2) each of these risks can be measured in terms of likelihood of occurrence; (3) there are substantial opportunities to reduce these inherent levels of risk; (4) the impact of any of the risks, when occurring, on each business function can be determined or predicted before it occurs; and, (5) each risk, and its impact on any business function, can be managed in a manner consistent with the needs of the organization (p. 5).

While these steps appear fairly straightforward, organizations have had difficulty translating them into action. Various reasons have been cited for inaction. Some of these concern the cost of plan development, misunderstanding as to the nature of BCP, and the complexity of the process itself. In a study conducted by *Contingency Planning and Management* magazine and Ernst & Young LLP, 95 percent of companies surveyed report that they are either developing or have some type of BCP in place. On the face of it, this is a remarkable percentage. Further scrutiny, however, indicates that

> ... twenty-five percent of the respondents state this as currently developing which is of no help if a major disruption occurs in the meantime. Thirty-three percent say they have local plans in certain departments/divisions, yet to fully realize the value of a BCP, it must be implemented corporate wide. Therefore, it could be that only 38 percent who stated that they had corporate wide plans in effect are fully protecting their companies.[3]

## ISSUES IN DEFINING DISASTER

What is a disaster? The term "disaster" is context specific. For example, there are political disasters, business disasters, publicity disasters, and natural disasters. What may be a disaster in one context, may not be a disaster in another. In the business context, the term "disaster" has been applied to significant business losses, such as a loss in market share, loss of top executives, and loss in balance sheet figures. It has also been applied to low product acceptance or to poor product performance. In the information systems realm, the term "disaster" has been defined in many ways. A disaster can range from "a flood, fire or earthquake to labor unrest or erasure of an important file" (p. 569).[4]

Alternatively, a disaster has been described as "an incident of such severity and magnitude that emergency steps are needed to stay in business" (p. 259).[5] From a business continuity perspective, the definition of disaster is probably best described as "when the organization is unable to continue to function in a predetermined manner, or is unable to recommence such functioning after the lapse of a predetermined, tolerable, time lapse" (p. 44).[1] What is of paramount importance in any BCP development is that the definition of disaster be established and used consistently throughout the enterprise.

While floods, hurricanes, fires, and power, communication, and technological failures might be included in anyone's list of top disaster causes, Rothstein notes that if a careful analysis of corporate disasters were conducted, it would be evident that there are numerous disaster causes or potential causes which are largely overlooked.[5] Examples include a seven-figure dollar loss because of a single database corrupted by a programmer who updated a production program without following production sign-off or turnover standards or procedures; the loss of a hospital pharmacy database when a disk crash led to the discovery that backup tapes had been made of the wrong files; sabotage of a data center by a former disgruntled employee; and when employees were prevented, due to flooding around corporate offices, from retrieving backup files stored on site so that they could be delivered to the off-site recovery area. Potential disasters lurk every day in our organizations. They may not be of the newspaper headline type, yet they will effectively produce the same results as an earthquake or a fire. As often as not, disasters "are compounded failures gradually escalating from seemingly innocuous, recoverable glitches to near-tragedies. In most cases, human error (whether proactive or reactive commission or omission) is the single greatest factor in growing a large headache into a small disaster."[6]

Businesses have indicated that the greatest cause for business interruption could be attributed to problems with their electrical power grid. In one survey of 560 respondents, 72 percent reported power outages and 34 percent indicated lightning/storm-related interruptions. More than 46 percent reported telecommunications failure. In addition, 52 percent of these respondents reported hardware problems and 43 percent reported problems with software.[3]

What is apparent today is that "disaster" has a very broad meaning. No longer is disaster solely associated with headline events such as hurricanes, earthquakes, tornadoes, or floods. Indeed, as Jackson and Woodworth note,[7] even brief interruptions to information systems can mean the inability to deliver products and services to the customer, which then impacts revenue, productivity, and customer relations. No longer does it take the worst-case disaster scenario to adversely impact a company's business processes or bottom line.

## DEVELOPMENT OF THE BUSINESS CONTINUITY PLAN

There are a variety of methodologies available for development of the business continuity plan. Some are more structured than others; some are more complex than others; some are proprietary and some are not. Whatever methodology is used, however, must be predicated on the underlying philosophy that BCP first and foremost concerns risk prevention and management and then concerns recovery and resumption. The emphasis must be on saving the company, as opposed to saving the computer system. Ultimately, the outcome of BCP is to ensure that if an untoward event does occur, irrespective of preventative measures that have been taken, it will not result in the collapse of the organization.

**Fundamental Guidelines for Building a Culture of Business Continuity Planning**

While abundant methodologies exist for development of the business continuity plan, some straightforward guidelines should be applied to any planning process. These are not listed in order of importance, but rather compose a set of considerations that should be incorporated into any plan development.

The process used to develop the plan must be manageable in nature and in cost. Too frequently, organizations embark upon planning using complex methodologies that result in a high price tag in terms of time, resources, and personnel. Often this results in abandonment of the process entirely and the business continuity plan is never realized. The moral is to select a methodology that makes sense for the organization and is compatible with the culture of the enterprise. When the methodology used is out of sync with the company culture, the result is more often than not unfavorable.

Another guiding principle is that BCP will only be successful when it has the full support of executive management. When the focus is on saving the company rather than saving the computer system, top management support is required to secure cooperation among the various stakeholders and to ensure that they understand that BCP is a high company priority. Executive management support is essential to support allocation of resources to the project. No matter how simple the chosen planning methodology is, the project will require time and resources — and this translates into cost. The "kiss of death" to any project is insufficient allocation of resources at the onset.

The goals of BCP must be clearly understood by all stakeholders. This means that every player understands that business continuity is first a process for management of risk and secondly a process of contingency planning and recovery. The goal is to keep the healthcare enterprise operational, not to save the computer system. Understanding this goal includes every functional manager as a stakeholder in the process. As stakeholders, managers are expected to assume responsibility for identifying and managing risk within their business process areas and for developing alternatives for operation should an untoward event occur.

Irrespective of the methodology used, the planning process must include an effective awareness and education program. Executive and functional managers must be made aware of specific incidents to which the organization is vulnerable. They must also understand that reducing the level of vulnerability is the top priority of a business continuity plan.

Specifically, as Myers[5] notes,

> Senior management must be made aware of the following facts: the business is exposed to sudden disaster. It makes good business sense to have at least a set of guidelines as a point of reference should a disaster actually happen.
>
> The Contingency Plan strategy is to protect market share, cash flow, and the ability to service customers during a disaster recovery period. The methodology to be used in plan development should specifically be designed to yield cost-effective solutions (p. 39).

An important component in any business continuity plan development is focus on business process areas. A vanilla plan that is "one size fits all" simply does not work. While many vulnerabilities are enterprisewide, some functional areas may be at higher risk for certain out-of-course events or have unique vulnerabilities. In addition, it is important to identify alternative contingency approaches for each functional area in order to coordinate and integrate operations in the event of a crisis. Thus, a systemic view must be taken to ensure that the alternative approaches used in one business area will meld with, integrate, or support those taken by another functional unit.

Any business continuity plan must be built upon a companywide definition of disaster. As previously noted, a disaster must be defined in terms of what constitutes an unacceptable interruption in normal business process and what constitutes a tolerable time lapse before normal functioning is resumed. A disaster should be defined in terms of the specific business environment. For example, what may be considered a disaster in a university medical center may not be a disaster for a small clinic. Additionally, predictable events and those that cause minor inconveniences or that can be corrected in a short period of time should be addressed in standard operating and availability management procedures. A succinct definition of disaster should include type of incident (i.e., unplanned, local, regional) which results in disruption of normal operations for a specific period of time (i.e., twelve hours, twenty-four hours, two days, three days) and which has a significant impact (defined by specific criteria) on patient care, the bottom line, customer satisfaction, or cash flow.

Content of the BCP is also dependent upon the organization's size, processes, and amount of risk. The goal, however, should be toward simplicity and flexibility. The plan should be free of unnecessary detail, be easily updatable, and provide reasonable alternatives for continuing business processes. It should also include an organized response. Having alternatives is one thing; putting them into action is another. The plan should identify specific individuals who are responsible for decisions, actions, and issues during the response and recovery periods. Processes and procedures for recovery must be identified, along with a systematic plan for bringing up individual business process areas. Finally, any plan must include provisions for testing. Without a continuity exercise, an untested plan is unlikely to work during an actual disruption or, worse yet, could turn out to be even dangerous as a result of unverified processes or assumptions about integration.

### Steps Toward Building a Culture of Business Continuity Planning

The strategy chosen for business continuity planning will determine how well a business continuity culture is developed within the organization. Regardless of what vendors or consultants may lead one to believe, there is no one right way to approach planning. The strategies used are highly dependent upon the existing culture and politics within the organization, its size, the past experience and background of its stakeholders, and the nature of its processes. Therefore, the successful strategy used in a teaching facility environment may be an abysmal failure in a 100-bed acute care facility. Therefore, the steps discussed below must be viewed as a general outline for development of a strategy. The nuances in approach and dynamics and the content of each step will be different for each organization. Some organizations may wish to approach the process sequentially; others may do several steps simultaneously. Exhibit 1 shows the elements necessary for developing a company culture that supports the business continuity philosophy.

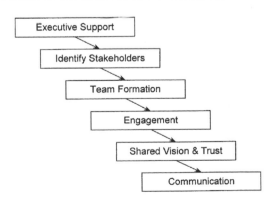

**Exhibit 1. Elements of a Successful Business Continuity Plan**

**Securing Executive Management Support.** As noted previously, securing executive management support is essential to the success of any business continuity project. Top management must support not only undertaking the planning process but must also support the creation of the infrastructure to install, maintain, and implement the plan. Too frequently, development of plans may be supported, but support for creation of the accompanying infrastructure to carry out the plan is not understood or negotiated from the beginning.

A critical question is how to secure top management support. First, management must understand that BCP is primarily concerned with risk management and keeping the company in business. Second, management must be educated that BCP concerns cost, image, and getting product delivered. It is not exclusively confined to recovering operations in the worst-case scenario but rather addresses minimizing the risk of even brief interruptions that can mean loss of revenue, productivity, or consumer goodwill. History from the individual organization can be compiled as well as innumerable examples published in the literature or on the Internet which detail adverse impact on revenue, costs, and customer service due to untoward events.

Management must also be convinced that the planning process will not turn into a "monster under the bed." A planning budget needs to be developed based upon "1) just how much plan you will need; 2) the net cost (planning expenditures less savings resultant from the plan); and 3) personnel time and costs that will be required in the planning, installation, and implementation activities" (p. 69).[1] To determine the planning budget, it is wise to initially secure funding for a feasibility or needs assessment study. Findings of this review will not only provide a solid basis for determining budget but will also provide basic facts on the current condition of the company's exposure to risk.

**Identifying the Stakeholders.** No BCP process should be started without identification of the major stakeholders. Because BCP is about keeping the company in business, every level of management must be considered a BCP stakeholder. Myers presents a tiered approached to garnering stakeholder participation.[5] The first tier is establishment of a steering committee composed of senior management staff. This group must be educated and committed to risk management and recognize the need to establish a plan that ensures an organized response should a disaster occur. The composition of the steering committee will depend upon the politics and culture of the organization. Normally, this committee should be composed of representatives from finance, operations, auditing, information systems, and executive management. The steering committee should serve as an advisory group on plan development and methodology, recommend policy changes, and set an expectation that department managers will participate in plan development.

The second tier of stakeholders includes department managers. Because BCP involves risk management and maintaining operations in the event of unplanned disruption, every functional manager or head of a business process area must be considered a stakeholder. Like executive and senior management, this tier must be educated as to the purpose and outcomes of BCP. They are also the needed link to obtaining access to first-line supervisors in plan development. A major role of this tier is to endorse the philosophy of BCP, participate in development of planning strategy, and to review and approve contingency plans and guidelines.

The third tier is composed of the first-line supervisors in each business process area. These are the individuals who are the most knowledgeable in current operations and who "know the business." It is the first-line supervisors who will examine alternatives to support operations should an untoward event and disruption occur.

**Setting the Stage: The Education Program.** The stakeholder education program is one of the most important steps to ensuring success of the BCP process. The education program must be deliberate. That is, like any education program, outcomes and instructional strategy must be identified and developed. This means more than conducting a one-hour meeting "telling" stakeholders about BCP. Rather, it means engaging stakeholders in the process through active participation and learning. Lectures, handouts, and memoranda do very little to engage the interest of people. Rather, the educational process needs to be placed in a discussion leadership context, where participants are presented with problems and scenarios and work as a group to develop solutions and outcomes.

**Forming the Team.** A several-tiered and team approach to BCP is recommended. This tiered approach consists of executive, senior, and department managers and front-line supervisors. Each tier must recognize its own value and discipline as well as that of the others. A systematic view must be incorporated so that team members see how each other's work contributes to the success of the BCP process. An important element of team success is the exchange of information and communication. Communication must be open and solution oriented. It must contain constructive feedback and, above all, trust must be cultivated among all team members. One of the most critical jobs of the business continuity planner and manager is to develop the team. With a good team all other elements of the planning process will easily fall into place. No amount of structure or methodology, however, can compensate for the lack of a functioning and healthy team.

**Identifying the Risks.** Because BCP is about risk management, an initial step in the process is to identify the exposure of the company. Once a functioning team is in place, risks to business operations that could result in the company's definition of a disaster need to be identified. Some of these vulnerabilities will cross departmental boundaries and be companywide; others may be unique to specific business process areas. While, in theory, any type of untoward event may occur, the emphasis should be placed on what events are likely to occur given the geographical location of the company, the processes that are performed, the physical facilities occupied, and the people who are present. Remember that the outcome of this step is to minimize risk. Therefore, events that have a higher probability of occurring within a specifically determined period of time should receive the attention for risk management. Those events that have been determined with a degree of acceptable certainty as unlikely to occur within a determined period of time should be dismissed. Thus, when risk assessment and subsequent management is approached in this manner, planning costs are reduced and a less complex and less costly plan to implement and maintain is developed.

**Identifying Impact.** Identifying the impact of out-of-course events is often referred to as business impact analysis or BIA. Impact needs to be assessed for each business process area. Some business areas may be minimally impacted by an event while for others the event may have catastrophic consequences. Impact should be assessed from the standpoint of how the event affects patient care, customer service, product delivery, cash flow, revenue, and productivity within each functional area. Assessment also needs to be systematic and interdependencies among functional areas identified. For example, the impact of an out-of-course event may be minimal to the admitting function. However, there may be interdependencies between admitting and other functional areas such that lower productivity or loss of a business process for any length of time in admitting might catastrophically impact the other functional areas.

Determining which functions are more critical than others is also associated with impact analysis. In other words, what functions, if lost, would have the greatest adverse impact on patient care, product delivery, customer service, cash flow, revenue, and the like? For example, the most critical processes may not be the admitting functions but rather those in the clinical laboratory. Patient care, cash flow, and revenue may be hardest hit by disruption of clinical laboratory services. The primary reason for identification of the most critical processes is to develop a priority restoration schedule in order to return to normal productivity.

**Identifying Interim Processes and Recovery Strategies.** Alternatives to regular business processes should be cost-effective solutions. The BCP team must recognize that the goal in meeting the crisis is survival, not business as usual. Therefore, supervisors and managers must recognize that alternatives are developed to continue business processes but that they will not necessarily ensure the same efficiency. Any front-line supervisor or department manager who is asked how long he or she can function given an unplanned interruption, will likely say that it would be impossible to carry out business processes or deliver services for any length of time. This perception often results in implementing costly backup solutions. Rather, front-line supervisors should be asked, "How could you survive given an event that impedes or interrupts your normal business process?" The answer to this question takes on a whole different perspective. Options may include suspension of an activity or living with less efficient alternatives. Supervisors are therefore encouraged to think first about developing cost-effective solutions rather than resorting to costly and redundant alternatives.

As Levitt points out, contingency plans most frequently provide for: (1) hot, warm, or cold sites; (2) provision of additional hardcopy-based information and/or magnetic-media-based data; (3) telecommunication paths via alternate routings, carriers, or mores; and (4) standby sources of electric power. However, "the importance of these provisions notwithstanding, organizations need to develop paper systems that will allow them to continue operating without the use of their computer systems" (p. 233).[1]

Alternative processes are only interim solutions. When a disaster is identified, recovery operations must go into effect immediately. These processes will be based upon a predetermined schedule of recovery actions. Depending upon the type of out-of-course event, restoration may include the relocation to a "cold" site, power generator activation, or retrieval of off-site stored media. Recovery also includes a schedule that identifies what processes come up first. This determination is often based on the criticality of the process, its interdependencies with other processes, and to what degree disruption will affect patient care, cash flow, revenue, and consumer satisfaction.

**Developing the Organized Response.** Alternative solutions and recovery schedules and processes are useless unless there is an organized process for their application. The organized response should include the immediate emergency response. This includes the plan for immediate situational assessment; criteria for determining and calling a disaster; notification of the emergency response team, vendors, and suppliers; and determination of what parts of the plan should go into effect and when. The BCP should outline the general emergency actions to be taken during an emergency response and who is responsible for each action. In addition, for each business process area, system descriptions should be available, interdependencies noted, hardware and software used cataloged, and interim processing strategies and processes identified.

**Compiling and Maintaining the Plan.** The BCP must be a well-annotated, usable, and visible physical document. This does not mean that the document must be complex. On the contrary, the intent of the BCP is that it be a useful and functional tool. It should be developed in such a way as to avoid unnecessary detail — containing only the elements necessary to carry out an emergency response to events that may impede, interrupt, or halt business functions. The plan should be well organized and, above all, be a communication tool. It should be designed so that it can be easily updated. A plan that is too complex impedes communication as well as hinders timely and necessary review and update. A simple approach to contingency plan content is suggested by Myers.[5]

Essentially this includes policy and strategy statements; executive summary; description of maintenance and user continuing education and preparedness reviews; general actions and responsibilities in the emergency response; interim processing strategies for each business process area; and restoration strategies. The plan should also include appendices as necessary, such as the emergency response notification list, list of vendors and suppliers, and restoration priority list.

## BUILDING THE BUSINESS CONTINUITY CULTURE: REVISITED

No program for business continuity can be totally successful without first considering the development of a company culture that supports the philosophy, goals, and outcomes of BCP. While executive management support is crucial to the success of the process, no plan can be accomplished without the engagement of managers, department heads, and first-line supervisors. Building a culture means developing a vision. It also means building a shared vision among all the stakeholders.

However, the culture cannot be realized until there is team learning and experience. Building the team, sharing the vision, and creating the culture will make all the difference in the world in the degree of success that is obtained from business continuity planning. Unfortunately, philosophies of organizational learning are rarely applied to endeavors that are considered on the "hard side," such as business continuity planning. Is it any wonder then that so many of these attempts fail and no one even understands why?

**References**

1. Levitt, A.M. 1997. *Disaster Planning and Recovery: A Guide for Facility Professionals.* New York: John Wiley & Sons.
2. Myers, K.N., *Total Contingency Planning for Disasters.* John Wiley & Sons, Inc., New York, 1993.
3. Levitt, A.M. and Ernst & Young, LLP. Information Systems Assurance and Advisory Services — Business Continuity Planning. http://www.ey.com/aabs/isaas/bcp/bcm.asp.
4. Stair, R.M. 1996. *Principles of Information System: A Managerial Approach.* Danvers: Boyd and Fraser Publishing Company.
5. Myers, K.N. 1993. *Total Contingency Planning for Disasters.* New York: John Wiley & Sons.
6. Rothstein, P.J. 1996. "Almost disasters," *InfoSecurity News Magazine,* January/February.
7. Jackson, J.A. and Woodworth, M. 1998. "Integrating disaster recovery into the high-availability agenda," *Contingency Planning and Management,* June: 22–26.

# Chapter 9
# Security Policies: The Foundation for Information Protection

*Cynthia M. Hemsoth*

I entered healthcare in the mid-1970s. This was the era of the mainframe. For most healthcare employees, the mainframe was known as a large computer that only a limited number of users had access to. Confidentiality was, of course, a concern; however, the focus was on physical controls for paper documents. As technology evolved, the 1980s brought the client/server environment, which provided a way to interconnect programs and computers that are distributed across different locations. This client/server environment opened up access to many users. By the end of the 1990s, the Internet/intranet had opened up data access to a larger number of users than ever thought possible.

Although the increased accessibility to patient information has contributed to better healthcare delivery, it has also posed serious security risks. The information age of the 1990s had many healthcare organizations struggling with information security issues. Exhibit 1 lists a sampling of healthcare security news events of the 1990s.

More than ever before, healthcare organizations need to share information with internal as well as external providers. The challenge is found in providing access to information to the parties who have a need to know, limiting access to only the information that is needed, and protecting the integrity and confidentiality of the information. Legal risks associated with failure to implement security measures are increasing. Federal and state regulations have brought attention to the need for a more structured security approach. Some of the regulations healthcare organizations need to consider include:

**Exhibit 1. Healthcare Security News Events**

| Topic | Date | Event |
|-------|------|-------|
| Medical data confidentiality | 02/97 | In Sheffield, England, a hospital gave 50,000 confidential gynecological records to a data processing firm that hired people off the street to transcribe the unprotected data.[1] |
| Medical confidentiality AIDS database | 04/97 | George Wentz was found guilty of anonymously mailing a list of 4000 names of AIDS patients to two Florida newspapers. In an effort to vindictively punish his ex-lover, William Calvert III, Wentz used the patient list he obtained from Calvert who worked in the Pinellas County Health Department. Calvert was charged with a misdemeanor for misusing the list, and Wentz faced up to 60 days in jail and up to $500 in fines.[a] |
| Patient confidentiality | 3/95 | A Massachusetts hospital employee was arrested for using a former employee's password to gain access to nearly 1000 confidential patient files, which he then used to make obscene phone calls.[b] |
| Online confidential records | 3/95 | Outraged patients found out that Harvard Community Health Plan physicians routinely put psychiatric notes into computerized medical records, which were accessible to many of the HMO employees.[b] |

[a] Kabay, M. E. Information security year in review — 1997. Available at http://www.icsa.net/library/research/iyir. Accessed 2/6/1999.
[b] News articles related to healthcare information security. Available at http://www.irongate inc.com/articles.html. Accessed 2/6/1999.

- JCAHO (Joint Commission on Accreditation of Healthcare Organizations)
- Privacy Act of 1974
- HIPAA (Health Insurance Portability and Accountability Act of 1996)
- MRCA (Medical Records Confidentiality Act of 1995)
- Medicare Conditions of Participation
- Other federal and state laws

Most healthcare organizations have implemented security measures to some extent, and conduct organizational audits to look at security controls. Security efforts are often decentralized, and issues are addressed on an ad hoc basis. Communication and enforcement of security processes and procedures are often weak. The goal and strategic direction for information security are rarely developed and communicated. To protect an organization's valuable information assets and to effectively meet regulations, a centralized coordination of security controls needs to be put in place.

## SECURITY CONTROLS

The National Institute of Standards and Technology (NIST) has defined three types of security controls:[1]

1. *Management controls.* Management controls address security techniques that focus on the management of a computer security program and the management of risk within an organization.
2. *Operational controls.* Operational controls are usually executed by people (rather than systems), and are implemented to improve the security of a particular system or group of systems. They often require special expertise and may rely on management and technical controls.
3. *Technical controls.* Technical controls are executed by a computer system and are dependent on the proper functioning of a system. Technical controls need to be consistent with the management of security within an organization and require significant operational considerations.

These controls are dependent on one another and should work together synergistically.[2] Computer security controls also need to work in conjunction with the traditional security disciplines, such as physical and personnel security.[3] Of course, all computer security measures need to be aligned with the organization's mission by protecting its information assets. It stands to reason that before technical or operational controls can be effectively implemented, management controls need to define the organization's strategic direction for its computer security program.

## ROLE OF SECURITY POLICIES

The management control that can best protect the organization is the establishment of key security policies. Developing security policies is one of the first steps in the implementation of an information security program. Without the appropriate policies in place, the effectiveness of security endeavors is compromised and is difficult to measure. In fact, at times technical solutions that are implemented without the guidance of a policy may not support the organization's business needs and could, in fact, open up the organization to a greater security risk. For example, many organizations are receiving numerous requests for remote access. Some of these requests are from third-party vendors, while others may be from employees.

There certainly are technology products with security features that can be installed to permit remote access. However, without providing guidance on the use of remote access through policies and procedures, the organization could be placing the security of their information at great risk.

Policies, therefore, play a critical role in how an organization begins to secure its information. The documentation that policies provide becomes a valuable tool when asking administrative staff to endorse and support the protection of healthcare data. If managers know which policies to turn to in the event of a security issue, they are not only more empowered to effectively address the issue, but will be more supportive of security efforts. Policies also serve as guidelines to be used during the development or implementation of systems. It is through policies that an organization can meet the requirements of regulatory agencies, such as those noted above.

The meaning or objective of a policy differs according to the type of policy it is. Below is a broad definition of a security policy:

> Security policy: a set of rules and practices that document an organization's security related decisions in regards to the management, access, and protection of information.

The three major categories of security policies are the *program policy, issue-specific policy,* and the *system-specific policy.* Some organizations refer to the three policies by a different name, such as plans or directives. Regardless of what they are called, they are the necessary building blocks for a security program.

## POLICY DEVELOPMENT

Policy development needs to be a joint effort with the input and approval of the appropriate parties. The role of the information security officer (ISO) is to ensure that the right people are involved, coordinate policy development activities, obtain necessary approvals, and communicate the policy to the organization. Without the role of the ISO as the central coordinator and overseer of policy development activities, most policies will result in incompleteness, inconsistency with other organizational policies, and lack of organizational commitment. A central force driving the process and providing direction is imperative to the successful development of key policies.

The areas of the organization that often have a role in policy development are listed below. Although the titles may differ between organizations, and some organizations may combine roles, the basic functions are usually present in most healthcare facilities.

1. *Senior management.*[1] Senior management has the ultimate responsibility for protecting the organization's information assets.[3] They establish the priorities of the computer security program to ensure that they support the mission and objectives of the organization. At times, the policy development and approval process is senior management's first opportunity to become involved in information security efforts. Obtaining the buy-in and support of senior management plays an essential role in the success of a security program.
2. *Physicians.* Although physician input may not be needed on all of the security policies, it is advantageous to obtain physician feedback

and direction on security policies directly related to patient care. Policies related to confidentiality, remote access to medical information, and electronic/digital signatures are some examples of policies that should at least be discussed with physicians.

3. *Chief information officer (CIO)*. The CIO is responsible for the daily management of information assets.[3] He or she defines the purpose and scope of the computer security program and assigns responsibilities for program implementation. The CIO works with senior management to ensure that the program's objectives are in line with the mission of the organization.

4. *Supporting areas*. The following departments need to either play a part in the approval process or to be informed on new security policies in order to ensure that the policies are in synch with other organizational objectives and are in line with other policies: information services (IS) management, human resources, legal, internal audit, risk management, purchasing.

5. *Managers/application owners*.[1] Managers or application owners are responsible for ensuring that a particular computer system has the appropriate level of security by working with the ISO. They usually supervise a staff member who handles the administration of the system. These individuals should be held accountable for security decisions and associated security risks related to the system.

6. *Information security officer (ISO)*. This individual manages the computer security program and facilitates security-related activities. Because he or she often serves as a consulting resource to those involved in security decisions, this individual should have knowledge and experience in data security. The ISO may also handle some of the administrative functions related to IS-supported systems.

7. *System administrators*. System administrators may work in IS or may work within an ancillary department, such as lab, radiology, or admitting. They are responsible for implementing, maintaining, and supporting the computer system(s) for their area. These individuals know how the system(s) are used in their area and can, therefore, provide valuable input to security policy. It is important that these individuals understand the security objectives and standards of the organization, so that they can implement the appropriate technical and operational security controls on the system(s) that they support.

8. *Information services technical and application specialists*. Representatives from the technical and application areas of IS should participate in the development of security policies. These individuals are responsible for communicating security endeavors and policies to their co-workers to help ensure that security policies and standards are addressed during system design and implementation. Some technical or application specialist roles that might be appropriate to

include in the policy development process include systems engineers, systems analysts, application project managers, and operations personnel.

9. *Supporting personnel.* Security policies need to be clearly understood by help desk personnel as well as training specialists. Both functions cross over in the manner in which they support computer security. The help desk, however, will have a greater need to be able to recognize security incidents, while the training specialists have the primary responsibility of educating users on computer security.

Involvement of the above parties in policy development and approval helps to ensure that the security policies are in line with the organization's mission and are supported throughout the organization. Integrating security policies with other organizational policies will help build an acceptance for these policies among employees. Human resources often has a process for communicating policies to administrative staff and employees. Working closely with human resources will assure that the standard policy-setting process has been followed. The distribution and education of information security policies will then eventually be received as a standard part of the performance management process and should be reviewed annually.

Exhibit 2 serves as a model for policy approval within an organization. A security committee can serve to bring together a number of the groups described above. The committee participants need to be genuinely committed to safeguarding information. In fact, a more appropriate committee name, and one that might be better received by the user community, is the information protection committee. This committee is directed by the ISO and becomes the driving force to document and implement information security policies. The ISO is responsible for educating the com-

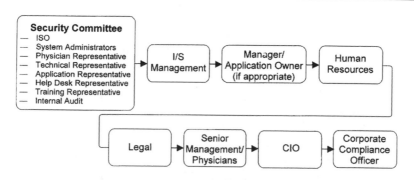

**Exhibit 2. Security Policy Approval Model**

mittee members on information security requirements and helping them to understand the security options that are available. Although this committee may recommend needed security policies based on the security issues that they have direct experiences with, approval from the CIO is often required to ensure that the committee's efforts are in line with the organization's strategic direction. The ISO serves as the key communicator between the CIO, senior management, and the security committee. In fact, the ISO is the central contact for facilitating the approval process and communicating security policies to all the parties involved.

The model above involves key areas within an organization that have a role in the policy development process. The involvement of these areas not only helps to establish buy-in and ownership throughout the organization, it also assures senior management, physicians, the CIO, and the corporate compliance officer that those areas responsible for monitoring and enforcing the policy have provided input and support the policy. Because of the corporate compliance officer's role in preventing violations of statutes and regulations, he or she should have a signature line on many, if not all, security policies. In fact, it is important to have a signature line on the policy for each key area that needs to approve the policy. This will clearly communicate to senior management who has been involved in the approval process.

## TYPES OF POLICIES

The degree of involvement each approval area has may differ according to the type of policy. There are three basic types of security policies: program, issue-specific, and system-specific policies. Each type of policy has a different purpose and should contain a set of basic components.

### Program Policy

> *Program Policy*: A high-level policy that sets the organizational strategic direction for security, defines the scope and purpose of the security program, assigns resources, and addresses compliance issues.[1]

The CIO is often responsible for developing the basic structure of the computer security program, defining the management structure supporting it, and setting the goals for the program based on organizational objectives. The program policy should address the areas of the organization that are most important to protect. For example, in a healthcare organization where maintaining confidentiality is of utmost importance, the policy might emphasize protection against unauthorized disclosure. Data integrity and availability of information also form the basis for a program policy. When developing the program policy, the National Institute of Standards and Technology (NIST) addresses the need for the following components:

- *Purpose.* The goals of the computer security program are defined here, setting the organizational direction for the program. The goals can be based on the three facets of security: confidentiality, data integrity, and availability.
- *Scope.* The boundaries for the computer security program need to be clearly defined. For example, the security program may encompass all systems and personnel within an organization, or it may focus on specific mission-critical systems and sites. The hardware, software, information, and facilities that the program will encompass are outlined in this section.
- *Roles and responsibilities.* How the program is to be managed and the organizational structure of the program needs to be documented here. The process for policy approval and for escalating issues is also included in this section. Defining the roles and responsibilities of areas and individuals involved in the program helps to maintain accountability. Employees, project managers, network engineers, information security officers, department managers, and upper management are just some of the individuals who often have a role in the security program. It is advantageous to also include the requirements that vendors, suppliers, and contractors have in complying with the organization's security policies. Expectations should be specifically defined in this section in order to establish ownership and follow-through.
- *Compliance.* There needs to be some means of ensuring that the requirements for the programs are met and that the responsibilities of the parties involved are carried out. To accomplish this, an outside party needs to periodically monitor security endeavors and to determine how well the organization is meeting its overall security goals. The implementation of management's security priorities should also be reviewed. The organization's internal audit department can handle this function. Also, for security measures to be effective, they need to be enforced. If there are no consequences for not following the policies or incentives for adhering to them, they are likely to be ignored. The program policy should address the consequences for not following security policies. Although the policy should clearly state that penalties would be incurred for infractions, it is best not to attempt to detail the specifics of the punishment. At times, human resources or legal counsel may need to be consulted regarding appropriate disciplinary action. For this reason, most policies will often state that the seriousness of the punishment will match the seriousness of the offense. Some organizations have a human resources policy book that can also be referenced in the policy.

The program policy addresses the high-level components of the program that remain fairly static once they are established. In effect, the program policy serves as the charter for the computer security program. For this reason, upper management should approve the program policy and, at times, will issue the policy. The program policy then becomes the framework for the computer security program. Additional policies and security activities are built upon this framework.

### Issue-Specific Policy

Another type of policy that focuses more on current security concerns is the issue-specific policy.

> *Issue-specific policy:* A policy that focuses on specific areas of security concerns and provides the organization's position on these issues. Issue-specific policies can also address new, emerging security issues. For this reason, these policies may need to be revised periodically as technology and regulations change.

Organizations can establish issue-specific policies to address new and changing federal regulations. Patient rights, the Health Insurance Portability and Accountability Act (HIPAA), electronic signature, and medical records confidentiality will all dictate the need for a healthcare organization to create or revise security policies. The utilization of the Internet as well as new technologies provides greater accessibility to information. With increased access to information, the implementation of tighter security measures and issue-specific policies becomes more important. Issue-specific policies help enable organizations to keep their information protection efforts in sync with the changing environment.

Just as the program policy should contain specific components, the NIST also recommends a structure for issue-specific policies. By breaking down issue-specific policies into components, changes that apply to only sections of the policy can be easily revised. Listed below are the basic components of an issue-specific policy:

- *Issue statement.* The issue statement defines the security concern and how it relates to the organization. The definition should be stated in easily understood terms so that all who are expected to adhere to the policy understand the issue at hand and the objective of the policy. Any exceptions or conditions also need to be explained. For example, an organization may have a system access policy that explains the need to maintain patient confidentiality and protect the organization's information assets. A condition of the policy would address the need to provide access to information and share information as needed to perform a job function.
- *The organization's position.* Management's stance on the issue is outlined in this section. To use the example of system access, management may decide that employees should be given access only to the information they need to perform their job and only after they are properly trained.

- *Applicability.* It may be necessary to indicate who in the organization is responsible for adhering to the policy and under what circumstances. For example, a system access policy may apply not only to any employee who has access to a computer system, but also contracted staff.
- *Roles and responsibilities.* Those individuals or areas within the organization that have a role in implementing the policy are identified in this section. The responsibilities of these individuals are outlined, which helps establish accountability. Using the example of the system access policy, some individuals responsible for the implementation of this policy may include the department manager, information security officer, system administrator, training specialist, and the user of the system.
- *Compliance.* As previously noted, there needs to be consequences for not adhering to a policy. The criteria for determining what constitutes an infraction or examples of unacceptable behavior should be documented. How infractions are handled should be consistent with the organization's personnel policies. The organization may choose to reference a personnel policy or specify within this policy some of the consequences resulting from infractions. If a personnel policy does not exist that addresses how an infraction should be handled, the organization's legal and personnel departments should approve any consequences noted in the policy. As for the penalties provided by law, it is not necessary to restate them in the policy; however, some organizations choose to do this when using the policy for training or for building security awareness.
- *Point of contact.* If employees have questions on the policy or need further clarification, they need to know whom in the organization to contact. This section of the policy is reserved for listing those who can provide guidance or additional information on the policy. It is often encouraged not to specify individual names, but rather to indicate the positions within the organization that can be contacted. Using employees' names will result in the need to revise the policy more often due to staff turnover. Including the contact's department, position, and, at times, their phone number should suffice.
- *System-specific policy.* Policy decisions that establish the rules and practices on how information is accessed, managed, distributed, and protected for a specific system based on the security objectives for that system.

Issue-specific policies are targeted at addressing a particular security threat or providing protocol based on regulatory requirements. Contingency planning can also take the form of an issue-specific policy. For example, as most organizations prepared for the transition to the year 2000, policies were put into place outlining the methodology for managing risks and addressing contingency plans.

As these contingency plans change, so do the policies. Because issue-specific policies are, in a sense, reactionary policies, they need to be reviewed for applicability and updated on a more frequent basis. Like program policies, issue-specific policies affect the organization as a whole. Therefore, when revisions are made to issue-specific policies, a mechanism needs to be in place for communicating the revision to the organization.

### System-Specific Policy

Unlike program and issue-specific policies, system-specific policies are focused only on a particular computer system. System-specific policies address issues such as who is allowed to inquire or modify data in the system, when information can be modified, and if remote access to the system is permitted. System-specific policies help outline how the system is actually used and the security put in place to protect the system.

The NIST has identified two basic components to system-specific policies: security objectives and operational security rules.[1] The rules of the policy are established from the security objectives. A management person is often held responsible for deciding which security rules should be implemented to meet the objectives. This decision process includes taking into account the goals for implementing the system, the manner in which the system should be used, the advantages and disadvantages of the controls available to secure the system, and feedback from both users and technical staff.

- *Security objectives.* When establishing security objectives, it is, of course, important to keep in mind the need to maintain confidentiality and to ensure the availability and integrity of the data. The objectives are to be specific and measurable. The objectives typically reference a function of the system and its corresponding security action. For example, a clinical system might include an objective that states that only authorized users can verify patient orders.
- *Operational security rules.* Once the security objectives are stated, the operating rules at which those objectives can be achieved are documented. These rules cover who can do what, to which data, and under what conditions.[1] Using the above security objective regarding the verification of patient orders, the rule might state that only RNs and physicians can verify patient orders prior to submitting the request to the appropriate service area. Usually the more specific the operational rule is, the easier it is to enforce, detect violations, and automate. However, one has to balance specificity with practicality to justify the level of effort and cost required to program a system to meet detailed security rules.

In addition to determining the level of detail that should be provided in the rules, the manner in which the rules are documented also needs to be determined. A formal written policy builds a better understanding of the security rules and is easier to enforce. However, at times, management may feel that a memo outlining the security rules is sufficient. Rules or policies that are not written down are very difficult to enforce. In general, rules applying to access controls and assignment of security responsibilities should be more detailed and formally documented.[1]

Because of various constraints, management more likely will not be able to meet all system security objectives. Decisions will need to be made as to which security objectives are most important and can be effectively implemented with available funds and technology. These types of decisions should be a routine part of any major system implementation. Reviewing security options and documenting system-specific policies needs to be incorporated in system implementation project plans. Some of the operational security rules that are typically created for and documented in system-specific policies include system access (who is allowed to access what functions where), the need to change passwords periodically, system security or administrative responsibilities, and remote access. The manager who is the key owner of the system should be accountable for signing off on the system-specific policy decisions, and thus held accountable for associated risks.

Although most systems should have documented security decisions, many do not. Because of the rush to get many systems up and running by a targeted deadline, with a limited budget, appropriate attention is not given to addressing and documenting security decisions. Obtaining management's support in requiring documentation of system security decisions for at least major applications will better ensure that appropriate system-specific policies are created. Also, providing project managers with an agreed-upon listing of the categories of security controls which should be documented for major applications will assist them in planning for system security controls, testing, and documentation.

Whereas the selection of system-specific policies is driven by the systems being implemented, issue-specific policies are often created as a reaction to new technology, current concerns, or regulatory requirements. As an example, some legislative efforts involving healthcare information technology (IT) that were started in 1998 were being carried over to 1999, which will require some healthcare organizations to develop or revise issue-specific polices. For example, patient rights legislation may require security policies and controls to be revised or created to provide patients access to their records, make confidentiality practices more visible and tighten the safeguards used to protect confidentiality and secure identifiable health information.

To determine what other policies are the most important to begin working on, the organization's IT strategic direction should be considered. For exam-

**Exhibit 3. Core Security Policies**

| Policy | Purpose |
| --- | --- |
| Confidentiality | To allow users appropriate and timely access to the information systems maintained at the organization while still establishing controls to provide protection for data that must be held in confidence and protected from unauthorized disclosure. |
| Electronic mail (e-mail) | To provide general rules for accessing electronic mail, using e-mail to conduct official or personal business, providing confidential protection of messages, and managing and retaining e-mail messages. |
| System access | To provide general guidelines for the process of requesting, creating, issuing, and closing user accounts. Password guidelines may also be addressed. |
| Virus protection | To implement appropriate software tools to safeguard the organization's computer systems from malicious code and to institute a process to handle computer virus incidents. |
| Internet/intranet use | To provide guidelines for accessing and using the Internet, as well as what services are allowed to both inside and outside users. |
| Remote access | To provide guidelines and mechanisms to control access between authorized users and the organization's computers/network and to establish levels of security to protect information assets. |
| Software code of ethics | To inform users that it is the policy of the organization to respect all computer software copyrights and to adhere to terms of all software licenses to which the organization is a part. |
| Backup and recovery | To outline and train appropriate personnel on emergency, backup, and contingency plans in the event of a system failure. |
| Security training and awareness | To maintain a security awareness program and provide training on security policies, guidelines, and procedures. To help ensure that employees understand their security responsibilities and how to report security incidents. |

ple, if an IT strategic objective is to increase remote access for physicians, security policies and controls need to be put in place to support this effort. At times, hospitals that have merged into a health system will have two sets of IT objectives. There will be institution IT objectives as well as health system IT objectives. As health systems begin to share information between institutions within the system, security risks increase. Therefore, there may be two levels of security policies and controls to support all IT objectives.

It is also important to keep in mind that as hospitals merge into health systems, more focus will be given to how information is managed between various institutions within a health system. JCAHO reviews how a health network/system ensures appropriate confidentiality across the system. How information is made available, transmitted, integrated, and protected across the health system is also of interest to JCAHO. This will require healthcare systems to have security policies at the system level as well as at the institution level.

Although security policies are developed to meet the security needs of a particular organization, there are some policies that can be thought of as core policies. These are the security policies that most healthcare organizations need to have. They address security concerns inherent to the healthcare environment. Exhibit 3 lists a sampling of some of these core policies.

In addition to developing new policies, it is just as important to keep current policies updated. Security policies should be reviewed at least once a year. At times, changes to technology or systems will require a policy to be revised sooner. Any revisions need to be communicated to those responsible for adhering to the policy. In fact, communicating updates to employees and educating employees on new security policies is a key factor to the success of a security program.

## AWARENESS AND TRAINING

It is often said that lack of employee awareness is one of the biggest roadblocks to improving an organization's data security. The fact remains that no matter how well your policies are written, if the user community is not aware of and does not understand the policies, they will not be effective. Employees need to understand how security fits into their job, the importance of security, and what happens if security fails. Individual responsibility and accountability are established by teaching employees the correct security practices.

Because management sets the example, awareness needs to start at the management level. By involving management and other key areas in the policy development cycle, there is a greater likelihood of ownership and support for security polices. However, not all managers are involved in policy development. For this reason, education needs to be provided to the management staff, so that they fully understand the security issues and the measures taken to protect the organization's information. Some organizations have standard management meetings with all of the management staff. Others have groups of managers that meet regularly. Periodically providing a presentation on a security topic or policy at an existing standard meeting can be used as a means to help educate the management staff. For organizations that have orientation for new managers, key security policies should be reviewed during orientation.

For some organizations, the implementation of security policies will be a cultural change met with resistance. The management staff is in a position to directly receive feedback from employees. They need to understand not only the organization's security policies and the importance of them, they also need to be clear on their role in establishing the right attitude as well as what the consequences are if policies are not followed. Management should help their employees understand the policies and how the policies apply to their daily activities. Managers also need to clarify their expectations of an employee's performance regarding security measures.

Although management staff plays an important role in supporting security policies and in helping their staff understand the policies, a security awareness effort for all employees needs to be developed and maintained. Just as security policies should be reviewed with new managers, they also should be part of a new employee's orientation. Some security policies requiring an employee's signature could be read and signed during the new employee orientation program. Other policies that are required to be reviewed within a specified number of days from the employee's start date could be included in a new employee packet and sent to the employee's manager.

The awareness effort should address not only new employees, it also should include the training of existing employees. In-house training sessions on computer systems should routinely include security procedures. Employees need to know how to secure their area, how to use and change passwords, and to whom they should report security violations. A roll-out of a new or revised security policy can follow the same approach used to disseminate other organization policies. If the policy requires further explanation, education sessions can be held requiring representatives from each area to attend. Depending on the type of policy being implemented, an informal "brown-bag" session can be scheduled during a mealtime to invite employees to bring their own lunch and join in on a conversation regarding the policy.

Security awareness efforts should go beyond the distribution of paper policies and manuals. In fact, the more visible, creative, and interactive the effort, the more successful it will be. Refresher awareness can be fun. For example, a little security awareness cartoon can be inserted in the organization's newsletter. The newsletter can also have security tips and an occasional article on current security events. Reminder security messages can be included on sign-on screens. Posters or banners can be displayed periodically to remind employees of important security practices. A contest can be organized with prizes awarded to those employees who correctly responded to a set of security questions or who made a significant contribution to a security effort. Using different types of awareness techniques will help employees to recognize and react appropriately to security situations.

Most healthcare employees feel they understand the need for patient confidentiality and are somewhat aware of security guidelines; however, they often do not connect just how many security scenarios are presented to them on a daily basis. A healthcare security video can often help raise the awareness of daily security concerns. Most organizations need to review various policies and procedures on a yearly basis. The inclusion of a security video and the review of important security guidelines would serve as a good yearly refresher.

Awareness helps employees understand how security helps to protect the organization's information assets. Training helps them understand what their security responsibilities are and how they can fulfill them. In addition to recognizing security breaches, employees must also know how to report security incidents. The procedure for reporting an incident should be easy, nonthreatening, and ensure that confidentiality will be maintained.

## ADDITIONAL TOOLS

Security policies provide the foundation for protecting an organization's information assets. To support those policies, standards, guidelines, and procedures often need to be developed. Security policies provide a high-level view of the organization's stance on security concerns. They serve as the governing principles to protect information assets. How those principles are implemented and applied to the daily work environment often requires more specific instruction.

For example, an Internet policy could provide the basic process for granting Internet access privileges and state the organization's stance on Internet usage. Standards would supplement the policy by providing uniform Internet usage methods that are mandated throughout the organization. For example, there is often a standard format used for access codes. The organization could also be standardized on a particular browser to assist in providing user support. Guidelines could then provide direction to help ensure good security practices. Protecting user codes and passwords from unauthorized access, honoring all rules of copyright and personal property laws, and refraining from using the Internet to communicate confidential information are examples of guidelines that could apply to Internet usage. Guidelines are usually generic enough that they do not necessarily have to be implemented in a particular way. The objective is to see that the guideline is met. How it is accomplished may differ between areas or systems. The actual step-by-step processes for implementing policies, standards, and guidelines are spelled out in the procedures. Procedures give a detailed account of the flow of activities to accomplish a particular task, and who is responsible for each activity. An Internet procedure would detail the steps and parties involved in addressing a request for Internet access. The flow of activities may involve many parties such as the requestor, department manager, help desk personnel, telecommunications personnel, a desktop support technician, and the purchasing agent, just to mention a few. The procedure is obviously the most detailed documentation and provides the employees with the clearest set of instructions.

Policies, standards, guidelines, and procedures can take on different formats. Some organizations may choose to combine the policy, standards, and guidelines in one document, and outline the detailed procedures in another document. Although formats may differ between organizations, there should be a standard format within the organization. Often the human resources department has a particular format for personnel policies and procedures. Because some security policies will coincide with other personnel policies, there is some merit in maintaining the same format as human resources. Standardizing on the document layout helps employees find the information they need faster. They become familiar with the structure of the document and can more easily locate the section that contains the information they are seeking.

## SUMMARY

The technology advancements within the past 20 to 25 years have greatly impacted the manner in which healthcare organizations access, manage, and use information. The systems and the information that is processed on them are considered valuable assets to the organization. As technology permits greater accessibility to information, security risks increase. Federal regulations, state laws, and regulatory agencies are imposing more information management guidelines and requirements. In most jurisdictions, civil law permits patients subjected to information protection failures to sue in civil court for redress, naming managers, physicians, nurses, and other employed staff in such lawsuits.

Senior management is left with the responsibility of protecting the organization's valuable information assets. The development and implementation of key security policies is the foundation for building a security program to protect those assets. A program policy sets the organizational direction for information security, assigns responsibilities, and addresses program compliance. Current issues or concerns are addressed in issue-specific policies, which may require more frequent updates due to changing technology or regulations. System-specific policies establish rules on how information is accessed, managed, and distributed for a particular system. Standards, guidelines, and procedures are often developed to support these policies and provide employees with a clearer understanding of how to apply the policy objectives to daily operations.

For security policies to be effective, support is needed at all levels within the organization. Involving senior management and key departments in the policy development and approval process is essential for establishing buy-in, support, and ownership. Working with the management staff and employees to build an awareness and understanding of the importance of the security policies to the organization's mission will help to foster a more secure environment. Training in security practices will help employees fulfill their security responsibilities and promote individual accountability. Employees should not only be able to recognize security breeches, they should also feel comfortable in the process for reporting them. Security awareness should be an ongoing activity so that security practices become a culture of the organization.

### References

1. National Institute of Standards and Technology. 1995. *An Introduction to Computer Security: The NIST Handbook*, Special Publication 800-12. Washington, D.C.: NIST, Technology Administration, U.S. Department of Commerce.
2. Swanson, M. and Guttman, B. 1996. *Generally Accepted Principles and Practices for Securing Information Technology Systems*, Special Publication 800-14. Washington, D.C.: NIST, Technology Administration, U.S. Department of Commerce.
3. Peltier, T. R. 1998. *Information Protection Fundamentals*. San Francisco, CA: Computer Security Institute.

# Section IV
# Standards and the Regulatory Environment

# Chapter 10

# Biometrics

*Philip J. Holt*

> And when any of the fugitives of Ephraim said, "Let me go over," the men of Gilead said to him, "Are you an Ephraimite?" When he said, "No," they said to him, "Then say Shibboleth," and he said, "Sibboleth," for he could not pronounce it right; then they seized him and slew him at the fords of Jordan. And there fell at that time forty-two thousand of the Ephraimites.
>
> Judges 12:5-6

Since biblical times, physical characteristics of the individual have been a means for identification and authentication. The unfortunate Ephraimites failed a simple behavioral biometric, a dialect test based on one word that everyone already knew.

Computing technology has finally reached a point where many more physical and behavioral attributes are becoming available for identification. Established techniques include fingerprint recognition, hand geometry, and retinal scanning. Emerging technology ranges from the surprisingly obvious — iris-scanning — to the stunningly arcane — human scent analysis. When combined with other security schemes, biometric technology offers a strongly reliable means for authenticating individuals.

Using biometrics as a sole means of identification presents many additional challenges that will take more time to solve. The greatest challenge to the strategist attempting to plan the impact of biometrics on healthcare technology will be to balance benefits and trade-offs. Improvements in security and in the authority of commercial transactions are obvious benefits. Diminishing anonymity and erosion of privacy remain constant concerns.

## BACKGROUND

Security represents a vast body of knowledge organized toward reducing risk of loss or theft to real (physical) and intangible (intellectual) property. Modern society, with its growing dependence on database technology, stretches this general definition further. Loss can include not only the physical loss of data but also logical loss where data is stored in the wrong place. For example, a credit card transaction inadvertently assigned to the wrong account is a type of data corruption that is the insidious equivalent of outright loss.

Healthcare has grown particularly data-intensive, yet the improvements to security infrastructure surrounding applications has been mainly limited to general access control techniques. Confronting several technical frontiers at a time, vendors of healthcare application software struggle to keep up with the requirements of a data-driven market. Where an application depends on the flow of transactional data about people — it could be financial or clinical data — reconciling the records authoritatively is essential to mining any useful information from the data. Eliminating duplicate identifiers for the same individual or preventing transactions from becoming associated with the wrong individual are a basic application challenge for designers of security infrastructure.

Technology is emerging that allows the use of biometric techniques to identify individuals more authoritatively than has been practical in the past. Biometrics defined broadly is the scientific discipline of observing and measuring relevant attributes of living individuals or populations to identify active properties or unique characteristics. Biometrics can look for patterns of change by measuring attributes over time or look for consistency by measuring attributes of identity or unique differentiation. When looking for patterns of change, biometric technology can be considered a tool for research, diagnosis, or even medical monitoring. When looking for consistency, biometrics becomes a useful vehicle for security.

## IDENTIFICATION APPROACHES

While the technology applied to the identification process has evolved and improved tremendously over thousands of years, the basic approaches have remained largely unchanged. The basis for identification has always been and continues to be the possession of a token by a requestor and the authentication of that token by a grantor. The degree of requestor anonymity typically measures how sophisticated a process will be, with the degree of anonymity and the concern of the grantor appearing to behave in an inversely proportional way. The more anonymous a requestor, the higher the probability of misidentification. Identification strategies generally follow one or some combination of the following approaches.

- *Simple token-based*. Something an individual has — some object or token — determines privilege or access. A house key is a simple example of token-based security. Whoever has the key can open the door. A security card is a more modern hybrid example. Typically, the card is encoded so that a machine intermediary can determine validity. It is used without specific knowledge of any information it may hold simply as a token. Because simple token-based schemes tend to be rela-

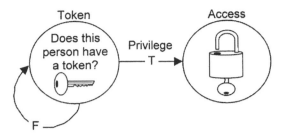

**Exhibit 1. Simple Security**

tively anonymous, they can fail easily if the token is lost or stolen. A token can be made difficult to lose or steal — for example, a radio frequency tag riveted to the fender of a vehicle or embedded under a pet's skin — but it remains a token all the same. It still can be removed and replaced. An identification card with a picture is merely a more complicated variant (see Exhibit 1).

- *Knowledge-based.* Something an individual knows — namely some fact or password — determines privilege or access. This is also a token-based approach, except that the token is intangible. Knowledge-based security requires some sort of intermediary to determine whether the individual actually knows the fact (has the token). Both the human guard to whom a secret password is given and a computer program into which a password or personal identification number (PIN) is typed are examples of intermediaries. Modern knowledge-based approaches are relatively anonymous and can fail if the passwords or facts are forgotten, disclosed, or stolen.
- *Two factor.* Both what an individual knows (some fact or password) and what he has (a token) determines privilege or access (see Exhibit 2). Automated teller machine (ATM) cards are a widespread example of two-factor security. Account holders are give tokens (mag-

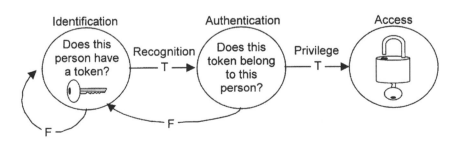

**Exhibit 2. Two-Factor Authentication**

netically encoded cards) and passwords (PINs) that allow them access to banking services. Neither the card nor the PIN is particularly useful by itself.

• *Biometric.* A permanent attribute, unique to an individual and not easily duplicated determines privilege or access — for example, a fingerprint, signature, iris, or voice pattern. Characteristic-based or biometric schemes vary from simple token-based schemes in that, rather than holding a token, the individual essentially becomes the token. A biometric technique examines a natively biological attribute of the individual. The individual possesses the characteristic; the characteristic is not added to the individual. The attribute is a permanent token. A radio frequency tag embedded below a pet's skin would be a permanently embedded token. Because biometric authentication can be quite authoritative, virtually no anonymity is possible in the transaction — each individual becomes self-authenticating, especially in a two-factor scenario.

## AUTHORITATIVE IDENTIFICATION

### Certainty as Probability

When an individual's claims of identity and privilege are verified or authenticated in a truly reliable way, that identification is authoritative. Unlike the sure match of character and case in a password, a biometric attribute is not subject to unambiguous permanence. The practical value of true reliability is that an authentication can be offered in one of three states — certain and unambiguous (deterministic), certain based on a low probability of error (probabilistic), uncertain and ambiguous and therefore false.

All biometric schemes are probabilistic, so design and implementation steps that can reduce the likelihood of an error are essential to orderly deployment of the technology. Biometric techniques are most reliable and effective when used as an authenticating technique as part of a multiple-factor scenario. For example, if an individual makes a claim of identity at the bank with his or her name, and that claim is supported by a biometric authentication, the probability of error is very low. Errors are much more likely to occur where the system must figure out on its own who an individual is (see Exhibit 3).

### Measures of Reliability

When evaluating a biometric identification scheme, several key measures reveal its ability to function reliably. When evaluating the reliability of a system for straight identification, the predicted number of rejections should be very small, but the predicted number of false acceptances should be improbable to the point of practical impossibility. Where a system will be used for authentication as part of a two-factor scenario, balance of false rejections and acceptance is more relevant. Here the system functions in a

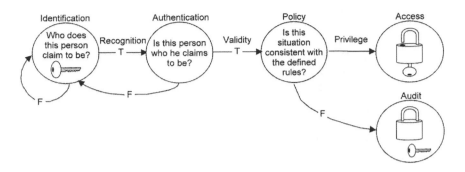

**Exhibit 3. Authoritative Identification**

context with other controlling factors — asserted identity, user facilitation, and so on — that can keep it functioning conveniently in addition to reliably. Three principal reliability measures for biometric systems are:

1. False accept rate (FAR) (also called type I error) indicates the percentage of unauthorized attempts that will be erroneously accepted. This number should always be as low as possible, although it should be interpreted in light of how many unauthorized attempts are expected on average.
2. False reject rate (FRR) (also called type II error) indicates the percentage of authorized attempts that will be erroneously rejected. This number should always be as low as possible. The more frequently authorized users are rejected, the more greater the risk to project acceptance.
3. Equal error rate (ERR), the point at which the lowest FAR and FRR intersect. A very low number for ERR indicates a system with a good balance of sensitivity.

## THE BIOMETRIC IDENTIFICATION PROCESS

In general, the simpler the identification process, the less authoritative it is. Put another way, the less anonymous a process is, the more likely the identification is to be correct and authoritative. Every system requires an enrollment step during which the identifier for an individual is read and stored in a database for future reference. (The paradox of this step is how to ensure that the individual is in fact whom he or she claims.) The enrollment process follows the same technical steps as the recognition process. The biometric attribute is acquired via camera or scanning device, computer software localizes the attribute so that it can be examined without extraneous noise or detail, a matching template is created, and the database is searched for duplicates. If no duplicates exist, the system will store the template for future use (see Exhibit 4).

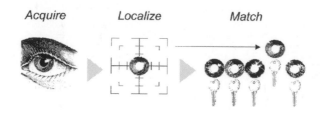

**Exhibit 4. Generic Biometric Recognition Process (Iris)**

Biometric systems can address recognition requirements two ways — identification and authentication. The exercise of identification involves isolating the biometric attribute and searching the database for matches from which to conclude the identity of the individual. Authentication is much simpler and more efficient in that the match need only be performed against the records of the person an individual claims to be.

## TYPES OF BIOMETRIC IDENTIFICATION

Approaches to biometric identification using current technology range from the quick and relatively conventional to slow and exotic. Fingerprint recognition is gradually becoming more widespread, mainly because it is noninvasive, the technology is simple to implement, and it requires no more processing power than what any conventional personal computer could spare.

Identifying an individual using genetic patterns, while quite reliable and authoritative, remains a time-consuming scientific process and is generally reserved for forensic purposes because it is invasive and requires highly specialized equipment and expertise. Human scent identification is emerging as yet another, although currently quite arcane, technology.

The rate of change in technology guarantees that what seems impossibly complex today can become practical, even a practical necessity, in just a few short years. The various available technologies differ mainly in their choice of identifier and the technical means to acquire and localize the necessary information about it. The current state of biometric identification technology includes numerous options, some capable of production use, others still emerging and not yet reliable or cost-effective enough for common deployment.

### Established Technology

Several approaches have entered the technical mainstream, although biometric identification has yet to cross the chasm into mass-market acceptance. The determining factors in establishing a biometric identification technology are typically reliability, convenience, and cost.

**Fingerprint.** The use of fingerprints as a unique characteristic has emerged as an early and popular method. This is due in part to its ubiquity in law enforcement applications. Fingerprint identification techniques fall into two major categories — automated fingerprint identification systems (AFIS) and fingerprint recognition systems. An AFIS generally uses computer and imaging technology to match actual fingerprint images to identify an individual authoritatively. Simple fingerprint recognition normally derives a unique template from the attributes of the fingerprint without storing the image itself or even allowing for its reconstruction. Fingerprint recognition is a more common biometric identification technique while AFIS installations tend to fall more into the domain of law enforcement.

Fingerprint recognition for identification acquires the initial image through live scan of the finger by direct contact with a reader device that can also check for validating attributes such as temperature and pulse. This can improve the authority of the image and makes the security more difficult to compromise. Because the finger actually touches the scanning device, the surface can become oily and cloudy after repeated use. This will affect the sensitivity and reliability of optical scanners. (Hand geometry, discussed below, is less sensitive to dirt.)

Solid-state sensors overcome this and other technical hurdles by offering virtual immunity to dirt and scratches because the coated silicon chip itself is the sensor. Additional local processing logic can be built into the sensor module at very low cost as well. Solid-state devices use electrical capacitance to sense the ridges of the fingerprint and create a compact digital image. In fingerprint recognition, the image is less critical than its differentiating characteristics or minutiae. While each fingerprint has 100 or more minutiae, an authoritative identification requires matches on only a fraction of them. The minutiae create a data template that is matched against the template stored in the database for an individual.

Because this comparison is mathematical and the technology for identifying minutiae is evolving quite rapidly, FRR and FAR percentages are low enough for practical use. Finger imaging (shown in Exhibit 5) is a variant of hand geometry discussed below.

**Hand Geometry.** No two hands are exactly alike, so the essence of hand geometry is the comparative dimensions of fingers and the locations of joints. Measuring hand geometry became one of the earliest automated biometric techniques with the introduction of the Identimat, installed at the Shearson-Hamill investment bank on Wall Street during the late 1960s. The system stayed in production for almost 20 years.

The popularity of hand geometry as a biometric identification technique for access control is due in part to a combination of practical reliability — relatively low FAR and FRR rates — as well as declining cost of technology.

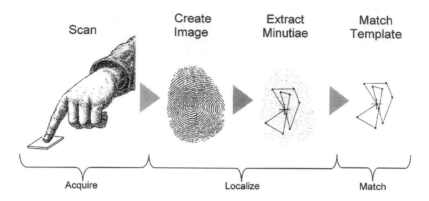

**Exhibit 5. Fingerprint Recognition Process**

Some systems perform simple, two-dimensional measurements of the palm of the hand. Others attempt to construct a simple three-dimensional image from which to extract template characteristics.

In one of the most popular descendants of the Identimat, a small digital camera captures top and side images of the hand. Reference marks on the platen allow calibration of the image to improve the precision of matching.

**Retinal Scan.** Retinal recognition (see Exhibit 6) remains one of the most authoritative techniques for biometric identification. It creates an "eye signature" from the vascular configuration of the retina. This is an extremely reliable attribute, especially considering that it is protected inside the eye itself and is not known to change significantly over time. An image of the retina can be captured easily without any physical contact, although the individual does need to look through a lens at an alignment target. Its visible/internal nature and the fact that a pulse can be discerned easily also

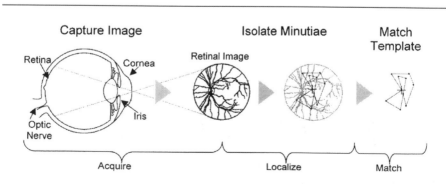

**Exhibit 6. Retinal Recognition Process**

make the retinal attributes extremely difficult to forge or steal. Diseases or injuries that would interfere with the retina are comparatively rare in the general population, so the attribute normally remains both consistent and consistently available.

**Voice Recognition.** Voice recognition techniques are generally categorized according to two approaches — automatic speaker verification (ASV) and automatic speaker identification (ASI). Speaker verification uses voice as the authenticating attribute in a two-factor scenario. Speaker identification attempts to use voice to identify who an individual actually is. Voice recognition distinguishes an individual by matching particular voice traits against templates stored in a database. Because it is a performance-based measure, the system must be trained to the individual's voice at enrollment time. So that extraction and matching algorithms can work properly, one or more enrollment sessions are necessary, each involving repetition of known words and phrases to be used for feature extraction and matching.

Feature extraction typically measures formats or sound characteristics unique to each person's vocal tract. More complex measures can involve the rate of speech or accent. The pattern matching algorithms used in voice recognition are similar to those used in face recognition.

## Emerging Technology

**Iris.** Iris scanning offers a less intrusive technique than retinal recognition, which requires the eye to be close enough to the camera lens to reveal its interior. The iris is easily visible from several feet away and seems to offer as much reliability as fingerprint or retinal recognition. Although longer empirical tests with the technology will improve its reliability, it appears quite promising and even practical for many applications, especially two-factor scenarios.

One of the benefits of this technology is that it should be less invasive than retinal scanning. Capturing an image from several feet away is feasible. While some of the technical issues of iris scanning seem pedestrian, they present implementation challenges. Light, distance, resolution, and contrast must all be balanced to acquire a useful image. With low available light, the lens aperture of the camera must be quite wide, drastically reducing the depth of field and requiring very precise focus. Too much available or ambient light can cause discomfort to the individual or extraneous reflections. This magic balance of light and distance determines resolution and contrast. Balanced resolution and contrast are necessary to extract the attributes or minutiae from the localized image. Color, the feature that most of us notice first, does not seem to be a significant differentiation except insofar as it provides a means to limit the number of templates to search.

A factor in the reliability of iris scanning is the point at which an individual's iris becomes stable enough to use an identifier. While the iris seems to be consistent throughout adulthood, it does vary somewhat up to adolescence. Responses of the iris to changes in light can provide secondary verification that the iris presented as a biometric factor is genuine.

**Face/Facial Thermogram.** In its simplest form, face recognition involves simply matching an image of the face that is presented with each of the available alternatives stored in a database. This technology is still in its early stages, and most tests and applications have been run against relatively small databases. The similarity score produced by each comparison determines the match — the highest score wins.

Acquisition for biometric identification purposes requires the individual's face to be presented to a video camera. An evident deficiency in some current schemes is that because the image is acquired in two dimensions, given perspective only by shadow, an individual could hold up a picture of a face and probably be accepted. A stereoscopic camera could determine that the face was actually three dimensional, but could still be fooled by makeup or a disguise. A combination of face recognition and thermogram offers a reliable alternative. A facial thermogram works much like face recognition except that the image is captured by way of an infrared camera, and the heat signature of the face is used to create the biometric template used for matching.

The algorithms used in face recognition can be quite complex and, in certain cases, result in high FAR/FRR values. A controlled environment in which lighting and facial orientation are uniform can improve results dramatically with this technology. The recognition process follows the common acquire-localize-match model. During localization the image is aligned and adjusted for contrast, facial features are isolated, and an eigenspace projection is typically created. This statistical technique creates a very compact, normalized representation of the face.

The normalized image is projected mathematically onto normalized eigenfaces stored in the database for matching. Some systems use neural network algorithms to solve the matching problem.

The U.S. Army Research Laboratory conducted the FERET Database Evaluation Procedure in September of 1996, comparing various technologies and algorithms side by side. While the results are promising and some approaches yielded impressive results, this technology is still considerably less reliable than some alternatives. As is the case with other technologies, practical usefulness increases dramatically in a two-factor scenario.

**Hand Vein.** Hand vein recognition attempts to distinguish individuals by measuring the differences in subcutaneous features of the hand using infrared imaging. This is a logical hybrid of face recognition, hand geometry, and retinal scanning. Like face recognition, it must deal with the extra issues of three-dimensional space and the orientation of the hand. Like retinal scanning, it relies on the pattern of the veins in the hand to build a template with which to attempt matches against templates stored in a database.

The vascular patterns of each individual's hand are unique and do not appear to change much over time, although they do not present as richly detailed and reliable a structure as the retina. The use of infrared imaging offers some of the same advantages as hand geometry over fingerprint recognition in manufacturing or shop-floor applications where hands may not be clean enough to scan properly using a conventional video or capacitance technique.

**Signature.** Signature is one of the oldest forms of biometric authentication. It is a simple, concrete expression of the unique variations in human hand geometry. Forensic experts have developed criteria over the years for verifying the authenticity of a signature. Automating this process allows computer automation to take the place of an expert in looking for unique identifying attributes. In addition to the general shape of the signed name, a signature recognition system can also measure both the pressure and velocity of the point of the stylus across the sensor pad. (Keystroke dynamics is a variation on this technique that measures the typing rates and intervals.) These subtle individual variations are extremely hard for forgers to mimic, especially under the scrutiny of computer software operating virtually in real-time. Signatures, however, are difficult to model for variation, and the reliability of these systems, especially when compared with other simpler alternatives, positions them mainly for specialty use.

## CHARACTERISTICS OF A GOOD BIOMETRIC IDENTIFIER

Casual observation of the incredible variety of human forms and attributes might seem to reveal a large number of potential attributes for biometric identification. Good biometric identifiers, however, share several characteristics that make them useful and reliable for recognition and identification applications (see also Exhibit 7):

- *Universal.* Everyone must have the attribute. The attribute must be one that is universal and seldom lost to accident or disease.
- *Consistent.* The attribute must not change significantly over time. The attribute should not be subject to significant differences based on age, or on episodic or chronic disease. Voice is a consistent measure assuming consistent health, but can vary considerably with colds and sinus conditions. The iris of the eye changes measurably between birth and adolescence. Retinas and fingerprints change very little over a lifetime.

| | Attribute | | | | | | | | System | | | Suitability | |
|---|---|---|---|---|---|---|---|---|---|---|---|---|---|
| | Universal | Consistent | Unique | Permanent | Inimitable | Collectible | Tamper Resistant | Comparable | Performance | Authoritative | Reliability | Relative Cost | Acceptability |
| **Fingerprint** | ◐ | ◐ | ● | ● | ● | ● | ● | ● | ● | ◐ | ● | ◐ | ◐ |
| **Hand Geometry** | ◐ | ● | ● | ● | ● | ● | ◐ | ● | ● | ◐ | ● | ◐ | ◐ |
| **Retinal Scan** | ● | ● | ● | ● | ● | ◐ | ● | ● | ● | ● | ● | ● | ○ |
| **Voice Print** | ◐ | ● | ◐ | ● | ◐ | ● | ◐ | ◐ | ○ | ○ | ○ | ◐ | ○ |
| **Iris** | ● | ● | ● | ● | ● | ● | ● | ● | ● | ● | ● | ◐ | ◐ |
| **Hand Vein** | ● | ● | ◐ | ● | ● | ● | ● | ◐ | ◐ | ◐ | ● | ◐ | ◐ |
| **Signature** | ○ | ○ | ○ | ○ | ○ | ◐ | ○ | ◐ | ○ | ○ | ○ | ◐ | ◐ |
| **Face Recognition** | ● | ◐ | ◐ | ◐ | ○ | ● | ◐ | ◐ | ◐ | ◐ | ◐ | ● | ◐ |
| **Thermogram** | ● | ◐ | ◐ | ◐ | ◐ | ● | ● | ◐ | ◐ | ◐ | ◐ | ● | ◐ |

High = ●

Medium = ◐

Low = ○

**Exhibit 7. Comparison of Representative Technologies**

- *Unique.* Each expression of the attribute must be unique to the individual. Height, weight, hair, and eye color are all attributes that are unique assuming a particularly precise measure, but do not offer enough points of differentiation to be useful for more than categorizing.
- *Permanent.* The attribute must be inseparable from the individual. The attribute must be integral and not viable for identification if removed.
- *Inimitable.* The attribute must be irreproducible by other means. A recording of a voice can be separated from an individual just as an image of his or her face. The less reproducible the attribute, the more likely it will be authoritative.
- *Collectible.* It must be easy to gather the attribute data passively. If a patient is unconscious, voice recognition would not be useful. If a patient is not particularly cooperative, fingerprint recognition or hand geometry would present limitations.

- *Tamper-resistant.* The attribute should be quite hard to mask or manipulate. Fingerprints cannot be changed and hiding them is difficult, whereas faces can be masked or made up.
- *Comparable.* The attribute must be reducible to a state that makes it digitally comparable to others. The less probabilistic the matching involved, the more authoritative the identification.

## ISSUES OF BIOMETRIC IDENTIFICATION

The widespread availability of consumer credit has helped turn the private details of individual lives into the currency and property of financial institutions, credit reporting companies, and mass marketers. Financial institutions assess credit risk using complex formulas fed with numerous details related to an individual's spending and payment habits. Marketing firms study the detailed buying patterns of individuals to both improve products and target their audience better. While privacy persists as a national concern, it is no longer a national debate. The flow of detailed private information underlies much of consumer convenience in developed societies.

The issues of privacy, anonymity, and community standards surface at the center of an implementation of biometric identification. It is in the nature of the technology to excite concerns about loss of control of information or of individuality. Like other technologies, biometric identification is a double-edged sword — each benefit includes a trade-off. While biometric identification itself is a reliable probabilistic scheme — the statistical chance that the security would be compromised is low — an implementation using two (or more) factor security could allow identification with scientific accuracy. In other words, the identification would be as close to a certainty as modern science would assert.

For all practical purposes, a two-factor security biometric security scheme could eliminate the external ambiguities that cause records to become lost or associated with the wrong individual. The potential reduction in fraud alone is driving some financial institutions to introduce biometric techniques associated with credit card verification. Transaction records this authoritative would have implications for how many transactions that demand high security are automated.

The consequences in terms of improved efficiency in our data-based society are already showing up in banking, the use of cash, and even taxation. The social cost can be assessed in the simple concession that authoritative identification expects — the loss of anonymity.

The loss of anonymity is a natural technical consequence of society's growing dependence on database technology. In developed countries, the sheer scale of the commerce involved in day-to-day living defies any manual alternatives. As business and government strive to improve the level of logical trust associated with their transactions, the pressure to shed personal anonymity increases. Trust ultimately means that an individual is whom he or she claims, and that claim can be verified authoritatively.

In healthcare, implementations of biometric identification where the scope is limited to controlling access to computer systems or to identifying employees authoritatively certain areas seem to offer the greatest immediate promise. While some anonymity is given up, it is for proprietary purposes and not typically useful beyond its application. Ironically, the absence of current standards related to biometric technology ensures that this will continue to be the case for some time. Rolling out a biometric identification scheme to the community at large, on the other hand, must navigate the discovery and definition of local community standards and whether or not such technology would be accepted. Finally, almost none of the legal aspects of biometric technology are adequately defined or tested, and most of the conversation on this front seems to remain the domain of privacy advocates and special interest groups.

The technical and operational benefits of implementing biometric identification finally appear to be aligning with the costs. The strategic opportunity for healthcare organizations is in implementing and gaining experience with these new technologies under the wary eye of the local community.

Chapter 11

# The Role of the Information Management Standards in the JCAHO Network Accreditation Program

*Marianne F. Miragia*

In this era of regulation and oversight of all industries, the Joint Commission on Accreditation of Healthcare Organizations (JCAHO) is not a newcomer to the field of healthcare accreditation and regulation. Although different than the federal regulators, in that JCAHO accreditation is voluntary, the JCAHO accreditation survey process has been recognized by the federal government to have a "deemed status." Therefore, a healthcare organization that is accredited by the JCAHO is not required to have a separate accreditation survey by the Centers for Medicare and Medicaid (CMS) to receive payment for Medicare and Medicaid patients. Most insurance companies, managed care plans, and employers prefer or require JCAHO accreditation, as well, for their healthcare reimbursement.

## JCAHO BACKGROUND

Founded in 1951, the JCAHO evaluates and accredits almost 18,000 healthcare organizations nationwide. Included in these organizations are

0-8493-1498-4/03/$0.00+$1.50
© 2003 by CRC Press LLC

hospitals and other healthcare entities that provide long-term care, home care, behavioral health, and laboratory and ambulatory services.

## Mission

The mission of the JCAHO is to improve the quality and safety of care provided to the public through the provision of healthcare accreditation and related services that support performance improvement in healthcare organizations.

## Corporate Members

The Joint Commission's corporate members consist of:

* American College of Physicians — American Society of Internal Medicine
* American College of Surgeons
* American Dental Association
* American Hospital Association
* American Medical Association

## Board

The Joint Commission has a board of 28 individuals, including nurses, physicians, consumers, medical directors, administrators, providers, employers, labor representatives, health plan leaders, quality experts, ethicists, health insurance administrators, and educators. They bring countless years of diverse experience in healthcare, business, and public policy.

## Staff

There is a cadre of more than 400 JCAHO surveyors comprised of physicians, nurses, healthcare administrators, medical technologists, psychologists, respiratory therapists, pharmacists, medical equipment experts, engineers, and social workers. A central office staff of more than 500 employees, who schedule the surveys, plan the agenda, and analyze the results, supports the surveyors. In addition, there are research and development staff, external relations, public relations, business development, information systems, statisticians, and account representatives to each of the accredited organizations.

The JCAHO has also created numerous task forces and customer-focused panels to ensure that the survey process and accreditation standards are addressing the needs of the patients, the clinicians, and the healthcare organizations.

## NETWORK ACCREDITATION

Always responsive to the needs of the industry, as many healthcare organizations began mergers, acquisitions, and affiliations, the JCAHO began to modify its accreditation programs and survey process to include the following types of organizations: assisted living facilities, ambulatory care, behavioral healthcare, clinical laboratories, disease-specific care, home care, hospitals, healthcare networks, long-term care, office-based surgery, pharmacy, preferred provider organizations, and managed behavioral healthcare.

In the 1990s, the JCAHO created a new accreditation program called "Network Accreditation" to accommodate integrated delivery systems, health maintenance organizations, preferred provider organizations, and managed behavioral healthcare. This type of accreditation evaluates the structure of an organization to determine and recognize the organization's ability to integrate its services to meet the healthcare needs of the population it serves.

Network accreditation standards assess the structure, processes, and policies the organization has put in place that drive how the organization functions (or does business).

By selecting this type of accreditation, the standards and the survey process act as "tools" for the organization to demonstrate its ability to work together as one organization, to deliver one level of care in all aspects and entities of the organization.

This type of survey does not involve visiting any patient care areas. Interviews are held with organization executive leaders who must describe how they function according to standards developed for this type of survey. Collaboration and communication are key in demonstrating compliance to these standards.

The core groups of functional standards for network accreditation are: leadership, human resources, improving network performance, patient rights, responsibilities and ethics, continuum of care, education and communication, health promotion and disease prevention, and management of information.

## STANDARDS DEVELOPMENT

Standards development at the JCAHO has always focused on statements that would indicate a level of excellence reflecting the "state-of-the-art" for the area to be evaluated (see Exhibit 1). Initially, the JCAHO standards were written and reviewed by experts in the field for the major departments, disciplines, and services and that would be found in a healthcare organization. Processes were defined that should be in place and that were identified as being important reflections of quality patient care. As the cost of healthcare escalated in the mid- to late 1980s, the focus of the industry began to examine the actual "performance" of an organization and the "outcomes" of the care provided as a measure of quality.

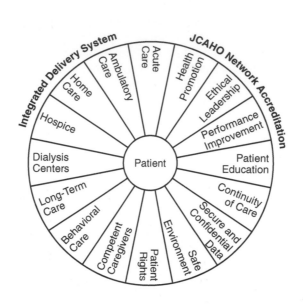

**Exhibit 1. JCAHO Standards Wheel**

---

Standards were reorganized and written to reflect acknowledged measures of performance. Instead of being organized by departments, disciplines, and services, they were organized according to key functions within an organization that are related and integrated with one another in order to demonstrate excellent outcomes of performance.

## NETWORK STANDARDS

As an organization makes the decision to become network accredited, it discovers that the standards are written to act as tools to assist an organization in sustaining the interdisciplinary teamwork needed to implement functions and processes effectively. Network functional standards (see Exhibit 2) promote components working together, with the patient/members being the driving factors.

## NETWORK MANAGEMENT OF INFORMATION STANDARDS

Key to the successful outcomes of the network survey process is the management of information standards. These standards promote current, accurate, and timely patient information that is accessible to all components within the organization, whether it be paper or electronic.

The complete set of information standards for networks is listed in Exhibit 3. Each group of standards addresses different aspects of how information needs are assessed, planned, designed, and implemented in various

**Exhibit 2. Goals for the Major Functional Areas of Network Standards**

| Functional Area | Goal |
| --- | --- |
| Rights, responsibilities, and ethics | To improve member health outcomes by respecting each member's rights and by conducting business relationships with members and the public in an ethical manner |
| Continuum of care | To define, shape, and sequence processes and activities to maximize coordination of care within a continuum |
| Education and communication | To improve member health outcomes by promoting healthy behavior, facilitating member and family participation in treatment, appropriately involving members and their families in healthcare decisions, and supporting recovery and a speedy return to function |
| Health promotion and disease prevention | To address maintenance of health, prevention of acute diseases and injuries, and avoidance or delay of morbidity and disability associated with chronic and degenerative diseases |
| Leadership | To plan, direct, coordinate, provide, and improve healthcare services that respond to community and member needs |
| Management of human resources | To identify and provide an appropriate number of qualified people to fulfill the network's mission and meet the needs of its members |
| Improving network performance | To improve member health outcomes throughout the network by improving performance of clinical, governance, and support processes |
| Management of information | To obtain, manage, and use information to improve clinical staff, licensed independent practitioners, and component performance in providing member care and the governance, management, and support processes |

aspects of the organization, as well as how security and confidentiality are to be provided. Although there is a separate interview in the network survey process that addresses management of information, the standards are also designed to be integrated into the other functional interviews.

The first set of standards, the IM.1 standards, addresses the assessment and planning needs of the organization for information. They are related to the leadership standards that require leaders of the organization to be involved in these processes. In the network survey process, compliance can be demonstrated in the Leadership interview by describing how leaders of the clinical, financial, and operational aspects of the organization participate in the assessment of the organization's informational needs. This would include identifying patient demographic needs, results of lab tests, physical assessments, physician dictation, development and approval of forms, composition of the patient record, information needs by third-party payers, and regulators. Other issues such as timeliness and access of information also require input from leaders. In the Informa-

141

## Exhibit 3 . Information Management Standards for Networks

| | |
|---|---|
| IM.1 | Information-management processes are planned and designed to meet the network's internal and external information needs. |
| IM.1.1 | Internal and external information management processes are appropriate to the network's size and complexity. |
| IM.1.2 | Appropriate individuals participate in assessing, selecting, integrating, and using efficient information management systems. |
| IM.2 | The information management processes in the network, its practitioner sites, and its components protect the confidentiality, security, and integrity of information. |
| IM.2.1 | The network, its practitioner sites, and its components determine appropriate levels of security and confidentiality of data and information. |
| IM.2.2 | Data can be easily retrieved in a timely manner without compromising security and confidentiality. |
| IM.2.3 | The network, its practitioner sites, and its components effectively safeguard records and information against loss, destruction, tampering, and unauthorized access or use. |
| IM.2.4 | Individuals (members, clinical staff, licensed independent practitioners) about whom data and information may be collected are made appropriately aware of what use will be made of the information. |
| IM.2.5 | All staff of the network, its practitioner sites, and components are effectively and continually reminded of the need for confidentiality of data and information. |
| IM.2.6 | The network determines how long health records and other data and information are retained. |
| IM.3 | Whenever possible, minimum data sets, data definitions, codes, classifications, and terminology are standardized throughout the network. |
| IM.3.1 | Data collection is timely, economical, efficient, accurate, complete, and sufficiently discriminating for its intended use throughout the network. |
| IM.3.2 | The network assesses data reliability, validity, and accuracy on an ongoing basis and verifies that data bias is minimized. |
| IM.3.2.1 | Member health records are periodically reviewed for completeness, accuracy, and timely completion of all necessary information. |
| IM.3.3 | The network and its components have an effective system for coding and retrieving financial information from appropriate sources. |
| IM.3.4 | The network's and component's data-collection systems provide timely and accurate information for operational decision making and planning. |
| IM.4 | Transmission of data and information is timely and accurate. |
| IM.4.1 | The network uses standardized formats and methods, whenever possible, to disseminate data and information and provide feedback to network components and participating practitioner sites. |
| IM.5 | The network has adequate capability to integrate and interpret data and information from various sources. |
| IM.6 | Information management processes enable the definition, capture, analysis, transformation, transmission, and reporting of individual member-specific data and information related to processes and outcomes of care. |
| IM.6.1 | The network's member information system routinely provides access to all needed member information during treatment. |
| IM.6.2 | The network requires that a record of member health information be initiated, maintained, and accessible for every individual assessed or treated. |

**Exhibit 3 (Continued). Information Management Standards for Networks**

| | |
|---|---|
| IM.6.3 | The network requires that the record of health information contains sufficient information to identify the member, support the diagnosis, justify treatment or services, document the course and results of treatment or services, and facilitate continuity of care among components. |
| IM.7 | The network defines, captures, analyzes, transmits, and reports aggregated data and information that supports managerial decisions, operations, performance improvement activities, and member care. |
| IM.7.1 | Occurrences of measures (indicators) of care processes and outcomes for assessing performance can be aggregated. |
| IM.7.2 | Summaries of actions taken resulting from networkwide performance improvement activities, including risk management and utilization review, can be aggregated. |
| IM.7.3 | Clinical staff-specific and licensed independent practitioner-specific information can be aggregated. |
| IM.7.4 | Data and information used to support clinical research can be aggregated. |
| IM.7.5 | Data and information used to provide feedback on performance to network components and participating practitioner sites can be aggregated. |
| IM.8 | The network provides systems, resources, and services to meet its informational, educational, and research-related needs for knowledge-based information or professional literature. |
| IM.8.1 | The network's knowledge-based information resources are authoritative and current. |
| IM.9 | Information management includes the definition, capture, analysis, transmission, reporting, feedback, and use of comparative performance data and information. |
| IM.9.1 | The network uses external reference databases for comparative purposes. |
| IM.9.2 | The network contributes to external reference databases when required by law or regulation and when appropriate to the network. |

tion Management interview, compliance with this set of standards is demonstrated by describing the processes used to identify organizational needs and the results.

The IM.2 standards address the confidentiality, security, and integrity of the data and information. This is addressed in the Information Management interview by presenting policies and describing processes that address how security and confidentiality of patient-specific data and information will be maintained at both the components of the system and any practitioner office sites within the system. Education of all staff concerning these policies and nondisclosure agreements would be included in this discussion. Evidence of training and presented documents used is also necessary for surveyors to review.

Policies, processes, and documents will also be needed to demonstrate how patient data can be retrieved in a timely manner without compromising security and confidentiality; how patients are made aware of how their information will be used; as well as how patient information will be protected against loss, destruction, and tampering. A demonstration of how paper records are secured and how access codes and passwords are distributed and maintained is very effective for the surveyors' review.

The IM.3 standards address standardization of how patient data is defined, collected, validated, aggregated, and reported to clinicians, financial staff, physicians, and quality and monitoring functions. In the Information Management interview, compliance with these standards requires policies, processes, formats, and evidence of education for these elements. Examples of how the validation of data collection is performed, and how medical records are secured after regular business hours or at practitioner office sites, will be of interest to surveyors.

Evidence of reports and how patient- and practitioner-specific data is collected is important to demonstrate in the Performance Improvement interview. Coding and financial reports will be important to present in the Utilization Review interview. Spreadsheets and databases will be needed in the Leadership interview to demonstrate data-driven decision making and planning.

The IM.4 standards address the formats and methods used in the transmission of data, both within the organization and to external organizations and agencies. Policies, processes, and a demonstration of data transmission will be effective for surveyor review in the Information Management interview. It will be helpful if the Information Management interview is held in a conference room where a network "hook-up" and computer are available. Many organizations also have the capability to project the computer screen onto an overhead projector for their demonstrations.

The IM.5 standard addresses the organization's capability to integrate and interpret data from various sources. As for the IM.4 standards, this can be demonstrated with the computer hook-up in the Information Management interview.

The IM.6 standards are the core of the IM standards. They require policies, processes, and documents that guide the content of a patient medical record and its timely availability during the patient's course of treatment throughout the various services and components within the organization. They support and facilitate the necessary availability and accuracy of the patient's diagnosis and treatment plan for the continuity of care.

Compliance is demonstrated in both the Information Management interview with policies, documents, and processes, and a demonstration where, if appropriate, in the Continuity of Care interview of how clinicians access patient information during care in the various services and different entities. This can be a very powerful statement by the organization in both interviews if done well.

144

The IM.7 standards are concerned with how data is aggregated and analyzed for the various functions of Performance Improvement, Utilization Review, Risk Management, Medical Staff Credentialing, and employee evaluation records. Compliance with these standards is best demonstrated in the above-mentioned interviews rather than in the Information Management interview. Policies and processes that outline the structure of how this is implemented are very important.

The IM.8 standards state that systems and resources must be in place to provide knowledge-based information for research and education purposes. The organization's librarians and in-service educators should be included in the discussion and demonstration of how this is implemented in the Information Management interview.

Finally, the IM.9 standards describe the use of data for external comparison and benchmarking and accessibility to external benchmarking databases to address regulatory compliance issues. A statement of which databases the organization participates in is an excellent way of demonstrating compliance.

## THE FUTURE OF INFORMATION MANAGEMENT IN HEALTHCARE REGULATORY COMPLIANCE

In the age of Web-based information, regulatory agencies are requiring more compliance data to be transmitted directly to their Web sites. The JCAHO already requires accredited hospitals, home care programs, long-term care facilities, and behavioral health facilities to transmit outcome measure results quarterly as a condition of participation. The JCAHO also requires external benchmarking as part of Medicare regulations and a list of healthcare organization-level compliance on the its Web site for the public to access. It is only a matter of time before regulators, in response to consumers, require all information to meet similar standards, as is evidenced by the pending HIPAA regulations to be implemented starting in April of 2003. Familiarity with the JCAHO Information Management standards for networks is the cutting edge of the role of information management in regulatory compliance for the future in healthcare.

# Chapter 12
# HIPAA Privacy in the Healthcare Industry

*Rebecca Herold, CISSP, CISA, FLMI*

## INTRODUCTION

In today's high-tech and increasingly network-connected world, depending on locking file cabinets to protect the privacy of health information is not feasible. In addition to technology challenges, the laws in force to protect personal patient information have historically been very patchwork and greatly diverse under the large collection of state and federal laws. In the past, personal patient and health information could be distributed without notice for almost any reason, including those not even related to health care or medical treatments. For example, such health information could be passed from an insurer to a lender, who subsequently then could deny the person's application for a mortgage or a loan, or even to the person's employer who could then consider it for making personnel decisions.

By enacting the Health Insurance Portability and Accountability Act of 1996 (HIPAA), the U.S. Congress mandated that organizations must take specific actions to protect personally identifiable health information. President Clinton signed the HIPAA on August 21, 1996. The Act was designed to protect health insurance coverage for workers and their families when they change or lose their jobs. Also known as the Kennedy-Kassebaum Bill, provisions of the HIPAA intend to ensure patient privacy and confidentiality for all healthcare-related information. This affects all healthcare organizations — from physicians and insurance companies to healthcare support organizations.

The HIPAA contains an important section called Administrative Simplification. Provisions of this section are intended to reduce the costs and administrative burdens of healthcare by standardizing many administrative and financial forms and transactions. Administrative Simplification includes sub-sections on the privacy and security of patient information that mandate standards for safeguarding for physical storage and maintenance, transmission, and access to individual health information. The privacy requirements are collectively referred to as the Privacy Rule.

The Privacy Rule was passed on April 14, 2001, and updated on August 14, 2002, with compliance required by most health plans and healthcare providers by April 14, 2003. Those entities that do not comply with these regulations will be subject to severe civil and criminal penalties.

The Privacy Rule intends to protect personal health information by:

- Giving patients more control over their health information
- Setting limitations on the use and release of health records
- Establishing safeguards covered entities must implement to protect the privacy of health information
- Holding those in noncompliance responsible through civil and criminal penalties for privacy violations
- Attempting to create a balance between public responsibility for disclosure of some forms of information and the personal information of individual patients
- Giving patients the opportunity to make informed choices when seeking care and reimbursement for care based on considering how personal health information can be used
- Enabling patients to learn how their information can be used along with the disclosures of their information
- Limiting release to only the minimal amount of information needed for required disclosures
- Giving patients the right to examine and correct any mistakes in their personal health records

## DEFINITIONS AS THEY APPLY TO HIPAA

When reading and interpreting the HIPAA Privacy Rule, it is important to do so within the appropriate context for which the terminology used was intended. Some of the terminology used leads to a great deal of confusion. The following summarizes the definitions, as provided within the Privacy Rule, of some of the more commonly used and misunderstood terms.

### Business Associate

A *business associate* is a person working on behalf of a covered entity performing a function or activity that involves the use or disclosure of personal health information, including:

- Claims processing or administration
- Data analysis, processing, or administration
- Utilization review
- Quality assurance
- Billing
- Benefit management

- Practice management
- Repricing
- Providing legal, actuarial, accounting, consulting, data aggregation, management, administrative, accreditation, or financial services for a covered entity
- Any other function or activity related to processing or accessing personal health information

## Covered Entity

A covered entity with respect to the HIPAA Privacy Rule compliance includes the following:

- A health plan
- A healthcare clearinghouse
- A healthcare provider who transmits any health information in electronic form

## Health Care

Health care is a broad term referring to any type of care, service, or supply related to the health of an individual.

## Privacy

Privacy, with respect to HIPAA, generally limits release of information to the minimum reasonably needed for the purpose of the disclosure. It means people are able to make informed choices when seeking care and reimbursement for care based on how personal health information may be used. Privacy enables patients to find out how their information can be used and what disclosures of their information have been made. Privacy gives patients the right to examine and obtain a copy of their own health records and request corrections.

## Protected Health Information (PHI)

PHI refers to virtually all types of individually identifiable health information that is transmitted or maintained in any form or medium. Examples of PHI include, but are not limited to, the following:

- Information created or received by a healthcare provider, health plan, public health authority, employer, life insurer, school or university, or healthcare clearinghouse
- Information that relates to the past, present, or future physical or mental health or condition of an individual
- Information about the health care for an individual
- Information about the past, present, or future payment for individual health care

## TPO

TPO is an acronym that stands for "treatment, payment, or healthcare operations." This acronym is used throughout many regulatory documents related to the HIPAA.

## OVERVIEW OF THE AUGUST 2002 CHANGES

The Department of Health and Human Services (DHHS) proposed several changes to the original Privacy Rule on March 21, 2002, under the direction of President George W. Bush. The changes are referred to as the Notice of Proposed Rulemaking (NPRM). The primary changes that comprised the Privacy NPRM included changes in the requirements for:

- Consent
- Notice
- Minimum necessary and oral communications
- Business associates
- Parental access rights
- Marketing
- Use and disclosure for research
- De-identification
- Disclosure accounting
- Disclosures for TPO of other covered entities
- Uses and disclosures requiring authorization

In addition to the above categories of changes, a spattering of several other changes were made throughout the Privacy Rule.

The published reasons Secretary Thompson gave for making Privacy Rule revisions was to "eliminate serious obstacles to patients getting needed care and services quickly while continuing to protect patients' privacy. For example, sick patients will not be forced to visit the pharmacy themselves to pick up prescriptions – and could send a family member or friend instead. Doctors will be able to consult with nurses and others involved in a patient's care to ensure that they get the best care."

The changes were approved on August 9, 2002, and officially released on August 14, 2002. The information that follows incorporates these changes. Since their proposal in March, the changes were generally favored by the entities covered by the regulation, while many other groups and organizations criticized the proposed changes. Some in the healthcare industry believe more changes are needed within the Privacy Rule to make their jobs easier and place less procedural and monetary stress upon them to meet compliance. Other groups, primarily privacy rights organizations, believe the Privacy NPRM changes were a blow to patient privacy rights and greatly eroded the assurances of privacy the rule was originally constructed to help ensure.

## GENERAL RULES FOR PHI USES AND DISCLOSURES

Covered entities may use or disclose PHI, for living and deceased individuals, only under certain conditions. Basically, these include:

- To the individual about whom the PHI applies
- With individual consent or other legal agreement related to carrying out TPO, depending upon the date the agreement was obtained and the conditions of the agreement
- Generally without individual authorization for TPO, with a few exceptions

The wording of the original Privacy Rule was changed in the update to clarify parental access rights to children's medical information. As it was originally written, parents of an un-emancipated minor did not have to be treated as personal representatives of the child if the child could lawfully obtain health care without parental consent. The Privacy NPRM allowed disclosure of medical information to parents if state law allows such disclosures. So, even if a minor has a legal right to certain types of medical care without parental consent, the Privacy Rule does not grant the child the right to keep this information secret from parents or guardians.

When using, disclosing, or requesting PHI from another covered entity, reasonable precautions must be implemented to limit PHI access to only those people who need the access to accomplish their valid job responsibilities related to TPO. PHI may be used without authorization by a covered entity to create aggregate information if the PHI cannot be connected to a specific individual, in other words, ensuring "de-identification" of the individual PHI.

With exceptions related to HMO and government programs, a covered entity generally may disclose PHI to a business associate and allow a business associate to create or receive PHI on its behalf if the covered entity can ensure that the business associate will provide adequate security over the PHI. The covered entity must have written documentation showing the evidence of adequate security within agreements or other types of contracts. When communicating PHI in any form, the covered entity must take measures to ensure that the confidentiality of the PHI is maintained. PHI may not be used or disclosed in any way that conflicts with the entity's notice.

## USES AND DISCLOSURES: ORGANIZATIONAL REQUIREMENTS

There will be situations in which a covered entity performs one or more other functions that are not related or covered by the Privacy Rule. Such an organization is referred to within the regulation as a "hybrid entity." Legally separate covered entities can be considered as a single affiliated covered entity if all of the covered entities designated are under common ownership or control. A hybrid entity must ensure that the healthcare component of the organization complies with the Privacy Rule. For example, such a covered entity must ensure that the healthcare component does not disclose PHI to the other component of the entity in the same manner as if the other component were distinctly and legally separate.

If a person within a hybrid organization has job responsibilities for both the healthcare component and another aspect of the organization, the person must ensure they do not disclose PHI within their nonrelated role. To help ensure protection of PHI in this and similar types of situations, covered entities must implement policies and procedures to ensure compliance and awareness of the Privacy Rule by all persons working with PHI.

Affiliates and business associates of a covered entity must also ensure that their use and disclosure of the entity's PHI complies with the Privacy Rule. The Privacy NPRM includes model business associate contract provisions. With the exception of small health plans, the Privacy NPRM gave covered entities up to an additional year to change existing contracts so it is more realistic to renegotiate contracts one or a few at a time instead of all at once.

If a covered entity knows that one of its affiliates or business associates is in violation of the Privacy Rule, then the covered entity will be considered to be in noncompliance if it does not take reasonable steps to end the violation. To help ensure such compliance, covered entities must ensure business associate contracts clearly establish the permitted and required uses and disclosures of the entity's PHI by the business associate. The regulations list specific activities that can and cannot be included within business associate contracts.

## USES AND DISCLOSURES: CONSENT FOR TPO

As stated within the original Privacy Rule, a consent agreement was intended to give healthcare providers who have a direct relationship with a patient, permission to use and disclose all PHI for performing TPO. The consent purpose was to give permission to that specific provider, and not to any other person.

The Privacy Rule as updated on August 14, 2002, no longer requires healthcare providers to obtain a patient's written consent before using or disclosing the patient's PHI to carry out TPO. Prior to passage of the Privacy Rule, many healthcare providers routinely obtained a patient's consent for disclosure of information to insurance companies or for other purposes. The Privacy Rule originally mandated such practices by establishing a consistent standard for covered healthcare providers to obtain patient consent for uses and disclosures of PHI to carry out TPO. However, the requirement to obtain a signed consent for uses and disclosures of PHI to carry out TPO was removed in the Privacy NPRM. Patient authorizations are still required to use and disclose information for non-TPO purposes. It is important to note, however, that covered entities may still choose to use consents if they believe the use of consents is beneficial to their business organization and environment, or if they want to continue their existing consent agreement practices.

If a covered entity chooses to use consents for use or disclosure of PHI, the consents can be combined with other types of legal documents from the patient if the PHI consent is clearly separated from the other legal permissions, and if it is signed and dated by the individual. Additional disclosures were allowed within the Privacy NPRM for certain types of payments and healthcare operations by a second covered entity. The Privacy NPRM removed the original restrictions and allows the general sharing of TPO information between providers concerning a common patient.

## USES AND DISCLOSURES: AUTHORIZATION

An authorization is more customized, detailed, and specific than a consent agreement and applies to all covered entities. An authorization gives covered entities permission to use specified PHI for specified purposes, generally other than TPO, or to disclose PHI to a specified third party. Covered entities cannot make authorization a condition of treatment or coverage for an individual. It covers only the uses and disclosures and only the PHI stipulated in the authorization, it has an expiration date, and it sometimes also states the purpose for which PHI can be used or disclosed.

Generally, an authorization is required for all purposes that are not part of TPO and are not described as acceptable uses and disclosures that do not require authorization. All covered entities must obtain an authorization to use or disclose PHI for these purposes. A provider may have to obtain multiple authorizations from the same patient for different uses or disclosures. For example, an obstetrician may, under the authorization obtained from the patient, send an appointment reminder to the patient, but may need another authorization from the patient to have her participate in a research project, or perhaps to send her name and address to a company marketing a birth announcement service.

The Privacy NPRM changes allow the use of a single type of authorization form to get a patient's permission for a specific use or disclosure that otherwise would not have been permitted under the original Privacy Rule. Patients still need to grant permission in advance for each type of use or disclosure, but the updated rule eliminates the requirement for covered entities to use different types of forms to obtain advance permission. The Privacy Rule requires providers to obtain authorization to use or disclose PHI maintained in psychotherapy notes for treatment by persons other than the originator of the notes, for payment, or for healthcare operations purposes.

In general, an authorization for use or disclosure of PHI cannot be combined with another document to create a compound authorization unless the use or disclosure is for research purposes, related to psychotherapy notes, or if the provider has conditioned treatment, payment enrollment in a health plan, or benefits eligibility according to the specific allowances within the Privacy Rule. The need for researchers to use multiple consent forms, one for informed consent to the research and one or more related to information privacy rights, was removed in the updated rule. The Privacy NPRM allows researchers to use a single, combined form to accomplish both purposes. Other changes were made to make the research requirements more closely follow the requirements of the "Common Rule" governing federally funded research, which applies to both publicly and privately funded research.

Individuals can revoke, in writing, authorizations at any time, except to the extent that the covered entity has taken action as a result of the authorization, or if the authorization was a condition of getting insurance coverage.

## USES AND DISCLOSURES REQUIRING OPPORTUNITY FOR THE INDIVIDUAL TO AGREE OR OBJECT

A covered entity may use or disclose PHI without the written consent or authorization of the individual in certain situations if the individual is informed in advance of the use or disclosure. The individual must have the opportunity in advance to agree to or prohibit or restrict the disclosure of the individual's:

- Name, location, condition, and religion within the entity's facility directory or to clergy or persons asking for the individual by name
- Medical condition to a family member, other relative, or a close personal friend of the individual, or any other person identified by the individual

The covered entity may orally inform the individual of this possibility and obtain the individual's oral agreement or objection to such use or disclosure.

## USES AND DISCLOSURES FOR WHICH AUTHORIZATION AND OPPORTUNITY TO AGREE OR OBJECT IS NOT REQUIRED

Covered entities can use and disclose PHI without individual authorization for certain national-priority activities. This is a long and detailed list, and health providers should ensure their understanding of these situations with their legal counsel. A general listing of such purposes includes:

- Quality assurance
- Emergencies or concerns affecting public health or safety
- Suspected abuse of the individual

- Research
- Judicial and administrative proceedings
- Law enforcement
- Next-of-kin information
- Government health data and specialized functions
- Workers compensation
- Organ donation
- Identification of the deceased, or to determine cause of death
- Financial institution payment processing for health care
- Utilization review
- Credentialing
- When mandated by other laws
- Other activities that are part of ensuring appropriate treatment and payment

Individuals may ask a covered entity to restrict further use and disclosure of PHI (with the exception of uses or disclosures required by law). The covered entity does not have to agree to such a request. But, if the covered entity and the individual agree to such a restriction, the covered entity is then bound by the agreement, even when the agreement is given orally.

## OTHER REQUIREMENTS RELATING TO USES AND DISCLOSURES OF PHI

The Privacy Rule makes many other requirements for a vast array of situations relating to virtually every conceivable type of PHI use and disclosure. Again, it is important for covered entities and their legal counsels to thoroughly review and understand the Privacy Rule and these many sundry requirements. An overview of the other requirements includes the following:

- PHI must be handled in specific ways for de-identification requirements. In general, if PHI is presented in such a way that it cannot be used to identify an individual, then it is considered to be de-identified. De-identified information does *not* include names, geographic subdivisions smaller than a state, dates, telephone numbers, fax numbers, e-mail addresses, social security numbers, medical records numbers, health plan numbers, account number certificate/license numbers, vehicle identifiers, device identifiers, URLs, IP addresses, biometric identifiers, photographic images, or unique identifying numbers or codes that could be translated to identify the individual. The disclosure of the limited data set within the Privacy NPRM depends on the condition of the covered entity obtaining a data use agreement, or something similar, from the recipient that would require the recipient to limit the use of the data set only for the purposes for which it was given, as well as not to re-identify the information or use it to contact any individual.
- Covered entities must ensure that minimum necessary requirements are implemented related to PHI use and disclosure. Such re-

quirements include the implementation of policies and procedures, documentation, awareness, and appropriate technologies and tools. Entire medical records may not be used or disclosed except when the entire record is specifically required for an authorized use or disclosure purpose. The Privacy NPRM changes preserved both the oral communication and "minimum necessary" requirements, but it now allows physicians to discuss a patient's treatment with other doctors and professionals involved in the patient's care without having this considered a violation of the Privacy Rule. If a covered entity meets the minimum necessary standards and is considered to take reasonable safeguards to protect PHI, then they will not be held liable for incidental disclosures, such as patients overhearing doctor conversations.

- PHI may not be used for marketing purposes without the specified authorizations described within the Privacy Rule. The Privacy NPRM increased controls on marketing communications. Now, authorization is required for all marketing activity and communications with patients. The only exceptions are face-to-face communications between physicians and patients or promotional items of nominal value.
- A covered entity may use or disclose demographic information relating to an individual and dates of health care provided to an individual for its own fundraising purposes without authorization to a business associate or to a related foundation. However, patients must be given the opportunity to opt out of such uses and disclosures.
- PHI used by a heath plan for underwriting, premium rating, or other activities relating to the creation, renewal, or replacement of a contract of health insurance or health benefits, may not be used or disclosed for any other purpose, except as may be required by law, if such PHI is not placed with the health plan.
- Before covered entities disclose PHI, they must verify the identity and authority of the person requesting PHI.

## NOTICE OF PRIVACY PRACTICES FOR PHI

Covered entities must provide individuals with a notice document specifying their information use and disclosure practices. The notice must include information describing how the information is protected, stored, used, and the conditions under which is it shared. More specifically, the notice must:

- Contain the following statement, prominently displayed:

THIS NOTICE DESCRIBES HOW MEDICAL INFORMATION ABOUT YOU MAY BE USED AND DISCLOSED AND HOW YOU CAN GET ACCESS TO THIS INFORMATION. PLEASE REVIEW IT CAREFULLY.

- Contain a description, including at least one example, of the types of uses and disclosures that the covered entity is permitted to make for each of the following purposes: treatment, payment, and healthcare operations
- Contain separate statements if the entity will use PHI for appointment reminders, information about treatment alternatives, to raise funds for the entity, in information sent to the HMO or health insurance insurer
- Contain a statement that the individual may revoke or restrict authorization for the covered entity to use PHI
- Describe the patient's right to inspect and copy PHI
- Describe the patient's right to amend PHI
- Describe the patient's right to receive an accounting of PHI disclosures and make formal complaints
- Contain a statement that the covered entity is required by law to maintain the privacy of PHI
- Contain the name, or title, and telephone number of a person or office to contact for further information regarding the handling of PHI
- Be made available at enrollment, within 60 days of a material revision to the notice, and not less than every three years

A covered entity must revise and distribute its notice without delay whenever there is a material change to the uses or disclosures, the individual's rights, the covered entity's legal duties, or other privacy practices stated in the notice. Except when required by law, a material change to any part of the notice cannot be implemented prior to the effective date of the notice in which such material change is reflected.

If a covered entity provides information about its customer services or benefits on a Web site, it must prominently post the notice on the Web site in addition to allowing requests for the notice from the Web site. The requested notice can be sent by e-mail if the requestor agrees to this type of response. If the covered entity knows that an e-mail transmission failed, a paper copy of the notice must be sent to the individual. Covered entities must document compliance with the notice requirements by retaining all copies of the issued notices.

## INDIVIDUAL RIGHTS TO REQUEST PRIVACY PROTECTION FOR PHI

Covered entities must permit an individual to request restrictions for uses or disclosures of PHI about the individual to carry out TPO and other disclosures. A covered entity is not required to agree to a restriction request. However, if the entity agrees to a restriction, then the entity is bound to comply with the restriction for that individual, except for emergency situations and as required by other laws. A covered entity may terminate its agreement to a restriction if:

- The individual agrees to or requests the termination in writing.
- The individual orally agrees to the termination and the oral agreement is documented.
- The covered entity informs the individual that it is terminating its agreement to a restriction. The termination is only effective with respect to PHI created or received after it has informed the individual.

Covered healthcare providers must permit individuals to request and must accommodate reasonable requests by individuals to receive communications of PHI from the covered healthcare provider by alternate means or at alternative locations if the individual indicates disclosure of all or part of the PHI could endanger the individual.

## INDIVIDUAL ACCESS TO PHI

An individual generally has a right to access, inspect, and obtain a copy of his or her own PHI for as long as the PHI is maintained. There are a few exceptions, including:

- Psychotherapy notes
- Information that is, or could be used for, a civil, criminal, or administrative action or proceeding
- PHI that is subject to access prohibitions described in the Clinical Laboratory Improvements Amendments of 1988

A covered entity can deny an individual access to PHI without providing an opportunity for review under certain circumstances. For example, providers for correctional institutions can deny an inmate's request to access PHI if it could jeopardize the health, safety, security, custody, or rehabilitation of the individual or of other inmates, or the safety of any officer, employee, or other person at the correctional institution or responsible for the transporting of the inmate. The individual can also be denied access if the PHI was used for research that does not allow such access, if the access is subject to the denial of access requirements within the Privacy Act, or if the PHI was obtained from another provider with the condition the PHI cannot be given to anyone else.

A covered entity can deny an individual access in other situations if the individual is given a right to have the denial reviewed by a licensed health care professional designated by the covered entity to act as a reviewing official. The reviewer must be someone who did not participate in the original decision to deny. Such circumstances include:

- Access is likely to endanger the life or physical safety of the individual or another person.
- The PHI references another person and the access would likely cause substantial harm to the other person.

- The request for access is made by the individual's personal representative and access to the individual's PHI is likely to cause substantial harm to the individual or another person.

A covered entity must provide or deny an access request, in writing, generally no later than 30 days after receipt of the request for PHI they maintain on-site, and generally no later than 60 days for PHI maintained off-site. If a denial, it must explain, in plain language, the basis for the denial, and if applicable, the individual's review and complaint rights. The covered entity must provide the individual with access to the protected health information in the form requested by the individual if it already exists in the form; or, if it does not, in another form agreed to by the covered entity and the individual. When providing an individual with a copy of PHI, the covered entity may impose a reasonable, cost-based fee, provided that the fee includes only the costs of copying, postage, and preparing an explanation or summary.

If a covered entity does not maintain the PHI requested but knows where it is maintained, it must inform the individual where to direct the request for access. A covered entity must document the PHI files that are subject to access by individuals, in addition to the titles of the persons or offices responsible for receiving and processing individual requests for access.

## AMENDMENT OF PHI

The covered entity must permit an individual to request amendment to PHI maintained in a designated record set. The entity may require the requests to be in writing and require a reason to support a requested amendment. A covered entity must honor requests to amend PHI for individuals for as long as they maintain PHI records. A covered entity can deny an individual's amendment request if the PHI was not created by the covered entity (unless the originator of PHI is no longer available), if the PHI is not part of the designated record set, or if the PHI is determined to be accurate and complete.

A covered entity must make the requested amendment, or deny the amendment, no later than 60 days after receipt of the amendment request. If the covered entity denies, in part or in whole, the requested amendment, it must give the individual a written denial. If the covered entity is unable to act on the amendment within 60 days, the covered entity can extend the time to take action by no more than 30 days, provided the entity gives the individual a written statement of the reasons for the delay and the date by which action on the request will be completed. The covered entity can have only one extension of time for action on a request for an amendment.

If the covered entity accepts the requested amendment, in whole or in part, it must make the appropriate amendment to the PHI or record by, at a minimum, identifying the records that are affected by the amendment, and appending or otherwise providing a link to the location of the amendment. Then they must inform the individual that the amendment is accepted and obtain the individual's identification of and agreement to have the covered entity notify the relevant persons with which the amendment needs to be shared. Notice of the amendment must be made to persons identified by the individual as having received PHI about the individual and needing the amendment, and all persons that the covered entity knows have the PHI that is the subject of the amendment.

If the covered entity denies the requested amendment, it must provide the individual with a written denial. The denial must describe the basis for the denial in plain language and describe the individual's right to submit a written statement disagreeing with the denial. The denial must also state that if the individual does not submit a statement of disagreement, the individual may request the covered entity provide the individual's request for amendment and the denial with any future disclosures of the PHI, and a description of how the individual can submit formal complaints. The description must include the name, or title, and telephone number of the designated contact person or office.

A covered entity must permit the individual to submit a written statement disagreeing with a denial of a requested amendment describing the basis of the disagreement, and the entity can prepare a written rebuttal to the individual, but this is not a required action. Whenever a rebuttal is prepared, the covered entity must provide a copy to the individual who submitted the statement of disagreement. The covered entity must also identify the PHI that is the subject of the disputed amendment and amend it with information regarding the individual's request for amendment, related denial, and any resulting statement of disagreement and rebuttal. These amendments must then be included with any subsequent PHI disclosures related to the disagreement.

A covered entity that is informed by another covered entity of an amendment to an individual's PHI must amend the PHI in designated record sets. A covered entity must document and retain the titles of the persons or offices responsible for receiving and processing requests for amendments.

## ACCOUNTING DISCLOSURES OF PHI

In general, an individual has a right to receive an accounting of disclosures of PHI made by a covered entity in the six years prior to the date on which the accounting is requested. The exceptions to this include accounting of disclosures:

- To carry out general TPO
- To individuals of PHI about them

- For the facility's directory or to persons involved in the individual's care or other notification purposes
- For national security or intelligence purposes
- To correctional institutions or law enforcement officials
- That occurred prior to the compliance date for the covered entity

The covered entity must temporarily suspend an individual's right to receive an accounting of disclosures to a health oversight agency or law enforcement official if the agency or official indicates in writing that such an accounting to the individual would impede the agency's activities.

If, during the period covered by the accounting, the covered entity has made multiple disclosures of PHI to the same person or entity for a single purpose, the accounting may include the number of the disclosures made during the accounting period and the date of the last disclosure during the accounting period.

A covered entity must act on the individual's request for an accounting no later than 60 days after receipt of the request. The action must either be providing the individual with the accounting requested, or a written statement explaining the reason for delay. If there is a delay, the time can be extended no more than 30 days, and the covered entity must provide the individual with a written statement explaining the reasons for the delay and the date by which the covered entity will provide the accounting.

The covered entity must provide the first accounting to an individual in any 12-month period without charge. However, the covered entity may impose a reasonable, cost-based fee for each subsequent request for an accounting by the same individual within the 12-month period, provided that the covered entity informs the individual in advance of the fee and provides the individual with an opportunity to withdraw or modify the request for a subsequent accounting in order to avoid or reduce the fee. In addition, a covered entity must document the information that will be included in an accounting, including the specific pieces of information and the titles of the persons or offices responsible for receiving and processing requests for an accounting by individuals.

The original Privacy Rule required that all covered entities keep a log of all authorized disclosures for disclosure-accounting purposes, except disclosures made to the individual, for TPO, "verbal agreement" disclosures, or national security or law enforcement disclosures. The Privacy NPRM added disclosures that the subject individual has authorized to this exception list. So, a patient who has signed an authorization to disclose the results of a pre-employment physical to a prospective employer would not see this event in a disclosure accounting report.

## ADMINISTRATIVE REQUIREMENTS

Covered entities are required to implement basic administrative procedures to protect PHI. They must:

- Designate a privacy official responsible for the development and implementation of the entity's policies and procedures.
- Designate a contact person or office responsible for receiving complaints and answering questions related to the notice.
- Document the associated personnel designations (for example, Privacy Officer, contact person, etc.).
- Train all personnel on the privacy policies and procedures with respect to PHI as necessary and appropriate to carry out their job responsibilities.
- Document training that has occurred.
- Implement appropriate administrative, technical, and physical safeguards to protect the privacy of PHI.
- Safeguard PHI from any intentional or unintentional use or disclosure.
- Provide a process for individuals to make complaints concerning the policies and procedures.
- Document all complaints received and their resolution.
- Consistently apply sanctions against personnel who fail to comply with the privacy policies and procedures, and document applied sanctions.
- Mitigate, as much as possible, any harmful effect that is known to the covered entity of a use or disclosure of PHI in violation of its policies and procedures by the covered entity or a business associate.

Covered entities may not intimidate or take any type of retaliatory action against any individual for exercising the right to submit a complaint, request a review, request an amendment for their PHI, or any other type of action described previously as being a right of the individual under the Privacy Rule. Additionally, covered entities may not require individuals to waive their rights as a condition of medical treatment, payment, enrollment in a health plan, or eligibility for benefits.

Covered entities must implement PHI privacy policies and procedures designed to comply with the Privacy Rule. The policies and procedures must be designed to take into account the size of and the type of activities that relate to the covered entity's PHI. When developing policies and procedures to meet Privacy Rule compliance, a covered entity needs to:

- Review and change its existing policies and procedures, as necessary and appropriate.
- Promptly document and implement a revised policy or procedure whenever there is a change in the law that necessitates a change. If the change affects the content of the notice, the covered entity must promptly make the appropriate revisions to the notice.

- Maintain the policies, procedures, and related communications in written or electronic form for at least six years from the date of creation or the date when it last was in effect, whichever is later.

A group health plan is not subject to most of the above requirements if it provides health benefits solely through an insurance contract with a health insurance issuer or an HMO, and does not create or receive PHI other than summary health information or information indicating whether the individual is participating in the group health plan, or is enrolled in or has dis-enrolled from a health insurance issuer or HMO offered by the plan.

## TRANSITION PROVISIONS

A covered entity may continue to use or disclose PHI under a consent, authorization, or other type of legal permission obtained from an individual before the April 14, 2003 compliance date, as long as the entity complies with all limitations placed by the permission. For example, a provider that obtained consent for use or disclosure for billing purposes would be able to continue to use PHI obtained prior to the compliance date and covered by the consent form for all TPO activities to the extent not expressly excluded by the terms of the consent.

If a permission obtained prior to April 14, 2003, is a general consent to participate in a research project, and a covered entity is conducting or participating in the research, the entity may continue to make use or disclosure of PHI for purposes of that project. If a covered entity agrees to a restriction requested by an individual, subsequent use or disclosure of PHI is subject to that restriction.

## COMPLIANCE DATES AND PENALTIES

The following are the compliance dates for initial implementation of the HIPAA Privacy Rule standards:

- Healthcare providers: no later than April 14, 2003
- Health plans: no later than the following date, as applicable:
  Health plans other than small health plans: April 14, 2003
  Small health plans: April 14, 2004
- Healthcare clearinghouses: no later than April 14, 2003

If a complaint is lodged against an entity and an investigation or compliance review determines that no violation exists, the Secretary for the Department of Health and Human Services will inform both the entity and complainant in writing.

If a complaint is lodged against an entity, and the resulting compliance review confirms noncompliance with the Privacy Rule, the entity will be informed by the Secretary in writing, who will attempt to resolve the situation by informal means if possible. If the situation cannot be resolved in this manner, a formal noncompliance report will be issued to both the complainant and entity.

For noncriminal violation of the Privacy Rule, including disclosures made in error, civil penalties of $100 per violation up to $25,000 per year, per standard may be issued. Additionally, criminal penalties may be applied for certain violations done knowingly as follows:

- Up to $50,000 and one year in prison for obtaining or disclosing PHI
- Up to $100,000 and up to five years in prison for obtaining or disclosing PHI under false pretenses
- Up to $250,000 and up to ten years in prison for obtaining PHI with the intent to sell, transfer, or use it for commercial advantage, personal gain, or malicious harm

## CREATING A COMPLIANCE ACTION PLAN

Preparing for HIPAA compliance is complex and requires thorough planning. Planning should involve the entire organization; it is not just an information technology issue or a business application issue. It certainly involves these issues, but also much more. HIPAA compliance is both a project to be implemented as well as an ongoing practice to oversee. Most organizations will already meet some of the HIPAA requirements. Other requirements will still need to be addressed. Organizations must accurately review their state of HIPAA compliance, identify the outstanding requirements, and create a functional plan for implementation. A baseline compliance assessment needs to occur to determine where the organization is presently at with regard to compliance. A successful assessment will have the beneficial side effect of creating an information flow document.

The following are recommended actions for addressing HIPAA compliance:

1. Identify and appoint a qualified Privacy Officer to address HIPAA and other privacy-related issues.
2. Assign a HIPAA compliance team.
3. Understand the HIPAA regulations:
   a. Read the regulations thoroughly.
   b. Analyze the requirements.
   c. Make top management aware of the issues and obtain their documented commitment to compliance.
4. Identify and assess all the PHI used throughout the organization:
   a. Collect and review printed documentation.
   b. Conduct interviews.
   c. Review electronic information.
   d. Create a directory of all information, placed into appropriate classifications if possible.

5. Perform a baseline HIPAA compliance and risk assessment:
   a. Document current policies, procedures, and documentation related to HIPAA.
   b. Analyze gaps between the existing organizational (human) environment and HIPAA requirements.
   c. Analyze gaps between the existing technical and networking environment and HIPAA requirements.
   d. Analyze gaps between the existing information policies and procedures and HIPAA requirements.
6. Identify all business associates and map data flows with them.
7. Negotiate business associate contracts to ensure PHI is adequately protected.
8. Create a compliance plan for closing gaps and meeting compliance:
   a. Update existing policies and procedures, and create new privacy policies and procedures, if necessary, to comply with HIPAA requirements.
   b. Update organizational procedures, systems, and documentation to match policy and procedure requirements.
   c. Develop notice, consent (if applicable for your organization), and authorization documents.
   d. Develop employee privacy training programs and awareness materials.
   e. Develop formal documentation procedures and standards to ensure information is adequately maintained for the appropriate time limits.
9. Implement the plan!
   a. Implement and maintain training programs.
   b. Implement, communicate, and maintain policies.
   c. Implement, communicate, and maintain procedures.
   d. Implement and maintain the use of notice, consent (if applicable), and authorization forms.
   e. Implement and maintain the use of business associate contracts.
10. Keep current with changes in the HIPAA regulations.

The HIPAA compliance plan will require ongoing maintenance. Unlike a project such as Y2K compliance, when the project was essentially finished shortly after January 1, 2000, HIPAA compliance does not have a termination point. HIPAA requirements will impose strict penalties for noncompliance from the compliance date forward. One cannot expect to meet all the HIPAA compliance requirements on one date and be done; this must be a long-term commitment your organization makes.

## THE PRIVACY OFFICER ROLE

It will sometimes be difficult to clearly separate the roles and responsibilities of the Privacy Officer from the rest of the organizational responsibilities.

Healthcare organizations often assign privacy responsibilities to the Chief Information Officer. The risk of doing this is that privacy may then be perceived as a technology-only issue. Addressing privacy is truly a business issue and must be integrated into and addressed by all areas of the organization, including each business practice, and within all processing systems.

Ideally, the privacy function should be a separate function within the organization, reporting directly to the CEO, with communication and integration into all other areas of the company. But, is this a function that one person can accomplish alone? Perhaps, but it really depends on if you can find all the skills necessary for this job within one person, as well as the size of your organization. It may be impossible to find someone with all the necessary skills within a small- to medium-sized organization. In these situations, the responsibilities are often included within the responsibilities of another executive role, such as CIO. However, consider how difficult it may be for this person to perform all the privacy responsibilities in addition to all the other responsibilities of such a role. What is probably more effective and realistic within smaller organizations is to divide the roles among several positions, and create a Privacy Oversight Council to ensure all privacy issues are appropriately addressed. Establish a Privacy Oversight Council, with the Privacy Officer acting as leader of the group, regardless of your organizational size. The Council should consist of representative leaders from the business units, law, information technology, human resources, marketing, public relations, and information security.

In complex or large organizations, however, the Privacy Officer is more likely to be a full-time position reporting to the CEO, possibly even with a small staff of his or her own to address all the organization's privacy issues, in addition to having the Privacy Oversight Council. If staffing does not make having dedicated personnel feasible, then you must seriously consider hiring a consultant to spend some time reviewing your privacy practices, evaluating your situation, and getting you on track with all the assorted privacy requirements applicable to your organization. Or, outsource your privacy functions to a qualified and experienced organization that provides such a service.

Now you are ready to choose your Privacy Officer. So, what is the typical background of a Privacy Officer? An October 2001 survey revealed that most Privacy Officers in organizations, both within and outside the healthcare industry, have tremendous business experience, are well qualified, and have direct access to the top executives. Over half of the respondents had annual salaries greater than $100,000, and an impressive 82% of the Privacy Officers reported directly to senior management. The importance of reporting to senior management cannot be stressed enough; this is necessary for the Privacy Officer to have the appropriate influence to get unpopular, but necessary, privacy actions and initiatives implemented.

Privacy Officers must have a solid base knowledge of information technology, legal savvy, the ability to research and understand new laws and emerging technologies, be a great communicator, and be able to occasionally be the bearer of news business managers or marketers would rather not hear, such as telling them they cannot use protected information in a way they would like! A nice example of a Privacy Officer position description is located at the American Health Information Management Association (AHIMA) Web site: http://www.ahima.org. Here is another example for you to consider; it was created for the Computer Security Institute's August 2002 *Alert* newsletter. It incorporates many of the ideas found within the AHIMA example, but has additional responsibilities from which you may choose. The items you choose from this full list of responsibilities will depend on the nature of the information processed and handled by your organization and your organization's size.

The responsibilities of the Privacy Officer involve a much wider scope than just privacy and related legal compliance. Privacy Officer responsibilities also involve security, which is necessary for ensuring privacy (see Exhibit 1). Also, the corporate privacy plan can be used as a market differentiator, can be a sales tool for attracting and keeping clients, and is important for satisfying em-

**Exhibit 1 . Example Chief Privacy Officer (CPO) Job Description**

**This position reports to the:** <Chief Executive Officer, President, Board of Directors>
**Goal:** The CPO is responsible for ensuring the implementation, compliance and ongoing activities within the company as they relate to employee and customer privacy. The CPO will promote a corporate-wide privacy philosophy supporting a comprehensive and practical set of privacy policies, procedures, and technology to not only protect the organization from privacy-related liability, but also to use privacy practices as a way to create customer goodwill and market returns.

Qualifications:
<5, 10, X> years knowledge and experience in information privacy laws, access, security, release of information, and access control technologies
<5, 10, X> years knowledge and experience in the <financial, healthcare, manufacturing, government, etc.> industry
Demonstrated organization, facilitation, communication, and presentation skills
Experience in creating and following a departmental budget
Experience and effectiveness in leading initiatives and projects
CISSP or CISA preferred, but not required.

Roles and Responsibilities:
Know, understand, and ensure corporate compliance with all relevant privacy laws, regulations and standards that apply to the company. This includes the laws of any jurisdiction in which the company conducts business, including international locations.
Keep current with local, state, federal, and international privacy related laws and accreditation standards, and monitor privacy technologies.
Provide leadership and oversight for all privacy-related activities of the company.

*(continued)*

**Exhibit 1 (Continued). Example Chief Privacy Officer (CPO) Job Description**

Communicate and work with corporate senior management and corporate compliance officers to establish, maintain, and provide leadership for a corporate Privacy Oversight Committee.

Coordinate the development, implementation, and maintenance of corporate customer and employee privacy policies and plans with the Privacy Oversight Committee.

Create and implement procedures to help prevent loss and inappropriate distribution of corporate information.

Work with Public Relations and Marketing to increase the public awareness of the company's privacy efforts, and address privacy-related issues and incidents.

Analyze and assess information flows across and between business units, and address the privacy implications of the flows.

Investigate and handle every privacy-related incident and consumer complaint.

Ensure privacy compliance benchmarks and regularly scheduled information privacy risk assessments and compliance monitoring activities occur.

Coordinate and work with law, business department leaders, and appropriate committees to ensure the organization has and maintains appropriate privacy and confidentiality consent, authorization forms, and information notices and materials reflecting current corporate and legal practices and requirements.

Promote essential privacy policy elements organization-wide, including the following common regulatory requirements: Notice, Choice, Access, Security, Recourse, and Verification.

Ensure procedures are implemented to allow customers to view and correct their personal data files processed by the organization.

Oversee and ensure the development of ongoing corporate privacy orientation, training, and awareness activities and communications for personnel at all levels and business partners.

Ensure all trading partner and business associate agreements include privacy requirements and responsibilities, and address all related concerns.

Ensure procedures are implemented to track access to information protected by regulations.

Oversee and work with the Privacy Oversight Committee to create, implement, and maintain procedures for receiving, documenting, tracking, investigating, and addressing complaints concerning the company's privacy policies and procedures.

Oversee and work with the human resources and law departments to ensure compliance with corporate privacy policies and procedures and consistent application of sanctions and disciplinary actions for noncompliance throughout the organization.

Participate in and review information security plans throughout the organization to ensure alignment between security and privacy practices, and act as a liaison to information security and information technology departments.

Understand the organization's technical infrastructure, and promote the use of privacy-enhancing technologies.

Advise and work with corporate personnel involved with any aspect of access to personally identifiable information, or any other type of regulated information, to ensure compliance with the corporate privacy policies and procedures and applicable laws.

Cooperate with law enforcement and regulatory groups in privacy-related compliance reviews and investigations.

Represent the company's information privacy interests to third parties, privacy commissioners, and other officials responsible for the development, oversight, and enforcement of privacy legislation to update or adopt privacy-related legislation, regulations, and standards.

ployee concerns. The Privacy Officer role is one that will be of critical importance within your organization.Creating an Effective Awareness Program

Ensuring organizational awareness of privacy policies and practices is a requirement of the HIPAA regulations. It is also a good idea, and has been for many years. Your staff members are the foundation of ensuring your policy compliance. If they do not know and understand what is expected of them with regard to meeting HIPAA and other privacy and security requirements, then they will probably, unaware, do things that could very well put your organization at risk.

Healthcare organizations must develop and implement an awareness program that meets the following goals:

- Ensures compliance with HIPAA privacy awareness regulations
- Is supported by executive management. Establish an executive owner or sponsor to champion, maintain, and ensure senior-level involvement. This will be necessary to get the message across and secure support for HIPAA compliance activities throughout the organization.
- Instills the privacy and security requirements and concerns into the organizational culture
- Clearly communicates the HIPAA privacy and security issues and challenges
- Supports your strategic and tactical HIPAA implementation strategies

Your awareness strategy should include the following:

- An awareness budget that accounts for the communications, planning, and implementation activities that will be proportionate to this piece of the total amount of the HIPAA compliance budget
- A timeline indicating target dates for all phases of the awareness and training program
- A procedure or tool for measuring the overall effectiveness of the awareness program
- Identification of integration points and implementation windows to effectively coordinate the privacy and security awareness and education practices within the overall HIPAA compliance plan
- A strategy to integrate the awareness processes throughout all departments and teams of the organization to help ensure a successful awareness program
- Execution of an awareness risk assessment to identify awareness compliance gaps and form the baseline to use for measuring future awareness compliance success
- A description of the tactical objectives of the awareness and education program
- The development, implementation, communication, and enforcement of policies and procedures to mitigate risk and ensure ongoing compliance with HIPAA privacy and security regulations

The privacy awareness and education program you create needs to address your organization's interpretation of the HIPAA and support the activities your organization will take to mitigate risk and ensure patient privacy based upon the results of the baseline assessment. Creation and delivery of a common message, interpretation of the regulations, and a process for addressing and communicating issues will speed the implementation and reduce the overall cost in complying with the HIPAA. Exhibit 2 shows a high-level HIPAA awareness plan that you can use to build upon for your own unique plan that meets your organizational requirements. Follow a structured process for the development and maintenance of your awareness program:

- Clearly define your HIPAA privacy message (why, value, strategic approach, policies, procedures, contacts, etc.).
- Clearly document the desired tactical outcomes.
- Clearly document the details of what will be done (awareness activities and tasks).
- Provide examples of case studies and suggestions.

Continue to assess, refine, and update the awareness program throughout all phases of developing and maintaining your organization's HIPAA compliance.

Does your organization have the resources necessary to develop and deliver a privacy and security awareness and education program? If not, you will need to allocate or contract resources necessary to develop an awareness program. In the event you must obtain external resources, or an outsourced arrangement is desired, be sure to establish guidelines for qualifying an experienced consultant to develop your privacy and security awareness program, in addition to any other help you outsource for HIPAA compliance activities.

## CONCLUSION

Until comparatively recently in the history of health care, physicians personally hand-wrote their patients' medical records and they were typically locked in a file-cabinet with very little access by anyone other than the nursing and support staff within the immediate office. Today, healthcare delivery and payment systems are some of the biggest industries within the United States, with many intermediaries touching the systems and associated data. Integrated processing systems and networks have virtually replaced the pen, paper, and locked file cabinets. There are now so many players, public and private, involved with the processing and handling of health information, that it is almost impossible for all but the very smallest healthcare office to do business without some type of data processing. The HIPAA regulations are leading the industries in many ways with privacy and security mandates. Complying with the multitude of requirements

## Exhibit 2 . HIPAA Awareness Plan

***Step One:*** Identify the baseline awareness assessment target populations. For most
healthcare industries, your populations will consist of the following groups:
Management
IT staff
Care providers (physicians, nurses, etc.)
Support staff
***Step Two:*** Determine the sampling size to reach an agreed-upon point of accuracy for the
size of the audience. The sampling size can be determined by coordinating with
corporate audit, marketing, or human resources. Human resources should be able to
provide the list of names. Keep a record of the audience group surveyed for the baseline
to use for follow-up measuring.
***Step Three:*** Identify the topics for the survey. For HIPAA privacy requirements, these
topics should include:
Consent (if applicable)
Authorization
Privacy notices
Use and disclosure
Individual access to PHI
PHI amendments
Accounting
Compliance dates
***Step Four:*** Identify how to measure awareness. Possibilities include:
Telephone survey
Written survey distributed via printed memo
Written survey distributed via e-mail
Measurement tool (such as PentaSafe's VigilEnt Policy Center product, etc.)
***Step Five:*** Prepare survey questions. Structure the survey to determine the level of
awareness, knowledge, and compliance for the chosen survey topics.
***Step Six:*** Submit the survey to Privacy Oversight Council for review and approval.
***Step Seven:*** Utilize established awareness distribution channels, announce the upcoming
survey, and solicit the support of users chosen to participate.
***Step Eight:*** Conduct the baseline survey.
Coordinate with the human resources department to establish the survey start date.
Depending on the size of the sample populations, the survey should last between two and
five days.
***Step Nine:*** Analyze and summarize survey results.
Graphically depict survey results to show percentages of correct answers to questions.
Show the demographic breakdown of target groups.
Discuss results with CEO and Privacy Oversight Council
***Step Ten:*** Prepare and deliver an executive presentation on survey results.
***Step Eleven:*** Communicate survey results to the organization.
Disseminate appropriate portions of the results to the organizations.
Present results to indicate where more awareness is needed, within specific HIPAA topics
and target populations. Deliver in a positive way to motivate, not to humiliate.
Evaluate the results, identify gaps with HIPAA requirements, and then plan appropriate
training and awareness activities to close gaps.
***Step Twelve:*** Schedule follow-up survey.
Determine an appropriate amount of time for the awareness program to effectively
address the risk issues.
Conduct another random sampling survey of the same segment.
Analyze and summarize results and compare to previous survey. Chart the trends between
the surveys.

within all the HIPAA regulations, let alone just the Privacy Rule, will be a great challenge for most, if not all, healthcare organizations. Every healthcare organization covered by the HIPAA must know, understand, and address the requirements set forth by the Privacy Rule if they want to remain a viable healthcare entity and maintain their patients' trust.

# Chapter 13
# Getting Started with HIPAA Security Compliance

*Kevin Beaver*

## OVERVIEW OF THE HIPAA SECURITY RULE

### It's All about Best Practices

In August 1998, the U.S. Department of Health and Human Services (HHS) published the Security and Electronic Signature Standards; Proposed Rule (Security Rule). The Security Rule covers all healthcare information that is electronically maintained or used in electronic transmissions. It is defined by HHS as a set of requirements with implementation features that providers, plans, and clearinghouses must include in their operations to assure that electronic health information pertaining to an individual remains secure.[1] The Security Rule is merely a set of common best practices that is intended to be comprehensive, technology neutral, and scalable for different-sized organizations. It is a high-level information security framework that documents what needs to be done to secure healthcare information systems. At the same time, and much to widespread chagrin, the Security Rule is not a set of how-to instructions outlining the exact steps for securing healthcare information systems.

When the Security Rule was originally developed in the late 1990s, there were limited information security standards upon which a comprehensive information security framework for the healthcare industry could be developed. In fact, it is documented in the proposed Security Rule that no single standards development organization (SDO) is addressing all aspects of healthcare information security and confidentiality; and specifically, no SDO is developing standards that cover every category of the security framework.[1] Enter the Security Rule. Since 1998, several standards have evolved, such as the ISO/IEC 17799 Information Technology — Code of Practice for Information Security Management, among others. It is not currently known whether the final Security Rule will be based on any well-known standards, but healthcare organizations can benefit from utilizing these standard guidelines nonetheless.

## Covered Entities

As with the other HIPAA rules, the covered entities that are required to comply with the Security Rule are as follows:

- *Healthcare Providers.* These include hospitals, clinics, nursing facilities, laboratories, physicians, pharmacies, and most other entities that provide healthcare services.
- *Health plans.* Generally speaking, these are any individual or group plans that provide or pay for medical care. Examples include private and governmental issuers of health insurance, HMOs, PPOs, Medicare and Medicaid programs, and certain employer-sponsored health plans.
- *Healthcare clearinghouses.* These include entities that process or facilitate the processing of nonstandard data elements of health information into a standard format for electronic transactions.
- *Business associates.* A person or organization that performs, on behalf of a covered entity, an activity involving the use or disclosure of individually identifiable health information. Examples include financial advisors, accountants, auditors, lawyers, and consultants.

The list above basically boils down to any entity involved in accessing, electronically transmitting, or storing individually identifiable health information.

## Value Created by the Security Rule

Staying out of hot water in civil and criminal actions and protecting critical business assets is reason enough to secure information for some, but not all. The Security Rule, like information security in general, is often viewed as a cost center and a barrier to providing effective healthcare. Many doctors, clinicians, and nurses find that information security policies and procedures are an impediment to getting their jobs done. This is accurate when information security is poorly implemented. In fact, when implemented and managed with business processes in mind, information security can have quite the opposite effect. The Security Rule actually provides business value that can be leveraged to lower healthcare costs, increase the efficiency of healthcare operations, and help build long-term customer loyalty.

The Security Rule provides ways for healthcare organizations to leverage information technology in order to offer services that were not previously possible. For example, certain healthcare providers can allow patients to access and administer their private healthcare information via the Internet, knowing all along that their information is being protected from unauthorized use. In addition, wireless technologies that were traditionally insecure can be leveraged to make physicians' jobs easier and more efficient while protecting them from various liabilities. Secure wireless infrastructures will allow these users to rest assured that the health information on their PDAs (personal digital assistants) is stored, administered, and transmitted securely via access controls and encryption. In addition, information security that is managed properly can create value by giving patients life-long confidence that their private healthcare information is being managed securely and responsibly.

### The Security Rule's Relationship with the HIPAA Privacy Rule

The Security Rule has a close relationship with the HIPAA Privacy Rule, in which covered entities are required to comply with by April 14, 2003. In fact, a significant portion of the privacy requirements relies on a solid information security infrastructure in order to be implemented properly. The Privacy Rule mandates that appropriate administrative, technical, and physical safeguards be in place to protect the privacy of health information. That is, information security technology, policies, and procedures must be in place in order to comply with the privacy requirements. The bottom line is that one cannot have privacy without security. Perhaps the original rule makers at HHS did not think about this when they established the privacy requirements long before the security requirements were finalized, much less enforced. Regardless, it would behoove all covered entities to start studying the Security Rule, or at least some published information security best practices (e.g., ISO/IEC 17799). They then must make certain minimal efforts to deploy the policies, procedures, and technologies required for a basic information security infrastructure in order to be fully compliant with the Privacy Rule in 2003.

### INSIGHT INTO THE SECURITY RULE

Like any well-designed information security system, the focus of the Security Rule requirements revolves around the confidentiality, integrity, and availability (CIA) of electronic data. At the time of this writing, the proposed Security Rule is divided into four different categories:

1. Administrative Procedures
2. Physical Safeguards
3. Technical Security Services
4. Technical Security Mechanisms

Each category has a corresponding set of requirements that covers all aspects of the business and technical systems that make up an overall information security infrastructure. In the current version, there is a fair amount of overlap between the four different categories, which may cause confusion. In addition, it has become public knowledge that the electronic signature requirement in the proposed Security Rule is going to be dropped in the final version. Given that these categories are based on various best practices and information security standards, it is most likely that they will not change much in the final Security Rule. Either way, perhaps the final version will be clearer and illustrate that the requirements do not have to be quite as confusing or complicated as initially thought.

There is nothing new or magical about the Security Rule requirements. In fact, even if slight modifications are made in the final version, the proposed rule, if followed and implemented properly, consists of the majority of all information security best practices. That is, covered entities can use the information currently available to get started on their security initiatives now and be well on their way to full Security Rule compliance once the deadline is reached and the rule is enforced.

To ensure the CIA of healthcare information, the Security Rule outlines various technologies, policies, and procedures that must be implemented. From a high-level perspective, these policies and procedures include the following:

- Assigned security responsibility
- Instructions and procedures for secure computer usage
- Formal mechanism for processing and handling data
- Procedures for handling and controlling various media
- Incident response plan
- Disaster recovery plan
- Security configuration management
- Security awareness training
- Personnel termination procedure
- Ongoing security management

In addition, technology-based systems include:

- Logical access controls
- Physical access controls
- User authentication controls
- Authorization controls
- Audit controls
- Data encryption mechanisms

Given the technology-neutral stance of the Security Rule, there are no detailed requirements for specific technologies such as firewalls, authentication systems, or even encryption methods that must be deployed. However, their use is implied because technologies such as these must be used to enforce and support certain policy and procedure requirements.

Because information security is not a specific product or one-time event, care must be taken to ensure that ongoing risks are properly managed. The growing complexity of information systems leads to a multitude of unknowns. If one combines poorly written software, a general lack of consequences and liability, and security expertise that is difficult to find, then effective information security management is quite difficult to achieve — but it is not impossible. The keys to effective security management are ongoing information risk assessments and audits, regular security training for staff members, and consistent system maintenance and monitoring. It is the combination of these that make up the backbone of a solid information security infrastructure and also make good business sense.

## MOVING FORWARD

### Forming the Team

The first step toward Security Rule compliance requires the assignment of security responsibility — a Security Officer. The Security Officer can be an individual or an external organization that leads Security Rule efforts and is responsible for ongoing security management within the organization. To maximize the success of this Security Officer role, this person or organization must have authority and decision-making power, be able to provide guidance on security initiatives, and ultimately take full responsibility for Security Rule compliance. Credibility and sound judgment are very important, and upper management support for this position is absolutely essential.

Once this security responsibility has been established, it is essential to form a team of individuals to assist with compliance efforts. Because Security Rule compliance is not just an IT issue, it is important to bring in individuals from all departments who have a stake in this — legal, HR, operations, IT, etc. At some point, this team will likely include representatives from the entire organization. The team can be comprised of members external to the organization, but there must still be points of contact from within in order to accurately gather information on current business processes and systems.

Keep in mind that there are pros and cons to forming an in-house compliance team versus outsourcing the compliance efforts. An in-house team requires specific technical and business-related security expertise that may not exist in the current staff or that may require costly ongoing training. In addition, an in-house team may require that employees are regularly pulled away from their normal daily tasks to handle information security issues, and this may not make good business sense. On the other hand, an internal staff tends to know much more about the organization's information systems, which can help to streamline the implementation. It may also be easier to trust in-house personnel than outsiders, because the relationship has already been established.

In choosing to outsource Security Rule compliance efforts, there are four main things to consider. First, it is essential to find firms that specialize in information security, and specifically HIPAA security compliance. You will need highly skilled experts, not IT generalists. Firms that specialize are where the experts work. Second, you get what you pay for — within reason. If you search around, you can find expertise in smaller firms that will suit you just fine without having to pay the higher overhead costs associated with larger firms. Third, external experts have less exposure to internal politics. They can stay away from — for the most part — departmental bias and can provide fresh and impartial insight into what really needs to be done. Fourth, watch out for conflicts of interest that could possibly occur if you deal with vendors that try to push specific security products without considering the whole picture or your best interests.

### Assessing the Gaps and Risks

Once the Security Rule regulations and information security best practices have been studied and are well understood by the entire compliance team, the next step will be to perform a gap analysis and an information risk assessment. From a high-level perspective, this should help you understand where you are now with your information security initiatives compared to where you need to be according to the Security Rule requirements. In addition, it will help identify current information risks as they relate to the Security Rule. This analysis will help determine the impact the Security Rule has on your the organization. It will also help you understand the scope of your upcoming compliance efforts. Some key steps involved in this process are:

- Interviewing key personnel to gather facts
- Documenting existing information flows within the organization
- Taking an inventory and classifying all electronic health information
- Determining which assets you need to protect
- Assessing the threats and vulnerabilities you are trying to protect against
- Evaluating existing security policies and procedures
- Determining and documenting what technologies and processes are currently in place to protect your information systems
- Reviewing and documenting all electronic information that is shared with business associates

Once this information is gathered, you will be able to identify and prioritize your gaps and information risks in order to get started on creating the compliance plan.

### Creating and Implementing the Plan

Once the security gaps and information risks are identified, management should be briefed and a budget created. The next step is to create a compliance plan. It is essential that this plan contain documented roles and responsibilities, along with a prioritization of specific needs, a timeline, and a list of all deliverables involved. It may be difficult to estimate and secure these resources initially, but not to worry; this can be fine-tuned over time once the team becomes more accustomed to the workload. It is important, however, that everyone on the team, including the Security Officer, buys into and completely understands the plan.

One recurring requirement in the proposed Security Rule, and a general best practice, is to document everything involved with the compliance plan. This plan cannot exist only in the minds of the stakeholders. It must be written clearly and regularly updated. It is also a good idea to keep a backup copy of the plan offsite for disaster recovery purposes. This is not going to be a document that you will want to recreate from scratch! The documented plan will not only prove to be a valuable source for future reference, but will also be used to hold people accountable and serve as proof that the organization is working toward Security Rule compliance.

When the plan is in place and the time is right, the compliance initiatives can commence. Keep in mind that there is no need for perfection initially. All that can be expected is for you to create a good plan and show that you are working on it. Depending on the size and complexity of the organization and current information systems infrastructure, the implementation process could range from being fairly straightforward and simple, to being quite complicated and resource intensive. Either way, a project such as this can be made less daunting with proper planning, execution, and management.

## CONCLUSION

Complying with the HIPAA Security Rule is similar to any other compliance program. It revolves around designation of the responsibilities, establishing the appropriate policies and procedures, and maintaining these initiatives from a risk management perspective on an ongoing basis. Preparing for the Security Rule requirements does not have to be that complicated, especially if covered entities start early and certain information security best practices are already in place. The sooner that HIPAA covered entities start on their Security Rule initiatives, the cheaper and easier it will be. Some covered entities will have to overhaul their current information security infrastructure. Others that have a fairly simple IT infrastructure may have to start from scratch. Either way, organizations can save time, effort, and money by integrating information security and Security Rule compliance with current IT and HIPAA Privacy Rule initiatives.

By laying a solid information security foundation now, instead of layering it on top later when resources are slim and expertise is difficult to find, covered entities will be in a much better position to manage Security Rule compliance more effectively and minimize their costs. The key is to go into this with the attitude that the Security Rule, and HIPAA in general, make good business sense. Moving forward, remember to document everything to support your decisions. This documentation will prove very valuable in the future when it is needed.

### References

DEPARTMENT OF HEALTH AND HUMAN SERVICES, OFFICE OF THE SECRETARY, *Security and Electronic Signature Standards; proposed rule*. Federal Register document 45 CFR part 142, 1998.

# Chapter 14
# HIPAA Transactions and Code Sets Rule: Overview and Implementation

*Steve Endow*

The Health Insurance Portability and Accountability Act of 1996 (HIPAA) is federal legislation that seeks to improve several aspects of the healthcare system in the United States. HIPAA addresses many healthcare related issues, such as improving access to healthcare, improving the availability of health insurance, and simplifying the administration and delivery of healthcare services. This chapter addresses one "rule" within Title II of HIPAA. Title II is the Administrative Simplification section of HIPAA that establishes requirements for the healthcare industry intended to improve efficiency, patient privacy, and information security through the development of industry standards.

The Electronic Transactions and Code Sets Rule (Transactions Rule) is one of the four rules mandated by the Administrative Simplification provisions of HIPAA. The Transactions Rule is intended to improve the healthcare system by establishing a set of standard electronic healthcare transactions, replacing many proprietary electronic transaction formats that have been developed throughout the industry. The Department of Health and Human Services (DHHS) states that there are about 400 different transaction formats currently in use for electronic healthcare claims[1] — just one of the many different types of electronic healthcare transactions. In addition to developing standard electronic transaction formats for nine specific healthcare transactions, the Transactions Rule also includes requirements that specify who must use these formats, which standard data codes may be used within the transactions, how the transactions may be transmitted, and certain responsibilities of entities that transmit and receive the transactions. This chapter provides a high-level overview of the HIPAA Transactions Rule and serves as an introduction to the general transaction implementation process.

## KEY DEFINITIONS

The Transactions Rule, perhaps due to the fact that it relies on information technology, uses numerous acronyms and terms that can be intimidating and confusing. The following is a list of some of the primary terms related to the Transactions Rule and a brief explanation of each.

- *EDI: electronic data interchange.* EDI is a general technology standard for the electronic transmission of data by computer systems. EDI predates the current public Internet and has been used for decades by thousands of very large, established businesses throughout the world to electronically transmit data for documents such as purchase orders and invoices. Although EDI lacks some of the technical conveniences of newer data transmission technologies based on Internet standards, it is a mature, stable technology that is well known by many businesses and computer programmers.
- *ANSI: American National Standards Institute.* ANSI is a private organization that facilitates the development and certification of various standards used in the United States. The HIPAA transaction standards are among the 15,000 different standards maintained by ANSI. (http://www.ansi.org)
- *ASC X12: Accredited Standards Committee X12.* The ANSI ASC X12 committee was chartered in 1979 by ANSI "to develop uniform standards for interindustry electronic interchange of business transactions,"[2] which resulted in the development of EDI. This is the governing committee responsible for the development and maintenance of EDI standards. The HIPAA Transactions Rule refers to "ANSI X12N" transaction formats. This simply means that HIPAA EDI transactions are developed and maintained by Subcommittee N of the X12 Committee, which focuses on "all aspects of insurance and insurance-related business processes."[3] (http://www.x12.org)
- *Covered entity.* Covered entity is a term frequently used by all of the HIPAA rules. For the purposes of the Transactions Rule, the simple definition reads as follows: "*Covered entity* means one of the following: (1) A health plan. (2) A health care clearinghouse. (3) A health care provider who transmits any health information in electronic form in connection with a transaction covered by this subchapter."[4]
- *Transactions implementation guides.* These are documents, developed by the ASC X12N Insurance Subcommittee, that specify in great detail the format of each of the HIPAA EDI transactions. These documents discuss things such as "headers," "loops," "segments," "elements" and "positions" to describe the exact format and sequence of data in an

EDI transaction. Although these guides do contain some general information describing the transactions, they are primarily a technical reference for computer programmers and system administrators. These guides are available for free at http://www.wpc-edi.com.

- *Trading Partner Agreements.* Trading Partner Agreements are contracts that define, in detail, how two businesses will transmit HIPAA EDI transactions with each other. Despite the extensive detail provided in the implementation guides, there are numerous items that still must be negotiated between two businesses to ensure the smooth communication of HIPAA transactions.
- *Transaction set* — A transaction set is a pair of transactions that would typically be used together to complete a two-way communication and corresponds to the transactions covered in the HIPAA implementation guides. This term is not an official HIPAA definition, but is helpful in clarifying the identification of the different transactions.
- *WEDI: Workgroup for Electronic Data Interchange.* This organization helps businesses in the healthcare industry implement electronic commerce by facilitating the creation and adoption of EDI-related technologies and processes for healthcare. WEDI's Strategic National Implementation Process (SNIP) is specifically focused on facilitating the adoption and implementation of the HIPAA, and offers several helpful resources for healthcare organizations. (http://www.wedi.org)

## HIPAA TRANSACTIONS

The Transactions Rule does not attempt to mandate standards for all healthcare transactions. It focuses on a specific segment of electronic healthcare transactions shared by most healthcare organizations. Seven of the nine HIPAA transactions focus on financial transactions related to healthcare delivery, or processes that support those financial transactions. From initial patient contact through the payment of a claim, these transactions aim to streamline electronic transactions that will result in a faster, more reliable billing process. The other two transactions focus on improving the efficiency of the health plan enrollment and premium payment processes, thereby reducing administrative costs for health plans and health plan administrators.

The Transactions Rule does not require all healthcare organizations to comply with all of its provisions. It only mandates that when a covered entity conducts one of the HIPAA transactions electronically with another covered entity, "the covered entity must conduct the transaction as a standard transaction."[5] For example, a small, independent healthcare provider does not necessarily need to invest thousands of dollars in an electronic billing system to conduct HIPAA-compliant electronic transactions. Alternatives such as third-party billing services, paper-based billing, and Web-based data entry systems are still viable options, but these

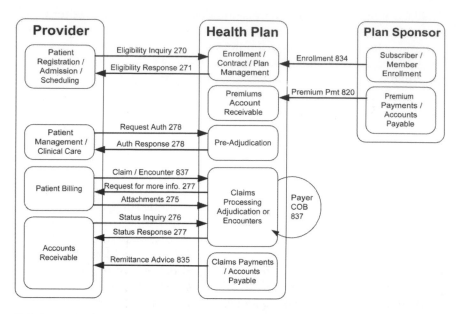

**Exhibit 1. HIPAA Transactions and Processing Flow WEDI SNIP Transactions Work Group, Sequencing Sub Work Group, "Transaction Sequencing, Version 2," 2/28/2002, p. 13. (Courtesy of WEDI SNIP Workgroup for EDI)**

are less practical and more expensive for many organizations with large transaction volumes.

Exhibit 1, developed by the WEDI SNIP Transaction Sequencing group, depicts the HIPAA transactions in the context of the business process of a healthcare provider, a health plan, and a plan sponsor. The transactions are arranged from top to bottom following the general sequence of the billing process for a healthcare provider. The individual transactions have been assigned numbers for identification, but the HIPAA implementation guides sometimes group a pair of transactions together due to their roles as requests and responses. This grouping is an important part of understanding which of the HIPAA transactions should be selected for implementation. Exhibit 2 lists the transaction sets and the associated transactions that would typically be implemented for each set.

In addition to the transaction sets in Exhibit 2, there is one additional transaction that has been proposed but is not yet finalized. It is the 275 transaction, referred to as the "Claims Attachment" transaction. Officially, the 275 is called "Additional Information to Support a Healthcare Claim or Encounter," and would be used as a response to a 277 request for more information. The potential benefits of this electronic transaction are tremendous, but so are the corresponding challenges. Given the broad range of information that may need to be transmitted as part of a claim attachment,

**Exhibit 2. Transaction Sets and Corresponding Transactions**

| Transaction Set | Transactions |
|---|---|
| Eligibility Benefit Inquiry and Response | 270 + 271 |
| Services Review Request and Response (Authorization) | 278 |
| Health Care Claim and Remittance Advice | 837 + 835 |
| Claim Status Request and Response | 276 + 277 |
| Health Plan Enrollment | 834 |
| Payroll Deducted and Premium Payment | 820 |

this transaction set has dozens of outstanding issues that must be resolved before organizations attempt to implement it as a standard.

Exhibit 1 illustrates how the transactions relate to three different types of healthcare organizations. Naturally, organizations will need to assess which transactions are relevant to them and how they might benefit from implementing each. A typical healthcare provider will focus primarily on the billing department and billing system as part of its HIPAA transaction implementation. The billing department will have many opportunities to reduce or eliminate manual tasks through the automation of certain transactions. Hundreds of telephone calls, faxes, and paper documents processed each day could eventually be replaced by a few electronic transactions. On the other hand, a plan sponsor, employer, or third-party administrator will likely have a different perspective as they consider the 834 Enrollment or 820 Premium Payment transactions. Such organizations that import and process data in dozens of formats can look to saving many hours each month by converting to the HIPAA transaction formats.

Naturally, such efficiencies come at a price. Organizations must invest in the computer systems and software to make such transactions a reality. Implementing these transaction formats is a significant project, requiring skilled individuals and perhaps even expensive software. Many organizations must also accept the potentially dramatic impact that such changes will have on employees' job functions through significant changes in internal business processes and possibly even headcount reductions. The costs of software and hardware, implementation, and training are also significant. Organizations with large transaction volumes and cumbersome business processes will likely realize the greatest return by fully embracing the transaction set as an opportunity to reengineer business processes and save time and money over in the long term. The following sections discuss each of the transaction sets in more detail.

## 270 + 271 Eligibility Benefit Inquiry and Response

This pair of transactions is intended to facilitate the process of verifying demographic information and insurance eligibility for a patient. The

**Exhibit 3. Request Types for the 270 + 271 Transaction Set**

| General Requests | Specific Requests |
|---|---|
| Eligibility status (active or inactive) | Procedure coverage dates |
| Maximum benefits (policy limits) | Procedure coverage maximum amounts |
| Exclusions | Deductible amounts |
| In-plan/out-of-plan benefits | Remaining deductible amounts |
| C.O.B. information | Co-insurance amounts |
| Deductible | Co-pay amounts |
| Co-pays | Coverage limitation percentage |
| | Patient responsibility amounts |
| | Non-covered amounts |

*Source:* ANSI ASC X12N Subcommittee, National EDI Transaction Set Implementation Guide: Health Care Eligibility Benefit Inquiry and Response 270/271, May 2000, p. 16, 17.

270 transaction is typically sent from a provider to a health plan to inquire about the eligibility and specific insurance benefits for a patient, while the 271 transaction is the response from the health plan. If adequate information is supplied in the 270 request and the patient is identified as a member of the health plan, the 271 transaction will confirm that the patient is enrolled in the plan and may also include specific benefits information for the patient.

Despite the general title of transaction "standard," the 270 + 271 transaction set may vary significantly, depending on the particular nature of the request. The implementation guide for the 270 + 271 transaction set indicates that "General Requests" and "Specific Requests" are supported and provides the examples listed in Exhibit 3 for each.

The implementation guide provides a standard data format for these requests, but obviously the quantity and type of data contained in the transaction will vary, depending on the nature of the request. Given the different requests that the transaction set must support, organizations and their EDI software must be capable of sending and receiving the transactions in a flexible manner and handling the variations appropriately without requiring frequent human intervention.

### 278 Services Review Request and Response

The 278 request and response transaction, generally referred to as an authorization, is identified with a single transaction number. The implementation guide provides the following examples[6] regarding the different uses of the 278:

- Admission certification review request and associated response
- Referral review request and associated response
- Healthcare services certification review request and associated response

• Extend certification review request and associated response
• Certification appeal review request and associated response

If an organization is burdened with calls to health plans to receive authorization for services, or frustrated with rejected or denied claims due to authorization issues, this transaction has the potential to improve both operational efficiency and billing accuracy.

### 837 + 835 Health Care Claim and Remittance Advice

The 837 claim will likely be the most widely implemented transaction format. Because many healthcare organizations already transmit and receive electronic claims, and because electronic claims often offer benefits such as faster processing and payment, the 837 will be a high priority for healthcare providers. The familiarity with electronic claims throughout the healthcare industry should also help the transition to the 837; but given the complex data sets involved with an 837 + 835 transaction set, it is anticipated that the adoption will not be smooth for every organization.

For billing departments that have been forced to implement unwieldy processes to trace payments to their claims and paper explanation of benefit statements (EOBs), the 835 remittance advice transaction offers hope. The introductory section of the HIPAA Transactions Rule states the following:

> Health care providers need to have adequate details on the ASC X12N 835 transaction that they receive in order to enable them to not only post accounts, but to decide whether an appeal should be filed, or further action taken in response to the health plan's decision on a claim. A failure to supply adequate reasons for denial or reduction would undermine the effectiveness of an ASC X12N 835 transaction.[7]

This brings a wealth of information to billing departments that previously had to make telephone calls to determine why claims were denied and should dramatically improve payment posting times.

### 276 + 277 Claim Status Request and Response

The elusive question for all billing departments is: "When will this claim be paid?" Plenty of other questions, such as "Has the claim been accepted?", "Has the claim been reviewed?", "Has the claim been rejected?", and "Do I need to resubmit the claim?", also come to mind. The good news is that the 276 + 277 transaction set should answer these questions, and more. Certain payers may even offer pre-adjudication processing in conjunction with the 276 + 277 to notify providers of invalid claims before they are even accepted.

Some additional good news is that the HIPAA Transactions Rule is firm on the adoption of the 276 + 277 when it states that "All health plans, including state Medicaid plans, must have the capability to accept, process, and send the ASC X12N 276/277 transactions."[8] This is great news for billing departments that have been frustrated with tracking a claim's status. The 276 + 277 implementation guide also states that "Status information can be requested at the claim and/or line level,"[9] which will be a wonderful benefit for most billing departments.

### 834 Health Plan Enrollment

The 834 transaction implementation guide is succinct in its statement of purpose:

> The intent of this implementation guide is to meet the health care industry's specific need for the initial enrollment and subsequent maintenance of individuals who are enrolled in insurance products. This implementation guide specifically addresses the enrollment and maintenance of health care products only.[10]

Although relatively simple in concept, the benefits of this standard transaction are significant for organizations that must accept, process, and transmit large quantities of enrollment and subscriber data. Rather than process dozens of different data formats, the 834 transaction should provide a means to standardize the format and dramatically simplify the process of sharing enrollment data.

### 820 Payroll Deducted and Premium Payment

The 820 transaction allows an organization to send an insurance premium payment request to a bank, along with remittance advice that will be supplied to the payee healthcare organization. For payments, the 820 can be sent directly to a bank with or without remittance data; and if a payment is sent via check or another electronic or nonelectronic means, the 820 transaction can be used to send remittance advice directly to the payee organization independent of the payment. Due to the involvement of a third-party financial institution, this transaction may be more challenging and time-consuming to implement, because three organizations must be involved in the implementation process. In addition to direct uses by large organizations, this transaction will likely be implemented by third-party payroll processors, allowing them to report payroll deductions and corresponding premium payments for their customers.

### TRANSACTION SEQUENCING

In addition to understanding the different HIPAA transactions, it is important to understand the applicability and importance of each transaction for your organization. Once applicable transactions have been identified, one must prioritize the transactions to facilitate the development of a project plan that will provide the most value to the organization.

Although it is possible to simultaneously implement multiple transactions, many organizations do not have the resources to effectively manage multiple large projects, and must therefore prioritize the transaction sets for sequential implementation.

First, consider which transactions must be implemented; this usually includes transactions that are currently performed electronically. These will typically be implemented first in order to comply with the HIPAA implementation deadlines. Next, for those transactions that are not currently performed electronically (telephone, fax, mail), which transactions would provide the greatest financial or operational benefit? For some organizations, eligibility is a pressing issue; for others, it is authorization; and for some, it is claim status. Prioritize these transactions based on estimated cost reductions or operational efficiencies, and also consider that some processes may not benefit at all from using a HIPAA transaction due to high implementation costs or lack of support by other trading partners. For each transaction, the potential benefits need to be weighed against the cost of the implementation as well as a consideration of alternatives, such as outsourcing or the use of a clearinghouse for submission of nonstandard transaction formats.

As an example, consider a hypothetical healthcare provider. This provider currently submits over 1000 electronic claims per day. Efficient claims processing and payment receipt is a top priority, and the receipt and review of paper EOBs are one of the biggest impediments to payment posting. Eligibility is not a major concern because this provider does not have any direct contracts with health plans and operates on a fee-for-service basis, but it would be beneficial in order to verify patient demographics and ensure accurate billing information. Finally, because this provider does not have any contracts with insurance companies or managed care organizations, authorization is rarely an issue. This provider uses a third-party payroll service and a third-party administrator for its insurance programs. Based on this information, Exhibit 4 is an example of the likely transaction sequencing for this healthcare provider.

Because claim status and eligibility transactions are currently handled by telephone, fax, or mail, the provider is not required to implement these

**Exhibit 4. Transaction Sequencing Example**

| | | |
|---|---|---|
| 1 | 835 + 837 Claims | Required |
| 2 | 276 + 277 Claims Status | Strong desire |
| 3 | 270 + 271 Eligibility | Moderate desire |
| 4 | 278 Authorization | No desire |
| N/A | 834 Enrollment | Not applicable |
| N/A | 820 Premium Payment | Not applicable |

transactions, but believes that the benefits of the two transactions outweigh the implementation costs. Because the provider handles almost no authorizations, there is little financial justification for implementing the 278 transaction, but might reevaluate it in the future if the business decides to pursue HMO contracts. Finally, because this provider outsources benefits and payroll, it has no plans to implement the 834 and 820 transactions.

## CODE SETS

In addition to developing standard transaction formats, the HIPAA also identifies certain "code sets" that should be used to standardize the encoding of certain medical information. The following list summarizes the HIPAA code set requirements,[11] which are comprised of existing industry-standard code sets:

- Codes for diseases, injuries, impairments, other health problems, and associated causes must be from ICD-9-CM volumes 1 and 2 (International Classification of Diseases, 9th edition).
- Codes for prevention, diagnosis, treatment, and management must be from ICD-9-CM volume 3, Procedures.
- Codes for drugs and biologics must be from the NDC (National Drug Codes).
- Codes for physician services and healthcare services must be from CPT-4 or HCPCS (Current Procedural Terminology or Health Care Financing Administration Common Procedure Coding System).
- Codes for medical supplies, orthotic and prosthetic devices, and durable medical equipment must be from HCPCS.

Most healthcare organizations currently use one or more of these existing standards; however, the rule recognizes that not all medical and related services will be fully covered by these code sets. Unfortunately, the rule states that organizations that require additional codes not covered by the standard must work with the respective publishers of the standards (called DSMOs, or Designated Standard Maintenance Organizations) to add appropriate codes to support their transactions.

As for implementation of code sets, most billing systems and healthcare software packages already use and support one or more of the code set standards. Some organizations may need to transition off of proprietary codes or other "non-HIPAA" code sets, but overall, these transitions will be just one portion of an organization's transactions implementation project.

## IMPLEMENTATION OF HIPAA TRANSACTIONS

Once one has an understanding of which transactions are appropriate for an organization and an implementation sequence that makes sense, a project plan must be developed to guide the implementation. Given the importance of HIPAA transactions and the likely investment of a considerable amount of time and money, the transaction implementation should be treated as a significant project. And, just like any other projects that involve technology, certain steps should be taken to minimize risk.

One of the biggest challenges for technology projects is defining and controlling project "scope." What, specifically, will the project accomplish? How many hardware and software systems are going to be involved? How many people from which departments are involved? How many trading partners are involved? These questions begin to define the scope of the project. Ultimately, all of this information should be documented in a project plan that clearly states, in as much detail as possible, what the project will deliver, and just as important, what the project will not deliver. Items such as new software, hardware, program interfaces and data translators, telecommunications, transaction certification processes, trading partner agreements, and employee training should all be considered. Documenting this information will not only provide the basis for a project plan, but it will encourage one to think through the project and develop questions along the way, hopefully anticipating potential issues before the project begins. If the project plan does not include a list of unanswered questions and concerns, it should not be considered complete.

Once one has a good understanding of the project scope and a general project plan, the next step is to develop a timeline to schedule the implementation. With the passing of the original October 2002 implementation deadline for HIPAA transactions, organizations that have not completed their implementations were required to submit an application for the transaction deadline extension by October 16, 2002. Submission of a properly completed application automatically delayed the deadline for transaction testing to April 16, 2003, and allows testing and certification activities to continue until October 2003. Even with the extension, organizations only have six additional months from the original October 2002 deadline to complete the implementation process.

Given the mandated compliance dates and limited time for implementation, the project timeline is somewhat fixed. To meet the deadline, obtaining adequate resources and achieving proper resource allocation become the final piece of the implementation planning process. Resources need to be chosen based on their ability to assist with a rapid implementation. For example, purchasing packaged software from a vendor will likely reduce implementation time and associated project risk, compared to attempting custom software development. Working with experienced vendors or consultants should also be faster than training employees. The selection of these resources may cost a significant amount of money, but if properly managed, they should facilitate a rapid and successful implementation.

In addition to the direct resources required to facilitate the HIPAA transactions, external organizations will definitely be an important part of finalizing the project. Following the implementation of software or systems to handle the new transaction formats, the transactions should be tested and certified by a recognized organization. This process is intended to ensure that transaction formats comply with the HIPAA standards and that data is transmitted as expected. The process also helps minimize costly troubleshooting and debugging when real transactions begin to flow between trading partners. Make sure to contact all trading partners to identify the transaction certification process that each requires, and at the same time, take the opportunity to begin developing trading partner agreements for each of the trading partners.

## ANTICIPATED ISSUES

It is widely accepted that there will be significant challenges during the implementation of the HIPAA transactions and the several months following the deadline. There will certainly be many issues that were unforeseen in the development of the transaction implementation guides that will need to be addressed. By being prepared for such contingencies, organizations can have relatively simple and effective means to deal with the issues as they arise.

One of the most widely anticipated issues will be a lack of specific instructions or requirements for certain transactions and processes that occur in several specialized areas of healthcare. Alternative care, homeopathic medicine, clinical laboratory services, pharmacy services, dentistry, and at-home healthcare are just a few of the services that will likely face challenges when trying to implement and process certain transactions. Perhaps the best approach to handling these issues is to stay in contact with informed organizations. Healthcare industry organizations such as WEDI and specific industry groups will likely provide updates regarding specific issues and recommended resolutions. The DHHS and the Designated Standard Maintenance Organizations for the HIPAA transactions will also have direct information bulletins regarding issue resolutions and changes to standards to address such issues.

There are a few other points to consider when preparing to send transactions and develop a long-term HIPAA transaction strategy for your organization. First, as any organization that has EDI experience can attest, each trading partner will likely have unique or unusual requirements that will require your organization and computer systems to handle dozens of unique circumstances when processing transactions. Prepare for this by ensuring that your software, systems, and procedures are flexible enough to accommodate these needs.

Second, be aware that the transaction implementation guides will be updated on an annual basis, and will probably have considerable changes the first few years following the implementation deadline. Ensure that your software can easily accommodate these format changes, perhaps through vendor updates, template uploads, flexible field mappings, or other mechanism. In addition to changes to the transaction formats, the HIPAA mandated code sets will also likely undergo significant changes to accommodate a broader array of industry-specific needs. Again, make sure that your software and systems are flexible and can handle these situations through a simple upload or input of new code sets on a regular basis.

Finally, consider the reliability of the vendors with which you work. Ensure that professional service firms and consultants have strong references, qualified and experienced personnel, and the ability to provide proper support when an issue arises. For software or system vendors, make sure that you are comfortable with their financial status and ability to provide ongoing support, upgrades, and maintenance in the future. Given the current volatile business environment, it is important that a significant investment in software or computer systems be protected with some type of assurance that the investment will last for several years. If a software vendor is unable to provide adequate assurances regarding its ability to provide support in the years to come, inquire about a source code escrow program or other types of agreements that will allow you to support yourself should the vendor go out of business or discontinue support for its product.

## CONCLUSION

Implementing HIPAA transactions can certainly appear to be a daunting prospect; but in reality, such a project is not much different than implementing a complex financial accounting or billing system, or a patient management and electronic medical records system. It requires thorough research, planning, and diligent project management. Perhaps what makes the HIPAA implementation more challenging is the looming implementation deadline and the possibility of fines or penalties for noncompliance.

It seems clear that once the issues are worked out and the healthcare industry as a whole is comfortable processing electronic transactions using the new HIPAA formats, the efficiencies will provide a measurable benefit to healthcare organizations and patients alike. Achieving such benefits naturally comes at a price; but the sooner the implementations are completed, the sooner we can begin to appreciate the rewards.

## HIPAA INTERNET RESOURCES

Below are a few Internet resources that the author found helpful in learning about and keeping current with HIPAA. When reviewing information from any source that offers HIPAA advice (including this one!), be sure to verify the information you obtain. Many analyses of HIPAA exaggerate the impact of the requirements, or portray the requirements in situations that will not apply to your organization.

Rather than spending time reading others' interpretations of HIPAA, the author strongly recommends reading the actual government publications to obtain accurate, first-hand knowledge of the HIPAA requirements. The documents can appear daunting due to their size, but each HIPAA rule offers simple and well-written narratives that explain every requirement and how those requirements should be applied to different organizations. After spending just a few days reading and understanding the official documents, you should have a mastery of the subject that will give you confidence as you bring your organization into compliance.

http://aspe.hhs.gov/admnsimp/ — This is the official source for HIPAA documents and government publications. These documents should be the primary reference for all of your HIPAA implementations and are invaluable for any HIPAA project manager.

http://www.hipaadvisory.com — Operated by Phoenix Health Systems, this site is one of the most popular vendor-sponsored Web sites for up-to-date HIPAA information and guidance on HIPAA compliance.

http://cms.hhs.gov/hipaa — Formerly known as HCFA, the new CMS Web site offers some general HIPAA information. CMS also handled the deadline extension applications for the HIPAA Transactions Rule.

**Notes**

Department of Health and Human Services, Health Care Financing Administration, "45 CFR Parts 160 and 162 — Health Insurance Reform: Standards for Electronic Transactions; Announcement of Designated Standard Maintenance Organizations; Final Rule and Notice," August 17, 2000. p. 50312.

Accredited Standards Committee X12 (ASC X12) Web site, http://www.x12.org.

ASC X12 web site, X12N Subcommittee home page, http://www.x12.org/x12org/subcommittees/sc_home.cfm?strSC = N.

Department of Health and Human Services, op. cit., p. 50365.

Department of Health and Human Services, op. cit., p. 50369.

ANSI ASC X12N Subcommittee, National EDI Transaction Set Implementation Guide: Health Care Services Review — Request for Review and Response, May 2000, p. 10.

Department of Health and Human Services, op. cit., p. 50334.

Loc. cit., p. 50337.

ANSI ASC X12N Subcommittee, National EDI Transaction Set Implementation Guide: Health Care Claim Status Request and Response 276/277, May 2000, p. 11.

ANSI ASC X12N Subcommittee, National EDI Transaction Set Implementation Guide: Health Care Benefit Enrollment and Maintenance 834, May 2000, p. 7.

Department of Health and Human Services, op. cit., p. 50325 and 50370.

# Section V
# Improving Quality, Reducing Risks, and Understanding Costs

# Chapter 15
# A Tool for Evaluating Healthcare Plans from a Quality Perspective: HEDIS

*Donald M. Jacobs*
*Jim Peterson*

Increasingly, managed care has been equated with managed cost. Yet, when it was introduced, managed care was supposed to be a new way to make the healthcare system more cost-effective. It also was supposed to help to ensure that quality of care was not adversely affected and was, perhaps, even improved. The creation by The National Committee of Quality Assurance (NCQA) of the Health Plan Employer Data and Information Set (HEDIS) is an attempt to provide purchasers of care the information they need to select the right health plan. It also provides a health plan the opportunity to have a report card on the quality of the services that it provides its members.

Selecting a managed care plan has been a complicated endeavor and may even be a risky one. Fortunately, a group of large managed care organizations (MCOs) and large employer groups came together and formed a private, not-for-profit organization called the National Committee for Quality Assurance (NCQA).

NCQA had two basic goals. First, purchasers would be given access to information on managed care plans that would allow them to distinguish between different plans based on quality and value rather than on just price and a slogan. Second, when MCOs realized that purchasers would ask them for their quality grades, they would have to implement policies and practices that would ensure they could compete based on quality as well

0-8493-1498-4/03/$0.00+$1.50
© 2003 by CRC Press LLC

as price. Achieving these goals would hopefully improve the overall quality of the entire healthcare industry.

To achieve these goals, the NCQA concentrates its efforts on two complementary activities. One is the accreditation of MCOs. The second is the measurement of their performance. Although both activities are intertwined, and the discussion of one is difficult without the other, the purpose of this chapter is to discuss and explain the latter.

In 1992, the NCQA began using a tool for performance measurement called the Health Plan Employer Data and Information Set (HEDIS). To establish a basic understanding of HEDIS, this chapter is divided into two parts. Part one is a description of HEDIS consisting of a discussion of the following six basic questions:

1. How and why was HEDIS developed?
2. What is included in HEDIS data?
3. Who submits HEDIS data?
4. Who uses HEDIS data?
5. How do you access HEDIS data?
6. How is HEDIS data validated?

Part two uses the framework of these questions to detail the issues surrounding them.

## PART ONE: A DESCRIPTION OF HEDIS

### How and Why Was HEDIS Developed?

In contrast to the NCQA accreditation process, which examines a health plan's structures and systems, the purpose of HEDIS is to measure the results actually achieved by individual health plans. The problem for the developers of HEDIS was to determine which questions should be asked and what services should be measured to give a purchaser as valuable an insight into an MCO quality as possible.

In 1992, the NCQA formed a committee made up of representatives from several large employers and MCOs. Its purpose was twofold: the first task was to develop a standard set of questions applicable to MCOs for measuring the quality of their services. The second task was to develop a technical guide for MCOs to use for tracking, extracting, and reporting answers to these questions. In 1993, the NCQA released the first set of questions, HEDIS 2.0. The second version, HEDIS 2.5, was released in 1995; HEDIS 3.0 was released in 1997. The current release is HEDIS 1999; and according to NCQA President Margaret E. O'Kane, "With HEDIS 1999, we're turning up the lights in the health plan marketplace to show consumers and employers just what they're getting. Strong plans will look strong, weak plans will look weak, and they'll all work hard to get better. For purchasers, shopping without HEDIS data is shopping in the dark."[1]

### What Is Included in HEDIS Data?

HEDIS contains performance measures divided into the following seven basic categories: effectiveness of care, access/availability of care, satisfaction with experience of care, health plan services, use of services, cost of care, and health plan descriptive information. Exhibit 1 lists set measures under these categories.

Since the release of HEDIS 2.0 in 1993, these measurements have changed and have been updated with each subsequent version. The measurements shown in Exhibit 1 are included in the HEDIS 1999 reporting set. Prior to 1999, there was another category called the testing set. As measurements in the reporting set became irrelevant or outdated, they were replaced by those from the testing set. But, beginning with HEDIS 1999, the testing set was eliminated. In its place the NCQA established the Committee on Performance Measurement to monitor, evaluate, and ensure the continued relevance of HEDIS measurements. The committee surveyed 1700 organizations and individuals and requested suggestions for improving the performance measurement questions and processes. In addition, the NCQA formed a HEDIS user group to provide users with a continuous forum for discussion regarding the HEDIS initiatives. The NCQA is committed to all activities that ensure HEDIS continues to provide relevant information to all users, employers, consumers, regulators, and health plans.

### Who Submits HEDIS Data?

The available HEDIS data (plan year 1997) contains information from approximately 370 health plans covering about 40 million people. A recent NCQA survey indicated that almost 90 percent of all health plans collect and report at least some HEDIS data. The number of plans submitting this data has increased with each new HEDIS version.

The Health Care Financing Administration (HCFA) requires all managed care plans serving the Medicare population to submit data on HEDIS measures relevant to Medicare. These are listed in Exhibit 2. In addition, some states (e.g., New Jersey and Maryland) have made HEDIS submissions a requirement for all state HMOs. Most state Medicaid agencies require Medicaid HMOs to submit HEDIS information as well. In 1996, the American Public Welfare Association (APWA) completed a survey of state Medicaid agencies asking whether they currently had in place provisions for collecting HEDIS data, either in the form of measures reported directly to the state by participating health plans or in the form of encounter data reported by the plans to the state. The results of the survey showed the following:

## Exhibit 1. HEDIS 1999 Reporting Set Measures

**Effectiveness of Care**
•Childhood Immunization Status
•Adolescent Immunization Status
•Advising Smokers to Quit
•Flu Shots for Older Adults
•Breast Cancer Screening
•Cervical Cancer Screening
•Prenatal Care in the First Trimester
•Low Birth-Weight Babies
•Check-ups after Delivery
•Beta Blocker Treatment after a Heart Attack
•Cholesterol Management after Acute Cardiovascular Events
•Eye Exams for People with Diabetes
•Comprehensive Diabetes Care
•Follow-up after Hospitalization for Mental Illness
•Antidepressant Medication Management
•The Health of Seniors

**Access/Availability of Care**
•Adults' Access to Preventive/Ambulatory Health Services
•Children's Access to Primary Care Practitioners
•Availability of Primary Care Providers
•Availability of Behavioral Health Care Providers
•Availability of Obstetrical and Prenatal Care
•Providers' Initiation of Prenatal Care
•Low Birth-Weight Deliveries at Facilities for High-Risk Deliveries and Neonates
•Annual Dental Visit
•Availability of Dentists
•Availability of Language Interpretation Services

**Satisfaction with the Experience of Care**
•HEDIS/CAHPS 2.0H Survey (Adult Medicaid, Commercial)
•HEDIS/CAHPS 2.0H, Child (Medicaid, Commercial)
•HEDIS/CAHPS 2.0, Medicare

**Health Plan Stability**
•Disenrollment
•Practitioner Turnover
•Years in Business/Total Membership
•Indicators of Financial Stability

**Use of Services**
•Frequency of Ongoing Prenatal Care
•Well-Child Visits in the First 15 Months of Life
•Well-Child Visits in the Third, Fourth, Fifth and Sixth Years of Life
•Adolescent Well-Care Visits
•Frequency of Selected Procedures
•Inpatient Utilization — General Hospital/Acute Care Ambulatory Care
•Inpatient Utilization — Non-Acute Care
•Discharge and Average Length of Stay — Maternity Care
•Cesarean Section Rate
•Vaginal Birth after Cesarean Rate (VBAC-Rate)
•Births and Average Length of Stay, Newborns

**Exhibit 1. HEDIS 1999 Reporting Set Measures** *(Continued)*

- Mental Health Utilization — Inpatient Discharges and Average Length of Stay
- Mental Health Utilization — Percentage of Members Receiving Inpatient, Day/Night Care and Ambulatory Services
- Readmission for Specified Mental Health Disorders
- Chemical Dependency Utilization — Inpatient Discharges and Average Length of Stay
- Chemical Dependency Utilization — Percentage of Members Receiving Inpatient, Day/Night Care and Ambulatory Services
- Readmission for Chemical Dependency Measure — Retired Outpatient Drug Utilization

**Cost of Care**
- Rate Trends
- High-Occurrence/High-Cost DRGs

**Health Plan Descriptive Information**
- Board Certification/Residency Completion
- Practitioner Compensation Arrangements with Public Health, Educational and Social Service Organizations
- Total Enrollment
- Enrollment by Payer (Member Years/Months)
- Unduplicated Count of Medicaid Members
- Cultural Diversity of Medicaid Membership
- Weeks of Pregnancy at Time of Enrollment in the Health Plan

---

- Thirty of the thirty-three states responding to the survey and the District of Columbia are, or will be, using HEDIS specifications, at least in part.
- Eleven states reported they were currently requiring health plans to report HEDIS measures.
- Fourteen states indicated they would require plans to report HEDIS data in the future.
- Medicaid programs overwhelmingly intend to use HEDIS as a key tool for plan performance monitoring and for establishing goals for internal plan quality improvement efforts.
- Eleven states expected to have some initial HEDIS data by the end of 1996, the earliest date such data would be available given the release date of Medicaid HEDIS. Eleven states expected to have HEDIS data during 1997, and five during 1998.

## Who Uses HEDIS Data?

The NCQA intention for its accreditation and performance measurement activities is to provide purchasers with quality information about healthcare choices. For most people, healthcare is either received through their employment, or through a government agency such as Medicaid and Medicare. Subsequently, the purchasers most likely to use HEDIS data are corporate benefit managers, federal agencies such as HCFA, and state Medicaid agencies.

### Exhibit 2. Medicare Applicable HEDIS Measurements

**Health Plan Stability**
•Performance Indicators
•Years in Business/Total Membership
•Disenrollment
•Provider Turnover

**Cost of Care**
•High-Occurrence/High-Cost DRGs
•Rate Trends
•Health Plan Descriptive Information
•Provider Compensation
•Total Enrollment
•Enrollment by Payer (Member Years/Months)

**Effectiveness of Care**
•Breast Cancer Screening
•Beta-Blocker Treatment after a Heart Attack
•Eye Exams for People with Diabetes
•Follow-up after Hospitalization for Mental Illness
•The Health of Seniors

**Access to/Availability of Care**
•Adults' Access to Prevention/Ambulatory Health Services
•Availability of Primary Care Providers
•Availability of Mental Health/Chemical Dependency Providers
•Availability of Language Interpretation Services, Part II

**Use of Services**
•Frequency of Selected Procedures
•Inpatient Utilization — General Hospital/Acute Care
•Ambulatory Care
•Inpatient Utilization — Non-Acute Care
•Mental Health Utilization — Inpatient Discharges and Average Length of Stay
•Mental Health Utilization — Percentage of Members Receiving Inpatient, Day/Night and Ambulatory Services
•Readmission for Specified Mental Health Disorders
•Chemical Dependency Utilization — Inpatient Discharges and Average Length of Stay
•Chemical Dependency Utilization — Percentage of Members Receiving Inpatient Day/Night and Ambulatory Services
•Readmission for Chemical Dependency
•Outpatient Drug Utilization (For Those with a Drug Benefit)

**Informed Health Care Choices**
•Language Translation Services

**Health Plan Descriptive Information**
•Board Certification/Residency Completion
•Preventive Care and Health Promotion

---

Of the approximately 1500 buyers of HEDIS 3.0, most were large employers such as AlliedSignal, Chrysler, Federal Express, Ford, General Electric, IBM, and PepsiCo. These employers use HEDIS information and require the health plans they contract with to provide HEDIS information. In addition, some companies like GTE offer reduced premiums to employees who choose one of the highest ranking plans of the many plans with which they contract, in the case of GTE, over a hundred. The Managed Health Care Association, which comprises approximately a hundred Fortune 500 companies, has also issued statements in the past urging employers to use HEDIS measurements in evaluating health plans.

HCFA and state Medicaid agencies also use portions of the HEDIS data to help select the health plans eligible to receive service contracts for their covered populations.

In addition to purchasers of healthcare, many HMOs have used HEDIS data and results internally. For example, US HealthCare used HEDIS 2.0 and 2.5 data to award over $2 million in bonus checks to obstetrics/gynecology providers who scored well against their regional peers on five of the HEDIS measurements concerning Ob/Gyn services. Furthermore, the HEDIS measurements on member satisfaction, immunization rates, mammogram rates, and pap smear rates have also been used by HMOs in the calculation of capitation rates and bonuses.

### How Do You Access HEDIS Data?

One of the first problems facing the NCQA in regard to its HEDIS performance measurement tool was getting information collected in HEDIS into the hands of the purchasers. In its first attempt to solve this problem, NCQA launched the Report Card Pilot Project in January of 1994. It contained the externally audited data on plan performance. What resulted was a 296-page technical report comparing and analyzing the voluntarily submitted HEDIS data of 21 health plans. The report basically found that the health plans performed reasonably well on most of the report card's measurements. Some of the plans, in fact, performed very well. For example, while the U.S. Public Health Service targeted as its goal a 60 percent mammography rate for women over 50, the HEDIS Technical Report showed that a 74 percent mammography rate for women of this age group had been achieved by some plans.

In 1996, the NCQA developed two means by which to communicate HEDIS results to purchasers. First, it created a national database called Quality Compass. This database is designed to help make it easier for purchasers to receive comparative information regarding participating health plans and to provide national and regional averages for specific HEDIS measurements. The Quality Compass database can be accessed through the NCQA Web site, and reports can be purchased individually or on CD-ROM.

Second, in the fall of 1998, the NCQA released its second annual State of Managed Care Quality Report. This extensive, detailed report provides insights and interpretations of the HEDIS 3.0 data. It provides comparisons of HEDIS data to national benchmark percentiles by year and by region. The report contains both graphs of HEDIS data and data interpretations. Below are two examples taken from the report.

### Cesarean Sections.

*What did we measure?* The percentage of women who delivered by cesarean section rather than vaginal delivery.

*Why is it important?* Between one third and one half of all C-sections performed in the United States each year are probably unnecessary. C-sections are more expensive than vaginal deliveries, the recuperative period is longer, and there are more complications associated with them. Public health officials are working to reduce the U.S. C-section rate to 12 to 15 percent by the year 2000.

*How is the managed care industry doing?* See Exhibit 3 for the rates of C-sections.

*What would it mean if all health plans performed as well as the best plans?* The estimated risk of a woman dying after a C-section is four times higher than the risk of death following a vaginal delivery. C-sections are also typically followed by longer hospital stays and longer recovery times. Currently, 80 percent of all health plans report C-section rates between 14.8 percent and 38.4 percent.

*What can health plans do to make C-section rates more appropriate?* Many women and physicians incorrectly assume that after a woman has delivered via C-section, all subsequent deliveries should also be via C-section. This belief is not supported by available evidence and likely contributes to overutilization of this procedure. Health plans should educate women and providers about the option of delivering vaginally even after a C-section. Health plans may also lower C-section rates simply by providing practitioners with an analysis of how their own C-section rate compares with other practitioners' rates, thus high-

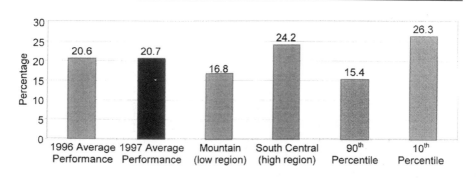

**Exhibit 3. Cesarean Section Rates**

lighting any atypical practice patterns. Medical directors should also consider developing educational outreach programs or labor management seminars targeting physicians who have unusually high C-section rates.

**Childhood Immunizations.**

*What did we measure?* The percentage of two-year-old children who received appropriate immunizations by their second birthday. The completed series of vaccines includes many different components. Included here are: four diptheria-tetanus-pertussis, three polio, and one measles-mumps-rubella vaccination.

*Why is it important?* Childhood immunizations help prevent serious illnesses, such as polio, tetanus, whooping cough, mumps, measles, and meningitis. Vaccines are an easy, proven way to help a child stay healthy and avoid the potentially harmful effects of childhood diseases. It is estimated that one million children in the United States do not receive the necessary vaccinations by age two.

*How is the managed care industry doing?* See Exhibit 4 for childhood immunization rates.

*What would it mean if all health plans performed as well as the best plans?* If all health plans were brought up to the 90th percentile benchmark of 83 percent, unnecessary morbidity and mortality among children would be prevented, thus saving lives, life years, and associated costs. The Children's Defense Fund estimates that providing immunizations yields a ten-to-one economic return on investment in terms of reduced medical expenditures.

*What can plans do to improve childhood immunization rates?* Plans should attempt to educate parents about the benefit of childhood immunization and send reminders to parents encouraging their children to become vaccinated. Incentive programs featuring gift certificates or other giveaways have proven to be an effective tool in

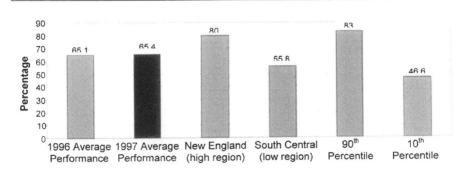

**Exhibit 4. Childhood Immunization Rates**

encouraging parents to have their children appropriately immunized. Health plans should also develop systems to remind parents of the need to immunize children while they are in the doctor's office. Similarly, health plans should also develop systems, such as immunization checklists on medical records, to help remind practitioners of recommended immunization schedules and whether or not individual patients are up to date. Some health plans have also developed effective partnerships with state governments to promote childhood immunizations.

## How Is HEDIS Data Validated?

A sound audit program is one of the key elements for any database project. It will ensure that the data being input is consistent and meaningful. One of the main criticisms of the HEDIS database has been the lack of an audit program, not to mention the lack of audit standards. Although all MCOs that provide data use a detailed HEDIS technical specifications guide, methods and processes for obtaining data, individual interpretations of data, and potential for errors vary considerably from one MCO to the next. Also, because these data are self-reported and do not go through an independent, unbiased audit process, questions are raised regarding the integrity and usefulness of the HEDIS data.

To address these concerns, the NCQA set up an audit committee in 1996 to develop a precise audit methodology to verify both collection and calculation of HEDIS data for an MCO. This standard methodology is called the NCQA HEDIS Compliance Audit and consists of two parts. (The audit methodology can be purchased from the NCQA Publications Center or through a NCQA Certified Auditor program.)

The first part defines the information systems standards designed to assess the MCO system capabilities for collecting and extracting the required HEDIS data elements. These standards address the basic capabilities an MCO has in the place for collecting, sorting, analyzing, and reporting health information. For example, the organization must have the capability to process medical information for members and providers as a foundation for accurate HEDIS reporting. If the processes are not computerized, the organization must demonstrate the adequacy of its procedures, including its method for obtaining information from a medical record.

The second part defines steps to achieve compliance with HEDIS specification standards (HD standards). To begin, the auditor must have completed the information systems capabilities assessment. Once the auditor understands the MCO's information systems, he or she designs the appropriate verification audit steps for each of the specific HEDIS measures. Specifically, these measures include the following:

- Effectiveness of care
- Access/availability of care
- Satisfaction with the experience of care
- Health plan stability
- Cost of care
- Health plan descriptive information
- Use of services

To establish an unbiased, independent audit process, the NCQA licenses organizations and individuals as NCQA-certified auditors. Individuals must pass a qualifying exam developed specifically for certifying NCQA auditors before they obtain this designation. The auditor must then take the exam every two years to remain certified. The NCQA has also set up a process for monitoring its certified auditors by reviewing a portion of their audits each year.

An organization may also become licensed if it has a group of certified auditors. Both individuals and organizations are required to complete an application and pay a fee for certification.

NCQA-certified auditors use the NCQA HEDIS Compliance Audit methodology to assess the following areas in the information systems (IS) and HD categories:

1. Information practices and control procedures
2. Sampling methods and procedures
3. Data integrity
4. Compliance with HEDIS specifications
5. Analytic file production
6. Reporting and documentation

Although auditors do verify a small sample of HEDIS data for accuracy, the audit is designed to verify only the compliance with HEDIS-based processes and not to assess the overall accuracy of an MCO's data.

Currently, there are two types and three designations of certified HEDIS audits. An MCO can choose the first type, a partial audit, where a subset of HEDIS measurements is selected and audited. Or, it may request a full audit, the second type, where at least 15 HEDIS measurements are audited while the findings are extrapolated and applied to the remaining measurements.

When an audit is completed, a final report is drafted and provided one of these three designations: Report, Not Report, or Not Applicable. The NCQA defines these designations as follows:

- *Report.* The plan produced a reportable rate for the measurement (or a reportable denominator and numerator for a Medicaid measure where the denominator was less than 30). The plan followed the HEDIS technical specifications.

- *Not Report.* The plan did not calculate the measurement when a population existed for which the measurement could have been calculated. Or, the plan did the measurement but chose not to report the result. Or, the plan did the measurement but the result had significant bias according to the NCQA HEDIS Compliance Audit.
- *Not Applicable.* The measurement is not applicable to the particular population. Or, there was insufficient denominator population to support a reported rate. Or, the plan does not offer the benefit to the population.

## PART TWO: SOME CONCERNS

As with any project or initiative, especially one dealing with an industry as large and varied as healthcare, there are many critics of the current NCQA accreditation and HEDIS programs. In relation to the basic set of questions defined earlier, the following are some concerns with the current system.

### What Is Measured?

Although the areas and questions included in the HEDIS 1999 specifications are extensive, critics have concerns about whether the answers to these questions truly provide usable information for choosing a health plan. HEDIS is not completely relevant to all consumers. For example, critics cite as deficiencies of HEDIS 1999 the exclusion of such significant areas as pain management, cultural awareness, and infection control. Other critics state that because of the ever-changing and increasingly varied structure of the healthcare delivery system, measuring performance using only one set of questions is becoming increasingly difficult.

### Who Submits the Data and How Is the Quality of the Data Determined?

At the present time, participation in HEDIS is voluntary (although many state agencies are requiring it as a condition of participating in the Medicaid program). Although a significant number of health plans will submit data for HEDIS 1999, this number still represents only about half of the nation's health plans. Many regions of the country are experiencing an even smaller HEDIS compliance percentage for the plans available in their service area. Therefore, although HEDIS data is desired, it is unavailable for some purchasers.

In addition, criticism also arises because participation in the audit process is also only voluntary. This situation is being addressed, however, because in 1999, for the first time, the NCQA accreditation process required an NCQA-certified audit report with the submission of HEDIS data.

The most significant concern, however, involves questions about the quality of the submitted data. First, the NCQA does not require the submission of all HEDIS data elements. Therefore, plans can simply omit data for certain HEDIS measures if they are either unable or unwilling to include the data. Furthermore, plans can also choose to submit their data for NCQA to use only for the calculation of national and regional averages while preventing the release of this data for public use. As long as MCOs are allowed to exercise these options, the validity of the HEDIS data is compromised.

Lack of participation in HEDIS can be explained four ways. First, many health plans use managed care software systems that do not have the functionality to track HEDIS data elements. Second, some plans do not have the internal IS and healthcare expertise and resources to ensure accurate HEDIS submissions. Third, because some health plans have multiple computer systems, they do not have one computer-based database for recording and extracting the HEDIS-specific data. Fourth, while a patient's medical record is considered the most reliable and comprehensive source of much of the HEDIS data, most medical records today are still in paper format; and for this reason, chart auditing to obtain and submit HEDIS data is too complex and, therefore, not feasible.

If an MCO participates, it must rely on its claims or administrative systems for extracting HEDIS data. This situation presents other problems for submitters. First, there is a lack of standard procedure codes for some HEDIS-specific measurements. For example, claim coding for a mother's obstetrics services includes prenatal care, delivery, and postnatal care. Therefore, to track specifically whether there was prenatal care in the first trimester or a post delivery check-up is an impossible task using a claim-based submission process. Second, some medical services measured by HEDIS are not always submitted as claims. For example, some states offer vaccines to patients at no cost. In a case like this, a claim is never generated and submitted.

All of these problems affect the validity of HEDIS data. The greater the number and types of sources an MCO must use to submit the data, the more likely data integrity is to be compromised. As a result, and because the widespread of electronic medical records is still a few years away, critics feel that HEDIS should attempt only to measure services typically tracked in a typical MCO administrative system.

**Who Uses the Data?**

There are many employers who claim they use HEDIS data for helping them make their healthcare choice. However, these are almost all employers of very large populations. Smaller employers, who make up a significant portion of the NCQA audience for HEDIS, are not even aware of HEDIS or the NCQA. Furthermore, many of these employers use brokers for obtaining healthcare, and many of these brokers are also unaware of the existence of HEDIS. Those brokers who are aware of HEDIS cannot reasonably apply HEDIS results to each small company employer for whom they present healthcare choices.

There is also a question of the usefulness of HEDIS. A survey completed by the Washington Business Group on Health with Watson Wyatt Worldwide showed that only 37 percent of employers ask HMOs for HEDIS measures; and when employers rated HEDIS, only 25 percent found it very useful.

## CONCLUSION

There are problems existing in the NCQA current system, and the full potential of HEDIS has not yet been realized. Still, purchasers and consumers of healthcare services need to know the quality of health organizations. Purchasers need to know that these organizations compete with each other based on quality of service and not just cost of service. Without a process like NCQA accreditation and HEDIS performance measurements, decisions about healthcare plans are often left to chance.

## HOW DO I LEARN MORE ABOUT NCQA AND HEDIS?

NCQA and HEDIS have a very comprehensive Web site at www.ncqa.org, which will provide additional information. You can contact the NCQA if you have any questions or comments about its programs or activities at this address:

NCQA
2000 L Street, NW
Suite 500
Washington, D.C. 20036
Telephone: 202-955-3500
Fax: 202-955-3599

To order HEDIS 3.0 requirements, call the NCQA publications center at 800-839-6487. For information about NCQA conferences, call 202-955-5697.

### References

1. O'Kane, M.E. (personal communication).
2. Sennett, C. 1996. "An introduction to HEDIS," *Hospital Practice*, 31(15 June): 147.
3. Ullman, R. and Spoeri, R. K. 1997. "Measuring and reporting managed care performance: lessons learned and new initiatives," *Annals of Internal Medicine,* 127(15 Oct.): 726.
4. Greene, J. 1998. "Blue skies or black eyes? HEDIS puts not-for-profit plans top," *Hospitals and Health Networks*, 72 (20 April): 26.
5. Schwartz, M. P. 1995. "As HEDIS develops, so too must interpretations," *National Underwriter Life and Health,* Financial Services Edition (10 April): 2.
6. Bell, A. 1996. "Draft of new HMO standards," *National Underwriter Property and Casualty: Risk and Benefits Management*, 15 July: 16.
7. Stoil, M. J. 1996. "HEDIS over heels?" *Behavioral Health Management,* 16 (Sept./Oct.): 4.
8. NCQA Web site: www.ncqa.org.
9. Partridge, L. 1997. *Performance Measurement in Medicaid Managed Care: States' Adoption of HEDIS*. Princeton: Center for Health Care Strategies.

# Chapter 16
# Understanding and Implementing Computerized Physician Order Entry

*J. Marc Overhage, M.D., Ph.D.*

Look in many doctor's pockets and you will find a large-barreled, expensive fountain pen. They carry these pens because they spend much of their day writing — writing notes and writing orders. Physicians' orders result in diagnostic tests, treatments, and other things needed for the care of their patients. Traditionally, they write these orders on order sheets in the patient's chart and then, through a complex sequence of steps involving several individuals and a considerable amount of time, these orders are communicated to the various departments and service areas that implement these orders. A second set of processes then assures that no orders are missed and that all of them are accomplished as the ordering doctor intended.

## DEFINITIONS: WHAT IS CPOE?

Computerized Physician Order Entry (CPOE) is simply a system for direct entry of patient care orders by a physician into a [computer] system.[1] Sometimes, these systems are referred to as "Computerized Provider Order Entry" because physician assistants, nurse practitioners, dentists, podiatrists, and pharmacists all write orders as well. CPOE is often thought of in the context of inpatient care but it has also been implemented in outpatient settings and a few emergency departments and nursing homes.

**BRIEF HISTORY OF CPOE**

In 1970, Morris Collen identified CPOE as an essential component of a clinical information system and recommended that physicians enter the orders directly. Technicon (commonly referred to as the TDS system) developed one of the earliest commercial systems. Many TDS clients are still using this early system. Academic medical informatics programs have been responsible for much of the advancement of clinical decision support in CPOE. The Regenstrief Institute for Health Care in Indianapolis, Indiana, and the program at Intermountain Healthcare's LDS hospital in Utah were among the earliest to develop and test the effectiveness of CPOE systems. Investigators at the Regenstrief Institute published several studies about the effects of CPOE in the outpatient setting[2-4] as well as the first randomized controlled trial to examine inpatient order entry in which they demonstrated reduced charges, decreased length of stay, and some evidence that care was improved. Investigators at IHC demonstrated improved use of blood products as a result of an order entry system they developed for blood products.[5] Other academic programs have also made contributions in this area. In the 1990s, the Brigham and Women's Hospital in Boston demonstrated reduced medication costs and significantly reduced adverse drug events.[6,7]

**DESCRIPTION OF MODERN CPOE SYSTEMS**

**Technology Platforms**

CPOE has been implemented on nearly every technology platform imaginable. Many user interfaces are character based, but more recent products are based on the Microsoft Windows platform. A few have even been developed using a Web interface. CPOE is available on nearly every kind of hardware, from mainframes to midrange servers, personal computers, and handheld computers. Successful examples of each of these interfaces can be found on each of their platforms, with the possible exception of handhelds.

**Relationship to Other Healthcare Information Systems**

CPOE is usually integrated with a collection of other clinical information system components such as a clinical data repositories, clinical decision support systems, laboratory systems, or pharmacy systems. The degree of integration can vary from being part of a monolithic software program to a very loosely coupled arrangement in which orders are passed to other systems using standard message structures such as HL7. Order entry itself can be subdivided further into order creation and order management. Order creation includes the process of creating, modifying, or discontinuing orders while order management includes processes related to order routing, maintaining a profile of a patient's

Care Processes

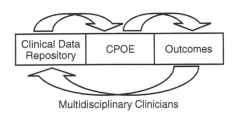

**Exhibit 1. CPOE: A Component of the Overall Care Process**

---

orders, and reporting. These functions are often combined in a single program but this is not essential (see Exhibit 1).

## Functionality

The basic functions a CPOE system can provide include:

- Order creation, modification, and discontinuation
- Order dictionary management
- Management of a patient's order profile
- Order routing to various departments and programs that carry them out
- Reporting and summarization

Order Creation, Modification, and Discontinuation.Creation, modification, and discontinuation of orders are the core functional ties that any order entry system must provide. In its most basic form, order creation involves creating a new transaction or record that specifies who the patient is, what item is being ordered and the details related to that item, when it was ordered, from where it was ordered, and by whom. This simple view belies the difficulties inherent in the process. There are at least four major difficulties that a CPOE system must overcome.

First, the user has to select the patient. This sounds easy until you try to find the right patient out of the several million who may be registered in an order entry system. Names are inadequate. The user needs to review additional demographic data such as date of birth, medical record number, or social security number in order to identify the correct patient. Ideally, the system assists the user in selecting the correct patient by displaying a list of patients the user is likely to use — those scheduled to see them in the office that day or the patients in the ward where the device and the logged-in user are located. Selecting the wrong patient is one of the most common errors seen in order entry. Undoing or voiding an order entered for the wrong patient in an order entry system can be much more difficult than in a paper-based system because the order is so widely distributed before the mistake is recognized. Whereas in the paper system it is difficult to write orders for a patient who is not in close physical proximity (the Sam Jones on ward C4 is very likely, but not certainly, the Jones whose room the provider just waked out of), and there are long lag times during which the mistake can be recognized.

Second, the user has to select the item to be ordered. The challenge here is primarily the "pick from thousands" problem. Because there are thousands of drugs, thousands of tests, hundreds of nursing interventions, and many, many other things that can be ordered, it can be difficult for users to find the item they want to order. Drop-down choice lists are not good tools for selecting from so many items. Most CPOE systems rely on partial name look-up to find the item to be ordered. A variety of tricks can be used to make this easier. These include choice lists of commonly ordered items, mechanisms to limit the scope to specific domains such as radiology tests or medications, and personal favorites.

Third, the items to be ordered have to be properly conceptualized. Medications, for example, have to be conceptualized at the level of clinical use such as sustained release verapamil (a calcium channel blocking drug in a dosage form that releases the drug slowly into the body) rather than as a specific product such as Calan SR 120 mg tablets. Medications and laboratory tests are easier to conceptualize at the proper level than nursing and other orders. Activity level could be represented as a single concept that would require the user to specify the details such as bed rest, but this level of granularity may make communication between the user and those who have to carry out the order more difficult. In addition, decision support systems will not be able to determine that the patient is at bed rest and cannot remind the user that the patient is a candidate for heparin prophylaxis to reduce the risk of DVTs.

Fourth, the details required to specify each orderable item are unique, which makes creating a user interface challenging. The common first-pass solution is to specify a list of fields that the user must enter data for in order to complete the order. This approach uniformly fails! It fails both because it is too tedious and cumbersome to be usable and because there are so many variants that users become confused and never become proficient.

Order Dictionary Management.A typical CPOE system will maintain a dictionary or catalog containing on the order of 10,000 orderable items. The system requires a wide variety of information about each orderable item, such as the department that provides the service, what details are required, whether a medication is a DEA Schedule III drug, and what other synonyms or alternate names might be used to identify the orderable item. Managing this dictionary of items and associated data is a very important function of a CPOE system.

Management of a Patient's Order Profile.After order creation, management of a patient's order profile is the most important function a CPOE system provides. As orders are created, modified, and discontinued, the system must maintain a profile or list of the patient's current orders. It must also manage conflict resolution. That is, the system must manage multiple users entering orders for the same patient. Some systems solve this problem by allowing only one user to write orders for a specific patient at one time. Others provide feedback to users about potential conflicts (for example, "You just wrote an order for verapamil SR but user 1123–9 discontinued verapamil SR while you were writing orders") and provide options for the users to cancel their order or overwrite the other user's orders.

Other profile management functions include expiring orders that have a defined lifetime (Benadryl 25 mg PO 1x only now for itching), prompting the user to renew expiring orders (Narcotic analgesic medications expire after 72 hours. Renew the order for morphine SR if still needed) and integration of multiple order profiles (Patient was discharged from Community Hospital East 08-Aug-02 and has discharge orders. Choose discharge orders to integrate them with the patient's profile or to replace the patient's current profile.).

Order Routing to Various Departments and Programs that Carry Them Out.Some of the earliest and even some current commercial CPOE systems are primarily order communication systems rather than order entry systems. Automating the communication of orders from the patient's location (hospital ward, for example) to the department that provides the services (transportation and radiology, for example) is a key benefit of CPOE. Depending on the scope, this function can be simple or very challenging. In a small hospital where all laboratory tests get routed through a central laboratory, it is fairly easy to send the orders for a laboratory test (this is an attribute of the orderable item that has to be stored in the order dictionary) to the laboratory, and even to transfer these orders electronically to the laboratory system. In an outpatient setting, this routing may be much more difficult because the specimen may need to go to one of several different laboratories, or the test might be performed in the office; the patient may get a specimen drawn in the office or at a laboratory draw site and different requisition forms may be required.

Reporting and Summarization.There are a variety of needs for reporting and summarization of orders. In the inpatient setting, for example, nursing staff may want to print a report summarizing the patient's order profile in order to ensure that all of the orders are being carried out or to carry with them as a quick reference. Departments or programs responsible for specific functions or orders may need reports of patients for which relevant services have been ordered and organized by location or in other ways. A smoking cessation counselor in a hospital might obtain a list of all patients who have an order for smoking cessation counseling organized by hospital ward, starting on the highest floor and descending to the lowest floor.

Decision Support.One of the key benefits from CPOE is the potential to provide clinical decision support at the point of care. Some CPOE systems provide basic decision support, such as:

- Drug allergy checking
- Drug duplication checking
- Cost or charge information

Advanced decision support is provided by some systems in the form of:

- Drug lab interaction checking
- Drug disease checking
- Guidelines/care pathways
- Formulary management
- Automatic suggestions for medication dosage calculations based on age, sex, weight, lab values, etc.

Usability.Response time is probably the most important factor that determines whether users, particularly physicians, will use a particular CPOE system. Moving from one step to the next, or one screen to the next, must occur at sub-second speed. Providers will become expert users and readily sacrifice ease of use for speed. Another very important determinate of usability is whether users can understand how to complete the task they need to get done. They must be able to guess how to order a medication or place an activity restriction.

One example is how to order a Purified Protein Derivative (PPD) test for tuberculosis. Many users will think of this as a nursing order, others as a test, and yet others as a medication order. In fact, all of these conceptualizations are correct — the PPD is a test done by nursing using a medication that has to be obtained from the pharmacy. A usable CPOE system will help the user discover how to properly place a PPD order by allowing them to place it as a medication order, a nursing order or as a test, or by directing the user to the proper category if the user tries to order it under the wrong category.

## RATIONALE FOR IMPLEMENTING CPOE

CPOE offers several advantages over traditional paper-based systems, including process improvements, improved resource utilization, and clinical decision support. First, CPOE improves the process of order writing by generating legible orders that require less clarification. The order workflow is streamlined by eliminating valueless steps such as order transcription. Second, CPOE can improve resource utilization by modifying provider ordering. Studies have shown reductions in charges after the implementation of CPOE systems. These savings result from a variety of features, including faster administration of medication, more effective monitoring, more appropriate test and medication choices, and reduced redundancy. Third, perhaps the most important advantage of CPOE over paper systems is the ability to provide clinical decision support at the time of ordering. Meta-analysis of recent published studies has convincingly shown that these systems with clinical decision support are able to improve physician performance in both the inpatient and outpatient settings.[8-10]

For all its potential, CPOE carries some risks. CPOE can introduce new errors. For example, in one study, errors related to the administration of potassium increased due to an unfortunate structuring of the potassium order details.[11] In addition, CPOE systems can mask errors; orders created using the system "look" correct and may go unchallenged for example.

## IMPLEMENTATION

Despite strong evidence that CPOE can reduce resource utilization and improve quality, there are only a few examples of successful implementations. One survey indicated that, although 32 percent of the hospitals had some form of order entry, only 6 percent overall had at least 50 percent usage by physicians.[12]

The benefit of CPOE to the individual physician is primarily that his or her patients will get better care, more efficiently, but at the cost of the physician changing how he does his work, and probably, taking longer to do it. In addition, most physicians practice in a variety of care settings — their office, the nursing home, and frequently more than one hospital. If only one of these settings has CPOE, the physician has to work differently in that setting than in others. Worse yet, these settings may have different CPOE systems, thus requiring the physician to learn multiple user IDs and passwords, user interfaces, order vocabularies, and workflows. The implementation challenge may be increased even further when the physician has limited contact in the care setting where CPOE is implemented. Imagine a community-based pediatrician who, once or twice a month, cares for a newborn at a hospital across town.

To date, no one has identified a formula for successfully implementing CPOE, but a few critical areas have emerged. First, management is very important. The organization's senior leadership must be fully committed to the project's success and must have realistic expectations about the benefits that will result. In addition, a strong clinical leader almost always plays a central role. Strong continuity of this leadership is also critical. Second, while return on investment analyses are difficult, CPOE systems must demonstrate value. This is important not only at an organizational level, but also at the user level. If a CPOE system solves a user's problem, the user will be grateful for several weeks. If, on the other hand, a CPOE system creates a problem for a user, that user will never forget it. The system must show value again and again. Third, processes will almost always have to be reengineered. In fact, processes should be reengineered before implementing CPOE. If reengineering is done at the same time as CPOE implementation, the system is often "blamed" for the change; and if they are not changed, a sub-optimal process will be automated, which is an even bigger mistake. Fourth, it is almost impossible to get all the configuration and processes right to begin with. Ongoing modifications and refinements to the system will be required. Fifth, the focus has to continually be on solving real problems that the organization faces rather than on broad, nebulous goals.

Finally, it is almost impossible for physicians to complete. Successful CPOE implementations requires "help at the elbow" or on-the-spot training to identify problems, help users overcome barriers, and refine processes. When mainframe computers were introduced, the hardware accounted for most of the cost, the software a smaller component, and implementation was almost unnecessary. In today's environment, hardware is free, software is expensive, and implementation is very costly. This is money well spent — without it, a CPOE system will not provide the value it should.

## RESOURCES

Sittig and Stead provide an outstanding summary of the state-of-the-art of CPOE which, while written in 1994, still provides many valuable insights.[13] The Computer Based Patient Records Institute Nicholas Davies Award (http://www.cpri-host.org/davies/index.html) conference proceedings are a good source of additional information about CPOE. The Davies Award winners provide detailed descriptions with good insights into their local implementation. The American Medical Informatics Association Annual Fall Symposium (http://www.amia.org) proceedings include many important papers that describe lessons learned about implementing CPOE in addition to providing insight into essential functionality and characteristics. Other meetings that focus on computer-based patient records often include material on CPOE.

### References

AHA Guide to Computerized Physician Order Entry Systems, White Paper. Chicago, IL: American Hospital Association, 2000.

Tierney, W.M., Miller, M.E., and McDonald, C.J., The effect on test ordering of informing physicians of the charges for outpatient diagnostic tests, *New Engl. J. Med.,* 322(21), 1499–1504, 1990.

Tierney, W.M., McDonald, C.J., Hui, S.L., and Martin, D.K., Computer predictions of abnormal test results. Effects on outpatient testing, *J. Am. Chem. Soc.,* 259(8,: 1194–1198, 1988.

Tierney, W.M., McDonald, C.J., Martin, D.K., and Rogers, M.P., Computerized display of past test results. Effect on outpatient testing, *Ann. Intern. Med.,* 107(4), 569–574, 1987.

Lepage, E.F., Gardner, R.M., Laub, R.M., and Jacobson, J.T., Assessing the effectiveness of a computerized blood order "consultation" system, *Proceedings — The Annual Symposium on Computer Applications in Medical Care,* 33–7, 1991.

Bates, D.W., Leape, L.L., Cullen, D.J., et al., Effect of computerized physician order entry and a team intervention on prevention of serious medication errors, *J. Am. Chem. Soc.,* 280(15), 1311–1316, 1998.

Bates, D.W., Miller, E.B., Cullen, D.J., et al., Patient risk factors for adverse drug events in hospitalized patients, *Arch. Intern. Med.,* 159, 2553–2660, 1999.

Bates, D.W., Cohen, M., Leape, L.L., et al., Reducing the frequency of errors in medicine using information technology, *J. Am. Med. Inform. Assoc.,* 8, 299–308, 2001.

Teich, J.M. and Wrinn, M.M., Clinical decision support systems come of age, *MD Comput..,* 17(1), 43–46; 49(10), 938–943, 2000.

Hunt, D.L., Haynes, R.B., Hanna, S.E., and Smith, K., Effects of computer-based clinical decision support systems on physician performance and patient outcomes: a systematic review, *J. Am. Chem. Soc.,* 280(15), 1339–1346, 1998.

Bates, D.W., Cullen, D.J., Laird, N., et al., Incidence of adverse drug events and potential adverse drug events: implications for prevention. ADE Prevention Study Group, *J. Am. Chem. Soc.,* 274 (1), 29–34, 1995.

Ash, J.S., Gorman, P.N., Hersh, W.R., Lavelle, M., and Poulsen, S.B., Perceptions of house officers who use physician order entry, *Proc. AMIA Symp.,* 1999, 471–475.

Sittig, D.F. and Stead, W.W., Computer-based physician order entry: the state of the art, *J. Am. Med. Informatics Assoc.,* 1,108–123, 1994.

# Chapter 17
# Clinical Decision Support Systems

*Eneida A. Mendonça*
*Robert Jenders*
*Yves A. Lussier*

Imagine a situation: A patient goes to the doctor with symptoms that are causing discomfort. The physician will talk to the patient and perform a physical examination to identify the cause of the symptoms. She also will consult the patient's history as recorded in an electronic medical record. She thinks that one of several diseases may explain this patient's history and examination findings, but she is not certain. Moreover, she has never actually treated a case of a few of these possibilities. To improve her knowledge and help identify the disease, the physician uses an electronic consultation system, into which she enters the initial clinical findings and which provides suggestions regarding diagnoses and diagnostic tests to order.

In an attempt to identify the correct diagnosis, the physician orders some tests. Subsequently, the laboratory reports the results of one of the tests. Another software application, monitoring the transmission of results to the electronic medical record used by the physician, detects that the results may represent a dangerous condition that requires urgent action. The system then pages the physician. However, the physician, uncertain of the significance of the results, looks up medical journal articles and chapters in electronic textbooks in order to refresh her knowledge. Using the test results, the physician identifies the likely diagnosis and, using a clinician order entry application, prescribes a new medication. However, the application detects a potential interaction with a medication that the patient already takes and warns the physician at the time of prescribing, allowing safe selection of an alternative drug and initiation of appropriate therapy.

These events — reviewing data organized in an electronic medical record, using a consultation application, alerting regarding abnormal laboratory tests, reading electronic textbooks, using bibliographic knowledge bases and warnings regarding potential adverse drug events — all represent types of clinical decision support. Considering the massive volume of published medical research — over two million articles a year in over 20,000 journals[1] — no individual can amass or stay entirely abreast of all medical knowledge. Moreover, the amount of clinical information that a physician must track for every patient (i.e., demographic data, medical problems, allergies, medications, test results, and more) compounds the problem. Ensuring patient safety requires attention both to general medical knowledge and patient-specific data. Indeed, preventable medical errors may cause 44,000 to 96,000 deaths a year in the United States and cost $29 billion.[2]

Employed to address these problems, clinical decision support systems (CDSS) are software applications that use embedded clinical knowledge to help physicians process patient data and make decisions regarding diagnosis, prevention, and treatment of disease. They may be stand-alone systems, or they may interact with other tools such as an electronic medical record or a clinician order entry system. They may provide a list of journal articles or general medical knowledge, or they may deliver a recommendation for action tailored to the circumstances of a specific patient. They may generate alerts regarding potentially dangerous conditions for a patient, or they may remind clinicians to perform routine tasks such as immunization. Not all clinical decision support is provided by computer-based applications; manual techniques, such as written reminders based on chart reviews, have been employed. However, this chapter focuses on computer-based CDSS. In exploring this topic, this chapter reviews the history of CDSS, describes the various types of systems, discusses how CDSS acquire medical knowledge, explores how that knowledge may be represented in the system, and identifies future trends.

## HISTORY OF CDSS

Work on computer-based CDSS dates to the 1950s and focused initially on the development of diagnostic systems.[3] Early systems can be classified into three generic categories: neural and belief networks, probabilistic, and logical/deductive (rule-based). In addition, hybrid systems use more than one generic CDSS category. Neural and belief networks are algorithms that require training a set of solutions to a problem and that can make decisions on new problems with incomplete facts. They are commonly used in biomedical pattern recognition. Probabilistic systems incorporate rates of disease in a population and likelihood of various clinical findings in order to calculate the most likely explanation for a particular clinical case. These systems typically employ Bayes' rule: a mathematical formula that accounts for the prevalence of disease in a population and the characteristics of a particular patient to calculate the probability that a particular patient has a particular disease. Logical/deductive systems use branching logic, a collection of if-then rules, to make decisions. Hybrid systems use features of several or all the previously described systems, along with heuristics or "rules of thumb" to assist clinicians in making decisions.

Neural networks (NNs) were first invented in the 1940s[4] as a biological model of the brain. The NN methodologies have been particularly successful for narrowly well-defined clinical problems such as classifying textual output of images,[5] diagnosis support,[6-8] and prognosis evaluation.[9,10] For such specific problems, NN models are economical and can be modified, trained, and fine-tuned to obtain competitive accuracies. In additional, NNs have also been commercialized for image recognition (automated image analysis systems), and are found in uterus cervix cytology labs.[11]

While the advantage of probabilistic systems is that their output reflects the relative likelihood of diagnosis or success of treatment, they may be limited by the fact that the necessary probabilities either are not known or are derived from a population at least somewhat different than the patient in a particular case. On the other hand, while the if-then rules of a logical/deductive system allow representation of the branching questions used by experts to make clinical decisions, they may overemphasize certain diseases if they are not adjusted for the rarity or prevalence of particular diseases. Hybrid systems attempt to overcome these drawbacks by combining both deductive rules and probabilistic reasoning in the same CDSS.

One of the earliest examples of a successfully used probabilistic system, tested in emergency departments in the United Kingdom between 1969 and 1974, was a CDSS created by de Dombal and colleagues that diagnosed the cause of abdominal pain. Noteworthy early logical/deductive systems include Bleich's software that diagnosed acid-base disorders and Shortliffe's system MYCIN. The latter system suggested both diagnoses and treatments of bloodstream infections and meningitis. Finally, work on hybrid systems dates to HEME, a system used to diagnose blood diseases in 1950s. Perhaps the best-known hybrid systems are the general medical consultation systems QMR (1985), DXplain (1986), and Iliad (1987).

More recent work has focused on integration of CDSS with clinical databases. These integrated systems take advantage of data already recorded for other purposes in order to avoid redundant data entry in the provision of alerts and reminders. These CDSS may monitor data in a large healthcare organization or may be part of an electronic medical record installed in a single medical office.

## TYPES OF SYSTEMS

The basic components of a CDSS are identified in Exhibit 1. The core of any such system is the inference engine (IE). The IE applies knowledge of

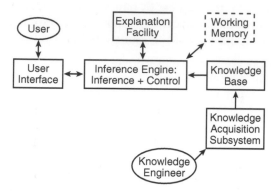

**Exhibit 1. Elements of a Typical CDSS**

clinical medicine represented in the knowledge base against a collection of data regarding individual patients. This data may include demographic details (date of birth, sex, etc.), laboratory test results, medication prescriptions, allergies, a list of the patient's medical problems, and other information. Data may exist in the form of messages or be represented in a clinical database, collectively known as "working memory." The inference engine uses knowledge of medicine and knowledge of the patient to draw conclusions, some of which may require other actions, such as notification of a clinical decision maker. The inference engine also performs control features of the system, such as determining the route of alerts and reminders based on the urgency of a condition.

The formalism used to represent knowledge in the knowledge base (KB) of the CDSS may take one of a variety of forms. In the typical situation, a knowledge engineer familiar with the CDSS and the kinds of clinical data available to it works with a clinical domain expert and some type of knowledge acquisition (KA) software to create, edit, and maintain the KB. The CDSS uses an explanation facility to compose justifications for conclusions drawn by the IE in applying the knowledge in the KB against patient data in the working memory. The CDSS can communicate with the user through a variety of mechanisms, including e-mail, fax, pager, and messages posted to an electronic medical record, all managed through the user interface (UI) of the CDSS.

A CDSS can operate in synchronous or asynchronous mode. In synchronous mode, the CDSS is communicating directly with a clinical user who is waiting for the output of the system. A typical example of synchronous decision support is checking physician medication orders written using an order-entry system for drug–drug interactions or to ensure that the patient has no known allergy to the prescribed medication before the order is finalized by that system. In asynchronous mode, the

CDSS performs its reasoning independent of any clinician awaiting its output. An example of this processing mode is the generation of a reminder to perform a periodic screening test, such as mammography.

Another way to characterize CDSS is by the degree to which a human decision maker mediates any action recommended by the system. In an open-loop system, the CDSS draws conclusions but takes no action directly on its own. Instead, it transmits its recommendation in the form of an alert or reminder to a clinician. The clinician then must assess that information and decide what action, if any, to take. The action may include ordering a treatment, performing a test, or gathering additional information. In a closed-loop system, the CDSS can implement action directly without the intervention of a human decision maker. For example, a CDSS can monitor the parameters of a respirator that is breathing for a patient. Based on sensors within the device and applied to the patient, the CDSS may conclude that different settings would improve the patient's respiration. In part because of the potential risks to the patient that such software may pose, closed-loop systems are not common. However, data does suggest that systems such as respiratory monitors may prove useful.[12]

While no quantitative survey of the numbers or kinds of CDSS in use has been published, the most common kind of system seems to be the event monitor. This is software that receives copies of all data available in electronic format in an institution and uses its knowledge base — usually a collection of deductive rules — to send alerts and reminders to clinicians when deemed appropriate.[13] This kind of "intelligent assistant" attempts to use data already captured for other purposes to advise clinicians instead of entirely replacing their judgment. Typical alerts and reminders include warnings regarding interactions between medications, suggestions to order screening tests such as mammograms, and messages regarding laboratory results that may suggest the presence of a disease or worsening condition. This model typifies the development of clinical decision support at academic medical centers (such as LDS Hospital, the University of Pittsburgh, and Columbia-Presbyterian Medical Center, among others) and has been incorporated into the decision support functions of electronic medical record software supplied by commercial vendors.[14] In addition to event monitors, another major kind of CDSS is the consultation system. Archetypes of this class of CDSS are DXplain, QMR, and Iliad.[3] To use such a system, a clinician will enter details of a case — patient demographic information, clinical history, physical examination findings, and test results — into the system. The CDSS, in turn, will provide a list of diseases that may explain the case and may suggest which tests might be useful in narrowing the list of possible explanations.

With emphasis on prevention of medical error and encouraging best medical practice, increasing emphasis has been placed on clinical guidelines.[15] Clinical guidelines, typically developed by groups of clinical experts and promulgated by the government or by professional organizations, represent a formal statement of recommended practice with regard to diagnosing or treating a particular medical condition. Workers who develop CDSS have been devising ways to incorporate guidelines into CDSS so that the advice provided by a system can represent the best medical evidence available. As an outgrowth of this effort, researchers are devising standard forms of knowledge representation so that the KBs that include clinical guidelines may be shared widely with minimum adaptation or rewriting required. Efforts include a standard formalism such as the Arden Syntax[16] and emerging standards such as the Guideline Interchange Format.[17] This effort to improve knowledge shareability will be an active area of research in the coming years, and this research will contribute to the utility of CDSS.

## KNOWLEDGE ENGINEERING

CDSS are systems comprising some form of knowledge and mechanisms to generate a solution when presented with a clinical input/problem. Domain experts, such as biologists or clinicians, interact with software analysts and programmers to develop such systems. These knowledge base software development experts are referred to as *knowledge engineers*. The *knowledge engineering* process is tightly related to the form of artificial intelligence employed to capture, represent, and reuse the knowledge. For example, software engineers "train" a neural network using different sets of problems represented as inputs to the system and "test" the output against curated gold standards. They compare different mathematical models of neural networks in order to optimize the system's performance. In the case of probabilistic or logical/deductive systems, the knowledge engineering process is fundamentally different and consists of three steps:

1. *Knowledge acquisition:* the extraction of knowledge from journals, books, and the minds of domain experts in a reusable form.
2. *Knowledge representation:* the translation of the acquired knowledge into a computable form.
3. *Knowledge optimization and testing:* the fine-tuning of a knowledge base destined to be used by a decision support system.

The remainder of the chapter focuses on the first two steps of the knowledge engineering process: acquisition and representation.

## KNOWLEDGE ACQUISITION

The first phase of knowledge engineering consists of harvesting the knowledge from an expert source (domain experts, books, journal articles, etc.). This knowledge is collected and stored in natural language; this is the knowledge acquisition process that precedes the formal representation in a declarative language. Acquired knowledge is usually articulated in *tacit natural language* or *domain-specific symbolic language*. Therefore, a knowledge engineer must understand enough about a domain to elicit knowledge from domain experts. This knowledge would otherwise remain subconscious and ignored or buried in inextricable implicit statements. In addition, the knowledge engineer must represent and test the knowledge base as well as master the computational principles of ontology.

Creators of knowledge bases focus on their content and structure to such a degree that many knowledge bases also require the use of taxonomy, and, in the long run, *high-level concepts*. The latter is referred to as *ontological engineering*. Visibly, this collection of skills is not acquired from any single undergraduate degree; thus, first-class knowledge engineers are usually trained in multiple disciplines via additional degrees or a unique mentorship. This section first describes the task of knowledge acquisition (KA) and then provides examples from the biomedical domain that illustrate the methods and skills sets required to build a knowledge base.

Here are steps that help understand the methodology used by knowledge engineers to acquire knowledge (knowledge representation issues have been relegated to the next section):

1. *Problem(s) to solve.* As a preliminary step, characterizing the problems and insuring that CDSS can reasonably solve the problem(s) are also crucial. For example, consider a CDSS that will assist a clinician to choose the most appropriate medications for patients having a history of myocardial infarction (heart attack). Because the solution comprises dozens of different medications for which the therapeutic indications may change over time (as new medications enter the market or new studies modify the former indications of medications), this is an example where solving the problem with a *declarative CDSS* appears more maintainable than alternate approaches, such as neural networks or a *procedural* programming language.

2. *Specific domain of interest for the knowledge.* While identifying the domain for the knowledge to be acquired seems obvious, there are examples of projects that failed because they acquired the essential knowledge of a sub-domain that incompletely solves the generic problem of interest.[18] From our previous example, acquiring the knowledge pertaining to the "indications" of each medication would be sufficient to derive a list of medications for a specific patient. Unfortunately, it would not provide the best choices to assist clinicians because it omits knowledge of contraindications of each drug — reasons why the drug should not be prescribed. These include interactions with other drugs that the patient already is taking and interactions with diseases that the patient may have that can wors-

en his or her condition. Thus, the domains in which we need to acquire knowledge span both the indications and contraindications of the medications.

3. *Style and granularity of the intended representation.* Because the knowledge of the expert must be translated into a computable form, the knowledge engineer must choose a declarative language in which to represent the knowledge. More importantly, he or she will subsequently reduce knowledge in chunks of predicates, axioms, functions, constants, concepts, vocabulary, and other essential computable components of knowledge bases using this language. Without prior knowledge of the representation, acquiring the knowledge can be severely impacted. Indeed, the breadth and depth of the knowledge acquired must be coordinated with the granularity for the intended representations. A mismatch where the knowledge acquired is superficial as compared to the granularity of the representation leads to a flawed or incomplete knowledge base, whereas the reverse leads to unwarranted efforts spent characterizing useless knowledge in an already resource-intensive process. In addition, as with any language, there are many styles of editing for the same representation language, and some ingenious redaction styles can be clearer or more efficient than others. Thus, choosing the granularity is usually coupled with representation choices on the language as well as the style of representation schema.

4. *Acquisition of knowledge, per se.* As previously described, knowledge sources vary, from textbooks, to journal articles, to domain experts. Techniques involving biomedical domain experts are described in depth by Kushniruk and Patel and include interviews, computer-based interactive techniques, rating and sorting tasks, protocol analysis, and cognitive task analysis. Because this step is the most resource intensive of the entire knowledge engineering process and often of the entire development of a decision support system, readers are encouraged to explore the topic further or train with knowledge engineers before engaging in knowledge acquisition endeavors.

5. *Acquired knowledge analysis and validation.* The acquired knowledge is usually stored in textual form, ordered, and maintained in a form that can be related to its future representation in the declarative language (formally, represented knowledge). This allows the knowledge engineer and expert source to analyze the text, identify concepts expressed in natural language, and render their implicit relationships explicit in a process called conceptual analysis,[19] which produces declarative knowledge. In addition, knowledge engineers extract procedural knowledge: how one reasons with the declarative knowledge.[20] This can be followed by the validation of the actual knowledge acquired against the expert source(s) for completeness, consistency, clarity, and correctness.[18]

While the knowledge acquisition process is usually described as occurring prior to knowledge representation, in practice, these steps are intimately woven together. Indeed, domain experts such as clinicians have been trained in knowledge engineering to kick off the initial development of large clinical knowledge bases[21,22] and singly develop the initial knowledge content as domain experts and knowledge engineers. During the knowledge acquisition phases of Purkinje[22] and SNOMED-RT, these initial efforts led to the identification of the best knowledge engineers, refinement of the original work product with the "best-of-breed," and eventually to a proper separation of tasks between domain experts and knowledge engineers. Additional information on knowledge acquisition can be found in the ISO SC32 project on Conceptual Schema Modeling Facilities (CSMF) that is developing standards for appropriate languages and tools.[19]

## KNOWLEDGE REPRESENTATION TECHNIQUES

Newell and Simon[23] describe intelligent activity through the use of three mechanisms: (1) symbol patterns to represent significant aspects of a problem domain, (2) operations on these patterns to generate potential solutions to problems, and (3) search to select a solution from among these possibilities. These mechanisms are the interrelated issues of knowledge representation and search; together, they are the center of research in artificial Intelligence (AI).[24]

The foundation of AI is multidisciplinary: it inherits ideas and techniques from other disciplines such as philosophy, psychology, mathematics, linguistics, and computer science. From philosophy, AI takes advantage of the theories of reasoning and learning. From mathematics, it uses formal theories of logic, probability, decision-making, and computation. The investigation of the human mind comes from psychology, and the theories of structure and meaning of language from linguistics. Finally, from computer science, AI uses the data structures, algorithms, programming techniques, and tools needed for the implementation of automated processes.

Knowledge representation studies how to convert knowledge to a form with which a computer can reason. It studies the conceptual symbols and the structures for arranging these symbols in meaningful ways. Much of the initial work in knowledge representation was tied to language and the connection between the language and the reasoning mechanism that goes with it.[18] In building a knowledge base, it is necessary to think about the significant objects and relations in the domain and mapping them to a formal language. Various representation schemas have been proposed and implemented, each having its own strengths and weaknesses.[24] Minsky[25] defends the position that, to solve really difficult problems, we need to use several different representations, because no single representation by itself seems to be adequate for all the different functions involved in representing a particular domain. The various schemas have been classified into four categories: logical, procedural, network, and structured representation.[26]

Logical representation schemas use expressions in formal logic to represent a knowledge base. Inference rules and proof procedures apply this knowledge to problem instances. First-order predicate calculus is the most widely used logical representation. One virtue of logic is clarity — its lack of ambiguity. Another advantage is the preexistence of technical theories about logic. But logic is limited. Logical generalizations only apply to their literal lexical instances, and logical implications only apply to expressions that precisely instantiate their conditions.[25] This representation is not suitable for complex domains, where one has to deal with gray scales, uncertainties, and fuzzy variables.

Procedural schemas represent knowledge as a set of instructions for solving a problem. Instructions may be of type "if-then," for example, and may be interpreted as a procedure for solving a goal in a problem domain. In an if-then rule, whenever a description of the current problem precisely matches the rule's antecedent "if" condition, an action is performed based on this rule's "then" consequent. In contrast, declarative schemas use rules that are appropriate for representing logical implications or for associating actions with conditions under which the actions should be taken.[27] This approach usually works very well for small, simple algorithms and has the advantage of being easily understood by experts. Whenever the system gets complex, and more and more rules accumulate, problems can occur. Each added rule is increasingly likely to interact in unexpected ways with the others. Another disadvantage of rules is the difficulty representing uncertainty. The General Problem Solver[28] and DENDRAL[29] are examples of the use of production rules.

Neural and belief network representations capture the knowledge as a graph in which the nodes represent objects or concepts in the problem domain and the arcs represent relations or associations between them. Examples include semantic networks, conceptual dependencies, and conceptual graphs. This approach can represent relationships between concepts even in a complex domain. It can handle abstraction mechanisms as generalization and specialization, aggregation, and association. Sowa's[30] research in conceptual graphs illustrates the work in network representations.

Structure schemas extend network representations by allowing each node to be a complex structure. This structure may consist of named slots with attached values. Examples include scripts, frames, and objects. This approach is appropriate for defining terms and describing objects. If well defined, this type of representation has the capability of inferring the class/membership relations between frames based on their definitions. Minsky's[31] work provides an example of frames and their use in reasoning, and Schank's[32] work provides an example of scripts and its organization. Other important works in structured knowledge representation include KRL[33] and KL-ONE[34] languages.

## KNOWLEDGE REPRESENTATION IN HEALTHCARE

The use of computers to assist health professionals in their activities has been studied since the 1950s. Ledley and Lusted[35] were the first to address this possibility. They described the use of punch cards for indicating relationships between diseases and their manifestations. An experimental prototype was described in a later publication.[36] Problems prevented the widespread establishment of the system, including the limitations of the scientific foundation and the resistance by practitioners to accept a system that was not integrated into their usual workflow.[37]

Since then, researchers have applied the various knowledge representation schemas to provide clinical applications with knowledge. De Dombal and colleagues[38] studied the diagnostic process using Bayesian probability theory. Their system, the Leeds abdominal pain system, used sensitivity, specificity, and disease-prevalence data for various signs, symptoms, and test results to calculate the probability of seven reasons for abdominal pain (appendicitis, diverticulitis, perforated ulcer, cholecystitis, small-bowel obstruction, pancreatitis, and nonspecific abdominal pain). In a controlled prospective comparison study, the system's overall accuracy (91.8 percent) was significantly higher than that of the most senior member of the clinical team to see each case (79.6 percent).[38] This system was used in a variety of settings but never obtained the same degree of accuracy in other environments as it did in the original settings, even after adjustments were made for different prior probabilities of disease.[37]

Shortliffe and collaborators used a different approach in the development of the MYCIN system.[39] Knowledge of infectious diseases in MYCIN was represented as a set of production rules, each containing content derived from expert collaborations. It was one of the first programs to address the problem of reasoning with uncertain or incomplete information, incorporating calculus of uncertainty called *certainty factors*. The system performance was evaluated on therapy selection for cases of bacteremia[40] and meningitis,[41] showing that the program's therapy recommendations met experts' standards of acceptance 90.9 percent and 65 percent of the time, respectively. Many of the expert system development techniques currently in use were first developed or based on the MYCIN project.[24]

Several other representation schemas were also used in medical applications. Medical logic modules in the HELP system and applications developed at Columbia University are examples of procedure representation schemas.[14,16,42,43] The Pathfinder system[44] for diagnosis of lymph node pathology, a Bayesian system, was built on the foundation laid by de Dombal and colleagues. Starren and Xie studied different representations for cholesterol management: first-order logic, frames, and production rules.[45] Cimino and collaborators[46] used a frame-based representation for terminology, as did Masarie and colleagues.[47] Conceptual graphs were also used for this purpose, as well as logic-based descriptions.[21,48,49]

The examples presented illustrate the use of the different approaches in representing not only the organization of symbols into knowledge, but also the representation of the symbols themselves. Lessons learned from these systems revealed the feasibility of encoding medical knowledge, and helped researchers to clarify both the strengths and limitations of knowledge representation approaches. There is a gradual change in attitudes and increasing acceptance of computer decision tools by healthcare professionals. However, this enthusiasm can diminish if researchers do not ensure that the products of their research respond to real-world needs and are sensitive to the logistical requirements of the practice settings in which clinicians work.[37]

## THE PRESENT AND FUTURE OF CDSS

Thus far, advances in CDSS have been painstakingly slow. As rule-based clinical expert systems, such as MYCIN, have pioneered the use of decision technologies for clinical use and delivered the earliest evaluation showing efficacy in clinical use, the systems were exposed to obstacles on all fronts: validity of a new technology, arduous data entry, inauspicious perceptions, outdated knowledge, etc.

The validity of CDSS is regularly established in narrow niche domains under varying conditions and technologies. Some CDSS follow the costly development path of medical devices and FDA approval, while the majority of systems are not bound to these stringent criteria. Generally, CDSS proliferate as fragmented and isolated systems, with a few hospital-wide exceptions in academic centers. We can already observe a multiplication of NN CDSS for effective predictions in molecular pathology and medical imaging. In parallel, the public awareness of safety and quality stemming from the reports of the Institute of Medicine has contributed to the acceleration of the comparably slow adoption of generic knowledge-based CDSS, especially for computerized physician order entry (CPOE) and drug prescription. While this trend in POE implementation has strong political support, its usefulness requires additional, expensive backbone integration with fragmented medico-administrative and ancillary systems. These inapparent integration problems hinder the diffusion of POEs and reduce their functionality; however, well-implemented systems will lead to additional integration of CDSS. Because NN systems are independently implemented in post-genomics laboratory medical devices, hybrid systems stemming from POEs and NN systems are foreseeable.

Another former barrier, the structured data entry process, has remained challenging for all clinical information systems, including CDSS, but clinicians are increasingly adopting vertical clinical systems such as palm-based prescription and desktop-based ordering systems providing additional computable facts for CDSS. Encouragingly, a significant portion of relevant clinical facts are progressively more computable and additional gains are expected from voice recognition coupled with language understanding. In the early days of CDSS, expert systems were viewed as challenges to the clinical thought process, whereas they are currently perceived more favorably as enabling additional and relevant decision making.

Finally, of all the above-mentioned barriers, the intrinsic substantial cost of knowledge acquisition and knowledge actualization remains the most challenging problem for the sustainability of CDSS. Indeed, the considerable societal investments in biomedical research contribute to the ephemeral "truths" of clinical evidence that translate into rapidly outdated knowledge bases. Fortunately, new models of knowledge engineering methods are being formally evaluated from knowledge acquisition to knowledge representation and reuse. These approaches will solve the technical reuse of knowledge, but the legal and economical implications of sharing expensive up-to-date knowledge bases have not been sufficiently explored. Nonetheless, the cost of building or maintaining even a small portion of all clinically validated guidelines is prohibitive to any single institution, yet the major clinical system vendors persist in selling "empty" CDSS with no knowledge bases. While some businesses have begun to specialize in selling knowledge bases, their pricing is also prohibitive for most institutions Hopefully, coopetition between clinical institutions sharing knowledge bases via a not-for-profit broker will provide sufficient market pressure to decrease the cost of commercial knowledge bases to competitive levels.

In conclusion, a fragmented development of NN-based CDSS stemming from molecular medicine will most likely precede and coexist with integrative probabilistic and logical/deductive systems in clinical institutions. This period will most likely be followed by hybrid systems. Finally, novel knowledge engineering technologies and business models will progressively reduce the previously unaffordable cost of maintaining current large-scale clinical knowledge bases.

### References

Mulrow, C.D., Rationale for systematic reviews, *Br. Med. J.,* 309(6954), 597–599, 1994.

Kohn, L.T., Corrigan, J.M., and Donaldson, M.S., Editors for the Committee on Quality of Health Care in America. Institute of Medicine. To Err Is Human: Building a Safer Health System. Washington, D.C.: National Academy Press, 2000.

Miller, R.A., Medical diagnostic decision support systems — past, present, and future: a threaded bibliography and brief commentary, *J. Am. Med. Inform. Assoc.,* 1(1), 8–27, 1994.

Rosenblatt, F., The Perceptron: a probabilistic model for information storage and organization of the brain, *Psychol. Rev.,* 65, 386–408, 1958.

Baker, J.A., Kornguth, P.J., Lo, J.Y., Williford, M.E., and Floyd, C.E., Jr., Breast cancer: prediction with artificial neural network based on BI-RADS standardized lexicon, *Radiology,* 196(3),817–822, 1995.

Ohno-Machado, L. and Musen, M.A., A comparison of two computer-based prognostic systems for AIDS, *Proc. Annu. Symp. Comput. Appl. Med. Care,* 1995; 737–741.

Speight, P.M., Elliott, A.E., Jullien, J.A., Downer, M.C., and Zakzrewska, J.M., The use of artificial intelligence to identify people at risk of oral cancer and precancer, *Br. Dent. J.,* 179(10), 382–387, 1995.

Doyle, H.R., Parmanto, B., Munro, P.W., et al., Building clinical classifiers using incomplete observations — a neural network ensemble for hepatoma detection in patients with cirrhosis, *Methods Inf. Med.,* 34(3), 253–258, 1995.

Farmer, R.M., Medearis, A.L., Hirata, G.I., and Platt, L.D., The use of a neural network for the ultrasonographic estimation of fetal weight in the macrosomic fetus, *Am. J. Obstet. Gynecol.,* 166(5), 1467–1472, 1992.

DeFigueiredo, R.J., Shankle, W.R., Maccato, A., et al., Neural-network-based classification of cognitively normal, demented, Alzheimer disease and vascular dementia from single photon emission with computed tomography image data from brain, *Proc. Natl. Acad. Sci. U.S.A.,* 92(12), 5530–5544, 1995.

Brown, A.D. and Garber, A.M., Cost-effectiveness of 3 methods to enhance the sensitivity of Papanicolaou testing, *JAMA,* 281(4), 347–353, 1999.

Dojat, M., Brochard, L., Lemaire, F., and Harf, A., A knowledge-based system for assisted ventilation of patients in intensive care units, *Int. J. Clin. Monit. Comput.,* 9(4), 239–250, 1992.

Hripcsak, G., Clayton, P.D., Jenders, R.A., Cimino, J.J. and Johnson, S.B., Design of a clinical event monitor, *Comput. Biomed. Res.,* 29(3), 194–221, 1996.

Jenders, R.A., Hripcsak, G., Sideli, R.V., et al., Medical decision support: experience with implementing the Arden Syntax at the Columbia-Presbyterian Medical Center, *Proc. Annu. Symp. Comput. Appl. Med. Care,* 1995; 169–173.

Audet, A.M., Greenfield, S., and Field, M., Medical practice guidelines: current activities and future directions, *Ann. Intern. Med.,* 113(9), 709–714, 1990.

Hripcsak, G., Ludemann, P., Pryor, T.A., Wigertz, O.B., and Clayton, P.D., Rationale for the Arden Syntax, *Comput. Biomed. Res.,* 27(4), 291–324, 1994.

Ohno-Machado, L., Gennari, J.H., Murphy, S.N., et al., The guideline interchange format: a model for representing guidelines, *J. Am. Med. Inform. Assoc.,* 5(4), 357–372, 1998.

Russel, S. and Norvig, P., *Artificial Intelligence: A Modern Approach,* Upper Saddle River, NJ: Prentice Hall, 1995. (Prentice-Hall Series in Artificial Intelligence.

Sowa, J.F., *Knowledge Representation — Logical, Philosophical, and Computational Foundations,* Pacific Grove, CA: Brooks/Cole, 2000.

Kushniruk, A., Patel, V., Cimino, J.J., and Barrows, R.A., Cognitive evaluation of the user interface and vocabulary of an outpatient information system, in *Proceedings/AMIA Annual Fall Symposium,* Cimino, J.J., Ed., Philadelphia: Hanley & Belfus, 1996, 22–26.

Spackman, K.A., Campbell, K.E., Côté, R.A., SNOMED RT: a reference terminology for health care, In *Proceedings/AMIA Annual Fall Symposium,* Masys, D.R., Ed., Philadelphia: Hanley & Belfus, 1997, 640–644.

Lussier, Y.A., Maksud, M., Yale, P.P., and St-Arneault, R., A Computerized Patient Record Software for Direct Data Entry by Physicians Using a Keyboardless Pen-Based Portable Computer, in *Proceedings of the Sixteenth Annual Symposium on Computer Applications in Medical Care,* New York: McGraw-Hill, 1992.

Newell, A. and Simon, H.A., Computer science as empirical inquiry: symbols and search, *Communications of the ACM,* 19(3), 113–126, 1976.

Luger, G.F. and Stubblefield, W.A., *Artificial Intelligence. Structures and Strategies for Complex Problem Solving, 3rd ed.,* Harlow, England: Addison Wesley Longman, Inc., 1998.

Minsky, M., Logical versus analogical versus symbolic versus connectionist or neat versus scruffy, *AI Magazine,* 12(2), 34–51, 1991.

Mylopoulos, J. and Levesque, H.J., An overview of knowledge representation, in *On Conceptual Modeling: Perspectives from Artificial Intelligence, Databases, and Programming Languages,* Brodie, M.L., Mylopoulos, J., and Schmidt, J.W., Eds., New York: Springer-Verlag, 1984.

Davis, R., Shrobe, H., and Szolovits, P., What is knowledge representation?, *AI Magazine,* 14(1), 17–33, 1993.

Newell, A. and Simon, H.A., GPS: a program that simulates human thought. in *Computers and Thought,* Feigenbaum, E.A. and Feldman, J., Eds., New York: McGraw-Hill, 1963, 477–523.

Lindsay, R., Buchanan, B., Feigenbaum, E., and Lederberg, J., *Applications of Artificial Intelligence for Organic Chemistry,* New York: McGraw-Hill, 1980.

Sowa, J.F., *Conceptual Structures: Information Processing in Mind and Machine,* Reading, MA: Addison-Wesley, 1984.

Minsky, M., A framework for representing knowledge, in *Readings in Knowledge Representation,* Brachman, R.J. and Levesque, H.J., Eds., Los Altos, CA: Morgan Kaufmann Publishers, 1985, 246–262.

Schank, R.C. and Abelson, R.P., *Scripts, Plans, Goals, and Understanding : An Inquiry into Human Knowledge Structures,* Hillsdale, NJ: L. Erlbaum Associates, 1977. (The Artificial intelligence series.)

Bobrow, D.G. and Winograd, T., An overview of KRL, a knowledge representation language, *Cognitive Science,* 1(1), 3–46, 1977.

Brachman, R.J., On the epistemological status of semantic networks, in *Readings in Knowledge Representation,* Brachman, R.J. and Levesque, H.J., Eds., Los Altos, CA: Morgan Kaufmann Publishers, 1985.

Ledley, R.S. and Lusted, L.B., Reasoning foundations of medical diagnosis, *Science,* 130, 9–21, 1959.

Warner, H.R., Toronto, A.F., and Veasy, L., Experience with Baye's theorem for computer diagnosis of congenital heart disease, *Ann. NY Acad. Sci.,* 115, 2–16, 1964.

Musen, M.A., Shahar, Y., and Shortliffe, E.H., Clinical decision-support systems, *Medical Informatics, Computer Applications in Health Care and Biomedicine. 2nd ed.,* Shortliffe, E.H., Perreault, L.E., Wiederhold, G., and Fagan, L.M., Eds., New York: Springer-Verlag, 2001, 573–609.

de Dombal, F.T., Leaper, D.J., Staniland, J.R., McCann, A.P., and Horrocks, J.C., Computer-aided diagnosis of acute abdominal pain, *Br. Med. J.,* 2(5804), 9–13, 1972.

Shortliffe, E.H., Axline, S.G., Buchanan, B.G., Merigan, T.C., and Cohen, S.N., An artificial intelligence program to advise physicians regarding antimicrobial therapy, *Comput. Biomed. Res.,* 6(6):544–560, 1973.

Yu, V.L., Buchanan, B.G., Shortliffe, E.H., et al., Evaluating the performance of a computer-based consultant, *Comput. Programs Biomed.,* 9(1), 95–102, 1979.

Yu, V.L., Fagan, L.M., Wraith, S.M., et al., Antimicrobial selection by a computer. A blinded evaluation by infectious diseases experts, *JAMA,* 242(12), 1279–1282, 1979.

Haug, P.J., Gardner, R.M., Tate, K.E., et al., Decision support in medicine: examples from the HELP system, *Comput. Biomed. Res.,* 27(5), 396–418, 1994.

Gardner, R.M. and Lundsgaarde, H.P., Evaluation of user acceptance of a clinical expert system, *J. Am. Med. Inform. Assoc.,* 1(6), 428–438, 1994.

Heckerman, D., Horvitz, E., and Nathwani, B.. Update on the Pathfinder project, in *Proc. 13th Annu. Symp. Comput. Appl. Med. Care,* Kingsland, L.W., Ed., Washington, D.C.: IEEE Computer Society Press, 1989, 203–207.

Starren, J. and Xie, G., Comparison of three knowledge representation formalisms for encoding the NCEP Cholesterol Guidelines, *Proc. Annu. Symp. Comput. Appl. Med. Care,* 1994, 792–796.

Cimino, J.J., Hripcsak, G., Johnson, S.B., Clayton, P.D., *in Designing an Introspective, Controlled Medical Vocabulary,* Kingsland, L.W., Ed., Washington, D.C.: IEEE Computer Society Press, 1989, 513–518.

Masarie, F.E., Jr., Miller, R.A., Bouhaddou,. O., Giuse, N.B., and Warner, H.R., An interlingua for electronic interchange of medical information: using frames to map between clinical vocabularies, *Comput. Biomed. Res.,* 24(4):379–400, 1991.

Campbell, K.E. and Musen, M.A., Representation of clinical data using SNOMED III and conceptual graphs, In *Proc. 17th Annu. Symp. Comput. Appl. Med. Care,* 1993, 354–358.

Bakken, S., Cashen, M.S., Mendonça, E.A., O'Brien, A., and Zieniewicz, J., Representing nursing activities within a concept-oriented terminological system: evaluation of a type definition, J. Am. Med. Inform. Assoc., 7(1), 81–90, 2000.

# Chapter 18
# Risk Management in Information Technology Projects
*Patricia S. Collins*

Healthcare information systems projects are looked at as a set of activities that are done only once and in a finite timeframe. Because of this self-limiting impact-time, organizations very seldom analyze and make risk management a key component of the project plan. As a result, risk is relegated as a part of doing business and not something that can be controlled. Risk identification is the process of documenting potential problem areas, assigning a factor of probability and a factor of consequence to the issue. Risk management is the process of monitoring for the occurrence of a risk event and mitigating the impact. In general, risks in healthcare information technology (IT) projects can be found in a few major categories. Risk begins with the project ownership (or lack of ownership!) and follows with events occurring in planning, contracting, procurement, resource management, scheduling, quality assurance, deliverables, and communications.

## UNDERSTANDING RISK TAKERS AND RISK AVOIDERS

How much risk is acceptable in a project? Risk acceptance or risk aversion in the team players should be evaluated at the onset of the project. This would allow each event to be resolved in proper perspective. In the healthcare industry, and correctly so, there is a philosophy that any event that could adversely affect patients will be avoided and considered high risk. Time in healthcare projects is not always considered a high risk factor. Although everyone may agree that the project is very important and cannot suffer delays, the urgency to get a healthcare IT project done is not on the same plane as releasing the newest version of a software package before your competitors do.

Risk takers are those team players who consider living on the "bleeding edge" the only way technology can stay ahead of rapidly changing de-

0-8493-1498-4/03/$0.00+$1.50
© 2003 by CRC Press LLC

mands in the industry. Risk avoiders are those players who consider the status quo as the strength of the organization. Those players like to take small bite-sized changes and evaluate the impact on the organization. The result is larger changes over greater time.

Assessing the team players at the beginning of a project for their risk perspective can give the project team two distinct advantages. First, if the one player (the CFO?) is a major risk avoider then, in that player's estimation, budget and cost related events would rate very high. Ask the chief nursing officer and the answer will probably be that quality of patient data is a far higher risk than budget and cost.

The key to successful risk management in healthcare projects is to identify the risk level of each of the team players and make sure that the team is balanced. In a team of 20 diverse players if 18 are risk takers, the project may end up with major arteries bleeding! Risk takers make shining-star accomplishments but leave a definite battle trail behind. If, on the other hand, the project team has 18 risk avoiders, the project will have great difficulty getting anywhere. Their goals are usually very defined, very limited, and well tested before the next step is started.

These groups find it very difficult to keep up with the rapid changes demanded in the healthcare industry. Accomplishments are often unrewarded or unrecognized because by the time they are done, the strategic goals have changed or the problem was resolved through some other mechanism. The project team should have a decided balance between risk takers and risk avoiders. If the players cannot be changed, at least the team will know the nature of the team's risk personality.

## DEFINING RISK FACTORS

The process of defining risk factors is unique to each project. Although there are risks common to most projects, each project brings its own set of problem areas. The project team needs to define the scope of risk that will be included in identifying risk factors. Scope of risk is accomplished by establishing a simple probability grid as in Exhibit 1.

Although anything may happen during a project, the events that will be actively managed will fall in the risk level $x$ or greater where the project team defines $x$. During the initial risk determination, many events may be documented that are later determined to have a relatively low impact. Risk management can be dispersed among team members by assessing the level of risk and delegating the monitoring of lesser impact risk events to someone other than the project manager. Risk factors are present in every task associated with the project. Knowing this, the most useful tool to assist in defining risk factors is the project work breakdown structure. After each task is identified and entered into the project plan, the risk team assesses:

**Exhibit 1. Determining Risk Event Impact**

| Risk<br><br>Event* | A<br>Probability of<br>Occurring (0–100%) | B<br>Level of Impact<br>1 low to 5 high | C<br>Risk Impact Level<br>$A \times B = C$ |
|---|---|---|---|
| Hardware will be late | 20 | 2 | 40 |
| Network cannot handle load | 40 | 5 | 200 |
| Oracle DBA not available | 50 | 3 | 150 |

*Each event must have a contingency plan to minimize a negative effect should the event occur.

- What could delay this task from being completed on time?
- What resources are required to accomplish this task, and are those resources readily available to the project team?
- What interdependencies occur with other tasks that could affect this task?
- How will the project manager know that this task is completed (are the deliverables measurable)?
- What impact will noncompletion of this task have on the rest of the project?
- What options are available to minimize any negative effects relative to this task?

One caution about identifying risk factors: there may be several reasons why team members disagree about whether an event should be considered a risk or not. Estimation of the ability of an individual's team members may be overstated, the team member may not be able to visualize the negative impact others are concerned about, or a negative event may have recently happened which is coloring the focus of the team. The risk manager's role is to watch for bias and minimize the effect it has on the process of good risk determination.

## RISK IN THE PROJECT LIFE CYCLE

During the project life cycle, project risk should decrease as the amount at stake increases. The project life cycle has four basic phases: (1) conception and approval, (2) planning and feasibility, (3) implementation and roll-out, and (4) closure and transition to support. During each of these phases, common risk events can be identified which should be evaluated for probability occurrence and impact, as displayed in Exhibit 2.

### Project Ownership Risks

One major factor encountered by healthcare IT projects is who owns the project. Ownership and associated stakeholders are a vital part of the

## Exhibit 2. Phases of a Project Life Cycle

**Conception and Approval**
- Poor definition of the problem
- Poor scope definition
- Lack of subject matter experts
- Unclear ownership
- Poor contract development
- Inadequate commitment of resources
- Unrealistic timelines

**Planning and Feasibility**
- Lack of a risk management plan
- Inadequate planning
- Poorly written design specifications
- Lack of integration planning
- Lack of change control
- Unprepared skilled resources
- Lack of experience in project management
- Insufficient input from all stakeholders

**Implementation and Roll-out**
- Lack of skilled resources
- Lack of training
- Lack of support documentation
- Availability of materials
- Changes in scope
- Changes in ownership
- Poor quality control
- Lack of integration skills
- Lack of migration from old to new policies and procedures

**Closure and Transition to Support**
- Undefined closure (when is the project done)
- Unsatisfied user acceptance
- Unresolved technical issues
- Lack of planning for ongoing support
- Lack of planning for 'phase 2' or after-life commitments

---

project's success. The risk associated with ownership starts with determining if this is a single department project or if it crosses the entire enterprise. With many degrees in between, the level of probability that events will occur rises dramatically as the project involves more players. In the event of enterprisewide projects such as telecommunications, networks, or computerized patient records the event probability is higher that negative events will occur, and when they occur, it will be more difficult to minimize the impact. Multi-facility projects bring their own level of complexity and the ownership across facilities may be a very high-risk area to define. The less defined the absolute owner, the higher the risk of events regarding decision making and acceptance of deliverables. Outside or third-party players may have a stakeholder's role in the project that could present risk events. Interfacing with external vendors always presents the risk of compatibility and additional costs to resolve negative communications events. Identifying and estimating the impact during the planning phase can mitigate these events. Defining ownership risks in the project risk plan creates a factual, documented way of dealing with very difficult interpersonal issues if they arise as the project progresses.

## Contract Risks

Establishing working agreements with outside parties is often handled as a necessary evil of paperwork. To minimize risk associated with contracts, the event should be handled as any other well-run project. There are phases, activities, and tasks associated with developing well-written, useful contracts. The most common areas of risk associated with the contract are when one party is not fulfilling the obligations expected by the second party. In healthcare IT projects, common problems that cause a consumer to resort to the contract are a lack of functionality or lack of performance. In developing the contract project plan, sufficient task detail should be given to minimizing the impact on the consumer should the product fail to perform as expected. Some key areas to assess risk or the probability that the contract will be the article of settling a dispute include:

- Poorly defined deliverables (who, what, where, when, in what condition)
- Undefined functionality (details of the functionality expected by the user)
- Unclear terms of payment
- Unclear terms of when support payments initiate
- Undefined terms of support during the implementation
- Undefined roles at the task level for the consumer and the vendor
- Undefined responsibility for unanticipated cost overruns
- Undefined third-party performance standards
- Unclear escalation procedures for contract disputes
- Unclear responsibility should the project be abandoned
- Lack of penalties for failure to perform

## Integration Risks

Implementation of healthcare IT projects is most risky when assumptions are made about disparate systems. Bringing a new system into any healthcare environment can be fraught with difficulties in getting the systems to work together well. In many projects the focus is so heavily centered on the principal project that the ability to communicate and function with peripheral systems is left for a late phase in the project. Many times the events that occur should have been addressed in a much earlier phase. In conducting a complete risk assessment, the probability that these events will negatively impact the project plan can be assessed. Common risks associated with integration include:

- Lack of sufficient infrastructure
- Software version incompatibilities
- Operating system incompatibilities
- Architectural inconsistency (Oracle and Sybase)
- Unstable or absence of test environments
- Discrepancies in data ownership
- Coordination of multiple system upgrades
- Unexpected impact on another system
- Lack of skilled integration resources

### Scheduling Risks

Scheduling risks involve first looking at the reality of the task level assignments in the work breakdown structure. During the estimation process in project planning, many teams use Delphi techniques or consensus to determine the most likely time for a task to be completed. Using a pessimistic, optimistic, and most likely formula, the team comes up with a time to be entered into the project work breakdown structure:

$$\frac{\text{Optimistic time} + (2 \times \text{Most likely time}) + \text{Pessimistic time}}{6} = \text{Task time}$$

Example: $\dfrac{3 \text{ days} + (2 \times 5 \text{ days}) + 7 \text{ days}}{6} = 3.3 \text{ days}$

If the estimated times do not appear to be risky, the second step is to look at relationships. As tasks are assigned predecessors or successors, an evaluation should be made of the resources required to accomplish the task. With a large number of project hours being outsourced to contract employees, the need to conserve project budget depends on the ability to keep resource-related tasks together and avoid contractor downtime. Because scheduling is dependent on the task level of the plan, the project next needs to be analyzed for float time or contingency time. The absence of any contingency time produces a higher risk factor than one with some flexibility. Another area to consider in scheduling risks is the learning curve associated with the resource assigned to the task. For short intensive tasks, the risk is higher if the resource is less skilled. For tasks that occur over time, the ability for the resource to add additional skills is more acceptable. Another risk common to healthcare IT projects is having key resources work on more than one project. It is virtually impossible to maximize a resource's time and optimize the project plan on two different projects. Identifying the degree to which this event may impact the project, is an important assessment. When multiple resources work on multiple projects the risk of impacting the schedule is exponential.

### Quality Risks

Quality assurance risks are identified throughout the project and are often the line items in the risk management report that gain upper management attention. If it is objectively documented that the project, as it is proceeding, will result in poor quality, a reaction of some kind is usually the result. Quality risks are closely linked to the planning, schedule, and resource issues. Some areas that identify poor quality in the final outcome include:

- Lack of end-user input in the planning phase
- Resource shifting on similar tasks
- Lack of feedback on testing and feasibility events
- Changes in scope and objectives
- Lack of owner support
- Changes in upper management expectations
- Lack of stakeholder participation in the project process

### Resource Risks

Someone very familiar with the strengths and weaknesses of the resource pool best accomplishes assessing resource risks. Experience is the best teacher for skill assessment, reliability of contract services, and performance of equipment. Planning four hours to copy 60 training manuals is not realistic if the copier is known to continually break down! The biggest risk in healthcare IT projects is the learning curve associated with new technology. As newer systems replace legacy products, resources are being requested to learn new skills. Many healthcare IT projects are requiring outsourcing for the implementation and counting on staff resources to learn enough new skills to maintain the system once it is installed. This is evident with database administration roles in many current projects. Experienced database administrators are doing the implementation work and the regular healthcare staff members are learning to be support database administrators. Reviewing each task in the work breakdown structure will identify the key areas of risk for the resource per task level. Then each resource should be reviewed to determine if there is an equal workload distribution across resources.

### Cost Risks

Estimating cost risks in the process of the project is very relative to the structure of the contract and the resource requirements. Analyzing the contract for license fees, and implementation fees, support fees, software and hardware costs, will assist in identifying any areas of risk that should be documented. If large segments of the budget are set aside for purchasing services and equipment over the life of the project, the risk that presents is the skill of the project manager best utilizing that money. Assessing the project manager's experience in procurement of peripherals (PCs, printers, etc.) and services, such as contract help, will determine the level of exposure the project budget has.

## Scope Risks

Defining and understanding the scope of the project at the onset is the key to minimizing risk from the worst of all foes, "scope creep." Risk assessment of the scope of the project involves analyzing the various factors for boundaries and limitations. The risk associated with the scope of the project is directly associated with the clarity of what is included in the project and, very importantly, what is not included. Verbal understandings and misunderstandings often affect scope. Having a formal change management plan in place will assist in effecting and controlling change requests. In assessing the risk factors, project team members should include an evaluation of the following:

- Poorly written scope documents
- Absence of a change management plan
- Verbal understandings and agreements
- Changes to the project plan without documentation

## Communication Risks

Risks to the entire project often are related to poor communications. Identifying risk associated with communications is usually looking for what is not present. Every project should have clear communications on a minimum of three major components: first, a regular status report utilizing the project work breakdown structure with delayed or incomplete tasks for date; second, the project budget should be documented and presented to stakeholders, as appropriate, while there is still time to react to any discrepancies; third, issue logs or reports on all items that are outstanding, escalation status, and responsible personnel. The degree of risk the project will encounter regarding communications is dependent on the existence of these types of communications on a regular basis.

## SUMMARY

Risk management is the process of reviewing and interacting with all facets of the project, for the life of the project. Successful risk management depends on having a risk-balanced team that can review the progress of the project and has the power to intervene before significant negative results occur. Participation by the risk management team members begins in the conceptual phase and continues until the support systems are established. Nonplanned events will occur. The rapidity with which the project team is able to respond will determine the outcome of the project.

### References

1. Bennatan, E. M. 1995. *On Time, Within Budget: Software Project Management Practices and Techniques.* New York: John Wiley & Sons.

2. Jenkins, George. 1997. *Information Systems, Policy and Procedure Manual.* Princeton: Prentice Hall.

3. McLeod, Graham and Smith, Derek. 1996. *Managing Information Technology Projects.* Cambridge, MA: Course Technology.

4. Wysocki, Robert K., Beck, Robert, Jr., and Crane, David B. 1995. *Effective Project Management.* New York: John Wiley & Sons.

# Chapter 19
# How Much Does This System Really Cost?

*Richard J. Linderman*

The purpose of this chapter is to assist prospective hardware and software purchasers to identify the various costs associated with their prospective action. Seldom is the total cost of an information system installation represented in the purchase order or vendor proposal. As you will see, several potential areas of additional expenses are identified in the ensuing pages. The specific expense areas encountered by your organization will be dependent on several variables. These include, but are not limited to, the following: the specific product, current technology versus required technology, project scope, organizational support, customization, etc.

## SYSTEM PURCHASE SCENARIO

The widget department (management engineers love widgets) at a facility wants to order a new "system" that will do everything shy of managing the department. This new widget information system (WIS) has a price tag of $300,000 for software, requires another $150,000 expenditure on hardware upgrades, and $50,000 for training and installation. The widget department manager brings the $500,000 proposal to his or her respective senior executive for approval. Both agree with the cost estimates and the system's need, but then the senior executive asks, "How much is this *REALLY* going to cost?" The widget manager thinks to himself, "Can't this idiot add?" and then answers $500,000. In defense of the senior executive, we assume that the inquiry was not from a lack of simple math skills. The executive wanted to know the "real" or "total" cost of installing WIS, not the purchase price.

In the example, the easily identified costs are calculated by adding the three identified costs. These expenses probably equal the WIS vendor's purchase order(s). However, few systems are installed without incurring additional expenses (hardware, software, and training costs, etc.). By exploring these "costs" areas, one can see that installing WIS will probably exceed the $500,000 estimate.

0-8493-1498-4/03/$0.00+$1.50
© 2003 by CRC Press LLC

## PURCHASE ORDER EXPENSES

### Hardware Costs

Our example calls for hardware costs of $150,000. Chances are this only includes what the WIS vendor is selling or requires the facility(s) to purchase in order to run WIS. This may or may not include upgrades to the mainframe, client/server, or existing PCs. Other potential hardware costs include cable installation costs (cable, construction/renovation, and labor). Does it include workstation modification costs or PC upgrades? Does it include all potential peripheral equipment that may need to be purchased to get WIS running? There is a high probability that the purchaser will incur significant other costs related to this purchase.

### Software Costs

Our example calls for software costs of $300,000. This typically only includes the WIS vendor's software. Seldom will it include additional software required for your facility to purchase in order to run WIS. The author's experience is that if applicable, only the first year "enhancement fees" and "maintenance fees" are included in a vendor's proposal. These are typically paid in perpetuity over the life of the software package contract. If both are $12,500 per year, $100,000 has been added to the software costs over the next four years! Additionally, will there be licensing costs to migrate to a new operating system (such as Windows 98 from Windows 95)? Will this migration require upgrading other existing software packages on PCs?

### Training Costs

Our example calls for training costs of $50,000. Typically, training expenses only include the direct cost of the training requirements. Seldom are related travel, lodging, and meal expenses included in the purchase order. Training expense is one of the most understated costs incurred in most system installs. For example, a client hospital purchased a system requiring four days of vendor training for each of the six modules purchased. The contract required that at least two employees per module take the vendor training. The cost of training was $2000 per employee plus expenses. Twelve employees were to be "trained" by the vendor. The contract had training expenses listed at $24,000 (plus expenses). A minimum of 12 employees had to fly from Kansas City to Atlanta, resulting in incurring 48 days of living expenses (motel, meals, phone calls, local transportation in Atlanta, etc.). If we assume the following conservative per-person expenses, you will see some significant additional costs:

Our conservative expense estimate adds $15,120 to our training costs that will not show up in any purchase order. Additionally, the hospital is not getting any direct labor from these employees for these days. If we

| Expense | Cost Estimate ($) |
|---|---|
| Airfare (round trip) | 500 |
| Motel (4 nights) | 500 |
| Meals (4 nights) | 160 |
| Telephone calls | 20 |
| Local transportation (to and from airport only) | 40 |
| Airport parking (home airport) | 40 |
| Total per person | 1,260 |
| Times 12 persons | × 12 |
| Estimated expenses | 15,120 |

assume that the average employee being trained earned $37,500 and we add 25 percent for benefits, it costs this hospital approximately $50,000 annually (approximately $190/day). If we assume one day for travel plus the four days of required vendor training, an additional $11,400 has been added to the training expenses.

## THE "OTHER" EXPENSES

In the ensuing pages, we will show examples of where the purchase order expense will not accurately reflect the true costs of a system installation. In this section, we will identify where other expenses will be incurred. Some will be direct and others will be indirect. No universal formula exists to determine which of the following expense types will be incurred. Generally speaking, most of the following will be incurred.

### Additional Training Expenses

Let's go back to the example of my client from Kansas City. In this example, we estimated additional training expenses to be at least $35,500. The 12 employees sent to Atlanta represent approximately five percent of all employees who will eventually receive training in this product. Does this mean that the remaining 230+ employees are going to be sent to Atlanta also? Luckily, the answer is no. The 12 "trained" employees will serve as "trainers" back at the facility using vendor-provided training documentation (this was included in the original purchase order). Is the facility going to incur any additional expenses? The answer is a definitive yes. The software vendor recommended a minimum of eight hours of core training for all users. Because virtually every employee being trained will be replaced while in training, the company will incur additional labor costs. Training classes are limited to ten employees; 40 training sessions are necessary, which means the hospital incurs approximately 270 person-days of training. If we return to our original value of $190 per person-day, the hospital will incur an additional $51,300 in training expenses.

## The RFI and RFP Process

Two other overlooked expense items are the *request for information* (RFI) and the *request for proposal* (RFP) processes. The expenses incurred will be dependent upon the process at the respective facility and the type of product being considered. Most organizations will utilize some sort of committee process to determine an information systems purchase selection. For both phases of the purchasing process, employees will be utilized in the selection process. Obviously, a product that will affect one department will require fewer representatives than a product that will affect multiple departments. For example, purchasing a nursing acuity system may only have representation from nursing, information services, and management engineering. Conversely, a patient accounting system may have representation from multiple fiscal areas, nursing, information services, radiology, management engineering, and other departments.

For the RFI process, we will need to add up the person-days (and labor expense) required for this phase. For the RFP process, the same is true, plus whatever expenses are incurred in the process. These can include several potential expenses such as travel and living expenses during site visits, telephone calls, check out references, etc. Depending on the number of participants and the scope of the RFI and RFP processes, several thousand dollars can be expended.

## Decision-Making Expenses

How much can it cost for an organization to make the purchasing decision? Again, this will vary greatly by organization and product being purchased. Some organizations may leave the entire decision process to a department or to the committee assigned to do the RFI and RFP processes. Other entities may bring departments like management engineering or fiscal affairs into the process to perform various financial analyses functions. Regardless of the path taken, additional expenses will be incurred.

Seldom is any system purchased in a vacuum. The process often starts when a department manager (or senior executive) decides that the current environment is insufficient for the facility's needs. For example, a hospital client in Pennsylvania had a "homegrown" payroll system and no computerized human resource system. The CFO decided that a modern payroll and HR system was required. After reviewing budgetary questions with the CEO, the decision was made to start a committee to explore purchasing a system. A committee was established with representatives from payroll (1), fiscal affairs (1), human resources (2), information services (4), and management engineering (1). The CFO charged the committee to solicit prospective vendors for RFIs.

To initiate the RFI process, the committee had to determine (in general terms) what to purchase and who were the prospective vendors. To accomplish this task, the committee met several times and each member was given specific tasks. These included broadly defining department needs and calling peers at other facilities to see what systems were "out there." The committee decided to send for RFIs from five vendors. Between committee meetings and assignments, each committee member contributed approximately five person-days. This translates into 45 person-days. If we again use our $190.00 person-day charge, the RFI process cost this hospital $8550.00 in labor expenses.

The RFI process narrowed the selection process to four vendors. One prospective vendor chose not to submit information because it was leaving that market. After receiving the vendor information, the committee was tasked to narrow the choices to two vendors to submit RFPs.

The RFP process started with the same committee composition. All committee members had specific tasks to assist in narrowing selection to two companies. The committee presented all four RFIs to the CFO for review. The CFO eliminated one vendor because the price exceeded his budget (up to this point the committee had no known budget). Each committee member averaged approximately three person-days during the RFP process. Using our daily labor expense average, the RFP process cost $5130 in labor expenses. These costs do not include any miscellaneous expenses that might be incurred.

Two vendors were selected to submit proposals. Both vendors were required to send detailed proposals and references. Each vendor arranged for site visits at reference hospitals. Both reference hospitals were less than 100 miles from the client hospital. Because of the proximity of both site visits, all committee members traveled for the site visits. Direct travel costs were minimal because two cars were rented for each site visit. The committee used two single-day car rentals for transportation, and no overnight stays were required. Frequently, hospitals will incur commercial transportation and overnight expenses on site visits. Most organizations do not send the full contingent of committee members on site visits that require commercial transportation. If this hospital sent all nine committee members on a site visit requiring an overnight stay and airfare, it could have easily incurred an additional $5000 in travel expenses.

To reach a consensus recommendation and make the presentation to the CFO and CEO, committee members expended approximately six person-days each. Using the $190 per-person daily standard, the hospital incurred $10,260 in labor expenses in this phase of the project.

## Other Financial Consideration Expenses

In making decisions, management must compare all alternatives before them. There is more to a purchasing decision than just a product's pur-

251

chase price. Every alternative will have costs associated with it. In the above RFP process, the two selected proposals had different purchase costs. In accounting terms, the difference is known as *differential costs*. If the purchase price of product A was $600,000 and that of product B was $500,000, $100,000 is the differential cost. If both products are rated as equal (in terms of capability, functionality, and use) and all other costs are approximately equal, a hospital investing in the more expensive product would incur differential costs.

Let's change some of our components. If the two products were substantially similar, but the net installation costs of product A were $200.000 less than that of product B, product A would be less expensive. If there is a substantial differential cost between products, justification of the significantly more expensive product needs to be done. This justification needs to focus on the operational advantages of the more expensive product.

Another consideration is what is known as *opportunity costs*. Opportunity cost is the potential benefit that is lost or sacrificed when the choice of one course of action is weighed against another. Using the example in the RFP process, if the hospital accelerated its $1,000,000 purchasing decision by one year, it would realize opportunity costs of approximately $75,000. This opportunity cost was calculated by multiplying the expenditure times an expected rate of return ($1,000,000 × 7.5 percent). Opportunity costs need to be calculated for any differential costs that are incurred. Remember that a system purchasing decision consists of several decision points. These include product selection (which vendor to buy from), when to make the purchasing decision, and whether or not to make a purchasing decision.

*Sunk costs* also come into play in the decision-making process. Sunk costs are costs that have already been incurred and cannot be changed by any decision now or in the future. For example, if a facility spent $1,000,000 on brand X's widget information system two years ago and was debating replacing that system (for whatever reason), do you take that expenditure into consideration in the future decision-making process? From a financial perspective, the answer is a resounding no. If your facility needs to purchase another system, the former expenditure is gone and is not an issue. What has happened in the past is done. Your organization cannot recoup past expenditures and they therefore should not be factored into the purchase price of future systems.

*Depreciation expenses*, unlike sunk costs, may need to be considered in the purchase process. If your organization is considering replacing a system that is not fully depreciated, the remaining depreciation expense needs to be factored into the purchase price. Because of the ever-changing accounting standards and tax laws, an organization needs to consult its fiscal department to determine if there is any remaining depreciation expense to be incurred. It is important to remember that depreciation is a noncash flow account. It is purely an accounting expense spread over the "useful life" of a product (as defined by accounting standards).

### Installation Expenses

As previously stated, seldom is any system installed in a vacuum. Information systems are seldom installed "as is" from the vendor. Systems are not just plugged in, turned on, and operational. There are unit/system tests, parallel testing, audits, go/no go decisions, etc. Virtually every system has to undergo some sort of customization before going live. These expenses need to be captured to measure total system costs.

### System Design

Unless your facility is installing Lotus, Excel, etc., chances are there will be significant labor resources utilized in designing the final system. To track the labor costs, the facility again needs to quantify the amount of labor resources required for the system design phase. This will include employees required for the design function and the time contributions of the "system users." Some facilities utilize "consultants" during this phase. The author has seen consultants used in all aspects of system design, ranging from project leader to programmer. If consultants are used, be sure to include "billable time and expenses." If only five IS employees are utilized over a six-month period in the design phase, the hospital would incur at least $125,000 in labor expenses.

### System Testing

Before a system goes "live," testing should be done. The degree and amount of testing will vary, depending on the system being installed. All labor needs to be accounted for in this phase. It is important to include labor costs from all respective departments. Labor may come from the user areas, IS, accounting, and even auditing. Chances are, system testing may include overtime in addition to straight or regular time. The main purpose of this phase is to determine what "bugs" to work out and when to go "live" with the new system.

### System Installation

During the system installation phase, significant labor resources may be utilized. At a client in Florida, approximately 200 new PCs were purchased for the new system. These PCs had to be unpacked, tested, loaded with all the required system and standard PC software, repacked, and installed in their respective locations. This hospital utilized six employees over a three-week period to complete this function. This translated into approximately $18,000 in labor expenses.

253

### System "Go Live"

Once the system *Go Live* time has arrived, there usually will be significant labor resources utilized in a "help desk" function. It is not uncommon for a hospital to have a dedicated help desk open around the clock for a large system installation. At this Florida client, their new system-dedicated help desk operated 24 hours daily for the first week, 16 hours daily the second week, and eight hours daily the third week after going live. The number of staff per shift also decreased each week. The dedicated help desk was always staffed during some segment of the "off" shifts. This resulted in shift differential and significant overtime expenses. The CIO estimated that the dedicated help desk resulted in approximately $35,000 of additional labor expenses.

## CONCLUSION

It should be obvious that installing an information system will cost significantly more than the price on the purchase order. We have identified several areas that could potentially add to the total cost of the system installation. Although they are not universal, most of the expense categories identified will be incurred to some degree. The amount of expenses and categories of expenses incurred will be determined by both the specific software product and the organization.

# Section VI
# EMR and the
# Data Warehouse

# Chapter 20
# Electronic Medical Records (EMR)

*Mark Leavitt*

Over the past 30 years, the definition of an electronic medical record (EMR), also called a computer-based patient record (CPR or CbPR), has evolved considerably, in parallel with changes that have swept through the healthcare industry itself. The Computer-Based Patient Record Institute now offers these definitions that differentiate the record itself from the system for maintaining it:

> A computer-based patient record (CPR) is electronically maintained information about an individual's lifetime health status and healthcare. CPRs are not merely automated forms of today's paper-based medical records, but encompass the entire scope of health information in all media forms. Thus CPRs include medical history, current medications, laboratory test results, x-ray images, etc.

> CPR systems facilitate the capture, storage, processing, communication, security, and presentation of non-redundant health information. They are not massive databases, but independent computer systems at individual care sites with minimum connectivity requirements and appropriate security, specific data can be accessed from any system upon authorization of the patient. CPR systems provide availability to complete and accurate patient data, clinical reminders and alerts, decision support, and links to bodies of related data and knowledge bases. CPR systems can warn a caregiver when there is an allergy to a medication being prescribed, can provide the latest research on treatment modalities, and can organize volumes of information about a patient's chronic condition.[1]

Because medical information is stored in many places, by many entities, the definition naturally depends on the stakeholder's perspective. To a physician, it would be an electronic replacement for the manila folder he or she uses to gather and store office notes, lab results, and external reports pertaining to a particular patient over an extended period. In the hospital, the paper medical record has traditionally been admission-centered, but the electronic record presents an opportunity to move beyond that to create a more longitudinal, patient-focused database. To an insurance plan, it might involve primarily enrollment information, benefits descriptions, and claims history. To an enterprise attempting to coalesce several of these entities into one, thereby forming an *integrated delivery system (IDS)*, the creation of an integrated system of electronic records has emerged as a key strategic goal without which successful integration is unlikely.

Although some choose to define the record (calling it an electronic *health* record) as an all-inclusive collection of every bit of data regarding the patient's health, including billing and reimbursement for example, I prefer to limit the scope of the EMR to data that would traditionally be stored in the patient's clinical *chart*. The challenges of computerizing just this milieu are difficult enough and require focused attention if the problem is ever to be solved.

It is important to recognize that electronic records are "not merely automated forms of today's paper-based medical records." Some time ago, after presenting a seminar on EMR to an audience of medical group practice managers, one of the attendees proudly invited me to her office to see their "brand new electronic medical records system." Accepting the offer, I arrived to find the customary basement room full of file shelves brimming with thick paper charts. But when she pushed a button, a motorized system started mechanically transporting the file cabinets until the one bearing the letter "L" came to the front. It may have used some electronics, but it clearly did not fit the definition of an EMR. Neither does a system that only stores digitally scanned versions of paper documents, because it cannot provide the additional benefits of flexible display, searchability, and decision support that a true electronic record must offer.

## THE HISTORY OF COMPUTER-BASED RECORDS

Interestingly, a physician played a key role in the chain of events that led to the development of computers in this country.[2] Dr. John Shaw Billings, asked to assist the Census Bureau in the 1880 and 1890 census, suggested to an engineer, Herman Hollerith, that punched cards could be used to represent individual citizens, and that machines should be built to tabulate them. Hollerith, whose name later became synonymous with the punched data card, founded the Tabulating Machine Company, which later merged into the Computing-Tabulating-Recording Corporation, which in 1924 was renamed by Thomas J. Watson, Sr., to International Business Machines Corporation.

It was not until the development of the transistor, and its application in computers in 1958, that these machines became practical for commercial use outside of special laboratories. Soon afterward, in 1960, the first paper proposing the adoption of computers for patient data collection and storage was published.[3] By 1965, Lusted had built a remarkably complete computerized clinical record system, including identification data, physical examination findings, laboratory test results, radiology reports, and disease summaries. But this system contained the medical records of monkeys, not humans, and I find it both amusing and illuminating that computerization of the "objective" portions of the clinical record was accomplished within five years of the availability of computers, while efficient capture of that last elusive bit of information, the "subjective" patient history, still challenges us 40 years later!

During the 1970s, a number of clinical computerization projects were initiated by medical informatics groups at academic medical centers. Some of the most comprehensive systems were developed in Boston, at Beth Israel Hospital, Brigham and Women's Hospital, and Massachusetts General Hospital. Other notable implementations were found at Yale, Emory, Johns Hopkins, and LDS Hospital. Systems housing ambulatory care data were less common, but the COSTAR system at the Harvard Community Health Plan and a system at Kaiser Permanente in northern California were pioneers in this area. For the most part, these systems were deployed using mainframe or minicomputers in a data center, with video display terminals placed throughout clinical areas of the hospital. Clinical data was captured from diagnostic testing departments such as laboratory, radiology, and pathology. Although physicians found access to diagnostic data was facilitated by computer systems, direct computer *entry* of data by physicians quickly proved itself to be a problem, so physicians continued to write on paper and data entry was later performed by clerical staff working from these "input forms." Many papers and even entire books[4,5] have been written on the challenges of getting physicians to use computers.

Incremental progress continued during the 1980s. In general, the large comprehensive systems built and maintained as long-term projects by dedicated informatics teams at academic medical centers did not become commercially available, but the ideas embodied in them saw use as vendors developed several clinical departmental systems. Bedside clinical systems for use by nurses and order-entry applications that were actually used by physicians were two notable breakthroughs during this period. Furthermore, the availability of low-cost personal computers enabled more clinicians to experiment and become familiar with computers, providing growth in the much-needed cadre of computer-knowledgeable physicians. However, as managed care emerged, bringing new reimbursement schemes such as prepaid capitation and diagnosis related groups, a considerable share of information system capital budgets was devoted during this time to financial and administrative systems — such as DRG groupers and managed care information systems — needed to cope with these changes.

A turning point came in 1991 with the publication of a landmark book by the Institute of Medicine, and with the implementation of their recommendation to form the Computer-Based Patient Record Institute.[6] The Institute provided a much-needed forum for discussion of the challenge, definition of standards, and dissemination of information. But even more importantly, sweeping changes took place in the business of healthcare delivery, leading to a wave of horizontal and vertical integration moves, experimentation with new models of healthcare delivery, and most recently, the emergence of the Internet and the empowerment of the health consumer. These forces are the topic of the next section.

## FORCES DRIVING COMPUTERIZATION

### Healthcare Industry Trends

Healthcare, the largest single industry in the United States at more than $1 trillion in annual revenue, has been subjected to tremendous pressure and conflicting forces during recent years. Expanding medical technological and pharmaceutical developments made available new — and frequently expensive — treatments, and made it possible to keep patients alive who previously would have been lost. Emergent disease challenges such as AIDS also contributed to the increasing cost of medical care. Finally, the healthcare financing system in the United States, which was traditionally structured around cost-based reimbursement, lacked incentives to control spending. These factors combined to produce double-digit annual growth in healthcare spending during the 1980s. In response to demands from employers who found it difficult to fund the increasing cost of employee health benefits, as well as the government, which was facing a crisis in Medicare and Medicaid financing, managed care appeared on the scene and grew involved in more than half of the healthcare delivered. Initially, managed care focused primarily on costs, but healthcare purchasers quickly became concerned with quality and value, which led to a new emphasis on measuring actual clinical outcomes.

Managed care, in some cases, turned incentives, and therefore information system requirements, completely upside down. For example, in hospitals the shift from cost-based reimbursement to diagnosis-related group (DRG) payments transformed extra hospital days from a source of revenue into a financial liability. Driven by the need to lower costs and demonstrate measurable outcomes, a wave of horizontal as well as vertical integration moves swept the previously fragmented healthcare industry. Hospitals formed partnerships with other hospitals (horizontal integration) and acquired health plans and physician practices (vertical integration). It soon became clear, however, that healthcare integration could not become reality until clinical information flowed seamlessly between all parts of the delivery system, and it was here that the failure of the paper-based medical record system became painfully apparent.

**Failure of the Paper-Based Record**

In the midst of these new demands for information, the healthcare industry found it difficult to respond, with so much of the core clinical information about its processes and outcomes locked up in pages of illegible handwriting in paper charts. The time and cost involved in retrieving information from medical records made it impossible for most institutions to tackle anything other than a few focused programs, and cycle times for studies and quality improvement activities were long.

The inefficiency of paper recordkeeping for clinical information has been well documented. Studies have demonstrated that charts are unavailable up to 30 percent of the time, and that the data within charts is frequently inaccurate and incomplete, missing diagnoses, allergies, medication details, and plans for follow-up.[6] Besides the obvious impact on quality, these studies also showed evidence of cost consequences, such as duplicate laboratory studies ordered 11 percent of the time, solely because the results were misfiled.[7]

Despite having such an inadequate core information system, the healthcare industry has continued to function, probably because of the dedication of the professionals involved. They work around the problems, using their memories to recall facts that may be lost in the chart, making telephone calls to locate other missing data, and keeping *shadow charts* in their desks in anticipation of the inevitable occasion when the official chart fails to arrive in time for a patient encounter. But the new demand for quality and outcomes information has finally proven that the electronic medical record is an essential part of every healthcare provider's strategic plan.

## STAKEHOLDERS AND KEY CAPABILITIES OF THE EMR

### Stakeholders in the EMR

Because clinical information is the core currency of the healthcare delivery system, an EMR system must fulfill the demands of the numerous stakeholders involved. The stakeholders can be divided into *primary users,* who perform direct patient care and are usually involved in creating the record, and *secondary users,* who need to view selected elements of the record but do not generally enter data. Each of these stakeholders may work with the record on an individual patient basis or on a population basis. A matrix depicting the four types of stakeholders is shown in Exhibit 1.

Note that some stakeholders work in more than one capacity, and that some roles are new, becoming feasible only once an EMR is in place. For example, the hitherto unavailable capability of performing automated search and analysis of the entire clinical records database creates a new opportunity for *case detection specialists* whose role is to proactively find patients

**Exhibit 1. EMR Stakeholders**

| | Primary Users | Secondary Users |
|---|---|---|
| Individual patient basis | • Attending physicians<br>• Consulting physicians<br>• Students, interns, residents<br>• Nurses and nursing assistants<br>• Ancillary care therapists<br>• Social workers | • Case managers<br>• Billing specialists<br>• Quality assurance reviewers<br>• Utilization reviewers<br>• Payers<br>• Attorneys |
| Population basis | • Quality improvement teams<br>• Best practices investigators<br>• Preventive care managers<br>• Case detection specialists | • Quality analysts/reporters<br>• Utilization analysts/reporters<br>• Clinical researchers<br>• Epidemiologists<br>• Federal/state/local health departments<br>• Healthcare financing entities |

whose pattern of care events may predict a serious adverse incident such as a hospitalization, and to take action to prevent it.

For an EMR to succeed, it must deliver sufficient benefits across the entire spectrum of stakeholders. A number of EMR efforts have failed because the system or its implementation was perceived to focus more on the needs of the secondary rather than the primary users, or because promised benefits would only be available at some point in the future. Conversely, a system that satisfies the wishes of the primary users, but fails to capture data in a structured and coded format so that quality and outcomes can be measured and value can be developed for secondary users, is also a poor investment.

## Key Capabilities of the EMR

To deliver benefits to its stakeholders, the EMR must deliver substantial improvements over the paper record in the following areas:

- Facilitating access
- Presenting data
- Supporting clinical decisions
- Automating workflow
- Connecting to external entities
- Managing populations
- Integrating care

Probably the most obvious benefit of an EMR is facilitating access to the record. As mentioned above, numerous studies have documented the inconsistent availability of paper records. As health systems grow from single campuses into large geographically dispersed networks, the number of places a physical chart might be increases exponentially, exacerbating the problem of locating and delivering the paper chart. Costs of $10 and more, and waits of 4 to 24 hours, are not uncommon in large health systems. Contrast this with access to a single patient record in an EMR, which requires no more than typing the patient's name into the nearest terminal device. Most contemporary EMR systems respond in two seconds or less. In addition to ease and speed, multiuser concurrent access is offered by the more sophisticated EMR designs, allowing several care team members to collaborate in parallel on the same patient encounter via different workstations, a feat completely impossible with paper charts, which support only one-at-a-time serial access.

As any harried hospital medical resident will bemoan, the paper chart, once found, does not easily yield up its secrets. The medical chart is nothing more than a bound collection of pages, some typed, but many illegibly handwritten. Although there is some attempt at organization, with tabbed dividers separating various sources of reports and pages filed chronologically within each divider, the clinician frequently finds himself flipping frantically between these sections in an attempt to collate data into an order needed for an understanding of the case. Therefore, presenting data in various ways on demand is another great advantage of the EMR over the paper record. To facilitate analysis of trends, the EMR can quickly summarize quantitative data in a tabular format or in a graph. The clinician can choose a time-oriented view, with all activities integrated, in order to understand everything that happened to the patient during a selected time period. Or she may switch to a source-oriented view to focus on x-ray results alone, free from the distraction of other items. The quick presentation of summary data, such as a problem list or medication profile, is yet another benefit, allowing the physician to gain a basic familiarity with the patient's situation at a glance, a task that could require many minutes of tedious examination in a paper chart.

The prospect of computers supporting clinical decisions has always been exciting for the medical informatics community, but some of the more ambitious artificial intelligence efforts may actually have contributed to the resistance of practicing physicians to using computers. After all, what professional enjoys having it proven that he can be replaced by a machine? However, it has subsequently become clear that computer systems can be valuable assistants when providing reminders, alerts, protocols, guidelines, reference material, and even selective private critiques. Specific examples of these capabilities will be provided later, in the section on design. Probably the most clinically sophisticated and longest-running decision support capability is found in the HELP (Health Evaluation through Logical Processing) system at Intermountain Health Care Corporation.[8] Controlled studies have actually demonstrated reductions in morbidity and mortality in surgical and critical care patients as a result of the decision support offered by this system.

The need for automating workflow can be appreciated by simply visiting a clinic and looking at the desktops of the physicians and staff — assuming you can find the desktops, which are completely covered with charts, reports, message slips, forms, and more. To succeed, the EMR must not only manage the charts, but must also automate the clinical workflows that surround the chart.

The value of the EMR is further enhanced by electronically connecting to external entities such as laboratories, radiology departments, pharmacies, and payers. By eliminating manual filing tasks and accelerating the appearance of new data within the record the timeliness of care is enhanced.

Once clinical information is available in an electronic database, powerful new capabilities for managing populations are unleashed. Statistical analysis can provide valuable information on the characteristics of the population, such as the prevalence of certain conditions or the correlation between certain observations and conditions. Using data mining techniques, new knowledge can be developed, such as predictive factors for adverse events. This knowledge can be harnessed to proactively improve the health of the population.

Finally, EMR is essential for integration of care across the many entities that make up a healthcare delivery system. To function seamlessly as a delivery system, transmission of clinical information from the primary care physician to the consultant, from the consultant to the surgeon, from the surgeon to the hospital admitting department, from the admitting department to the bedside nurse, from the nurse to the operating room, from the operating room to the ward, and finally from the discharging physician back to the primary care physician must take place instantly and accurately. Until EMR, every one of these steps involved some combination of phone calls, handwriting, dictation, transcription, photocopying, fax transmission, and manual filing. The potential benefits of an integrated electronic record, with universal and instantaneous access by everyone caring for the patient, can be enormous.

## ISSUES IN THE DESIGN OF AN EMR

### Database and Application Architecture

A general principle of database design is that it should model the real-world entities and activities of the target organization. In the case of healthcare, however, it has been fervently hoped that the EMR itself will help transform the underlying healthcare system — which is in reality still fragmented and frequently ambiguous in its relationships — into a new integrated whole. Because of this, a clinical data repository (CDR), a database housing all the clinical data collected in every care setting throughout the enterprise, is often seen as the necessary first step for an integrated delivery system on the road to an EMR. However, obstacles are immediately encountered in its design and implementation. Besides the technical challenges of interfacing the different legacy systems, the various entities within the enterprise may not be prepared to give up ownership of their data. Some may appropriately raise ethical and legal issues regarding the sharing of data, or even ask the question outright, "Whose data is it, anyway?" Privacy concerns are heightened, and many might question the system's ability to maintain the required confidentiality of patient information when the entire enterprise potentially has access to it. When attempting to forge links with non-owned physician practices, further legal issues are raised because hospitals are prohibited from providing goods or services that might be construed as an inducement to refer patients to that facility. Thus, the CDR project can actually end up slowing down the process of integration rather than accelerating it as originally hoped.

This issue can be addressed through appropriate utilization of *centralized* versus *distributed* approaches to the data architecture, as illustrated in Exhibit 2. Note that this is a simplified diagram: the CDR generally includes an interface engine as well to facilitate data interchange with numerous departmental and legacy systems. In the distributed approach, a more flexible stance is taken toward the housing of data. Some fully integrated departments will have all their data stored in the repository, while other entities that have a more ambiguous relationship can have their own database, with selective interchange of data between the local database and the central repository. My experience indicates that the fully centralized approach to the database is practically impossible to implement without a fully unified underlying healthcare system, and since that degree of unification is rarely a reality, the more flexible distributed approach is

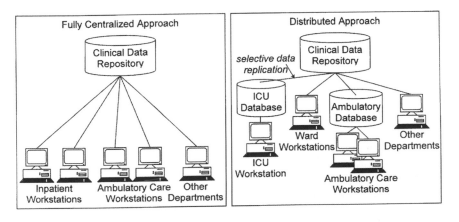

**Exhibit 2. Centralized versus Distributed Data Architectures**

more successful. The distributed approach also provides quicker results, delivering benefits in care settings such as the ambulatory environment long before a centralized CDR project can become a reality, providing necessary momentum to sustain the organization's energy and resources during the EMR project that will span several years. In the distributed approach, data integration can proceed at a pace matching the integration of the business elements.

Regarding application architecture, in IDS environments that include both hospitals and ambulatory care settings there has been a strong desire to have one application for clinicians to use across all settings of care. To some extent, this pressure came about because the different departmental applications have had different, idiosyncratic user interfaces, which clinicians found impossible to learn, but it is also in response to the gaps in information transfer that occur between inpatient and ambulatory settings. While a unified system may sound good in theory, dramatic differences in the workflows and perspectives of ambulatory care and inpatient care make it questionable whether such an idealized application can be created. As long as similar user interface paradigms are used by all programs, it may be most valuable to have focused applications tailored to each setting, with easy drill-across into the data from the other settings. For example, an inpatient system should be able to import a summary from the ambulatory care system for use as background material in the history and physical. Similarly, by clicking on a discharge summary document within an ambulatory care system, the user should be able to open up the details of the hospitalization. This kind of functionality can be delivered by separate, cooperative applications.

## Clinical Record Structure

The basic structure of clinical documentation has been established from years of paper medical recordkeeping tradition, consisting of little more than a binder, some section dividers, and a collection of paper documents fastened within the binder into the various sections. The sections generally divide the chart according to the source of the documents, such as physician notes, radiology reports, or external correspondence, producing a primary *source-oriented* organization. Within each section, the documents are filed chronologically, producing a *time-oriented* secondary sort order. There may be a problem list, but its usefulness is impaired because of the conflict between the need to keep the list accurate and up-to-date and the clumsy method of making serial revisions when erasures are forbidden. The paper chart offers no alternative sorting, grouping, or linking mechanisms between documents (except for the occasional staple!).

To completely reinvent the chart would require a drastic change in medical education and an extensive retraining of all clinicians, as well as

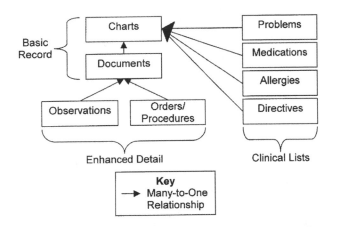

**Exhibit 3. Data Structure within an Electronic Medical Record**

revisions of laws and regulations regarding medical records. Accordingly, to be accepted, the EMR should respect these traditional metaphors, but to deliver value, it must in addition create a database of sufficient structure to allow searching, sorting, and displaying of information in ways that create new knowledge. A conceptual diagram of the data structure within an EMR is presented in Exhibit 17-3, which will now be discussed in greater detail.

The core of the EMR is the *basic record*, which contains the familiar concepts of the *chart* and of *clinical documents*. By retaining this model at its center, the electronic record and its legal status can be more easily understood by those familiar with paper-based records. If one were to print out all the documents, the familiar paper chart would be recovered, thus tying the electronic version back to known procedures, laws, and regulations governing their use.

Beyond this basic core, the EMR should capture enhanced detail, which can be classified into clinical observations, which represent finer-grained data gathered about the patient, and orders/procedures, which represent things done to or for the patient. The chief complaint, the patient's temperature, and the findings on palpation of the abdomen are all examples of observations obtained during a physician–patient encounter that can and should be stored as structured data. The technology for gathering structured data during the process of encounter documentation will be discussed in the section on data capture. Results of diagnostic testing, such as laboratory and imaging results, can also be stored as observations. Each observation has a number of attributes, including value, units, source, time and date entered, and more. The orders/procedures table contains detailed information about activities ordered and performed to diagnose and treat the patient.

While enhanced details let users "drill down" within a document, clinicians also need the ability to "zoom out" and gain an overview of the patient that spans multiple documents. To satisfy this important need, the EMR should support the maintenance of clinical lists for each chart. Created and updated by clinicians in the process of caring for the patient, the main benefit of the clinical lists is a reduction in the need to read the entire chart, because the lists offer a concise summary of the most important information. The most desirable lists cover problems, medications, allergies, and directives. The list maintenance functionality must offer an uncluttered view of the most current version of the list while retaining a complete audit trail of additions, changes, and deletions to support the medicolegal requirement of traceability.

To further increase the value of these additional tables, the EMR should attempt to capture relevant linkages between elements of the record. A laboratory observation could be linked back to the order that caused it to occur, the order could be linked back to the encounter during which it was placed, and the encounter could be linked backward to the problem being addressed, or forward to the medications prescribed for the problem. These linkages make it possible to analyze disease presentations, clinical processes, and outcomes to a much greater depth than could ever be done with paper records. Because clinicians are not accustomed to creating these linkages explicitly, the EMR application must create them transparently whenever possible.

Other concepts have been proposed as an organizing structure for the electronic chart. The *encounter* construct encompasses one distinct interaction between the patient and the healthcare system, such as, for example, an office visit, a hospitalization, or an outpatient procedure, including preoperative and postoperative care. The *episode* concept is one level higher, and might include several encounters that are all involved in the diagnosis and treatment of a particular episode of illness. However, these concepts break down frequently in real-world clinical situations. During a given office visit, several different conditions may be dealt with, destroying any neat hierarchical classification of encounters within episodes. Furthermore, episodes may not be apparent until they are well underway, or even until long after they are complete. Thus, while these constructs may have value for retrospective analysis, they have not proven practical for use at the time of care delivery. A similar difficulty emerged in earlier attempts to create a strictly problem-oriented record. This approach would require clinicians to select a single problem in order to create a document, and to create separate documents when multiple problems are addressed. Although such a system would certainly simplify retrospective analysis, it has proven impractical in practice because of the ambiguities and overlaps between problems in real-world clinical situations.

## Coding and Vocabulary

The next requirement of an EMR is to have a consistent coding system or vocabulary for the values entered in the above-described data structures, but this has proven to be one of the more daunting challenges. The potential knowledge space is extremely large and complex, and represents a wide spectrum of data from the most objective and quantitative, to the most subjective and "fuzzy" data imaginable. Nevertheless, progress has accelerated in recent years. Coordinated by the American National Standards Institute (ANSI), bodies such as Health Level 7 (HL7), the American Society for Testing and Materials (ASTM), and the American College of Radiologists/National Electrical Manufacturers Association (ACR/NEMA) have defined formats for interchange — and by implication, for storage — of many clinical transactions, clinical data elements, and radiographic images. Once formats are defined, the vocabulary to be used must be specified. The basic topic-focused vocabularies of the International Classification of Diseases (ICD) for diagnoses, and Current Procedural Terminology (CPT) for procedures, while popular standards for purposes of billing and reimbursement, are too limited to serve the needs of a comprehensive EMR. A more extensive vocabulary of clinical concepts, but one that still requires more work to become useful for direct clinician interaction, is the Systematized Nomenclature of Medicine (SNOMED). The Unified Medical Language System (UMLS) is an attempt to map between the various vocabularies. Blair has provided a useful and comprehensive overview of these and other healthcare information standards.[9]

## Displaying Clinical Information

The ability to find and display a chart quickly — with two seconds being a reasonable benchmark for response time — is a basic requirement for any EMR system. A higher level of benefit is delivered when the EMR also allows the clinician to view the chart data in illuminating and instructive ways that are not possible with paper. For example, on first accessing a chart, the system should present a summary view that takes advantage of the clinical lists. Exhibit 4 provides an example of such a screen. From the summary view, the clinician may choose to move to the documents list, but he should also be able to drill down directly, focusing on any of the clinical lists or documents.

When displaying the documents within a chart, the EMR should offer flexible ways to sort and filter them, and the clinician should be able to store these as reusable views. Examples of desirable views might include:

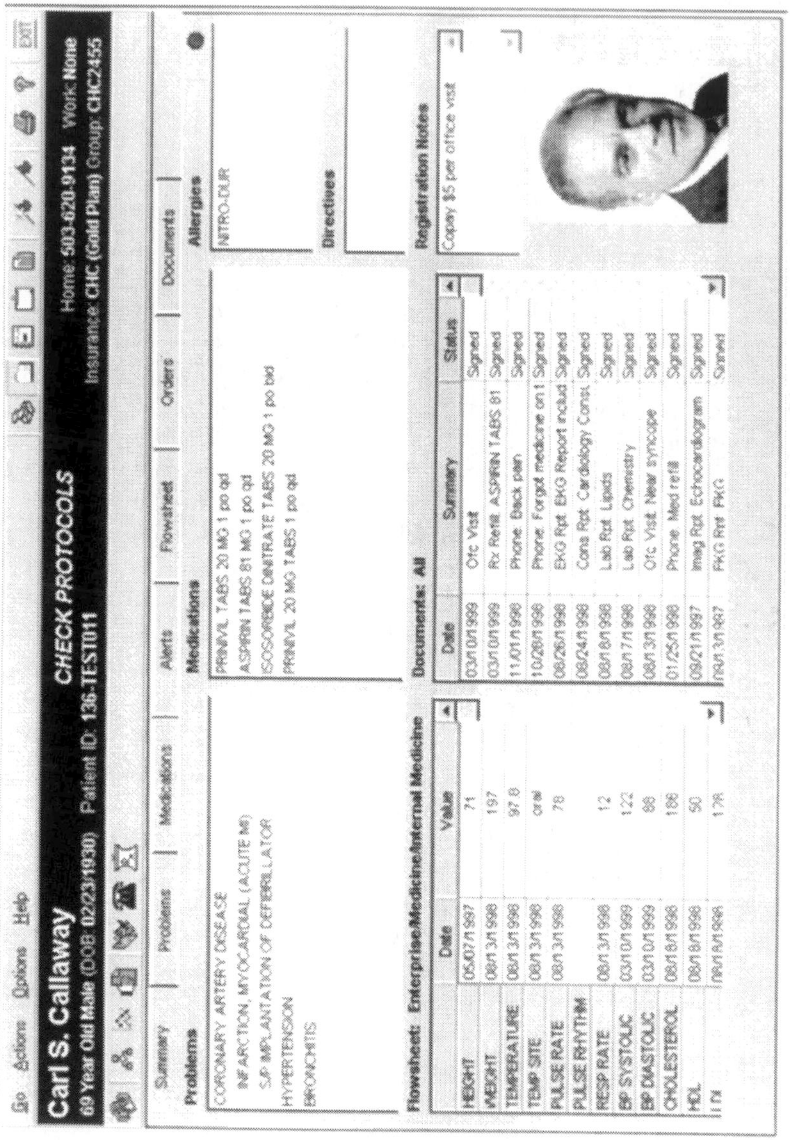

Exhibit 4. Summary View of a Chart within an Electronic Medical Record

- All documents, excluding obsolete revisions — a complete clinical view
- All documents, including all revisions — a strict medicolegal view
- Documents created by any particular clinician — "my own notes"
- Documents sourced from a given department, such as cardiology — a specialty-focused view
- Documents from several departments, such as laboratory, radiology, and pathology, collated together and sorted chronologically — "all diagnostic results"

Data from the enhanced detail tables should be offered in tabular and in graphical form. Clinicians are familiar with flowsheets as tools for collating information over time. Because no single organization of the data can suffice for all clinical situations, the concept of reusable views should be applied here also. For example, an anticoagulation management flowsheet view should include the patient's coagulation test results as well as the dosing levels of anticoagulant medication. An obstetric view should include all important parameters of maternal and fetal progress as well as an indication of the completion of interventions at the appropriate time during the pregnancy.

Display of the clinical lists appears on the surface to be a simple matter, but additional value can be delivered here as well. Clinicians value the ability to change the order within the clinical lists, sometimes preferring to sort by date of onset, but at other times wishing to sort by importance or by body system. Some more sophisticated users would wish to go beyond that and create hierarchical structures within the lists. Even more value can be provided by displaying an understandable history of revisions to the lists. Exhibit 5 illustrates the concept of a timeline display showing problem and medication clinical list entries along with their temporal histories, as well as a graphical display of blood pressure observation. At a glance over this five-year period, the clinician sees a patient with preexisting diabetes, who developed proteinuria and was placed on lisinopril, and who then developed hypertension, which has since been brought under control by the addition of atenolol. Deducing this information from dozens of notes and reports within a paper chart would take considerably more time.

### Data Capture

In the paper record, physicians are accustomed to documenting their encounters by handwriting or by dictation. Although there is a rough format to be followed, and for some documents such as hospital discharge summaries certain data elements are required, in general these creations vary tremendously in completeness and legibility. Medical record technicians are then tasked with deciphering doctors' notes, chasing them down to correct deficiencies, and obtaining missing signatures. Although it can

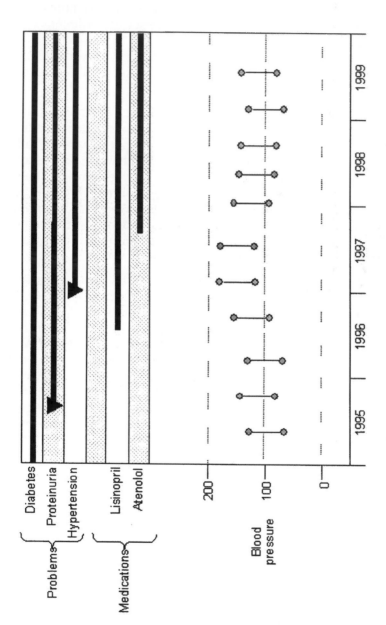

**Exhibit 5. Timeline Concept for Display of Clinical List Information**

certainly be argued that using clerical assistance to save physicians time makes economic sense, the traditional expectation that physicians can document their work any way they choose and that others will "clean up" after them is one of the major hurdles to clinical data capture in the EMR. Although one might be tempted to avoid this challenge altogether by building the EMR around scanned handwritten documents and transcribed notes, recall that most secondary users of the EMR expect the enterprise's investment in this technology to deliver large amounts of well-structured data for analysis.

In my experience, satisfying these conflicting expectations is probably the single most important negotiation to be accomplished in gaining enterprisewide acceptance of the EMR. Exhibit 6 illustrates this trade-off graphically. As the design moves from scanned paper (which allows clinicians to continue handwriting) to electronic free text (which allows them to continue dictating) to partial structure (which requires them to use the computer but only requires structuring of certain data) to complete structure (which forces them to enter all data by making choices from structured menus), the primary users — especially the physicians — perceive an increasing penalty, expressed on the graph as a declining value. Conversely, the secondary users see increasing value as more data become available in structured format. Combining the values delivered to both constituencies, an optimization peak occurs at some point between the two extremes.

Unless the EMR can eventually be operated near this optimum point, there will be insufficient value to justify the investment, or even to gain basic acceptance. However, it is essential to pay close attention to the primary users early in the process, since they are the ones who perceive

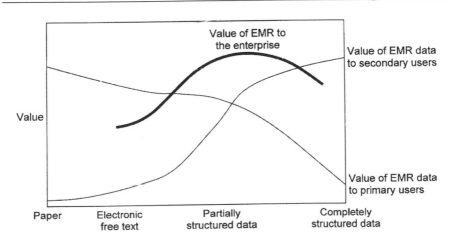

**Exhibit 6. Optimizing the Trade-off between Structured and Unstructured Data**

themselves as suffering a potential penalty. Therefore, it is advisable to "walk up" the curve from the left side rather than trying to strike the optimum balance immediately. Starting too far on the right side practically guarantees a violent uprising from the physician contingent. The situation is even more complex than can be expressed in a single graph. The various medical specialties have different levels of structured data inherent in their practice, and even within a specialty, various physician users have differing tolerance for change. However, I have found this graph very useful in bringing the inherent conflict to the surface for constructive discussions and to foster a mutual understanding of the opposing points of view.

New technologies for human–computer interaction promise some relief in this conflict. Voice recognition is approaching practicality, and handwriting recognition may some day reach that point as well, reducing the time and expense of capturing free text electronically. Farther in the future, progress in computer understanding of natural language could some day permit the extraction of consistent structured data from clinical free text. Until these become practical, the best approach is to offer a flexible choice of data entry methods to satisfy the widely differing needs of physicians that may be primary care or specialist, office or hospital based, young or old, computer-literate or technophobic. Dictation and transcription will continue to play a role for difficult and unpredictable elements, but wherever possible the adoption of point-of-care on-screen forms, using a mouse or pen to select from choices, should be employed. Forms that can be customized for the user are even more acceptable, but the time and effort of creating forms can be an obstacle. Building specialty-specific communities of users who share knowledge in their respective areas of expertise is helpful in overcoming this barrier.

## Decision Support

To be most effective, clinical decision support should be delivered at the moment of decision making, and the EMR provides the first real opportunity to deliver this information at the point of care. Decision support can take the form of reminders, alerts, protocols, guidelines, reference material, or critiques.

As an example, a reminder might take the form of a message that appears automatically when scheduling an appointment, informing the clerk that the patient is due for certain preventive care such as a pap smear based on their age and the interval since the test was last performed. Multiple studies have demonstrated that computerized reminders increase compliance for certain valuable but routine activities that are easily forgotten. In the primary care setting, reminders are generally focused on improving compliance with guidelines for preventive care. In procedure-oriented specialties, reminders can help ensure that all preoperative activities are performed, and that postoperative follow-up is thorough.

An alert can be defined as a warning of a potentially dangerous situation, such as a possible interaction between drugs on the patient's newly created medication regimen, or a worrisome trend in a particular lab result. It should be reemphasized here that alerts must be delivered immediately during the care process. If the processing time for alerts is long enough that the clinician has moved on to another patient context — and that could be a matter of just minutes — the alert is perceived as an interruption rather than as an assistance. Worse, if the alert arrives after the initial order has been transmitted, alerts may take on a nuisance or even a punitive connotation in the mind of the physician. This need for a tight feedback loop is one more reason why systems architectures with local databases and local decision support rules may prove more practical.

Protocols are predetermined pathways of care. Generally, patients are placed "on protocol" by virtue of having a particular condition or being on a certain therapy. The feedback mechanisms to the clinician can range from the very simple, such as a reminder that this patient is on a protocol, to the complex, such as a validation of every order against the protocol, or automatic entry of order sets to maintain the patient on the protocol. Guidelines are similar to protocols in that they recommend particular elements of care in a given situation, but they are generally delivered more as a unit of literature to be read by the clinician, instead of through a tight integration with the orders system. An even less formal type of decision support is the linkage of selected reference material to various elements of the electronic record. For example, an elevated serum calcium result in the EMR could have a button next to it that leads to a monograph on the common causes of this abnormality.

A number of papers have described critiques as a very sophisticated form of decision support, in which numerous rules are activated by several elements of the patient's data, and a computer-generated discussion tailored to the patient's situation is offered to the user. At present, these remain mostly in the research realm.

**Workflow Automation**

To deliver major gains in efficiency, the EMR must not only provide a replacement for the paper chart, but must also offer improved electronic versions of all the workflow processes that surround the chart. The equivalents of messages, attachments, inboxes (work queues), and routing must all be implemented within the electronic system. Each staff member should have an electronic desktop, typically containing scheduled events, such as patient appointments or meetings, and to-do lists of unscheduled tasks such as telephone messages, requests for information, and documents to be reviewed and signed. It is helpful if the electronic messages can be attached to particular items in the electronic charts, analogous to the use of paper clips or stick-on notes in the paper world. Thus, when a message is read, the system can immediately bring the relevant part of the appropriate chart into view.

The creation, signing, and routing of documents in the practice of healthcare can be quite complex. For example, in a training program, a note may be created by a medical student, with contributions from nurses and other allied health professionals. Each contributor initials his or her portion. The medical student must sign the document, but then route it to an intern or resident who has signing authority for medications and other orders before treatment can be given. The resident, in turn, must route it to an attending physician, who follows complex regulatory requirements to determine how much additional documentation he or she must append to the note before endorsing it with his or her own signature. The document may then be routed once more to several consulting physicians, for review only, and then perhaps — accompanied by a letter — it may be sent outside the health system to a referring physician for information purposes as well. All of these concepts and flows should be implemented in the EMR, or the staff will be forced to jump awkwardly between computer and paper systems. In examining an EMR implementation, a glance at the computer monitors will quickly reveal how successfully the system supports these workflows: if the monitor bezel is plastered with dozens of Post-It notes, the software is probably lacking in workflow features.

### Interfaces to the EMR

Unless the healthcare entity implementing an EMR is unusually self-contained, there will be numerous interfaces needed to import and export information to and from the system. Although a point-to-point interface to one or two other applications might be created in an isolated setting, the health enterprise generally requires an interface engine to efficiently manage data interchange between multiple applications.

The value of an EMR increases with the completeness of the clinical data it contains. Unless a critical mass of information is included, the need to maintain both paper and electronic records can make the system less efficient than paper alone. The EMR should be able to send and receive fully electronic documents with sufficient structure and context to enable them to be directly filed in the record, or placed in an appropriate inbox in the workflow system. It is extremely important to accomplish this for sources of detailed, quantitative data, such as laboratory reports, as manual entry into the EMR would be unacceptably laborious and inaccurate. An EMR should accept, and a laboratory should provide, such data in the common reporting formats defined by the ASTM or by HL7. Demographic data should be exchanged with practice management systems or hospital ADT systems, and clinical data should be interchanged with a clinical data repository if one exists. HL7 standards exist or are under development for these transactions. For incoming textual reports, digital transfer is preferred; and although there is an HL7 format defined, paper will probably not be eliminated for many years, so the EMR and its peripherals should include the capability to either scan and store the report as an image, or convert it to digital form using optical character recognition. Hybrid solutions in which some incoming paper reports are abstracted and the summary entered into the EMR, while the original report is filed in a seldom-needed paper file, can be cost effective during this transitional period. The ultimate goal, however, should be a near-paperless workflow.

In some cases, data from external systems is better left in place and simply referenced in the EMR database. For example, a picture archiving and communications system (PACS) for storing radiology images requires specialized, high-volume storage technology. The image data should remain within that system, while the EMR simply stores a reference pointer that allows the clinician to seamlessly call up the PACS viewer to display the file.

## Consumer Access to the EMR

Although in most states, patients have a right to request a copy of their record, healthcare organizations generally have done little to ease the access of patients to the information concerning them that is housed in their records. The rapid penetration of the Internet into American households has led to rising expectations of consumers regarding access to information as well as the ability to communicate with the providers of their goods and services. Once an EMR is in place, there exists an exciting potential to offer patients self-service access to selected elements of their record. Exhibit 7 illustrates this concept.

Some of the information and services that can be provided in this manner include:

- Self-service maintenance of certain elements of demographics, such as telephone or emergency contact
- An accurate listing of the current medication regimen
- Graphs of weight, blood pressure, cholesterol, and other parameters
- Notification of preventive care that is due
- Self-service access to immunization records and other documents needed for school or work
- A printable wallet card summarizing the patient's medical problems, allergies, and diagnoses
- A more accurate and less labor-intensive means of receiving medication refill requests
- An alternate means of requesting non-urgent appointments
- Collection of patient interview data from home before an office visit

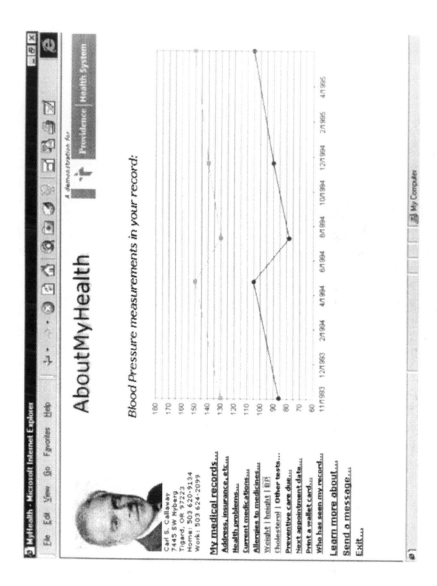

**Exhibit 7. Consumer Access to the Electronic Medical Record**

- Patient education by providing materials or directing them to other Web-based sources
- Improved follow-up of patients, by transferring home weight records of heart failure patients or home glucose data of diabetes patients

## CHALLENGES IN IMPLEMENTATION OF AN EMR

### Technological Challenges

In a paperless record environment, access to the EMR must be ubiquitous. The lack of a universal computing and network infrastructure in the clinical areas of most healthcare systems represents a major barrier to be overcome, and the number of access points that must be installed, the capital cost of equipment and wiring, and the ongoing costs of support and maintenance are formidable.

Healthcare presents a somewhat difficult environment for computing compared to other industries. For example, most healthcare services are not desk-oriented, taking place instead at bedside, in operating suites, or in examination rooms. Access devices that can be used comfortably in these environments have been slow to arrive, and their cost has not been driven down as quickly as the cost of the mass-market personal computer. Wireless portable devices, while attractive from an ergonomic and device count standpoint, bring additional technological problems such as the need for maintenance of reliable radio communications links and limitations in bandwidth. However, steady progress is being made and it is to be expected that compact, reliable devices with appropriate ergonomic characteristics will emerge.

The maintenance and support costs of workstations have been a major concern, exacerbated by the short technology cycles in this space. Personal computers, which initially appeared to have the potential to reduce computing, proved expensive to support because of the difficulty in controlling their configurations and resources, and because of basic immaturity in their underlying operating systems. This issue has been improved by remote hardware and software management features as well as a general maturation in desktop operating systems. Web technology offers another potential for simplification by limiting client code to a single, universal browser. However, Web technology itself is in a state of rapid evolution, particularly in the areas of structured data representation and support of robust client/server transactions.

The EMR must be recognized as a mission-critical service, especially when deployed in acute, intensive, or emergency care settings. Technologies such as redundant disk storage, redundant servers with automatic failover, self-healing networks, and auxiliary power supplies reduce the risk of hardware failure. Software reliability must be approached through rigorous testing and a disciplined approach to training, operations, and backup. High acuity departments require 99.9 percent uptime or better, while for ambulatory settings a 99 percent figure may be adequate.

In general, computing speed and storage capacity requirements of the EMR do not strain present technological limits unless an attempt is being made to store full diagnostic-quality images or video online. It is a good design practice to segregate the storage of large binary files such as images from the compact text and numerical data of the core EMR. Information from current EMR systems in use in ambulatory environments indicates that the core database, excluding images, consumes on the order of 10 MB to 50 MB of data per practitioner per year.

## Nontechnological Challenges

The nontechnological challenges are the ones most frequently underestimated when an EMR is implemented. The paper chart, clumsy as it may be, is a central organizing feature in practically all the activities of direct patient care. To put a completely new system in place, regardless of its advantages, a major reengineering effort is required. A complete description of the details of an EMR implementation project is beyond the scope of this chapter, but there are a number of critical success factors that have emerged as a result of experience.

First, there must be a strategic vision that motivates the organization to move to EMR. The project must be related to the strategic goals and objectives of the organization. During one such endeavor, I found it valuable to form small cross-functional groups, tasking them to create vignettes of the kind of patient care they wanted to deliver in the future. The need for an EMR should emerge naturally from the vision of quality care delivery.

Second, internal champions must be developed. Communication of the strategic vision may suffice to launch the project, but during the long and sometimes difficult course of implementation, champions who remain committed to the goal are crucially needed to urge along their less-enthusiastic colleagues. It is particularly important to have physician champions, and even better to have one for each major specialty area of practice. Beware of having physicians who are enamored with computer technology as your sole champions. Although they may display the best understanding of the technical issues, they are not always regarded by the average doctor as their representatives. The best champions are the clinical leaders, not the technical avant-garde.

Third, the project management must set appropriate expectations. Everyone must understand how long the project will take, what level of function will be available, and what limitations will exist. These expectations must be continuously reevaluated and corrected during the course of the project.

Fourth, all technical infrastructure problems must be solved, and high reliability achieved, before the clinical users are exposed to the system. For many users, this will be their first experience with a computer system, and first impressions can be difficult to change. It is a wise investment to allow a large safety factor when planning technical resources for support during this critical phase. Also, the first functionality activated should be one of the least mission critical, until the reliability of the infrastructure in everyday use has been proven.

Fifth, the interfaces should be developed, tested, and operational before users go-live on the system. The value of the EMR is increased greatly by its ability to display clinical data gathered from external sources, such as laboratories. During the first days after go-live, users will be struggling to adapt their working styles to enter data into the new system, and it is essential that they be receiving the maximum possible value from data presentation as a form of compensation.

Sixth, make a commitment to cultural and process changes that surround the introduction of the EMR. When access to the chart no longer requires intermediaries, and communication between staff becomes potentially instantaneous, the politics, power structures, and processes of the organization are all subject to change. This can be taken advantage of in positive ways, or it can prove disruptive if not managed well. Now that the physician can book a return appointment while still with the patient in the exam room, should he? How will the office appointment clerk react? Should the nurse be authorized to confirm routine medication refills now that the patient's compliance can be judged from the well-organized electronic chart? Or will physicians insist on retaining control of this task? Should patients be given a printout of their medication lists for review while waiting to see the doctor? Many process breakthroughs can be made; but at every step, the cultural and personal aspects should be addressed.

Seventh, do everything possible to simplify go-live. For example, the electronic record should be preloaded with basic data so that users do not face the daunting prospect of empty charts to be created from scratch on their first day of use. Another interesting practice that has proven valuable is to conduct a dress rehearsal just before go-live, complete with simulated patients enacting scripts, to let the staff work out details and reduce their anxiety about making mistakes in front of real patients.

Finally, there should be ongoing communication and continuous improvement in the use of the EMR. As a new system is rolled out to the organization, lessons are learned. These lessons should be shared throughout the organization through some communication instrument such as a project newsletter. Then they should be put into practice through a program of continuous quality improvement.

281

## THE RETURN ON INVESTMENT FOR EMR

### Economic Impact of EMR

While the costs of electronic record systems vary considerably, from about $5000 per physician per year to up to ten times that amount, they are always significant investments for the healthcare organizations considering them. Before making these commitments, healthcare organizations require justification in the form of a return-on-investment analysis. Unfortunately, no simple formula applies to all institutions; in fact, the return varies widely based on the ability of the organization to reengineer its processes to extract maximum value from the EMR. Some general guidance can be given, however. Financial returns can be classified into four types: *internal efficiencies*, which reduce the overhead costs of providing a given service; *revenue enhancements*, which may result from increased productivity or from more effective billing and reimbursement for a given service; *medical loss reduction*, which represents the potential decrease in the need for medical services as a result of greater clinical effectiveness; and ultimately, *competitive marketing advantage*, which is gained by health systems that deliver higher value as a result of more efficient clinical data management.

**Internal Efficiencies.** There are numerous areas of obvious savings for an EMR over paper record systems. Chart pulls as a cost factor can be practically eliminated after a period of time. Most paper-to-EMR conversions do not involve scanning of the entire paper chart, and as a result, the need to retrieve it falls off gradually after the go-live date. Experience in ambulatory care settings indicates that chart pulls fall off by 50 percent at six months after conversion and 85 percent at one year. The cost of a chart pull varies with the size and geographic dispersion of the organization, varying from a dollar or two in a small solo practice to $10–$15 in the large multisite health system. Another area of savings is the reduction in transcription necessary. This depends on physician willingness to use the computer as a documentation tool; but again, in typical ambulatory environments, reductions of 50 percent are common and cuts of 85 percent are achievable with motivated users. Clinical support staff requirements are reduced because fewer steps are needed to accomplish common processes such as medication refills or laboratory result follow-up. In a number of medium to large organizations, a reduction of 15 percent in the staff-to-physician ratio has been achieved. A number of professional liability insurers offer 5 percent premium discounts for clients using electronic records. Additional savings are achieved in physical chart supplies, chart storage, and photocopying. Taken together, annual savings on the order of $5000 to $10,000 per physician per year have been experienced in the second and subsequent years of EMR operation. Of all the financial impacts, internal efficiencies are the most predictable in terms of hard dollar amounts.

**Revenue Enhancements.** Analyzing the revenue enhancement effects of an EMR is complicated by the mixture of fee-for-service and prepaid reimbursement schemes. Nevertheless, in ambulatory settings in which an EMR capable of assisting in the assignment of appropriate billing codes has been installed, revenue enhancements of 8 to 15 percent have been measured. In addition, the reminder function of an electronic record increases compliance with preventive care guidelines, which represents not only an improvement in quality of care but also an additional source of revenue to the practice. Although revenue enhancements are somewhat more difficult to predict than internal efficiencies, the projections are fairly reliable in terms of hard dollar amounts.

**Medical Loss Reductions.** At the present stage of EMR penetration, a reduction in the total amount of medical services needed for a cohort of patients has yet to be demonstrated, although as mentioned earlier, an 11 percent savings in laboratory expenses has been reported simply by elimination of duplicated tests. Any attempt to measure healthcare economies is also complicated by a possible increase in services rendered in the cause of better preventive care compliance. Studies will have to be designed to measure clinical outcomes as well as medical expenses in order to draw comparisons between healthcare systems using EMR and those lacking automated records.

**Competitive Marketing Advantage.** The competitive marketing advantage produced by adoption of an EMR is the hardest return of all to quantify. In noncompetitive markets, the benefit may be undetectable, while in highly competitive environments, use of an EMR by one of the contenders could be a life-or-death strategic advantage. Buyers of healthcare services are becoming increasingly sophisticated in their demands for data that demonstrates quality and value. A healthcare organization that is unable to demonstrate its value could end up unable to compete at all. Each enterprise must evaluate its environment and determine the value of taking this step.

## THE JOURNEY TO EMR: WHERE ARE WE NOW?

### Prevalence and Adoption of EMR

Surveys of the usage of computers in ambulatory settings show considerable ambiguity in the definition of electronic records. From 13 to 20 percent of practices report using electronic records of some form, but only 1 percent report using them exclusively in place of paper records. Of those using some form of electronic record, less than half report their records include computerized problem and medication lists. The likely penetration of comprehensive, paperless EMR systems is probably at 1 to 5 percent, with partial systems that allow maintenance of problem or medication lists in about 5 to 10 percent of practices. In hospital settings, the prevalence of partial systems that allow laboratory result reporting and order entry is quite high, but it is still rare for these systems to have a means of capturing progress notes from physicians unless they are dictated and transcribed. A promising trend, however, is the growing usage of computers by physicians for other purposes such as e-mail, literature research, or personal finance. With more than half of physicians now having used a computer, the age-old problem of physician resistance to computers has probably been finally laid to rest.

## Vendor Marketplace

The electronic record has been referred to as the "holy grail" of healthcare information technology, and few established or aspiring vendors failed to notice the opportunity. However, the road to achieving a successful base of customers, revenues, and product profitability has proven a long and difficult one for all contenders. Considerable research and development work is needed to develop the product, followed by a long period of implementation experience to gain a customer base, and a number of hopeful companies with capital investments of over $50 million have failed and withdrawn from the market. As a result, the field has now narrowed to a handful of vendors with financial stability, a reasonably mature product, ongoing development efforts, and a base of customers who will share their experiences — good or bad — with prospective new adopters. The best approach is to initiate a competitive request for proposal process among the three leading vendors, and to include a visit to at least one reference site, and telephonic checks with several more, as part of the evaluation process. Because different products appeal to different areas within the organization, it is extremely important to involve all the stakeholders, especially clinician users, during the evaluation process.

## Where to Next?

What can be expected in the years to come? First of all, the pace of technology shows no signs of decreasing, and the following developments should have a substantial positive impact on the adoption of EMR:

- Advances in Web and browser technology that increase the capability of thin-client solutions, including XML and Java
- New workstation designs that emphasize light weight and portability, or improved ergonomics, with lower costs and higher reliability
- Improved automated recognition technologies for voice and handwriting
- Ubiquitous, high-bandwidth network connectivity
- Increasingly powerful server "appliances" with lower maintenance and administration costs
- Emerging standards for medical vocabulary and healthcare data interchange formats

In addition to these technical developments, a cultural shift is taking place among healthcare providers. It is no longer fashionable for a physician to scoff at the prospect of using a computer. That is progress! Sometime in the future, it will become embarrassing to think about the primitive way that patient information was managed in the days before EMR.

### References

1. Computer-Based Patient Record Institute. "Definition of Cpr," http://www.Cpri.Org/What.Html.
2. Collen, M. F. 1995. *A History of Medical Informatics in the United States.* Indianapolis, IN: American Medical Informatics Association.
3. Ledley, R. S. and Lusted, L. B. 1960. "The use of electronic computers in medical data processing," *IEEE Transactions in Medical Electronics,* 7: 31.
4. Anderson, J. G. and Jay, S. J. 1987. *Use and Impact of Computers in Clinical Medicine.* New York: Springer-Verlag.
5. Bria, W. F. and Rydell, R. L. 1996. *The Physician-Computer Connection.* Chicago: American Hospital Association Press.
6. Dick, R. S., Steen, E. B., and Detmer, D. E. 1997. *The Computer-Based Patient Record: An Essential Technology for Health Care.* Washington, D.C.: National Academy Press.
7. Tufo, H. M. and Speidel, J. J. 1971. "Problems with medical records," *Medical Care,* 9: 509–517.
8. Pryor, T. A., Gardner, R. M., Clayton, P. D., and Warner, H. R. 1988. "The HELP system," *Journal of Medical Systems,* 7: 87–102.
9. Blair, J. S. *An Overview of Healthcare Information Standards.* http://www.cpri.org/docs/overview.html.

# Chapter 21
# The Economic Justification for Electronic Medical Record Systems<sup>*</sup>

*Russell H. Sachs*

---

This chapter focuses on a study of the tangible economic impact of an electronic medical record (EMR) system on five ambulatory clinics. The goal of the study was to objectively quantify the benefits of an EMR system for practice administrators of small- to medium-sized ambulatory clinics. This study did not include intangible benefits of an EMR in the financial analysis. Any specific value cited in this study should not be considered definitive, but rather as a representative value to serve as benchmarks for any ambulatory practice wishing to assess its own potential return from EMR implementation.

## INTRODUCTION

Some physicians tend to be reactive in nature, especially with response to technology. As Larry Weed has said, "If physicians were in charge of airports, there would be no radar — just intensive care units all around the periphery."[1] For physicians to be more proactive in their approach to business planning they must take into account financial projections and analysis. One major decision facing most ambulatory clinics today is whether or not they should implement an EMR system and, if so, which one, and when. The decision to purchase an EMR system may be made solely on the merits of the considerable benefits achievable with an EMR.[2] Many smaller organizations may decide to proceed this way. In

---

* This study was designed by the former Healthmatics, Inc. of Cary, North Carolina, with assistance from Superior Consultant Company, Inc., Southfield, Michigan.

larger organizations, investment capital is more likely to compete with several other worthwhile projects and a financial analysis is required to compare the various options.

Any investment decision process must also evaluate risk. A detailed analysis of risk is not presented in this study but the risks are not trivial. The primary risk involved in the EMR implementation process involves the risk of an improper system selection. Selecting an information system that is incompatible with other information systems, or that does not fit well in the work environment, or that is based on obsolete or nonindustry-standard technology can be a costly error. However, assuming due diligence is conducted in the system selection process, the risk is minimized and is likely comparable to any other high-yield investment.

Clinic managers who are attempting to rate the relative value of an EMR investment may wish to prepare an analysis that includes the financial justification for an EMR in their environment. An attempt at the evaluation of the economic impact of EMR systems may prove difficult because of the variety of ways EMR systems impact workflow and productivity in physician practices.

A review of some published articles may only increase the confusion because of the preponderance in the literature of incomplete, sketchy, or anecdotal reports originating from a variety of clinical environments. Some reports even highlight the failures of certain EMR systems to work as expected.

## INPATIENT ENVIRONMENT DIFFERENT

Many published studies document a case for a favorable return on investment through projections that measure a single variable. For example, in the inpatient environment, reduction in lab test reordering was the basis for a finding of positive return on investment by one study.[3] Alternately, some vendors have developed multivariate models for the calculation of return on investment that are extremely difficult to use, while others are too simplistic to be of any real predictive value.

Most large-scale return on investment analyses of EMR systems reported in the literature were originally performed in an inpatient environment.[3] The impacts of a clinical information system in an acute environment are quite different from those in an ambulatory environment. One major difference is that any loss of provider productivity in an inpatient environment may have little or no economic effect on the hospital. This is not likely to be true in the ambulatory physician's practice. For this reason, this study quantifies the initial reduction in provider productivity common among most structured data EMR systems, and assigns an economic value to the initial productivity loss for the evaluation of the net return.

**Exhibit 1. Clinic Size and Staffing Ratio**

| Clinic | Number of Providers | Number of Ancillary Staff | Staff:Provider Ratio |
|--------|---------------------|---------------------------|----------------------|
| 1 | 21 | 24 | 1.1 |
| 2 | 7 | 22 | 3.1 |
| 3 | 7 | 30 | 4.3 |
| 4 | 5 | 15 | 3.0 |
| 5 | 5 | 17 | 3.4 |
| Average | 9 | 21.6 | 3.0 |

Staff productivity gains are likewise different in an ambulatory environment. In practice, the physician-to-staff ratios vary significantly. Staff productivity gains may depend somewhat on the initial staffing ratios and possibly on staff turnover rate. This study did not look for, nor did it find, a definitive correlation between initial staffing ratio or staff turnover rate and savings realized from potential full-time equivalent (FTE) reduction.

## METHODS USED IN THE RETURN ON INVESTMENT STUDY

Data was collected over a period of two years at five representative clinics that had implemented a structured data entry type of EMR information system. The data was obtained prior to implementation of the EMR system and at periodic milestones after implementation. The five clinics in this study were geographically dispersed and varied in size from five to 21 providers (see Exhibit 1).

The practices involved in this study are generally high-volume, successful, and growing practices. The values displayed in the various tables may not necessarily be representative of average medical group practices. There was a significant amount of variability among many of the parameters measured. The values presented are averages across all five clinic sites, except where noted. Where useful, standard deviation from the mean is included as a rough guide to how closely the data were clustered. The financial impact of EMR systems on family practice or internal medicine ambulatory clinics is evaluated from direct and indirect measurements. The savings quantified include improved staff productivity, paper cost reduction, and transcription cost reduction.

Possible cost savings not considered in this study were medical record storage cost savings, the impact of decision support paradigms, reduction in lab test redundancy, malpractice premium reduction, or improved charge capture. The costs that were quantified include computer hardware and software cost, network installation and maintenance cost, network support, consultant cost, training cost, and the initial reduction in provider productivity. The net return was analyzed using net present value with an assumed compounded "hurdle rate" of 15 percent.

**Exhibit 2. Financial Impact of the EMR**

| Net Positive Financial Impact | Net Negative Financial Impact |
|---|---|
| Improved staff productivity | Computer hardware and software cost |
| Transcription cost savings | Network installation and maintenance cost |
| Paper cost reduction | Information systems personnel, network support, and/or consultants cost |
| Improved charge capture | Training cost |
| Medical record storage cost savings | Reduction in provider productivity |
| Clinical pathways/decision support | |
| Reduction in lab test redundancy | |
| Malpractice premium reduction | |

The study focused only on those benefits of EMR systems that result in actual savings or costs. Those benefits with economic impact include improved staff productivity, paper cost reduction, transcription cost savings, improved charge capture, medical record storage cost savings, savings resulting from the use of clinical pathways or decision support functionality, reduction in lab test redundancy, and malpractice premium reduction (see Exhibit 2).

This study attempted to quantify only the first three benefits (staff productivity savings, paper cost savings, and transcription cost savings). Because not all of the beneficial financial impacts were included in the analysis, the return on capital invested may be greater than that documented herein. The cost side of the equation includes costs for computer hardware, software, network installation and maintenance, information systems personnel or consultants, training, and any reduction in provider productivity (see Exhibit 3). All of these cost variables were considered in this study.

Of particular interest for this study was the impact of EMR systems on both staff and provider productivity, specifically the:

- Reduction in medical record staff time required to pull and file charts
- Reduction in staff time spent routing charts, chart requests, and phone messages
- Decrease in laboratory staff time spent routing laboratory test results as a result of using an electronic interface with reference labs
- Elimination or reduction of the need for transcription if providers use software to gather encounter data
- Decrease in staff time spent looking for "missing" charts
- Reduction in administrative staff time spent writing referral letters when EMR software is used to automatically generate the letters

Other benefits of EMR systems often described as "intangible" are actually tangible benefits that are merely difficult to quantify. For those

**Exhibit 3. Tasks for which Time of Completion Was Measured Directly**

- Phone calls that do not require a chart (switchboard returns call)
- Phone calls that do not require a chart (provider returns call)
- Phone calls that require a chart (switchboard returns call)
- Phone calls that require a chart (provider returns call)
- Dictation and transcription
- Recording and reviewing lab test results during an encounter (in-house labs)
- Recording and reviewing lab test results during an encounter (reference labs)
- Provider encounter with a scheduled patient
- Ancillary staff encounter with a scheduled patient

who may be interested in further quantifying the financial impacts of an EMR in their own environment, some of these additional potential cost savings are:

- Savings in time spent researching data for quality assurance reports mandated by hospitals, managed care organizations, and third-party payers
- Reduction in time spent generating reports on patients taking medications that have been recalled
- Reduction in the amount of repetitive testing due to laboratory test results that are "lost"
- Reduction in time spent correcting billing errors resulting from automatic transfer of billing codes from the computerized clinical record to the billing system
- Improved medical insurance claim reimbursement as a result of better documentation of services rendered during patient encounters
- Standardized care guidelines provided with a computerized record result in more efficient and higher quality patient treatment
- Automated alerts in the computerized record improve the quality of care by reminding caregivers to schedule mammograms, cervical cancer screening tests, and other preventive treatment procedures
- Better reporting methods allow providers to demonstrate positive outcomes for third-party payers demanding the data before approving contracts
- More efficient reporting methods result in improved financial risk assessment in negotiating capitated contracts
- Remote access to computerized records means fewer errors in recommending patient treatment
- Accessibility of summary information in the patient chart means that less information is missed during patient chart reviews
- Legibility, organization, and comprehensiveness of a computerized patient record reduce errors in treatment
- Avoidance of malpractice lawsuits as a result of medication dosage errors, prescription errors, or missed medication interactions

**Exhibit 4. Tasks for which Time of Completion Was Measured by Interview**

- Searching for charts
- Writing referral letters
- Writing quality assurance and audit reports
- Writing reports on patients taking recalled medications
- Performing laboratory "re-tests"
- Correcting billing errors

In this study the word "provider" designates physicians, physician assistants, and nurse practitioners directly involved in patient care. The term "staff" is used to indicate nonproviders. Wherever possible, generic job titles are given for the purpose of clarification. For example, the word "operator" is used to indicate any staff member who answers the phone, whether his or her actual job title is "switchboard," "triage nurse," or the like.

First, the study personnel observed workflow processes at each study site, then analyzed and documented the specific steps that comprise typical paper-based tasks at the study clinics. Focus was given to processes involving pulling, routing, and reviewing patient charts, processing phone messages, and transcription, since these tasks are most impacted by EMR systems.

Second, the study personnel identified the steps in the paper-based process and carefully timed the processes. Certain key tasks were directly measured for time of completion (see Exhibit 4). Occasionally, an estimate of time required to perform certain tasks was obtained through an interview process. The sample size for each task varied.

## RESULTS

### Workflow Diagrams

Exhibit 5 demonstrates the typical clinic workflow process prior to implementation of the EMR system. The diagrams are not exactly representative of each clinic studied but are representative of the typical clinic workflow processes encountered. The diagrams are provided here for reference and comparison purposes.

### Improved Staff Productivity

An important objective of this analysis was to determine the differential cost of paper medical record handling versus electronic medical records. Based on an average staffing level of 0.36 FTE medical record file clerks per provider and a measured number of average chart pulls per day of 54, as well as the known average salary figures, the cost per chart pull was calculated at $0.68:

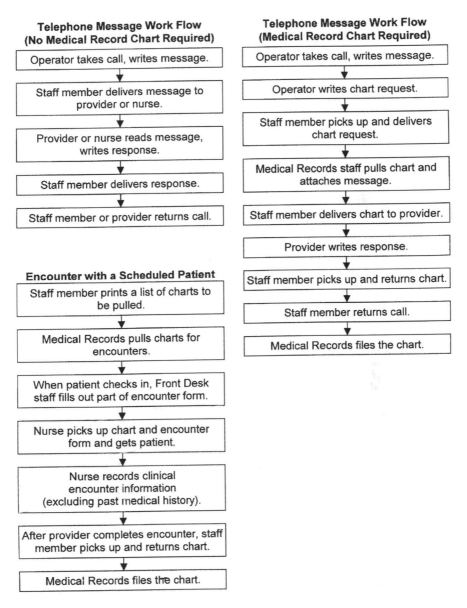

**Telephone Message Work Flow
(No Medical Record Chart Required)**

Operator takes call, writes message.

Staff member delivers message to provider or nurse.

Provider or nurse reads message, writes response.

Staff member delivers response.

Staff member or provider returns call.

**Encounter with a Scheduled Patient**

Staff member prints a list of charts to be pulled.

Medical Records pulls charts for encounters.

When patient checks in, Front Desk staff fills out part of encounter form.

Nurse picks up chart and encounter form and gets patient.

Nurse records clinical encounter information (excluding past medical history).

After provider completes encounter, staff member picks up and returns chart.

Medical Records files the chart.

**Telephone Message Work Flow
(Medical Record Chart Required)**

Operator takes call, writes message.

Operator writes chart request.

Staff member picks up and delivers chart request.

Medical Records staff pulls chart and attaches message.

Staff member delivers chart to provider.

Provider writes response.

Staff member picks up and returns chart.

Staff member returns call.

Medical Records files the chart.

**Exhibit 5. Workflow Processes**

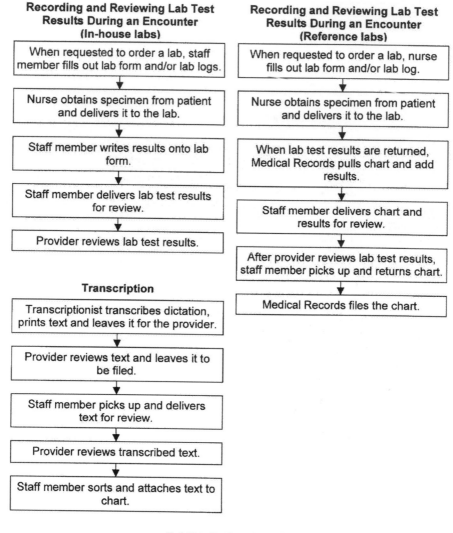

**Recording and Reviewing Lab Test Results During an Encounter (In-house labs)**

When requested to order a lab, staff member fills out lab form and/or lab logs.

↓

Nurse obtains specimen from patient and delivers it to the lab.

↓

Staff member writes results onto lab form.

↓

Staff member delivers lab test results for review.

↓

Provider reviews lab test results.

**Transcription**

Transcriptionist transcribes dictation, prints text and leaves it for the provider.

↓

Provider reviews text and leaves it to be filed.

↓

Staff member picks up and delivers text for review.

↓

Provider reviews transcribed text.

↓

Staff member sorts and attaches text to chart.

**Recording and Reviewing Lab Test Results During an Encounter (Reference labs)**

When requested to order a lab, nurse fills out lab form and/or lab log.

↓

Nurse obtains specimen from patient and delivers it to the lab.

↓

When lab test results are returned, Medical Records pulls chart and add results.

↓

Staff member delivers chart and results for review.

↓

After provider reviews lab test results, staff member picks up and returns chart.

↓

Medical Records files the chart.

**Exhibit 5.** *Continued.*

**Clinical Encounters and Chart Pulls**

| | |
|---|---|
| Average daily clinical encounters per provider | 33 |
| Standard deviation | 15.4 |
| Average total chart pulls per provider per day | 54 |
| Standard deviation | 24.1 |
| Average total chart pulls per provider per year | 11,340 |

**Cost per Chart Pull**

| | |
|---|---|
| Average number of file clerk FTE per provider | 0.36 |
| Standard deviation | 0.22 |
| Average file clerk salary and benefit cost | $21,453 |
| Standard deviation | $577 |
| Net file clerk cost per provider | $7,723 |
| Cost per chart pull | $0.68 |

This rate per chart pull is low compared to some published reports. For example, six physicians in Iowa measured the cost of chart pulls in their small clinic. They found 22 sites where charts might be located with an average cost per chart pull of $2.[1]

Other studies on EMR systems performed in inpatient environments point to a higher average cost per chart retrieval in this setting. One such study in the Milwaukee area reported a $5 savings per chart request at the hospital versus a $2.62 savings per request in the physician office environment.[4] At Intermountain Health Care, Inc., and Brigham and Women's Hospital, the cost of delivering a paper chart to a physician's desk averages between $3 and $5.[5]

The clinics varied in their approach to requiring medical record availability for telephone calls. Some clinics in this study recorded all telephone calls in the medical record, whereas other clinics charted only clinically relevant telephone calls. The average percentage of telephone calls that required a chart is 70 percent:

**Telephone Messages Requiring Chart Pull**

| | |
|---|---|
| Percent of telephone messages that require a chart pull | 70 |
| Standard deviation, percent | 22 |

The time of task completion for both paper records and electronic medical records was recorded at the five study sites. The largest productivity gains were in transcription, form completion, and the retrieval and the filing of medical records. Time savings of staff per provider averaged 3.39 hours (203.4 minutes) per day:

Average Staff Time Savings by Process per Provider

| Type of Task | Net Time Savings after 12 Months (Minutes per Day) | Standard Deviation |
|---|---|---|
| Writing forms | 30.5 | 41.9 |
| Routing forms | 9.6 | 9.5 |
| Pulling charts | 31.9 | 43.9 |
| Routing charts | 10.2 | 11.3 |
| Filing charts | 20.6 | 17.5 |
| Searching for charts | 39 | 71.6 |
| Writing referral letters | 18 | 40.2 |
| Transcription | 43.6 | 59.5 |
| Total (min) | 203.4 | |
| Total (hr) | 3.39 | |

The annual value of these time savings was calculated using an average hourly value of $14 per hour for salaries and benefits. The first-year savings are calculated at $9967 per provider:

**Dollar Value of Average Annual Staff Productivity Savings per Provider**
($14/hr for Salaries and Benefits + 5% Annual Increase)

| | |
|---|---|
| Year 1 | $9,967 |
| Year 2 | $10,465 |
| Year 3 | $10,989 |

For the purposes of the financial projection, a 5 percent increase in annual salary and benefits is incorporated.

## Paper Cost Reduction

Much of the data in the literature regarding paper cost reduction originates in an inpatient organization. The Medical Center at Princeton reported an 84 percent reduction in paper processes resulting in a reduction of 712,907 pages of charting that cost an average of $41,795, not including the $10,930 worth of lab reports thrown away each year.[6] In the study at hand, at each ambulatory clinic, all paper forms being replaced by EMR software were documented and the printing costs for each obtained. The average annual cost per provider for paper forms that were being replaced totaled $1575, with a standard deviation of $670.

## Dictation and Transcription

Two of the clinics studied do not use any dictation and transcription for documentation of patient encounters. The other three sites used transcription for a significant portion of their clinical encounters. In the three sites that rely on transcription, an average of 35 percent of a transcriptionist's time is spent sorting, attaching, and routing paper transcriptions. For the financial projection, an average of all sites was utilized. Thus, the transcriptionist time saving and resulting cost saving used in the financial projection will tend to be lower than the actual time and cost saving found in those sites that do use transcription:

| | Transcribing (Minutes per Hour) | Percent | SD |
|---|---|---|---|
| Sorting and attaching transcribed text to chart | 28 | 31.8 | 15.3 |
| Delivering transcription to providers | 2 | 3.2 | 1.4 |
| Total | 30 | 35 | |

## EMR Implementation Costs

The EMR implementation cost includes actual cost for hardware and labor for items, including:

- Workstation or PC upgrades
- Servers
- Telecommunications
- Software cost
- Hardware and software maintenance
- Training cost
- Network cable installation or upgrade
- Hubs, bridges, routers
- Printers, scanners
- Wireless equipment
- Technical support
- Consulting services
- Memory, processor, motherboard, or hard drive upgrades

The total average implementation cost per provider was calculated at $12,718:

### Hardware and Software Cost per Provider
(Including training, consultants, and network installation)

| | |
|---|---|
| Average total hardware and software cost | $114,458 |
| Hardware and software cost per provider | $12,718 |

## Provider Lost Productivity Cost

Providers at each clinic were carefully timed to determine how long it took to complete the four sections of a SOAP (subjective, objective, assessment, and plan) progress note during clinical encounters. Time of completion was measured for the subjective, objective, assessment, and the treatment plan.

The baseline values represent the time of completion for recording a patient encounter in the EMR system just after EMR implementation but before the providers develop significant familiarity with the EMR system. Times of completion showed provider productivity losses at all sites, with greater times of completion for all sections of the progress note than comparable times in the paper record. Providers took an average of a little over two extra minutes to record an encounter in the electronic clinical record which calculates to a 71.3 minutes per day productivity loss for the average of 33 patient encounters. The subjective complaint and review of systems were affected least (11.5 percent) by the change to an electronic format, whereas the recording of the physical exam added the most time to the task.

It was anticipated that the provider productivity loss would lessen as the providers gained familiarity with the EMR system. Twelve months after implementation, three of the test sites were measured for changes in provider productivity (see Exhibit 6). All sites demonstrated much improvement in efficiency in recording clinical data entry in the EMR. Average time of completion had been reduced significantly for all sections of the clinical record at all tested sites. Average times were equal to those previously recorded for the paper record.

The dollar value of lost provider time is estimated below using an average provider salary of $75 per hour. For the purposes of the financial projection, a constant rate of improvement of provider productivity was assumed, resulting in a net first-year value of provider productivity loss equal to the estimated six-month productivity loss:

| | Total Initial Provider Productivity Cost | | |
| | Time Savings per Day per Provider (Minutes) | Dollar Cost per Day (@75/hr) | Annual Value of Provider Productivity Loss |
| --- | --- | --- | --- |
| Baseline | −71.3 | $89.13 | $18,716 |
| 6 months (est.) | −35.65 | $44.57 | $9,358 |
| 12 months | 0 | 0 | 0 |

## Financial Projection

It seems prudent to expect that a rapidly developing technology such as an EMR information system would show an adequate return on investment within a three-year recovery period. Technology change is rapid and the cost of technology reduces exponentially over time. Computer hardware purchased today will likely become obsolete in three years.

**Exhibit 6. Average Baseline Provider Task Completion Time per Patient Encounter**

| Task | Time in Paper Record (sec) | Standard Deviation (sec) | Time in Electronic Record (sec) | Standard Deviation (sec) | Average Percent Increase | Net Time Savings (sec) |
|---|---|---|---|---|---|---|
| Complaint and review of systems | 69.4 | 45.8 | 77.2 | 56.4 | 11.5 | –8 |
| Physical exam | 46.7 | 37.3 | 127.2 | 97.6 | 172.3 | –80.5 |
| Assessment | 36.4 | 47.2 | 44.2 | 17.4 | 21.4 | –7.8 |
| Plan | 65.8 | 49.7 | 99.2 | 83.1 | 50.8 | –33.4 |
| Total | 218.3 | | 348 | | 59.4 | –129.7 |

PV = present value, assuming an expected rate of return of 15 percent (hurdle rate).

**Exhibit 7. Net Return per Provider**

|  | Year 1 | Year 2 | Year 3 | Net/Total |
|---|---|---|---|---|
| Hardware, software cost and training (with 20 percent of initial cost for estimated training, upgrades, and maintenance after first year) | ($12,718) | ($2,544) | ($2,544) | ($17,806) |
| Physician productivity cost | ($9,358) | $0 | $0 | ($9,358) |
| Total actual cost | ($22,076) | ($2,544) | ($2,544) | ($27,164) |
| PV cost (int = 15 percent) | ($22,076) | ($2,212) | ($1,924) | ($26,212) |
| Staff productivity savings | $9,967 | $10,465 | $10,989 | 31,421 |
| Paper cost reduction | $1,575 | $1,575 | $1,575 | $4,725 |
| Total actual savings | $11,542 | $12,040 | $12,564 | 36,146 |
| PV savings (int = 15 percent) | $11,542 | $9,104 | $8,261 | $28,907 |
| Net | ($10,534) | $9,496 | $10,020 | $8,982 |
| Net present value (int = 15 percent) | ($10,534) | $6,892 | $6,337 | $2,695 |

Thus, it would be proper to question any return on investment analysis for information technology based on any positive cashflow projected beyond three years. For this reason, the return on investment was projected based on collected data for three years using the net present value (NPV) method for the analysis.

The NPV method of return on investment analysis is one of the most accepted methods for evaluating investment decisions. Essentially, the NPV method involves a calculation of whether the expected rate of return on a capital investment meets the expected or "hurdle" rate set by an organization. The expected rate is compounded annually and factored into cost and revenue figures. An NPV of less than 0 indicates that the investment did not meet the expected rate, whereas an NPV of greater than 0 indicates that the investment exceeded the expected rate of return.

For the purposes of this analysis, an expected rate of return of 15 percent was chosen. The tabulated results indicate that for the first year the rate of return was less than 15 percent, with a net loss of $10,534 per provider, but succeeding years resulted in a return greater than 15 percent. In the third year, the overall return on all cash investments exceeded 15 percent compounded annually (see Exhibit 7).

## CONCLUSIONS

This study demonstrates a rate of return on capital investments in EMR information systems that exceeds 15 percent compounded annually over a three-year period. This rate of return would meet or exceed the expected return on capital for many organizations. In addition, this study did not measure, nor factor in, several variables that have the potential to increase the rate of return on the capital investment. Thus, based on the potential returns, an EMR system appears to be a worthwhile investment.

Another factor to consider is the timing of the purchase and implementation. Buying information systems too early will reduce the return on the investment in information systems since technology costs have historically decreased rapidly with time. However, buying systems too late may also cause serious financial losses due to noncompetitive work practices. With regard to EMR systems, it is likely that the risk of getting in too early has already passed in time, and the primary risk is that of implementing a system too late.

Thus, unless a physician practice could earn a return significantly greater than 15 percent on an investment of $22,000 per physician, with only moderate risk, then an investment in an EMR system would seem to be economically justified.

The results of this study reveal a staff time saving of over three hours per provider after implementation of an EMR system. Thus, it is feasible to project that one FTE of staff time can be reduced for every two to three providers based on improved staff efficiencies. The actual rate of achievable FTE reduction may depend on the initial provider-to-staff ratio but this could not be confirmed in this study. Likewise, no immediate correlation was found between initial staffing ratios and total potential cost savings, although it is suspected that this will turn out to be the case with a larger sample size. Future studies may be necessary to address this issue. An FTE reduction of one FTE for every two providers may be possible for clinics that are less efficient at the baseline (those with relatively high staff overhead), whereas more efficient clinics might only be able to reduce one FTE for every three providers.

In the future, the need to financially justify the purchase of an EMR system will in all probability become a moot issue as the competitive benefits of an EMR system become more widely realized; documentation requirements stiffen; and the paper medical record, like paper currency, gradually becomes a thing of the past.

### References

1. Proceedings of the TEPR '98, "Toward an Electronic Patient Record," 1998.
2. Vrooman, W. 1996. "Benefits realization analysis of a CIS," *HIMSS Proceedings* 3:91–99.
3. Kian, L., Stewart, M., Bagby, C., and Robertson, J. 1995. "Justifying the cost of a computer-based patient record," *Healthcare Financial Management,* 49(7):58–67.
4. Morrissey, J. 1995. "Study shows value of Wis. CHIN," *Modern Healthcare,* 25(38):50.
5. Moad, J. 1996. "Dose of reality: Health care industry attempts to overcome problems with CISc," *PC Week,* 13(6).
6. Molfetas, L. 1996. "Strategic CPR issues: benchmarking paper documentation prior to implementation," *HIMSS Proceedings*.

# Chapter 22
# Data Warehousing: Design through Implementation for the Healthcare Professional

*Michele Lettiere*

For decades, healthcare information technology (IT) groups have been called upon to implement and support various software solutions throughout the organization. These types of applications assist in managing the organization by enhancing workflow and increasing productivity. By collecting and storing relevant data, all of these solutions have had an enormous impact on the healthcare organization. Historically, it was the responsibility of the end user (business and clinical analysts) to identify and retrieve the data required to measure the success of the organization.

Over the years, these business and clinical analysts have accumulated an armory of disparate data which is critical to providing executive management with the information required for accurate and timely decision making. An Excel spreadsheet here, an Access database there; all are important members of an information symphony that was successfully orchestrated to provide results. Then why the movement toward data warehousing? Simply put, each individual business or clinical analyst had been playing in his or her own symphony. Unfortunately, when the time came for all analysts to play together, each played a different piece of music, in a different key. One analyst was forecasting different numbers than another; the hospital administrator was using incorrect data in his or her business planning and revenue projections. An investment in a data warehouse is an investment in the intellectual property of the organization. This

0-8493-1498-4/03/$0.00+$1.50
© 2003 by CRC Press LLC

chapter is written to introduce the healthcare IT professional to the benefits and technologies of data warehousing. In addition, this chapter provides an overview of the technical processes required in getting the healthcare data warehouse project launched. Like healthcare, data warehousing follows similar principles: be patient and always consider a second opinion!

## THE HEALTHCARE DATA WAREHOUSE

Unlike most data warehousing teams that exist in fields such as retail, finance, or banking, healthcare IT groups have been given the unique charge not only to develop systems for running the organization and improving customer satisfaction, but to improve the quality of patient care. This is true for the IT professional in the hospital, provider, or payer setting. Regardless of the clinical discipline, data is now emerging that makes understanding quality of care possible. The healthcare IT manager must fully understand this responsibility and embrace the uniqueness of this field in the data warehousing arena.

In the past, the information made available to the healthcare data warehouse was mostly comprised of provider charges and payer reimbursement, hospital admissions and discharges, and, if fortunate, the listing of all drugs an individual patient received. Many important patient demographics were missing. The emergence of the electronic medical record (EMR) into the healthcare market significantly contributes to the value of the information previously available. The EMR, despite all controversies, provides the link to the element of data once unknown or unquantifiable to the payer and provider communities — clinical treatment and outcomes.

To begin, a discussion of the EMR may be necessary. An EMR is a fully integrated clinical software application, the purpose of which is to replace the paper chart in the physician's practice. The EMR electronically captures all encounters between the provider and patient, including diagnostic tests and treatments, along with the results of those tests and the outcome of given treatments. Electronically capturing all encounters with a patient and the results/outcomes of those encounters enables the analysis and reporting of all facets of clinical care. Performing various analyses, the healthcare institution is able to (1) understand treatment patterns and (2) measure the effectiveness of each treatment. Understanding such information ultimately leads to the overall improvement of patient care.

Many challenges arise during the development and implementation of such software. Physicians are not typically avid computer users, thus potentially making the initial learning curve quite steep. Many EMRs provide an outlet to dictate into the chart to ease the transition of a paper-based, highly dictated practice. This highlights another obstacle for the EMR: the collection of data. It is already known that the EMR collects all encounters with the patient; however, the important factor is how such data is collected. Every encounter with the patient must be electronically coded to uniquely identify one type of encounter from another. Codification of all clinical terminology within the system facilitates the analysis and reporting of all aspects of the clinical care.

Trends in the EMR market indicate that by the year 2005 healthcare providers are expected to be utilizing some form of an EMR. So, if the current scope of the healthcare data warehouse project plan does not include the integration of EMR data, the project plan will soon be expanded to include such data.

## DEVELOPMENT OF THE DATA WAREHOUSE

Several stages are involved in the development of the successful data warehouse. Each stage will be discussed in detail. These stages include project planning, staffing, data modeling, metadata, data extraction, data mapping and transformation, data warehouse maintenance, and data marts.

### Project Planning

Like any other IT project, the data warehouse requires a carefully documented project plan, preferably written in non-IT terminology. This document should be distributed to all involved IT professionals, as well as to all end users. End users include those individuals who benefit from the access to the information in the data warehouse and should be thought of as "customers" of the data warehouse and members of the data warehouse project team. It is important to note that the number-one reason why data warehouses fail is the lack of involvement of the end users. They are the most critical entity involved in the project. Historically, many data warehouses followed the familiar "build it and they will come" philosophy. It has been learned since then that these data warehouses required a significant amount of reengineering once they were released to the end users. Simply put, the earlier end users are involved in the project, the fewer the modifications to the released product.

In order to ensure acceptance of the data warehouse project, it is strategically critical to identify and describe the benefits of a data warehouse to the organization. Since data warehouses are not created equally and each serves many different purposes, it is difficult to list all of the benefits a data warehouse will provide to a given organization. However, most data warehouses provide the following benefits:

1. A single, consistent source for all data analysis
2. Accurate answers to questions that affect the organization
3. Easier access to information that was previously stored disparately

Another important position to be included in the project plan is the concept that the development of the data warehouse is an ongoing task. Just as the type of information utilized by the healthcare community is constantly changing, so is the architecture to the data warehouse. The data warehouse project will be better served if it is understood at the onset of the project that although various endpoints in the project timeline will be met, a true data warehouse is never complete.

Key components of the project plan include:

1. Description of a data warehouse (what it is and why one is needed)
2. Identification of the customers (end users)
3. Statement of the initial scope of the project highlighting which sources of data are within the scope
4. Listing of the roles and responsibilities of the project team
5. The process for implementation arranged in a "phased" approach
6. Listing of the objectives and deliverables for each phase of implementation
7. Project timeline
8. Budgetary requirements

During the development of the project plan, it is necessary to document the scope. By doing so, all sources of data must be identified and their place in the organization understood. Frequently, in the absence of adequate data, individuals within the organization have developed their own data source to assist them with their day-to-day responsibilities. These "stand-alone" sources are often unknown to most IT groups. The relevance of such stand-alone sources must be considered for integration when determining the content of the data warehouse. To facilitate the identification of all sources of data, face-to-face interviews with various individuals within the organization should be conducted. The project manager should strive to interpret how each of the data sources fits in the organization. In addition, the interview process should result in a thorough understanding of upper management's requirements for "running" the business. The project team may find that the information needs of upper management are currently not collected in an organized, electronic manner. If this is the case, the conversion or update of such data should become a separate sub-project of the team and timelines adjusted accordingly.

### Staffing the Data Warehouse

While it is important to identify the individuals who will participate on the data warehouse team, it is more important to fill specific responsibilities. These roles exist in the development of all data warehouses.

**The Project Sponsors.** The project sponsors have a unique role in the development of the data warehouse. Project sponsors should be high-level individuals who possess the "big picture" within the organization. The two types of project sponsors are the IT project sponsor and the customer sponsor. The role of the IT project sponsor is to champion the data warehouse project to upper/executive management and to secure the required resources and financing. The customer sponsor represents the end-user community and can demonstrate the benefits of developing a data warehouse to upper/executive management. In addition, the customer sponsor should provide the final review of the high-level architecture to ensure that the overall goals of the project are met when all sources of data are integrated.

**The Project Manager.** The project manager is usually a member of the IT group. Experience with all facets of the organization is a critical prerequisite for this project team member. The project manager writes the project plan, coordinates the appropriate interviews, determines timelines and budgetary requirements, and, along with the project sponsors, selects the members of the data warehouse project team.

**The Subject Experts.** The subject experts are both end users and critical members of the project team. The subject experts are just what the title implies: the individual(s) who are most familiar with the source application/system, the data collected by the source, and understand the requirements for utilizing these data, once integrated into the data warehouse. Generally, the three functions of the subject experts are found in one individual per source. Their level of participation will also vary, based on the relative size of the data source they represent.

**The Data Architects/Engineers.** The architects/engineers are responsible for the technical delivery of the data warehouse. Their role spans data modeling, development of database tables, extraction of data from source application/system, mapping of all data into the modeled table architecture, and ongoing monitoring of database performance issues to ensure scalability. The number of data architects and engineers varies, based on number of data sources and expected data volume.

## Data Modeling

As in software application development, the database must be designed (modeled) before the software is written and data entered into the tables. Data modeling, otherwise known as entity relationship modeling, is a graphically depicted design methodology based on the adherence to several logical rules that are applied to clarify and document business policies and workflow. A required component of database designing for the data warehouse begins not with the details of the data, but with the business model. The business model provides a thorough understanding of the business and business-related processes within the organization. Beyond the

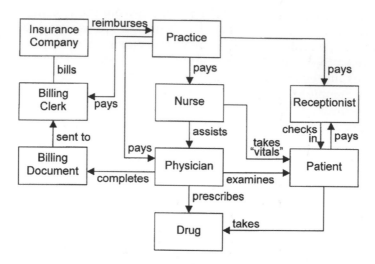

**Exhibit 1. The Business Model**

business model, a logical model representing the source data is developed, followed by the final product, the analytical model.

**The Business Model.** To begin the business modeling process, all project sponsors, subject experts, and data architects/engineers work together to document the business and related workflow. During this process, all participants are asked to define the purpose of the business. For example, the purpose of a physician's practice may be as simple as "Our purpose is to provide the highest quality of care to our patients. This is achieved through developing 'gold standard' treatment protocols, treating our patients according to such protocols and measuring the results of each treatment to determine the best care available." This step is necessary to ensure that all project team members understand the overall goal of the business. Next, the group defines all entities within the business. Entities are defined as items or events about which we collect information. In the case of the practice, a few entities might include patients, drugs, equipment, nurses, receptionists, billing clerks, insurance companies, etc. To complete the business model, the relationship between each of the business entities is graphically depicted and defined using words to describe the action of how each entity relates (see Exhibit 1).

The purpose/benefit of the business model is to (1) document the known workflow/processes, (2) uncover new sources of information, and (3) identify areas of weakness within the organization that may be addressed prior to the development of the data warehouse.

**The Logical Model.** The logical modeling process is quite similar to the business modeling process; however, the logical model relates to the data that is available for inclusion in the data warehouse. It is advisable to build the logical model one data source at a time. For example, if the project plan scope includes integration of data from the billing/reimbursement system (often referred to as practice management system) and the electronic medical record, develop the logical model for one source system before beginning the other. Following this process allows for the more precise identification of "ovserlap" among source systems. The data warehouse team must consider which source provides most accurate information while considering their respective amount of manual maintenance. In data warehousing, manual maintenance of data should be kept to a minimum.

To begin the logical modeling process, as with business modeling, all project sponsors, subject experts, and data architects/engineers work together to understand and document the type of required data that was identified through interviewing and developing the project plan. The first step includes a purpose statement for each source of data. The relevant subject expert will provide this statement of purpose. In addition, the subject expert should also provide a demonstration of the source application/system, examples of the types of analyses and reports that are generated from the source, and a description of how each analysis/report adds value to the organization. Next, the team identifies the data entities that are required for the organization to operate.

For example, the entities for a practice management system might include patient demographics, patient encounters, insurance companies, insurance plans, procedure codes (CPT and HCPCS), etc. Again, entities are items or events for which data is collected. This definition varies slightly for logical and analytical modeling since these two types of modeling relate to data from source applications.

Next, the identified entities and their relationships are graphically documented as in the business model; however, additional rules are applied. Rather than documenting the "action" that forms their relationship, the team must now document the type of relationship utilizing one-to-one, one-to-many, and many-to-many relationships. The basics for identifying the types of relationships between entities are quite simple. First, choose two entities to be related. Next, draw a line between the two and relate them. For example, if patient and gender are to be related, consider while filling in the blanks, "A patient can have ___ gender; a gender related to ___ patient(s)." In this example a patient can have ONE gender; a gender relates to MANY patients. This is known as a ONE-TO-MANY relationship. Another example: if patient and charge are to be related, consider while filling in the blanks, "A patient can have ___ charge(s); one charge can be applied to ___ patient(s)." In this example a patient can have MANY charges; a charge can be applied to MANY patients. This is an example of a MANY-TO-MANY relationship. Generally, in logical modeling, most relationships are MANY-TO-MANY. This reasoning is discussed in the following section covering analytical modeling.

The purpose of the logical model is to (1) identify the type of data to be integrated into the data warehouse, (2) serve as the architectural foundation for the analytical model, and (3) provide a user-friendly, layman view of the data warehouse architecture.

Several helpful books have been written on the subject of data or entity relationship modeling. A listing of these sources can be found in the "References" section at the end of this chapter.

**The Analytical Model.** Once the logical model is complete and has been reviewed and approved by project sponsors, the analytical modeling process may begin. In this process, the project team will build an entity relationship model depicting each actual data element to be captured and accessed through the data warehouse. The logical model will serve as the foundation to be built upon. Begin this process by identifying all attributes for the entities having a one-to-one relationship, followed by the one-to-many and many-to-one relationships, and ending with the many-to-many-relationships. For example, begin with the logical model entity "patient." The team will identify all data elements that are attributes or descriptors of that entity. In this example, attributes may include patient name, date of birth, race, gender, etc. You will find that all one-to-one relationships in the logical model result in one entity being an attribute of another. In the example in the previous section, the one-to-one relationship of patient to gender on the logical model results in gender becoming an attribute of patient in the analytical model. The many-to-many relationship can exist on the logical model only. In a relational database design it is impossible to accurately capture data represented as many-to-many. Everywhere such a relationship exists on the logical model a new entity is created which combines data from the original two entities to create a one-to-many or many-to-one relationship. This new entity is known as a "junction table" (see Exhibit 2).

During the course of attribute identification, the project team will, from time to time, notice several instances where an attribute on one table would be very valuable to have stored on another, nonrelated table. Storing data in this manner is known as "denormalization." Not too long ago, when data storage was extremely expensive, denormalization was considered too costly for the desired benefit. Today, cost is not as much a consideration as the answer to the following question. Will analytical users be working directly against the data warehouse tables, as opposed

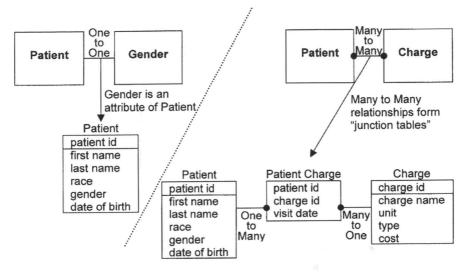

**Exhibit 19-2. The logical and analytical model.**

to data marts? (Data marts are discussed later in this chapter.) If so, denormalization is an accepted method of storage. If data marts will be developed from the underlying data warehouse, those valuable data elements may be represented in many tables.

### Metadata

As is the case with any technological implementation, documentation is critical. Data warehousing is no exception. Releasing even the most simplistic component of the data warehouse without metadata is like driving across-country without a road map. Metadata is the comprehensive dictionary that defines every table and every attribute within each table. One primary function of the data warehouse is to provide "analysis-friendly" information; therefore, it is vital that all customers of the data warehouse have access to the definition of each table and its related attributes. Three types of metadata should be created, one for each type of data model (business, logical, and analytical).

**Business Metadata.** Business metadata should include the names of all entities within the business, the organizational department of the entity, and a brief description of the responsibilities or purpose of each entity.

**Logical Metadata.** Logical metadata should include the names of all entities, the data source(s) that store information about each entity, and a brief description of the entity.

311

**Analytical Metadata.** At the analytical model level, metadata should include a table in which attributes reside, data sources of attributes, attribute names, and comprehensive definition of attributes.

During the data modeling process, the subject expert of each data source is responsible for the creation and maintenance of the metadata for their respective area of expertise. Keep in mind that metadata is an ongoing subproject, which requires updating whenever modifications to the database architecture are made.

Several software vendors offer both integrated tools (within the database modeling) and stand-alone metadata management software. Very often, a simple "homegrown" database to store metadata is sufficient for even the most complex data model. It is much more valuable to provide a simple graphical user interface to facilitate the understanding of data elements to end users.

## Data Movement

At this point the metadata is developed and electronically stored, the data model has been designed, and the actual data warehouse table architecture created in the database. Now the real work begins — getting data from point A (the source application) to point B (the data warehouse). Data movement consists of three separate and distinct processes: (1) data extraction, (2) data transformation, and (3) data population. Several software vendors offer data extraction/transformation/population tools for varying levels of complexity. These tools have propagated faster than any software segment in the data warehousing market. Prior to the development of such tools, data was moved via volumes of manually generated electronic code created the by the data warehouse (DW) engineer. Incidentally, many organizations that began development of a data warehouse approximately five years ago or later are now suffering the penalty for having done so on the cutting edge of the market.

**Data Extraction.** In addition to knowledge of the data warehouse architecture, it becomes critical for the DW engineer to thoroughly understand the source database, as well as the source software functionality. It is this comprehensive understanding that will allow for the accurate and timely integration of data into the warehouse. Data extraction is the act of tagging data that is required for integration into the warehouse. As part of this process, the DW engineer must account for all data elements and their respective data type.

Because the architecture of the data warehouse varies slightly to significantly from the architecture of the source database, the complexity of the data movement from point A to B is equally as variant.

**Data Transformation.** Realizing the major benefit of the data warehouse as a single source for all information helps define the need for data transformation. Through extraction from the source application database, the data needs to be standardized to "fit" into the data warehouse architecture. This occurs through varying levels of complexity.

*Simple Complexity.* In the event that data is extracted from the source application database and requires very little conversion or modification of the data type, a fairly straightforward extraction may occur. An extraction of simple complexity should allow for the data to move from point A to point B rather seamlessly. The only step involves the "mapping" of the unique source ID for the data to the unique data warehouse ID. Data of simple complexity is moved quite quickly, even in the presence of large volumes of data.

*Moderate Complexity.* Often, the data is extracted from a source application database and requires conversion to another data type or modification of a similar data type. Essentially, the data remains the same. In addition to mapping to a unique source ID in the data warehouse, the transformation requirements include the conversion/modification of the data type. These types of data are also readily handled with the use of an extraction/transformation/population tool.

*High Complexity.* Very often, similar data is collected from more than one source application. Due to such complexities, it may be necessary to add an interim destination for the extracted data to reside. This interim destination is known as the "load" architecture. The load architecture, a relationally "flat" architecture, acts as a "holding tank" for the extracted data prior to its ultimate transformation into the data warehouse architecture. This data is extracted from the source application database and transformed into the load architecture. The benefit of utilizing a load architecture is that it allows many and diverse data sources with the same context to be added or modified while "holding" the transformation of data into the data warehouse at a constant (see Exhibit 3).

**Data Population.** Once extracted and transformed, the data is now ready for population into the data warehouse architecture. As part of the population, the code that handles the process should be developed to (1) move data into the data warehouse architecture, (2) exclude those data elements that meet requirements for erroneous data, (3) write such exclusions to a log file for review, (4) document each successful and erroneous population record to a log file for review, and (5) apply categorization to data warehouse architecture.

*Categorization.* During the course of data modeling, new data elements may have been added to provide a more "analysis-friendly" environment. For example, if a drug is recorded as given to a patient, the project team may want to provide additional information about that drug to assist the

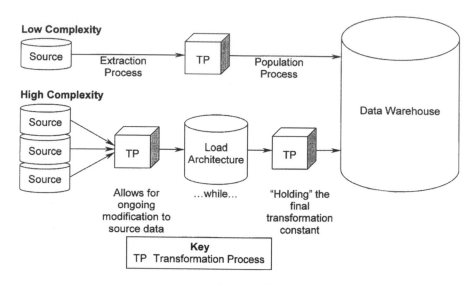

**Exhibit 3. The Extraction/transformation/Population Process**

end users. The drug may be related to a "type" or a "group." A type of drug may be a penicillin or chemotherapy, while the group for the drug may be antibiotic or antineoplastic. Categorization affords the end user the flexibility to query the database at varying levels of interest rather than creating such groups "on the fly." By omitting the necessary categorizations, the end-user communities will once again return to developing their own "stand-alone" entities to help resolve their problems. This action will result in inconsistent, erroneous information being utilized for corporate decision making, thus returning the process to its earlier state of disarray.

## DATA WAREHOUSE MAINTENANCE

Now that the data has been accurately populated into the data warehouse, the next population should be considered. Depending on several variables, the next population might consist of a complete "drop" and re-population of the data warehouse, transforming new data elements along the way. Another possibility includes the addition of new data only into the warehouse. This option requires that any modifications to source data elements that were previously populated into the warehouse be tagged and replicated into the warehouse as modifications. The driving factor in this decision is the current and future size of the data warehouse. Obviously, low volumes of data more easily lend themselves to frequent drops and repopulation, while large volumes of data tend to require replication. However, if the volume on the warehouse is not expected to grow for more than a year or so, beginning the project with a drop/repopulate strategy

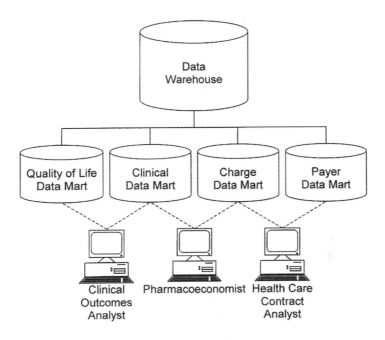

**Exhibit 4. Data Marts**

---

will provide a quick implementation time. When the process is a little more stable, the drop/repopulate approach can be abandoned in favor of the replication option. Be sure to include this strategy in the project plan.

## DATA MARTS

A data mart is a view of the data, one level removed from the detailed data warehouse architecture. The data mart is generally topic specific, such as the treatment data mart, the charge encounter data mart, or the payer reimbursement data mart. Development of data marts reduces the traffic of all users hitting the same database simultaneously, which tends to have a negative impact on performance and response of the database.

A data mart (see Exhibit 4) is similar to the warehouse in that it provides a query and analysis environment for end users. However, a data mart differs from a data warehouse because it is organized by topic to ease the performance burden of the data warehouse table architecture. One large benefit of data marts is that they provide an extremely easy-to-use environment for which the high-level end users, including executive management, can learn to query. What better public relations could the project team ask for than to have the project sponsors actively utilizing the data warehouse through data marts?

Data marts are developed similarly, on a small scale, to the data warehouse. The project team and selected end users identify those data elements that are most often utilized for analysis, a model of the desired architecture is created, and electronic code developed to extract the data from the warehouse into the appropriate data mart. Very often, new derived data elements are created such as patient age at diagnosis. In this example, the end users never have to bother with calculating this value from date of birth and date of diagnosis. This should be an encouraged practice, especially if one of the goals of the data warehouse is to provide a decision support environment for all levels of user analysis sophistication.

As discussed earlier, the decision to have end users working directly against the data warehouse is important for planning the architecture. If the project team decides to utilize the data warehouse architecture for their querying and reporting environment, then the data model may be organized to reflect the concept of denormalization (storing relevant data in multiple tables).

## ANALYSIS AND REPORTING TOOLS

If one element of the project has a large impact on the perceived success of the data warehouse, selecting and implementing the most appropriate analysis and reporting tools is that element. By virtue of the fact that the "rubber hits the road" with the implementation of such tools, it is crucial that the project team work with the end users to understand: what types of tools are currently used by the organization, why those tools were selected, and positive and negative values the current tools bring to the organization.

Once the history is understood, the team should:

- Identify the tool(s) that meet the criteria of the end users
- Invite each vendor to demonstrate the software functionality to the project team (including several end users)
- Select at least two products for evaluation
- Select an evaluation team comprised of end users and project team members
- Obtain pricing proposals from each vender to be evaluated
- Evaluate the products within a set timeframe
- Select and implement product(s) *quickly*

## MEASURING FOR SUCCESS

Throughout various stages of the data warehouse project, the project team is encouraged to plan a session that will allow the executive sponsors and upper management to review the progress and ensure that the project plan and timeline correspond with the needs of the organization.

For instance, if a member of upper management has recently decided to replace one type of software with another, the project team should be made aware and necessary modifications to the project plan and timeline should be made.

With this initiation, the healthcare professional is now empowered with the basic knowledge of data warehousing design, development, and implementation. Hundreds of books have been written on the subject of data warehousing and some recommended titles appear below. Good luck and happy data warehousing!

### Recommended Reading

1. Kimball, R., Reeves, C., Ross, M., and Thornthwaite, W. 1988. *The Data Warehouse Lifecycle Toolkit: Expert Methods for Designing, Developing, and Deploying Data Warehouses.* New York: John Wiley & Sons.
2. Inmon, W. 1996. *Building the Data Warehouse.* New York: John Wiley & Sons.
3. Hackney, D. 1997. *Understanding and Implementing Successful Data Marts.* Redwood City: Addison-Wesley.
4. Edelstein, H. and Barquin, R. 1997. *Building, Using, and Managing the Data Warehouse.* New York: Prentice Hall.
5. *DM Review,* Powell Publishing, 617 S. 94th Street, Milwaukee, WI 53214-1222. Web sites: dmreview.com and data-warehouse.com.
6. *The Journal of Data Warehousing,* The Data Warehousing Institute, 849-J Quince Orchard Boulevard, Gaithersburg, MD 20878. Web site: dw-institute.com.

# Chapter 23
# Critical Factors in Developing a Data Warehouse

*Duane E. Sharp*

Data warehousing has become one of the most significant technologies of the past decade, and has permeated virtually every business sector, from retailing to finance, in one form or another.

The International Data Corporation (IDC) estimates that revenue from the total worldwide data warehouse software market, including data access, warehouse management/storage, and data transformation/warehouse generation, will grow at a compound annual growth rate (CAGR) of 30.8 percent during the period from 1995 to the year 2000. Worldwide market revenue was $1.4 billion in 1995; based on this forecast, it will grow to $5.4 billion by the year 2000. This growth pattern is a certain indication that data warehousing is well beyond the stage of early adoption and has been accepted by pragmatic businesses as a proven technology for enhancing their business operations.

As an example of the proliferation of this major corporate application of information technology, it is worth noting that NCR Corporation, a world leader in data warehousing technology, had over 500 data warehousing installations worldwide in 1997, in a broad range of business sectors.

## ARE COMPANIES REALIZING A RETURN ON THEIR INVESTMENT?

A recent IDC return on investment study, published as "The Foundations of Wisdom: A Study of the Financial Impact of Data Warehousing" by Stephen Graham, interviewed 62 sites that have successfully implemented a corporate data warehouse. The study covers a wide range of industries, including financial services, healthcare, telecommunications, retail, government, and manufacturing. The average initial investment by the sites surveyed was $2.2 million. The major finding of the study is that organizations recouped their initial investment within an average of 2.3 years. The

0-8493-1498-4/03/$0.00+$1.50
© 2003 by CRC Press LLC

average return on the initial investment over three years was more than 400 percent, dramatic confirmation that data warehousing can be a good investment.

## INTERNAL ACCESS TO THE CORPORATE DATA WAREHOUSE

A data warehouse takes time-oriented data from multiple applications and organizes it according to subjects meaningful to the corporation or business. Corporations, concerned with informing their decision makers, are pursuing this strategy for two major reasons:

1. *Reduced complexity.* The data in the decision-support database or warehouse is made available in a form that is relatively easy to understand.
2. *Improved performance.* The warehouse can be tuned to provide better performance and faster response to complex queries and analysis.

## BUILDING THE DATA WAREHOUSE

From a qualitative perspective, according to the IDC survey, the key benefits of a corporate data warehouse are more streamlined systems administration, and more productivity for internal analysts. Building a data warehouse is one of the most complex processes a corporation can undertake. It will change the corporate decision-making process without necessarily reengineering the corporation. Traditionally, corporate decisions have been based on the analysis of data, without detailed information to support the data. Corporations analyzed data from reports and made decisions based on limited information. Data warehousing changes this process dramatically, by quickly transforming all available detailed data (irrespective of volume) into meaningful business information. The end results are timelier and better informed business decisions.

Experience based on successful data warehouse implementations points to five critical factors that are essential for a successful implementation. The following analysis of these factors describes why they are important to any data warehousing project.

### Focus on a Real Problem

It is a fundamental axiom that a successful data warehouse implementation needs to be based on solving a real business problem, and the corporation will have to solve this problem. A data warehouse that does not address a critical business problem is destined for failure.

The business problem selected must have senior management backing that correlates with the desire to solve the problem. Most successful data warehouses are cross-functional, because the return on investment increases with both the breadth of data they hold and the impact they have on the business. Business problems that have been solved by a data warehouse solution include credit card risk management; sales and inventory management; supply-chain management; exposure management; and target marketing.

Solving these business problems requires large volumes of data from many business functions and, in some cases, even from outside sources. It also involves structuring the data based on input from end users who will use the system, as to what data is important and how it should be presented.

History has shown that if a data warehouse is built without end-user input, end users will not use it and the development exercise will be a spectacular, expensive failure. Information technology professionals alone cannot build a data warehouse; user organizations must be involved from the beginning.

There are several approaches to implementing a data warehousing system. One solution that is often applied to solving a business problem is the so-called packaged data warehouse. A packaged solution is usually a single vendor solution, with a predefined front-end application, a standard database management system, and an industry-generic database design. It often fails because it does not solve the critical business problems of a corporation; however, it is implemented to prove the concept. Since it is designed to meet a variety of requirements, it usually fails to address the specific needs that are always a part of any organization's data warehousing business.

The data warehousing solution that is most likely to be successful is one that provides a solution to critical business problems, specific to the organization for which it is designed, with significant end-user involvement and senior management support.

### Select the Right Data Warehouse Champion

The second critical success factor is acquiring a strong champion for the data warehouse implementation. The complexities of the implementation are enormous, ranging from maneuvering the project through the corporate political environment to gaining consensus among cross-functional business users with different objectives. Usually, a data warehouse champion has to spearhead the project to ultimately make the data warehouse successful.

The data warehouse champion is typically a fairly senior business user with a strong understanding of the information technology environment. He or she must understand the political landscape, have the capability to bring tough issues to a consensus, and should report to a senior corporate sponsor during the data warehouse implementation. Meeting these criteria is the best way to ensure that the champion will prove to be a real champion when the chips are down.

The champion must be firmly convinced that a data warehousing solution will meet the requirement and solve the defined business problem, to the extent of betting his or her reputation on the implementation. He or she will also ensure that the right team of professionals is involved in defining the business problem to be solved, and ultimately in developing the data warehousing solution that will meet the requirements.

A key element in the champion's involvement is the requirement to challenge information system specialists, to work with them for the benefit of the corporation, and to represent the business users in defining methods of access and presentation of the wide range of information to be derived from the data warehousing system.

### Use Detailed Historical Data

The foundation of every successful data warehouse is the detailed historical data on which it is based, and this is the third critical success factor. One approach that has been used by information systems departments to manage the volume and complexity of the issues associated with navigating through weeks, months, or even years of detailed transaction data is summary data structures. Although these elements have often become a preferred strategy for implementing decision support systems, they frequently become a detriment to the data warehousing system and its original intent. Summary data structures inevitably fall short of meeting requirements, for several reasons:

1. *Obscuring data variations.* Because they are only summaries of information, they tend to obscure important data variations, masking important variations in corporate data which may point to problems, indicating areas where successful techniques have been applied in the past and may be applied in the future.
2. *Complex maintenance.* Another deficiency of summary structures is that their maintenance can be fairly complex and quite resource intensive, requiring a significant amount of updating to reflect adjustments to transaction data.
3. *Single static scheme.* A final deficiency of summary structures is that they are usually created using a single static scheme for organizing transaction-level details into a coherent and manageable information format. This limitation ultimately causes the summary structure to fall short because it prevents the business user from viewing the data in a manner conducive to a discovery process. In short, most of today's business problems or opportunities cannot be identified using a few, limited static views of the business activity.

Summary data tables do have a place in data warehouse design. However, they should not be considered as an alternative to storing detailed data, but rather as a technique for solving some very well-defined performance problems.

## Apply Technology

The fourth critical success factor is that a successful data warehouse implementation will apply technology to the business problem. One technology which has been applied to the data warehousing solution is symmetric multiprocessor (SMP) computer hardware supporting a relational, multidimensional, or hybrid database environment.

More advanced solutions use massive parallel processor hardware (MPP). In a decentralized data warehouse architecture, this solution will probably employ middleware to coordinate wide area access. Furthermore, it will entail the use of graphic user interface (GUI) application tools (either developed in-house or purchased off-the-shelf) and online analytical processing (OLAP) tools to present the volumes of data in meaningful formats.

There are a broad range of architectures that can meet the requirements of a data warehousing system, and the selection of the right technology is a critical factor. However, architectural issues should only be approached when the business problems to be addressed are clearly understood. The technology should always be applied as part of the solution.

Evaluations of different technology can consume significant amounts of time and energy. It is better to work with vendors who can provide references that relate to an organization's requirement. Other sources of information are technical publications, seminars, and conferences, and research organizations that have conducted studies and evaluated a variety of different issues around data warehousing. Knowledgeable individuals in organizations that have implemented a data warehousing solution are also a major and extremely useful information resource.

## Trust the Data — History Does Not Lie

The fifth and final critical success factor in a data warehousing implementation is realizing that historical data is a strategic asset, because it is a source of corporate truths that do not forget or deceive. Human perception and memory can be faulty, and the data warehousing system should not be entrusted to a process that relies on the human memory.

Precise point-in-time readings of key business indicators can help recreate a thumbnail sketch of past business events. They can also forecast the success of a future event, potentially reducing the probability of recreating previous business disasters.

However, data alone will not solve a business problem. Specialists with specific information system skills will be needed to scrub, load, access, and present the gigabytes and terabytes of transaction data generated each year by the business. Statisticians and business analysts can interpret the business information distilled from all the detailed data, and provide the business analysis and predictive models that project future business trends.

While history does not lie, it can sometimes mislead. Inconsistencies, incomplete or absent metadata definitions, data loss from media corruption, or unnecessarily restrictive retention cycles are potential serious threats to the quality of data residing in a data warehouse.

## CONCLUSION

There are no guarantees with data warehousing implementation; however, the probability of success will be increased significantly if these five critical success factors are addressed. Therefore, it is important to consider these critical factors long before the first query is run or the first gigabyte of data is loaded.

A data warehouse system is one of the most complex applications that an organization can implement, since it involves the core business of the organization and a large part of its transaction and business history. It will have a dramatic impact on each information user. While it is not in itself a solution to a business problem, it provides a means to a solution, one that will involve the entire organization in a major cultural change. This change will enable employees to use detailed information as a key to knowledgeable corporate decision making.

# Section VII
# The Changing Organization

# Chapter 24

# Healthcare versus Information Technology

*Phillip L. Davidson*

There are hundreds of texts dealing with the role of information technology (IT) in today's world. The realm of exploration of this chapter will be the adaptability of IT in that rapidly evolving world, and its relationship to healthcare.

## INTRODUCTION

The field of information systems (IS) may be the fastest developing field in the world today. Nicholas Negroponte, in his best-selling text *Being Digital*, effectively describes the exponential growth of computing and telecommunications. He states that "35 percent of American families and 50 percent of American teenagers now have personal computers."[1]

Personal computers (PCs)* are certainly one important indicator, but nothing can compare with the revolution caused by the Internet. "Surfing the Net" is becoming part of our popular cultural parlance. According to Negroponte, the number of people using Internet browsers grew 11 percent per week from February to December and the number of people using the Internet is increasing ten percent a month.[1]

What we are seeing are evolutionary changes in the technology, changes happening so quickly, no one can know or even be aware of all of them. However, perhaps partially because of the revolution, especially with connectivity (the Internet), other changes are taking place. "Now both technology and business directions are driving information systems management to a fundamentally new paradigm."[2]

---

*Personal computers (PCs) in this text refers to IBM computers and their clones and Macintosh computers.

0-8493-1498-4/03/$0.00+$1.50

The technology is certainly exciting and that is the topic covered by all the news. But IS or IT is a fairly recent development along the human timeline. In the 1960s, computers simply were not available, except as esoteric research tools. Punch cards were still the rule. The IS world, however, has exploded in 30 years. In 1999, I am typing this chapter on a laptop with enough memory to store four years of *The Wall Street Journal.* I carry a "palmtop" in my shirt pocket that has more memory and works faster than the first computer, which required an entire building to house.

Reading all of this, one might expect that the world of information systems and technology is one success story after another. The truth is, there are more failures than successes. "Contemporary research cites a high percentage of Information Systems Development (ISD) project failures."[3]

Lyytinen suggests that "the majority of reasons for ISD failures are social in nature."[4] Lyytinen derives his hypothesis from computer surveys searching the quantitative aspects of the IT culture. When he suggests that the failures have a "social" origin, he is using the term in the context of "culture." Both Heales[3] and Lyytinen[4] suggest that there may be issues within the IT culture that allow "failure" as a cultural norm. What we discuss later in the second section is that what Heales and Lyytinen are calling "failure" (i.e., the lack of completion of an information system implementation) is not viewed as failure within the IT culture and is, in fact, part of the norm for that culture. Hofstede et al. describe culture as consisting of the symbols, heroes, rituals, and values of an organization. They describe these as "layers of an onion" with values serving as the core.[5]

Christian Scholz suggests that IT culture "starts out with a strong bureaucratic culture, characterized by high values for standardization, security, centralism, order and individual avoidance."[6] These reflect similar core values in Hofstede's work.

The overview will look at the culture of IT. It is my suggestion that it is the organizational culture of IT that has set it up for failure and it is the organizational culture of IT that makes change so difficult. The business world of IT is entangled in a morass of trying to make the needed social changes while surrounded by the burgeoning technologies of client/servers and optical storage and SCSI hard drives.

The internal conflict being experienced by various IT groups also brings their culture into conflict with other cultures, especially cultures that are also going through tumultuous changes. A good example is medicine. Medicine, much like IT, has a technical culture that thrives on exclusivity. Medicine, however, needs IT to succeed in today's world, and that complicates the picture.

The first part of this chapter will look at the foundations of both cultures, but will focus primarily on the information systems perspective. Areas of conflict will be examined and discussed.

In the second section, I will look more closely at an example of a large IT culture and its conflict with an even larger medical culture, both parts of the same organization. We will look at specific pieces of the conflict and some recommendations for resolution.

In the third and final section, we will look at an attempt to combine these two cultures into a single working organization. Specific areas of conflict and methods of resolution will be discussed.

## Definitions

- Clinical medicine — that aspect of medical practice that uses quantitative, analytical procedures (as opposed to observation and intuition). Examples would be laboratory, radiology, and pathology reports.
- Clinical information systems — those information systems used to collect, store, quantify, and distribute clinical information.
- Culture — a pattern of shared basic assumptions (see Hofstede et al.[5] and Scholz[6] on values) that the group learned as it solved its problems of external adaptation and internal integration, that has worked well enough to be considered valid and, therefore, to be taught to new members as the correct way to perceive, think, and feel in relation to those problems.[7]
- Information systems (IS) — generally refers to the computer systems themselves, but the two terms (IT and IS) are frequently used interchangeably in the literature. This chapter will maintain the distinction between IT and IS.
- Information technology (IT) — for the sake of this chapter, that computer system technology required for the gathering, classification, and distribution of information. While there are other means by which one can gather, classify, and distribute data, the term generally refers to computers and computer systems.
- Provider — someone who provides medical care. The traditional provider is the physician. In today's work, this can also include nurse practitioners and physicians' assistants.

## THE CULTURE OF INFORMATION TECHNOLOGY

It has been suggested that IT may go clear back in time to the clerics of ancient Egypt. If one defines information technology as above, then one could make the case that modern IT is only different from that ancient gathering and classification and distribution of data in speed and connectivity. Where the ancient clerics counted and noted data on papyrus or clay tablets as they stood in a single location, modern technology allows us to collect data virtually at the speed of light from around the world and from multiple locations simultaneously.

There is an assumption that gathering this information has some value. In ancient times, for example, it allowed the rulers to know how much of a crop the farmers had produced, allowing them the ability to plan ahead. Clearly, misinformation could create serious problems, even famine. Therefore, the person who has control of the correct information can be assumed to have some degree of power.

Gareth Morgan addresses this in his text *Images of Organizations*:

> Power accrues to the person who is able to structure attention to issues in a way that in effect defines the reality of the decision-making process. This draws attention to the key importance of knowledge and information as sources of power. By controlling (emphasis added) these key resources, a person can systematically influence the definition of organizational situations and can create patterns of dependency.[8]

From the preceding, therefore, we can assume that one aspect of the IT culture is the issue around *control* of information.

Structure is another defining aspect of the IT culture. Morgan continues:

> Often the quest for control of information in an organization is linked to questions of organizational structure. For example, many battles have been fought over the control and use of centralized computer systems, because control of the computer often carries with it control over information flows and the design of information systems.[8]

What is the structure and how does information move through it? Edgar Schein gives at least one description of the basis for that flow.

> For an organization to cope effectively with a rapidly changing environment of the sort we see increasingly in today's global context, it must be able to (1) import information efficiently; (2) move that information to the right place in the organization, where it can be analyzed, digested, and acted upon; (3) make the necessary internal transformations to take account of the new information; and (4) get feedback on the impacts of its new responses, which starts the whole coping cycle via information gathering all over again.[9]

Translating Schein's description into IT language (1) we must be able to input and receive data across system interfaces that are accurate; (2) we must store that data in a format that is useable and accessible by those with permission to view it; (3) we must validate the integrity of the data as it is translated from analog to digital or from one digital code to another; (4) we must be able to monitor and measure system and user response to the data.

Structure may be the most defining characteristic of the IT culture. The design and structure of information systems directly reflects how control is manifest through system design. What does the classic information system look like?

- Data is entered into the system through keyboard, instrument interface, or through an interface with another system.
- The data stream must be structured so that tagging of individual segments of the information stream will match, identically, the same segments in other streams.
- The data is stored as either a batch file on a local PC or host or is transmitted to a larger collecting location where the batch file can be tagged and separated into its individual components.
- The transmission from a local host to a central collection point can involve a variety of individual points of transmission, such as timeplex, terminal servers, Ethernet connectors, microwave transmitters, plus transmission lines of varying sizes and speeds.
- Once the data has been collected and sorted, it can be displayed through the use of a separate display software and hardware system. The display software is written specifically to be able to display the collected data in the format the user expects to see.
- After a certain period of time, the data is archived either onto hard disk, or more likely tape or optical disks.

Each point along this line is managed by a separate individual or group of individuals. The *structure* is of foremost importance. IT is reminiscent of the assembly line mentality, taking to heart the principles of scientific management as described by Frederick Taylor.

Frederick Taylor's principles of scientific management, although developed at the turn of the century, are alive and well within IT. Taylor's primary emphasis was to place all responsibility on the shoulder of the manager, adapting the most capable workers to specific tasks. Using quantitative "scientific" methods, these tasks would be designed and monitored for maximum efficiency.[10]

Certainly the design of today's "systems" uses the scientific methods of electronics and physics. Schematics of geographic locations connected by specific pieces of instrumentation and wiring are created first. You then select the individual with the most skill at performing each task. Their tasks, however, are very focused. If you do not have an individual with the needed skills, you can train one or hire a contractor. Training can be fairly easy because you are only training one small segment. Monitoring and verification of worker performance is a constant within IT. Performance is easy to measure since, in electronics and computers, either it works or it does not.

The flow described above can easily have eight separate segments from data collection to display and archival. Each section is under the direction of a different manager and there might be multiple individuals under that manager. Each individual is responsible for a tiny segment of the chain of information with no one having the overall skill to physically create the entire system. This type of segmentation within IT is called "staging" and may be the biggest problem area within the IT structure that threatens the ability of IT to move quickly into the future.

Getting back to Taylor's first point, responsibility is taken away from the worker and given totally to the manager. This is part of the problematical structure that IT is trying to deal with today. The manager or administrator has total responsibility for the system. However, within the IT structure, that same manager or administrator has neither the skills nor the authority to make changes anywhere along the line except through proclamation. There may be a single manager responsible for an entire network, yet each component may have its own manager and individuals under that manager. Those last individuals are normally the only people who can make changes to the system itself, yet none have a picture of how the whole system works.

This philosophy of staging is a structural issue as well as a security issue. It comes primarily from the banking and military industries where various stages are inserted so that no one has the ability to affect the outcome through manipulation of the system.

We can see, therefore, that *structure* is an inherently important aspect of IT culture.

IT has one product — information. To lose control over that product — using the current mindset — means to lose your reason for being. The elaborate structure imposed helps prevent someone outside the IT organization from gaining control. The structure, in fact, is so elaborate that not even someone *inside* the IT organization can gain control. This is the Achilles' heel of IT. It is a problem that has not been ignored. The cost of IT and its pervasiveness in today's business have given IT a visibility unheard of in the past.

> The majority of organizational leaders are convinced that information management is the most important factor in organizational performance and competitive advantage. It is increasingly obvious that information management is too central to be controlled by information managers. Decisions about information networks and other uses of exploding technology are top management's responsibility today. But if top management is making these decisions, what is the role of the information division?[11]

> Information systems managers ... must prepare themselves for managing in an environment in which they may not directly control information resources — a corporate world in which the mystique of information technology is no longer the exclusive province of information systems specialists, line business managers increasingly take responsibility for information technology decisions, and computing and telecommunications are ubiquitous.[2]

These kinds of discussions are emotional, international, and omnipresent. IT managers are threatened and they must adapt or face extinction —

not an easy choice either way because adaptability is almost antithetical to the concept of structure within IT.

An absolute belief in the quantitative is also inherently part of IT. Computers are on or off. Switches are on or off. On and off switches are represented by simple 0s and 1s. Fuzzy logic notwithstanding, computers do not understand "about" or "approximately." Therefore, the individuals who spend their whole lives with these instruments tend to adopt the same mind set.

Schein describes seven basic assumptions about the nature of information commonly held by IT personnel:

1. It is possible to package and transmit information accurately in an electronic medium.
2. Information can be validly divided into bits.
3. Information can be frozen in time on a screen or on a printout.
4. Faster transmission and computation are always better than slower.
5. More information is always better than less.
6. The more quantifiable the information is, the better.
7. Ultimately, a paperless environment is more efficient and desirable.[7]

These seven points, along with the overriding belief in the need for control and structure, form the core of the IT culture and form the crux of the conflict with which IT is struggling.

> This belief in technology, which sometimes shades into a blind faith in technology, acts as a lens that distorts our perception of computers, leading to false beliefs or myths about them. These myths are often difficult to spot because they usually are partly true — they tend to be oversimplifications rather than outright falsities. In addition, computer myths are so deeply embedded in the culture of some companies and industries that they are taken for granted and pass unnoticed. Left unidentified, these myths are pernicious because they can silently shape expectations and guide decision making down inappropriate paths.[12]

The focus of this chapter is on how the IT culture conflicts with the culture of clinical medicine. IT tends to be extremely vertical with high authority expressed in very narrow vertical "silos." Clinical medicine is very horizontal, with authority vested in one person who has wide-ranging responsibility for patient care. IT feels access to information should be limited, whereas providers argue that it needs to be easily accessible for everyone. These are only a couple of the points of conflict. There are other conflicts with the seven points Schein describes above.

1. Is it possible to package and transmit information accurately in an electronic medium? We have found that "data," at least within clinical medicine, is highly interpretive. We might be collecting some kind of "information," but does it have value? If it has no value, is it

"information," or just junk? In addition, we know that different types of electronic media behave differently. Transmissions on twisted copper wire as opposed to fiber optic cable, with or without an Ethernet connection, are not the same. Traffic levels and how the electronic media cope with that traffic are a consideration. "Collisions" on the Ethernet can lose data.

2. "Bits" on a computer system are elements of information of a specific size. It is difficult, if not impossible, to quantitate qualitative data. Much of clinical medicine is qualitative.

3. Information displayed on the screen is already obsolete in a clinical setting. However, to "paint" or "refresh" the screen in real-time makes decision making impossible. The compromise is somewhere between a "frozen" screen and a fully active screen.

4. More hardware and faster hardware are on everyone's wish list. The fact than my computer operates at a speed nearly one million times faster that the first computer is irrelevant. Our data becomes increasingly complex; therefore processors must work faster, read faster, and display faster. In truth, however, there is serious doubt that one achieves benefits directly proportional to the costs of the faster systems. There is a point where we are buying speed only for speed's sake.

5. The idea that more information is always better than less information is highly debated within the medical field. We are now asked to remove data because too much data makes it difficult to make medical decisions. Data can be analyzed and comparisons between data points can be displayed. How much of this data has value? If IT can provide it and display it, does it automatically have value? The answer is no and providers within clinical medicine are overwhelmed with the volume of both electronic and print data they constantly receive.

6. Making information more quantifiable is related to point 5. Much of clinical medicine is intuitive and qualitative. Legalistic concerns continue to apply pressure on providers to use quantitative data, yet the sense of touch and smell and intuition still play significant roles in the practice of medicine.

7. Ultimately will we be paperless? There is tremendous pressure upon the medical community to go paperless. However, millions of patients' medical histories are wrapped up in thick "paper charts." The international drive to move to "paperless charts" has physicians in an extreme state of disquiet. The idea of looking up a chart, instantly, from any location is appealing, but there is something very solid about flipping through the patient's chart. Using the "page up" and "page down" keys on the computer has far from universal appeal. Probably no other issue has the potential financial and patient care impact than this issue currently has on the practice of medicine today.

We have looked at nine aspects of IT culture, and have discussed seven in detail. Control and structure — so intimately intertwined — may be the most relevant. It is important to reexamine the concerns over these two aspects that conflict with the practice of medicine.

The issue of control is probably the easiest to explain. Providers feel that the information on their patients belongs to them, the providers. They demand quick and immediate access to that information and have no tolerance for issues about security. IT, on the other hand, would like to control access to that information by allowing the provider to see her or his patients only. IT would like to segment security at a variety of levels so information is provided on a "need-to-know" basis only. This is in conflict with a medical culture that is used to complete and unobstructed access to any patient information at any time.

IT argues that it is an issue of patient confidentiality. The medical community, which treats patient confidentiality as an inherent part of the job, feels confidentiality is not the issue, but that access is the point of controversy. This issue is argued daily and with multiple clinical systems and methods of display. Many IT organizations maintain elaborate security groups within their internal organizations to deal with exactly these issues.

The issue of structure so closely relates to control and power that they are one and the same issue.

> Many of the hot issues regarding the merits and problems of microprocessing hinge on the question of power. The new information processing technology creates the possibility of multiple points of access to common databases and the possibility of local rather than centralized information systems. In principle the technology can be used to increase the power of those at the periphery or local levels of the organization by providing them with more comprehensive, immediate, and relevant data relating to their work, facilitating self-control rather than centralized control.[8]

> Today's end users want to get their hands on [patient] data, period. Whether it resides in local databases, remote servers or a central mainframe just does not matter. Try explaining the intricacies of incompatible networks, multiple operating systems, proprietary databases or other facts of client/server life, and their eyes glaze over. If they're not getting what they want from IS, they're likely to try building or buying their own proprietary applications.[13]

> Companies that currently face the issue of centralization versus decentralization must realize that the onslaught of technology and the consequent empowerment of end users is more powerful than any desire for IS management control. Managers must be cognizant of the reality of decentralized processing — it has invaded all organizations. However,

it is not technology alone that is driving the IS organization toward de-centralization; it is the customers of the IS function who are trying to find ways to better satisfy their business needs for information and business process support.[2]

One intermediary solution is to train "power users," specific users who have been selected by IT for extended training. This partially placates release of power from IT because they get to choose the users. However, as Santosus notes,

> The idea of supporting "power" users is not an altogether comfortable pill for many IS people to swallow. Some IS departments try to keep a tight rein on end users by establishing firm control over computing resources while others opt to placate them by handing out some of the tools now available that allow end users to access data themselves. However, simply throwing tools at end users or, worse, discouraging their empowerment will likely serve no one's needs. Both tactics are a Band-Aid solution to a much greater problem: that IS and end users too often find themselves working as adversaries when it comes to accessing and manipulating data.[13]

In the past, one obtained data from some central data repository. As illustrated above, providers can now "log on" from virtually anywhere, including their home, access the data repository or even directly connect with the patient. This decentralized structure is very bothersome for IT.

Structure is the way IT deals with the issue of control. The medical community, however, finds the structure of the typical IT community confusing. That may well be the point. These issues will be demonstrated in greater detail in the next section.

In summary, the ability to control the flow of information is a major point of contention between IT and the medical community. The issue is one with a long history. The very culture of IT treats information as quantitative and inviolable. IT managers view the control of information as their primary responsibility. However, things are changing and we will discuss this concept in the last section in greater detail. Suffice it to say that a two-page ad in a recent copy of a magazine directed toward chief information officers simply said "CHANGE OR DIE!" The need to change is known. How to change is still not clear for everyone.

## INFORMATION TECHNOLOGY AND CLINICAL CULTURES WITHIN A LARGE HMO

The focus of this section is on one division of a large, national HMO. The organization will be referred to simply as HMO so as not to identify the specific organization. The same issues have occurred in multiple HMOs; the same play reenacted multiple times.

### A Short Clinical Information System History

In the late 1970s, there was an attempt by HMO to create a clinical laboratory information system. There were no clinical information systems within the division at that time. The only information systems were database systems that tracked appointments, kept patient demographics, and provided multiple pathways for the transmission of business information. Since HMO is a prepaid healthcare plan, patients are not billed and billing does not have the major information system role typically found with other types of medical practices. The attempt to begin that first clinical system never got started due to internal conflicts over scope and control.

About five years later, a second attempt was started. Patient tests performed at the large central laboratory were being collected on punched paper computer cards that were manually typed. These punched cards were fed into a regionwide database for data collection and presentation. Physicians could view the data, but the manual entry was tedious and error ridden. Turn-around time was slow because transmission to the IBM mainframe was only by batch operations that occurred once every 24 hours. Not having patient data from all the facilities gave only limited value to the information that was collected. These were the reasons behind the attempt to create a regionwide system. However, politics and control issues killed attempts to create an integrated system. A stand-alone mainframe was installed at the central laboratory that processed most outpatient work. This eliminated the batch operations and improved the turn-around times. In addition, the ability to interface instrumentation directly to the mainframe helped with errors in transcription from the manual system. A few of HMO's laboratories used a PC-based data entry system that improved the amount of information available for viewing. The PC-based system, however, was still manual, error ridden, and personnel intensive.

In 1990, the decision was made that it was essential for HMO to have an integrated divisionwide computer system that provided complete patient data from any terminal in the division. That project is the subject of the third section of this chapter.

### THE INFORMATION TECHNOLOGY CULTURE

The IT organization within HMO consists of approximately 700 people. This IT organization is called the Information Systems Division (ISD). The total organizational description, including organizational charts, is issued semi-annually and is approximately 50 pages in length. This is a cultural artifact worth noting.

IDS (Integrated Delivery System) reports to the CIO for HMO. The physicians all belong to a separate corporation and report to the medical director of HMO. Both the CIO and the medical director report to the CEO and to the board of directors of HMO. Part of the conflict begins here, where there is argument as to which group within the division actually controls or "owns" clinical information systems.

In 1993, two issues drove HMO to examine its internal IT organization. First, the inability to implement a system over the past decade (1975–1985). Second, the pressure from competition and the potential reorganization of healthcare at the national level made it apparent that an integrated information system was essential for HMO to be able to compete in their marketplace.

In 1993, HMO began a serious reorganization of all its component parts. Outside consultants were invited to evaluate the current IT organization and asked to make recommendations for change. One of the most telling reports was presented to corporate management by an outside consulting group. This report will be referred to as the CSS report. The remainder of this section will deal with the issues that surfaced as they relate to the organizational culture and conflict between the IT and medical cultures.

The CSS report included observations, findings, and recommendations regarding their review of the clinical systems currently being developed or implemented. Information and interviews were taken from both the IDS and physicians' group. Other information, including innovation projects and future business and systems plans, were evaluated. CSS also reviewed similar projects being undertaken by other outside organizations.

CSS interviewed more than 100 personnel at 15 separate locations. They also interviewed numerous other vendors. They reviewed a considerable number of documents, including the HMO business plan and the strategic information systems plan.

The CSS report was brief, only 37 pages. The copy had obviously been edited down to a level where the language was very succinct.

In what might be seen as an attempt to relieve the large number of negative findings about to be reported, CSS listed a few positive points first. One, in particular, relates to this chapter.

> HMO has a significant number of physicians, nurses, administrators, laboratorians, and other system users who are more than willing to participate in and contribute to the development of clinical systems and other projects. These individuals wish to make a positive difference and contribute to the organization, the practice of medicine, and the effective care of patients (Internal HMO report).

This first point is crucial to the understanding of the conflict between the IT group and the medical staff. According to CSS (and this point is well documented internally to HMO), you have a large medical staff who are anxious, willing, and able to participate in the implementation of clinical information systems. The feeling that they are being ignored is a point of great frustration. When IDS does talk to the physicians, there is the feeling of resistance based on "well, they're listening, but they're not really listening." There is a sense that IDS is feigning interest. This issue is discussed in greater detail below.

## Problems Described by CSS that Relate Specifically to the ISD/ITS Issue

**Accountability and Responsibility.** Specific accountability and responsibility for clinical system projects are not supported by the organizational culture and reward structures, and a sense of urgency to perform is not apparent. The physicians perceived ISD (the Information Systems Division, now ITS) as being the main barrier to success; ISD perceived the lack of agreement, clear direction, and support from the business and operations side as the main barriers to success. According to the report, "There is a clear indication that no one is responsible for the successful completion of a project, and that no one is held accountable for either project success or failure. Clinical system projects don't fail; they are either renamed and started anew, or they simply cease to operate."

This reflects back to the "cultural norm" mentioned earlier in reference to the works of Heales[3] and Lyytinen.[4] Within the IT culture, *not* finishing a project is okay. It is not considered a failure but is within the normal values of the culture where employees frequently move from project to project without any particular ownership of completion. Add to this Scholz's comment that avoidance is a core value of the IT culture and project completion becomes a significant issue as shown here.[6] The reward structure within IDS is for the developing and "selling" of projects, not for the completion and implementation.

**Systems Development.** The typical systems development life cycle at HMO is around five years, provided specific deliverables and scope are established and adhered to. The life cycle can be much longer if the deliverables and scope continually change. Most likely, a five-year or more life cycle will no longer meet the requirement of an organization that must rapidly evolve to maintain its market advantage and superior care model.

There is a "norm" with the IDS culture that projects last five years. That is clearly stated among the staff and was a point acknowledged by CSS. However, few people actually stay through the entire five years. It is also a cultural norm within IDS that people never stay on a specific project (or at least not in the same position) for longer than two years. This sort of turnover makes project continuity very difficult.

The point made by CSS, however, is that HMO must be able to react more rapidly while still focusing attention and responsibility on completion and implementation. Another point that is not discussed is that there is little or no planning for post-implementation. All attention is focused on selling the project, with minimal effort focused on reaching actual completion and with no consideration about what to do if and when the project is actually completed.

**Credibility.** ISD clearly lacks the necessary level of credibility (required to achieve effective results) among the physicians and staff of HMO. Moreover, ISD is not integrated with the division; there is a clear perception that ISD does not share a common sense of mission and objectives with HMO.

ISD and the physicians and staff view each other as a barrier to success. "ISD does not clearly understand the clinical environment; and the physicians and staff do not clearly understand the development requirements for large, complex systems."

The physicians and staff view ISD as a separate entity that "seems to exist for its own purposes." ISD is viewed as not being accountable to its "customers." The ISD focus is viewed as developing systems without regard to true customer needs or trends in the medical care industry. CSS felt that this is at least partially due to the lack of direction given to ISD regarding its mission and role within the organization. According to CSS, "ISD took [historically] most of the responsibility with less than sufficient guidance and assistance from the physicians and staff. Now it appears that the physicians and staff have taken on much of the responsibility for developing clinical system requirements with less than sufficient guidance and assistance from ISD."

## THE MEDICAL CULTURE

There is an internal hierarchy within the medical community, starting with the physician on top, and that pyramid is part of the medical culture. It is this "owner" group that defines the medical culture for this chapter.

> "We're part of a long, proud medical tradition." Does that line not trigger a sense of pride and altruism in you? We are, after all, in an industry with caring at its heart. And medicine and medical care cultures have developed traditions that make us proud, perhaps blindly proud. Underneath, we have tied ourselves unquestioningly to past practices, whether they still serve our interests or not. We have worshipped and glorified our traditions so much so that we now have trouble differentiating between those that work and those that do not. Change and experimentation are very sensitive, even political issues, because so many healthcare professionals interpret them as rejections of the hallowed traditions of the past.[14]

The paragraph above may hint at some small note of criticism, but more realistically, it is a passionate description of the idealized physician. For many of us who grew up with a family physician who came to our homes and treated parents and children (and sometimes even grandchildren), the picture of the paternalistic, white-haired, good-natured, caring physician still exists. The memory of physicians who only used hospitals and laboratories and x-rays for the extreme difficulties still lingers.

Historically, we see a picture of an individual who treats teachers with respect and gratitude, who works with conscience and dignity, who treats the patient as his first concern and respects all confidences. While one can easily make a case that one or all of these attributes are on the endangered species list, the belief that these values still exist is still present and still resides at the core of the medical culture. We could summarize, therefore, by stating that at least one aspect of the medical culture is the aspect of personal involvement with the patient.

There is still a desire among many physicians to retain this potentially outdated image because it is a romantic image, less tarnished than the image of today's high-tech doctor. Nevertheless, today's doctors tend to be more inaccessible. They rarely remember a patient's name without looking at a chart. To diagnose without the aid of lab tests, x-rays, and an assortment of imaging equipment would be unthinkable in today's litigious society. How long caring and personal involvement can exist as a cultural value within medicine is unclear, but there is a real fear these values will be lost.

To be able to do the things required to perform as a physician, their roles and responsibilities are very horizontal (as opposed to the vertical structure of IT). The physician must be able to take broad responsibility for the patient's care — and, indeed, that is his charge. Especially in a case of critical or urgent care, the physician has wide latitude, answering only to peers and then only in the event of an obvious mistake. The broad dimension of the physician's responsibility is an important aspect of the medical culture and finds the narrow, vertical responsibilities held by IT personnel difficult to justify.

Therefore, one can expect that a primary area of potential conflict between medicine and IT is the understanding of each other's responsibilities. As stated above, the CSS report stated that "HMO perceives ISD as being the main barrier to success." The physicians cannot understand why talking to a manager is not sufficient to effect a desired change. They do not understand that the manager may have considerable authority, but probably only within a very narrow range. At the same time, ISD does not believe physicians have a clear understanding of the complexity of the issues involved. It is possible that the desired change requested by the physician might require the consensus of half a dozen IT departments.

The other major aspect of the cultural conflict has to do with control or "ownership." As stated above, most IT cultures believe that they own the information their systems collect and handle. When the IT world was more centralized and information was less accessible, arguments on this topic were rare. Now, however, with the ease of accessibility, the medical community becomes more and more demanding of instant access. Since they view the patients as "their patients," and since the patient's well being is under the direction of the physician staff, they believe they should also have total control of that information and how that information is made available.

There is a great focus on changing the patient care model to improve access and quality of care, while increasing market share and financial margins in a marketplace that is highly competitive and rapidly changing. In addition, there is a greater emphasis on furthering a sense of ownership and responsibility among the physicians and staff.

All of this is influenced by greater competitive pressures on rates and service quality, and significant demands for information by employer groups, regulatory agencies, marketing and research, on the potential effects of healthcare reform. This, in turn, is placing greater emphasis on high-quality, sophisticated, and flexible information systems that can be delivered rapidly and cost-effectively.

## THE ISSUE CAN BE RESOLVED

Reaching an understanding of the potential conflict in the cultures between the IT group and the physician group was a significant step forward. How to resolve the issue was a little more difficult.

With HMO, the decision was made at the highest levels to have a true joint effort between the IDS group and the physicians' group, with the physicians leading the way through a clinical administrator. The administrator was part of the physicians' group but also an acknowledged expert in the IT healthcare world.

The implementation team consisted of two equal parts from each of the two organizations, but both ultimately were responsible to the clinical administrator for implementation. And, while there were a few bumps along the road, the implementation of one of the world's largest clinical systems was effectively accomplished on time and actually under budget. The success was seen as being due to recognition of the needs and cultures of both groups but with attention and direction focused on the needs of the overall organization. Having the backing and authority of the highest authorities within the organization was seen as essential in the success of this implementation (see Exhibit 1).

This seems like a simplistic argument, and I have discussed this issue in many venues around the world. The topic was a major discussion point in Geneva in 1998 and the HCC-5 conference. However, it is not difficult to understand. Quite basically, the issue becomes one of who has the most pow-

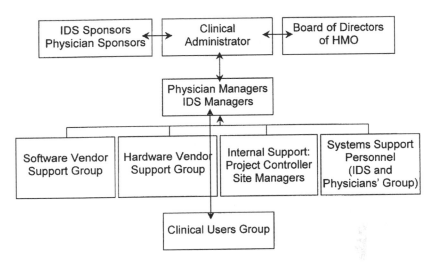

**Exhibit 1. An Ideal Approach to System Implementation**

er and who has the most control. Unfortunately, the issue of power and control is frequently established through traditional approaches. In the case of healthcare and information technology, IT has traditionally had the power and control in regard to computer information systems, regardless of the application.

Therefore, finding individuals who are willing to look to the benefit of the patient first is — in practice — difficult. Even within the healthcare community, cost and utilization seem to take preference over patient needs on occasion.

So finding someone in authority who is willing to look long-term, who understands the interrelationships among human systems and information systems and healthcare systems is and will continue to be difficult. However, it is possible. More and more people are beginning to recognize the need. More and more healthcare professionals are becoming extremely well versed in information systems and, I suspect, this will be the ultimate avenue for the evolution of the ideal healthcare system. However, it will be difficult to create a partnership in which all sides are truly partners because that is not how things have been done over the past 30 years. But it can be done.

**References**

1. Negroponte, N. 1995. *Being Digital.* New York: Alfred A. Knopf.
2. Fried, L. 1995. *Managing Information Technology in Turbulent Times.* New York: John Wiley & Sons, Inc.

3. Heales, J. 1995. *Measuring the Organizational Cultural Influence on ISD*. Research topic. Department of Commerce, The University of Queensland. Communication via Internet heales@commerce.uq.edu.au.
4. Lyytinen, K. 1987. "Different perspectives on information systems: problems and solutions," *Computing Surveys*, March: 5–46.
5. Hofstede, B. N., Daval Ohayv, D., and Sanders, G. 1990. "Measuring organizational cultures: a qualitative and quantitative study across twenty cases," *Administrative Science Quarterly*, 35: 286–316.
6. Scholz, C. 1992. *The Symbolic Value of Computerized Information Systems*. New York: Aldine de Gruyter.
7. Schein, E. H. 1992. *Organizational Culture and Leadership*. San Francisco, CA: Jossey-Bass, Inc.
8. Morgan, G. 1986. *Images of Organization*. London: Sage Publications.
9. Schein, E. H. 1980. *Organizational Psychology*. Englewood Cliffs, NJ: Prentice Hall.
10. Taylor, F. W. 1911. *Principles of Scientific Management*. New York: Harper & Row.
11. Beckhard, R. and Pritchard, W. 1992. *Changing the Essence: The Art of Creating and Leading Fundamental Change in Organizations*. San Francisco: Jossey-Bass.
12. Wessells, M. G. 1990. *The Computer, Self, and Society*. Englewood Cliffs: Prentice-Hall.
13. Santosus, M. 1995. "Sharing power safely," *CIO* February, 15: 50–58.
14. Leebov, W. and Scott, G. 1990. *Health Care Managers in Transition: Shifting Roles and Changing Organizations*. San Francisco: Jossey-Bass.

# Chapter 25

# Information Systems and Change: Which One Is the Chicken and Which Is the Egg?

*Rick Skinner*

Are information systems and change synonymous? Does one always follow the other? Which is ultimately more important for business process improvement? Organizations and entire industries have been struggling with these questions for as long as there have been information systems. In this chapter, we explore how change and information systems have been historically linked, look at different methods to couple process improvements with information systems, and finally, examine some actual health system cases.

Early in the history of information systems, they were seldom designed for, nor implemented to change, processes. Rather, they were deployed with the hope of simply automating existing processes to improve their speed or efficiency. If one person could process ten transactions per hour on paper, then automating the process should enable 12 transactions to be processed per hour. The format of the transaction, the skill set of the person processing the transaction, and the business validity of the transaction itself were seldom questioned, much less changed.

It was this implementation mindset (as well as the primitive nature of most of the applications) that kept automation from substantially improving productivity through the 1980s. While recordkeeping, access, and other characteristics did see dramatic benefits from automation in those years, business process productivity did not. An example of this type of automation is the billing systems for most hospitals then, and many still today. Charges were input manually, sometimes at the point of order, but frequently retrospectively, long after the service had been delivered, and in many cases after having passed in paper form through two or three processes. The billing system then calculated the bill and printed it, whereupon it was transmitted to the customer by mail. In most facilities, this process existed not once for all billing, but in multiple variations, by service line, supported by multiple, disparate information systems. So, while information systems supported the billing process, they did little to improve it.

Beginning in the mid-1980s, and continuing through today, the second wave of information systems inspired change, brought more advanced systems and the linkage of those systems with an expectation of a beneficial change in the processes they were designed to support. However, even at this point, the change expected (and that which typically occurred) was to individual processes. An example of such a change is the introduction of laboratory information systems, which, by linking laboratory instrumentation to computers, was able to eliminate many of the intermediate steps in delivering the results of laboratory tests. The process remained basically the same, overall, but the elimination of some of the steps improved its efficiency. Adding value to the process by linking laboratory results data with other clinical information, or linking the results delivery process to others, such as the order entry process, were seldom considered. Efficiency gains were limited to optimizing individual processes, which, while valuable, still did not produce the dramatic productivity improvements long promised by automation.

It was not until the late 1980s that industry began to couple comprehensive business process change with new information systems. It was this complete redesign of the business, supported by new and modern information systems, that produced industry revolutions such as banking ATMs, the overnight package industry, and others. For the first time, automation, coupled with dramatic business process change, was producing substantial productivity improvements. In large part, it is those improvements that fueled the United States economy in the late 1990s. Unfortunately, healthcare has few examples of this now-commonplace phenomenon in other industries. Examining the reasons why healthcare has lagged behind most other industries in coupling information systems with comprehensive business process change is beyond the scope of this chapter, but certainly cultural, social, and organizational issues have all played a part. One example where this has occurred is in the introduction of a computerized patient record in physician offices. Even with the introduction of this advanced technology, most offices have retained their traditional processes. However, some have now begun to take advantage of the technology by coupling the information systems with quality improvement efforts, dramatically impacting the delivery of care to their patients and their patients' outcomes from that care.

A fourth generation of information systems that enabled business process change is the increasing customer focus being achieved by many industries, mostly through the use of Web technology. This is not business process redesign, but rather the elimination of traditional business process in favor of more direct business-to-customer interaction. Booksellers and travel agents on the Web, online financial trading, and direct sales of automobiles on the Web are just a few examples. Again, in healthcare, there are few examples. Online scheduling, medical consultation, claims payment, and other uses of the Web to process traditional medical transactions are just emerging in a few organizations.

Now that it is well accepted that only by coupling business process change with information technology can substantial gains in efficiency, quality, and market presence be accomplished, how can a healthcare organization achieve results? The literature is full of examples of process change mismatched with information systems implementations and vice versa. How does a healthcare organization ensure that these changes remained linked and mutually supportive? Does one drive the other, or are they both to be accomplished in parallel? While there is not a universal prescription, here are two different approaches.

The classic (if something less then 20 years old can be termed classic) approach to improving a business process goes by the names of business process improvement, reengineering, process redesign, and a host of other popular names. Whatever the name, the process is similar and is characterized by a methodical, detailed, and lengthy analysis of the existing process, followed by an effort to invent or redesign an improved process. While the use of information technology is considered during both the analysis of the current process as well as in the design of the new process, the goal of the effort is to enable more efficiency or quality in the process itself. It is frequently assumed that the information technology can be invented or adapted to whatever the new, optimal process will be. While this approach has worked, and worked quite spectacularly in some instances, it is almost always expensive and lengthy.

Because those involved in the current processes seldom understand them in their entirety, and even if they do, have difficulty in designing improvements to them, outside help is frequently required. This always brings into play the possibility of misalignment between the organization and its outside assistance, as well as raising questions about accountability for the new processes. However, if done well, this approach is best at ensuring detailed requirements for the information systems that will support the new process. It can ensure that the process and its supporting information technology are designed and implemented with the same end result in mind. If done poorly, however, it will certainly drain the organization's resources with little return except frustration and failure. An organization must assess whether it has the will, the resources, and the commitment to undertake such a comprehensive approach, and whether the predicted end results justify the effort.

Implementations of enterprise resource planning systems are the most visible and dramatic examples of this approach. These implementations consist of complete process redesigns across entire corporations supported by entirely new, comprehensive information systems. They typically take three to five years, cost tens to hundreds of millions of dollars, and are reported to achieve their objectives only 60 percent of the time. Obviously, many smaller scale examples of this approach exist, but all share the characteristics of being expensive, lengthy, and high risk.

A second approach to coupling change with information systems is to lead with the implementation of a new information system, and then use its introduction as the foundation upon which to build new business processes. Some would call this the "slam dunk" approach to information systems implementation, but they forget the follow-on step of leveraging the new system to effect process change. This approach begins with the rapid installation of a new information system, either automating a process for the first time or, more typically, replacing an older system.

The new system is implemented "out of the box" with the major objective being to get it operational, not to change any processes. The implementation of the new system serves as the catalyst (and frequently the excuse) for introducing change into the organization. Its arrival serves as notice that process changes and performance improvements are soon expected. After implementation and a settling-in period, the organization begins to identify opportunities to combine the new functionality of the information system with process changes to improve performance. However, in order for this approach to work, the second step of benefits realization must be mandated and aggressively pursued by line management. All too frequently, victory is declared after the implementation of the system, and the benefits part is forgotten. Also, in order for this approach to work, the information services organization must be strongly supported by management during the implementation phase.

Information systems (IS) will be the lightning rod for any and all problems the organization encounters during an expedited implementation, whether related to information systems or not. Management must be resolute in insisting on compliance with schedules and participation in the project. Once the information system has been implemented and the organization has had a trial period in using it, it will be time to follow quickly with process changes and possibly some customization of the information system. Line departments will be quick to see and adopt process changes once issues with current processes become readily apparent with the implementation of the new information system. However, frequently they will need help in identifying specifically how changing their processes can optimize their new information system.

Many organizations schedule post-implementation audits or benefits realization studies shortly after the implementation of all new systems. The two biggest drawbacks to this approach are the danger of losing management commitment midway through the implementation, and the risk of not following through with an optimization process after the implementation.

Now we look at three different information technology-led projects exemplifying the approaches described above. All these cases are drawn from the Oregon Region of the Providence Health System. Providence (PHS) is a large, West Coast health system, operating in Alaska, Washington, Oregon, and California. In its Oregon Region, PHS operates six hospitals, employs over 150 primary care physicians, and owns a large managed care health plan. The state of Oregon is a highly competitive, well-organized, managed care marketplace and the PHS strategy has been to adapt itself to this market by optimizing each of its healthcare components, and deriving maximum market synergy from the interactions between the components.

Providence's initial reaction to the managed care transformation of its market was to standardize and consolidate its operations. In order to do so, it was recognized early in the planning process that information systems could play a major role. In the Portland metropolitan area, two of the three PHS hospitals used the same set of information systems already, and PHS decided to convert the remaining hospital (the largest) to that same set of information systems. However, PHS also saw the opportunity to design new business processes at the hospital to be converted, combine them with customizations to the information systems, and then to redeploy the customized system and the new processes to the other two hospitals. While PHS recognized the enormity of this undertaking, it felt that if it were successful, it could establish a new, dramatically more efficient baseline for its operations.

Almost a year was spent in planning both the information systems implementation, as well as the business process changes. The planning process recommended over 100 different customizations to the new information system, of which 60 were implemented at the cost of almost a million dollars. These customizations and the new business processes were designed by teams consisting of functional experts from the three hospitals, two of which, it must be noted, had been using the information system for years.

The scope of the new implementation touched just about everyone and every area of the hospital. The entire network was to be replaced, all terminals would be replaced with Windows personal computers, every single information system application in the facility was to be changed, and on the nursing units, the new systems were to be used for paperless documentation.

The actual conversion of the hospitals' systems was accomplished with few technical issues, with the exception of the nursing documentation system, which had performance and availability problems. However, the project team discovered within the first week after "going live" that the combination of new systems and new processes had almost incapacitated the facility. Few processes worked efficiently, either from lack of knowledge about the new process or its supporting information system, or both. This state of affairs lasted for 60 days after the conversion, and, toward the end of the period, it was only the personal activism of the senior regional administrator that enabled the facility to finally absorb the changes.

Three years after the conversion, less then 20 percent of the system customizations are in use at any of the hospitals, and most of the designed new processes have evolved quite differently than originally thought. In this case, the classical approach to systems implementation and process change ultimately succeeded, but at the cost of tremendous wasted time and effort trying to anticipate future needs without an understanding of the future environment.

Contrast the above case with the systems conversion at another PHS hospital in Oregon, three years later. This facility was a small, rural hospital that had been acquired by PHS four years earlier, but had retained its own business processes and information systems. Because it had yet to be integrated into the PHS information systems and business processes, Providence felt there were still performance opportunities from doing so. While the facility was much smaller and less complex than the one in the first case, the scope of the systems conversion was just as large. Virtually every information technology component in the facility was to be replaced. However, PHS had learned much from the initial hospital conversion described above, as well as others done since the first one. In this case, Providence decided not to use the classic approach, but rather to install the new systems, exactly in the configurations they were used in other facilities, and to continue to use existing processes to the extent they could be supported by the new systems.

This "slam dunk" approach was advertised to the hospital as a way to minimize impact on their operations, and also the method that would provide the hospital maximum opportunities for synergy with other PHS facilities after implementation. The entire conversion process for this hospital took only nine months, from the initiation of planning to the "go-live" date. No customizations were made to the systems, and very few process changes were necessitated by the introduction of the new systems. Those changes that were made were done to PHS standard processes, exactly as in use at other facilities.

Almost immediately after conversion, various departments began to explore how to change their processes, either to take maximum advantage of the new information systems or to be most like other PHS facilities, or both. For this facility and for the PHS Oregon Region, the "slam dunk" change process was extremely efficient in rapidly changing the hospital's systems to the regional standard, and then expeditiously moving to optimize their business processes.

The third case is an example of the classic approach to change being used to great advantage. Providence, after years of consolidation and integration in its Oregon operations, felt that its customers (members, patients, doctors, etc.) were not able to fully receive the benefits of that integration. Therefore, it launched an effort called the "Seamless Access" project to determine ways in which PHS could act more as a single organization with coordinated processes, providing better customer service. A very deliberate decision was made to use the classical change management approach to achieve these goals. The reason for selecting a structured, classic approach was that PHS recognized that it had little experience or knowledge as to the kinds of new processes and systems that would be required. Also, PHS recognized that much of this project would be experimental, and wanted to prove the concepts before embarking on large-scale system implementations.

A full-time internal project team was created and was matched to a project team from a consultant organization. The initial task of these teams was to evaluate the PHS current processes for customer service, and to recommend those with the most opportunity for improvement, either in terms of increased service or increased efficiency.

Once the targeted processes were identified, the team's mission was to design new processes, pilot and test them on a limited scale, and then if proven beneficial, to roll them out to the entire organization. All of this work was to be done without implementing new information systems, and with only minor changes to existing ones.

One of the processes identified for improvement was the registration and admission process for the hospitals and the clinics. The old process was somewhat different at each location, did not reuse information from previous contacts, was performed mostly on-site, and did not coordinate activities between locations or services. After a lengthy study (six months), the decision was made to disconnect the registration and admitting processes from the facilities and locations where service was rendered, and to consolidate those processes in one location.

There was a strong temptation to immediately begin systems design and selection efforts to support this new model. However, PHS decided to use its existing systems and to use its staff as interfaces between the systems, if necessary. A Central Access Unit was established to schedule, register, and admit patients into the PHS facilities. Staff was consolidated into a single location, new processes were developed to allow most activities to be done telephonically, access to all required information systems was created, and the required policy and procedures for the new unit were developed. No new information systems were introduced, and only a few minor modifications to existing ones were made.

PHS saw immediate benefits in both customer service and increased efficiencies. It was at this point, after the concept had been proven and the initial processes developed and deployed, that new information systems were considered. Benefits from a coordinated registration system for the enterprise became obvious and a project was started to implement one. The need for a single surgery scheduling system for the hospitals became apparent, and the subsequent conversion to one was made easier by this recognition.

Once the concept of operations was firmly in place for the new Central Access Unit, and initial processes had been designed and tested, the information systems requirements were quickly recognized and widely accepted. The end result was a new model for registration and scheduling that is now the foundation upon which to build further efficiencies and enhanced customer service. In this case, a classic approach proved to be best suited to a project where the outcomes were uncertain and experimental.

## SUMMARY

While in the past information systems and change were at best loosely linked, today it is the combination of the two that produce the benefits for which most information systems investments are made. In order to achieve those benefits, a rational approach to managing the changes in both information systems and process is necessary. In this chapter we have explored two of these approaches and examined some cases in which they were used.

# Chapter 26
# The Role of the Chief Medical Information Officer

*Victor S. Dorodny*

The chief medical information officer (CMIO) functions in a multidimensional, convergent environment defined by the clinical, financial, business, and information technology (IT) needs of the healthcare organization, without any particular aspect being more important than the other, and with a high degree of interdependency between them.

Because most healthcare information systems directly or indirectly affect clinical processes, some healthcare organizations are appointing physicians to oversee information technology initiatives. Increasingly, executives at these provider organizations believe that having a physician at the helm of automation plans is critical for success. In the past these physician/information technology specialists often were referred to by such titles as medical director of clinical information systems, director of medical (health) informatics, and medical director of computer services (systems). Today, physician leaders in such positions usually bear the title of chief medical information officer (CMIO). The functional description of the CMIO is that of a dedicated health "informatician," an emerging specialty in healthcare, which has not to date been definitively defined. For the purposes of this chapter, an informatician is an expert in applications of information within the integrated and secure clinical and business environments, encompassing the following responsibilities: gathering, monitoring, summarizing, merging and collating, deposition, release and exchange, transmission, storage and retrieval, analysis, and dissemination of information.[1]

These physicians usually head committees that define systems requirements and select information systems that will support outcomes research; develop, implement, and monitor clinical protocols; enable clinicians to access patient information at the point of care; and many others. The functional goal of CMIO participation on executive and user-level committees is to better integrate physicians into the delivery system to achieve lower cost and improve quality of care. The CMIO achieves this goal by helping physicians pinpoint their needs and desires and then working to educate them about information technology. The CMIO searches for, collects, processes, and understands the information needs of the enterprise so that these needs can be effectively communicated to all of the stakeholders, and acts as a catalyst for the processes that need to be put in place and activated for the economic survival of the enterprise.

## EXECUTIVE AND USER FUNCTIONS OF THE CMIO

On executive-level information services committees, the CMIO proactively participates in the performance of multiple functions:[2]

- Spearheads development of an IS strategic plan for the organization based on business strategy and goals
- Monitors the IS strategic plan in support of the organization's strategic and business plans; prioritizes projects and leads revisions as required
- Reviews and approves IS budgets
- Oversees progress of IS strategic plan implementation and overall status of specific application and technology implementations
- Communicates the IS strategic plan and the plan's implementation status to the board
- Approves IS contingency funding and other specific projects not planned
- Communicates the IS strategic plan and directives across the organization
- Approves overall corporation-defined IS policies and procedures
- Ensures the IS plan reflects the business plan of the organization on an ongoing basis

Having CMIOs chair the user-level committees helps ensure "buy-in" from the organization's stakeholders, which is critical to the success of clinical information initiatives. Their participation also promotes coordination of the multifaceted activities of the user-level committee:[2]

- Establishes user groups regarding specific IS projects based on the IS plan and scheduled implementation
- Has a working knowledge of business plan and understanding of the IS plan linkage
- Provides direction and recommendations for project implementation
- Monitors IS project implementation against established schedule
- Establishes task forces as required to support research into issues regarding project implementation
- Serves as mediation group for interdepartmental IS implementations

- Provides recommendations to the executive committee as needed for specific projects
- Reviews corporationwide IS policies/procedures and makes recommendations for approval to executive committee
- Evaluates and makes recommendations concerning IS issues and proposals that are directed by either the executive committee or recommended by the user group at large

The CMIO relies heavily on expectation and "wish" management, and strives to set reasonable, achievable goals without hindering enthusiasm for information systems. For instance, the chief executive officer (CEO) wishes to be freed from problems related to Y2K compliance, the Joint Commission on Accreditation of Healthcare Organizations (JCAHO), and physicians and nurses. The chief financial officer wishes problems would go away without capital expenditure. The CIO wants his or her IS problems to evaporate and, additionally, to have an unlimited budget to make it happen quickly so the CEO will stay happy. The CIO wishes medical personnel would become computer literate and use what they have without breaking it.

Generally, physicians and nurses are not concerned with the problems of the CEO or how much it is going to cost; they just wish the CIO would come up with something that is healthcare-friendly. Many physicians and CIOs prefer a part-time practicing physician for these positions because of the perception of better credibility with medical staff than an administrative physician. The rationale is that the CMIO sets an example, showing other clinicians that the person imposing the frequently unwelcome changes is being equally affected by them. Or, in the lexicon of managed care, the CMIO is "sharing risk" with providers regarding the implementation of IS.

When a healthcare organization reaches a critical mass, either through marketshare growth, mergers and acquisitions, or both, it requires a dedicated (nonpracticing) CMIO. When these physicians stop practicing, they may, arguably, lose some credibility, but the vast clinical and human interaction experience they bring to the job more than offsets the potential loss. It is this experience that enables them to understand and to communicate with all of the stakeholders in a healthcare organization. The CMIO fosters the ability of a healthcare organization to deal with the changing business environment and reconfigure itself when faced with amplifying levels of disturbance. A physician with strong interpersonal and communications skills and an inquisitive mind — one who is constantly searching for ways information systems can improve physicians' abilities to practice medicine as well as their quality of life — will do well regardless of whether he or she is an administrative or a practicing physician.

A word about the relevance of technical expertise. The level of computer literacy ("geekiness") is not a crucial factor in being able to obtain a position as CMIO. However, intensive on-the-job training would have to take place to enable the CMIO to perform his or her dual (clinical and techno-logical) functions. The technical experience is helpful, especially in the areas of evaluating vendors' products in the function of defining and selecting systems. It is less relevant in their larger, strategic role in an organization.

According to William Bria, M.D., who in 1997 co-founded the Association of Medical Directors of Information Systems (AMDIS), the CMIO is becoming a leader in defining medical information and its uses by the healthcare organization rather than defining the enabling systems.[3] The reason for this forward way of thinking is the prevalence of proven technologies available to the CMIO for implementation in the organization. Dr. Richard Kremsdorf, chief of medical informatics at Catholic Healthcare West, shares Dr. Bria's point of view and believes that the primary responsibility of the CMIO is defining the applications of IT to the care processes of an entire delivery system.[3]

## CHALLENGES FOR HEALTHCARE ORGANIZATIONS — YOU CAN MANAGE THINGS YOU CANNOT MEASURE!

Recent surveys of healthcare organizations and fellows of the Healthcare Information and Management Systems Society (HIMSS) estimate that between the present and year 2005, $200 billion will be spent by healthcare organizations on health information systems. Such unprecedented expenditures are driven by the healthcare industry's shift from medical risk/benefit decision-making to cost/benefit decision-making processes. In the face of continued distress in the managed care industry, healthcare organizations' reliance on information technology (IT) to reduce redundancy and inefficiency of operations is ever increasing. The implementation of IT has become the Achilles' heel of many managed care organizations. Oxford Health Plan, Pacificare, and Kaiser — in trying to explain their collective half billion dollars in losses in one year — have all pointed an accusing finger at their abortive efforts to modernize their information systems infrastructure.

Healthcare organizations are considering or embarking on countless initiatives to improve business office functions (billing, collection, coding, and patient registration); to integrate financial and clinical information (both transactional and analytical) into computer-based patient records that will be available across the enterprise; and to upgrade medical documentation (and inventory control) through handheld data entry devices (bar coding) (see Exhibit 1). Many of these organizations are introducing productivity-based co-pay, monitoring and controlling utilization, facilitating physicians' vacations, continued medical education rules, etc. And they are promoting adherence to and monitoring compliance with disease management protocols, measuring outcomes (clinical and financial) against national and regional benchmarks.

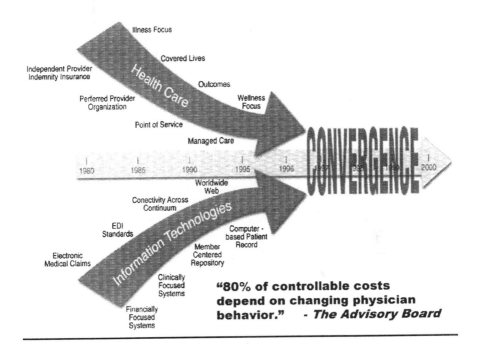

Point of Service

Managed Care

"80% of controllable costs depend on changing physician behavior." - *The Advisory Board*

**Exhibit 1. Convergence of Healthcare and Information Technologies**

Why are these healthcare organizations so involved? What are they striving for? They hope to be able to identify and analyze outliers and implement meaningful quality improvement methodologies to reduce variability. Informed decisions need to be based on real data and not on actuarial assumptions whether to accept the discounts on fee-for-service or restructure to accept capitation or global capitation (proper per-member-per-month), or to opt out of a particular contract.

By networking with hospitals, laboratories, outpatient facilities, home care providers, and skilled nursing facilities, healthcare organizations are expanding geographic access to patients or physicians with additional locations, advanced diagnostic and treatment technologies, and complementary and alternative medicine programs. In the process of developing leadership and communications skills for physicians and executives, and educating physicians to use the Internet, providers compete for quality, computer-literate support staff. The sustained growth of the health information technology sector, in part, is fueled by enormous healthcare deals that are rocking the world of enterprise integration. Mergers of mega healthcare organizations are unique in their multifaceted complexity. In order to merge two or more healthcare organizations into one cohesive enterprise, all strategic alliance partners and preferred vendors would have to afford the merging entity an optimal functional reality to avoid otherwise inevitable difficulties, complications, and related financial losses.

Seamless INFOgration, a cross-continuum, enterprisewide integration of voice, data, and imagery and secure information management, is the functional glue that would hold them together and assure their functionality and, ultimately, financial success.[4]

## INFORMATION TECHNOLOGY JEOPARDY

All healthcare organizations are undergoing chaotic changes at a much faster rate than in the pre-managed care era. The growing pains experienced by these organizations are exacerbated by the ever-increasing need to provide quality care (real and perceived and, most importantly, documented, verifiable, and repeatable), and by the core functions of profitability and economic survival. Some organizations are aware of their own problems and are actively seeking solutions. Others are playing "IT Jeopardy" while getting answers (IT solutions) that are looking for questions (growing pains). Healthcare organizations desire and must have customizable, scalable proprietary solutions based on nonproprietary products, driven by healthcare communications.

The ever-growing reliance on IT to deliver these solutions is responsible for the proliferation of physicians' active participation in other-than-clinical aspects of their organizations. Furthermore, constant changes in the architecture and nature of delivery systems, contracts, reimbursement schemes, and reporting and performance requirements need to be addressed rapidly and effectively. Otherwise, the business may suffer or a new opportunity may be lost. Software designed for legacy technology, such as COBOL, Mumps, and Business Basic, all of which have been popular in healthcare applications, are not easy to modify and do not fit the changing needs of managed care. Even when a more modern language like Visual C++ is utilized, the architecture of the software may become an impediment to growth and evolution.

## KNOWLEDGE-BASED HEALTH INFORMATION SYSTEMS

Knowledge-based health information systems (KBHIS©) can help fill the void in the healthcare decision-making process: the information you have is not what you need. The information you want is not what you need. The information you need is unavailable.

The concept of KBHIS was conceived and introduced to the American healthcare community to meet and specifically serve the increasingly complex requirements of healthcare information management.[5] KBHIS is based on the implementation of enterprisewide, virtual, computer-based patient record systems, providing the secure and accessible information, both analytical and transactional, that is crucial for the ability of healthcare organizations to maintain and increase their market share.

The complexity of knowledge-based health information systems resides in the "phase transition" — a class of behaviors in which the components of the system never quite lock in place, yet never quite dissolve into turbulence either. These systems are both stable enough to store information, yet evanescent enough to transmit it. Even though most systems are built from "out-of-the-box" components, like children's interlocking building blocks, the end result (in shape, form, and functionality) is unique to the builder (owner) organizations but is transplantable to a large degree. They are stable from the standpoint of supporting day-to-day functioning but are probably incapable of fully addressing the current needs of the organization, and obviously would not be able to support the emerging, future needs with "major" evolution.

Knowledge-based health information systems are characterized by feedback, resiliency, self-organization, evolution, and complexity, and are subject to all applicable principles of nonlinear dynamics. This breed of systems helps define the healthcare entity because the feedback speaks to the purpose of the organization. Whatever the type of feedback, it is a form of perception that defines the system in relationship with desired outcomes. Hospitals, for example, often use feedback for control rather than to foster change. When hospitals conduct surveys, the emphasis is on gathering feedback that informs the hospital it is deviating from the path to its goal: customer satisfaction within the hospital. This is a perfect example of a regulatory, or negative, feedback loop. The patients who give the responses may not share the hospital's enthusiasm over the fact that they are sick enough to require hospitalization. In fact, it can be assumed that the patients may not want to be in the hospital at all, and yet that information is not solicited by the hospital, probably because this kind of feedback does not serve the purposes of the hospital.

The distribution and "control" of information becomes key. Information is the currency of healthcare — a dynamic element that gives order, prompts growth, and defines what is alive. Information is a unique resource because of its capacity to generate itself. For a dynamic system to remain alive, information must be continually created. Isolated health information systems wind down and decay, victims of the law of entropy. In this positive feedback loop, information increases and disturbances grow. The system, unable to deal with so much magnifying information, is being asked to change. In other words, the demand exceeds the system's capability and forces the system's managers to look for solutions to ensure optimal functionality.

For those interested in system stability, amplification (of disturbances) is threatening, and there is a need to quell the noise before eardrums burst.

Yet, positive feedback and disequilibrium play a critical role in moving the healthcare system forward. True, disturbances can create disequilibrium, but disequilibrium can lead to growth. If the system has the capacity to react, change is not necessarily something to avoid.

Resiliency describes the ability of a dynamic system to reconfigure itself when faced with amplifying levels of disturbance in order to deal with new information. Neither form nor function alone dictate how the system is constructed. Instead, form and function mesh in a fluid process whereby the system may maintain itself in its present form or evolve to a new order. As the system matures, it becomes more efficient in the use of resources and better able to exist within its environment. It establishes a basic structure that supports the development of the system. Openness of information over time spawns a firmer sense of identity, one that is less permeable to externally induced change. As the system changes, it does so, in part, by referring to itself — just as centripetal force causes reversion to a center or axis. Changes do not occur randomly, but are consistent with what has gone on before — with the history and identity of the system. This consistency is so strong that in the biological system, for example, it is forced to retreat in its evolution. It does so along the same pathway, retaining a memory of its evolutionary past. This "self-reference" facilitates the inevitable "orderly" change in turbulent environments.

Self-organization describes a system's capacity for spontaneously emerging structures focusing on activities required to maintain their own integrity. Humans, for example, struggle to build layer upon layer of complex behavior, while dynamic systems unfold in a flat or horizontal fashion. In contrast to the emergence of hierarchical levels through the joining of systems from the bottom up, "unfolding" implies the interweaving of processes that lead to structure. A system manages itself as a total system through processes that maintain integrity. In health information systems, "relational holism" describes how whole systems are created among the disparate components. In this process, the parts of the information systems are forever changed, drawn together by a process of internal connectedness — hence, INFOgration (see Exhibit 2). It is no longer meaningful to talk of the individual properties of the constituent components (such as physician practice management systems or scheduling systems), as these continually change to meet the requirements of the whole system.

The implications for the enterprisewide information system is similar to those of the "rubber landscape," where a change (rise, fall, reflection, or deflection) in any part of the landscape causes material changes in the entire landscape. These changes are not reversible and are not repeatable, which is good news for those healthcare organizations that might consider going back. Similarly, any changes in the IT landscape cause changes in the clinical and business landscape of the enterprise. Evolution is unending

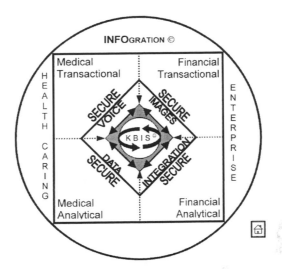

**Exhibit 2.** INFOgration (© 1997, 1998 Victor S. Dorodny, M.D., Ph.D., M.P.H. All rights reserved.)

change that is inseparable from learning. Resiliency and self-organization work in tandem, fed by information to create an ordered world. The result is evolution, the organization of information into new forms. In healthcare, this is represented by standards of care and new ways to deliver that care. The same enormous energy also can be seen as a constant organization and reorganization of health information into new forms: treatment guidelines, outcomes measurement and management, cost-effectiveness studies, telemedicine, and computerized patient record systems.

Unfortunately, the concept of evolution does not provide a way to *predict* the emerging future as if we were objective observers watching from outside the system. A greater knowledge of evolution and the other systems concepts, however, offers the means to make us more aware and foster strategies for change. Complexity can be seen as the path along which evolution proceeds, or the creative border between chaos and order. This zone between two realms is created by the dynamic between building order and destroying order, moving from order to chaos. Healthcare reveals a fascinating dynamic that is ordering the system on one hand, as providers aggregate and procedures become standardized; and chaotic disordering, as a result of market forces and information technology that disrupt traditional practices.

## THE CMIO AND THE BUSINESS OF HEALTHCARE

In a passage from the AMIA Proceedings 1995, the authors define the role of the information architect in medical centers. The medical informatician has a primary function "to steer the process [of clinical computing implementation] to fulfill stated objectives and build consensus where divergent forces are at work."[6] This is a challenging undertaking that can be well served by the cross-disciplinary nature of health informatics.

A 1997 survey of 140 leading provider organizations by the College of Health Information Management Executives (CHIME) revealed that 44 percent had assigned a physician to devote at least part of his or her time to information technology. It is rapidly becoming apparent that the CMIO is an important member of the executive team, and that regardless of an healthcare organization's IT strategy, closer harmony needs to be achieved among the CEO, CMIO, COO, CIO, and CFO. Each member of the executive team has his or her own "take" on the benefits of information technology. A recent study released by the Millennium Health Imperative, a think tank of executives from a variety of healthcare organizations, indicates that 71 percent of the CEOs believe there have been positive returns on their IT investment to date, but only 50 percent of the COOs and CFOs proclaim positive returns.[7] In addition, 64 percent of CEOs and 62 percent of CMOs/CMIOs say financial improvement, cost reduction, productivity, discussion support, process improvement, and integration should drive IT investment decisions. Only 27 percent of the CIOs share that perspective. CIOs who report to CFOs and COOs tend to emphasize financial and operational objectives for the next two years. Interestingly, 23 percent of respondents say the CIO reports to the CMO/CMIO.[7]

An industry survey targeted for executive-level administration of complex integrated delivery networks (presented at the HIMSS 1998 Annual Conference) revealed a spate of information with regard to medical directors of information systems (see the Appendix). Again, the role of the CMIO as an educator and consensus builder among the executive team could not be overstated since the organization's willingness and capability to make IT investments are the most important factors in gaining a competitive advantage.

## THE CMIO'S LIFE IN THE TRENCHES

Advocates of technology to their peers and acting facilitators between IS and clinical staffs, CMIOs may be perceived as a "magic bullet" to slay clinical computing demons. By approaching the issues from a wider bandwidth perspective (medical, IT, and management) as opposed to the perspective of people with careers focused in a single domain, the CMIO is bound to run into inherent cultural and organizational conflicts. A defined position on the organizational chart and levels(s) of reporting can simplify these issues if addressed by the CMIO prior to acceptance of the job offer, but will not solve the underlying conflict of real or perceived responsibility that exceeds his or her authority. In addition, the fact that most CMIO positions have no defined budget responsibilities exacerbates the imbalance. Further, such a conflict precludes the CMIO from optimally leveraging his or her skills for organizational success.

Some of the common pitfalls CMIOs encounter when working in the trenches is the IS department's perception of itself as the enabler that allows doctors to deliver medical care, while the CMIO is an outsider wielding the medical sword. In turn, the CMIO, as a physician, might view the IS department as a support service to the function of the healthcare organization. These subtle psychological nuances can be very important in setting the tone, and ultimately working relations, between clinical and IS parts of an organization. This is actually the most difficult aspect of the job of the CMIO — a never-ending balancing act 200 feet above the ground. The good ones generate consensus from all stakeholders and become known as institutional or organizational heroes; those who are not adroit at balancing may alienate some people.

Healthcare organizations adopt one of two general approaches to healthcare informatics. The least desirable approach is to strive for physicians becoming "computer proficient" and less uncooperative in the areas of database development and person–machine interaction. This approach is driven by the lack of recognition of the fact that while financial computing has not really changed much in the past few decades, clinical computing has become differentiated and highly complex. Further, many computer-proficient physicians recognize the fact that most of the "clinical" IT solutions on the market today are actually financial solutions masquerading as clinical. True to the dynamic nature of these systems, neither form nor function alone dictates how the system is constructed. Instead, form and function mesh in a fluid process where the system may maintain itself in its present form or evolve to a new order.

The most desirable approach is for IS to work within the constraints of the busy clinical setting, not the other way around. The demands of staying abreast of the developments in their respective clinical fields simply preclude most clinicians from suddenly and dramatically changing the way they think and interact (e.g., become more IT-friendly). Actually, IT is better suited to become more clinician-friendly, with user interfaces that are simple, logical, tailored to the clinical needs and accessible at the point of care.[8] These systems are self-organizing and manage themselves through processes that maintain integrity. It is here that the CMIO can impact the interaction, coexistence, and evolution of clinical computing within the constraints of a busy healthcare setting.

From a business of health standpoint, many physicians are somewhat uncomfortable with balancing practice and finance management under capitation, due to the inability to readily compare budgets to actual expenses, or to detect adverse selection or other variables resulting in abnormal expenditure patterns. Shadow capitation, or "managed care without inhaling," is the ability to convert fee-for-service data to equivalent capitation amounts. This allows physicians to compare, understand, and be able to manage changes in reimbursement and practice paradigms, and greatly eases the trauma of accepting reasonable managed care contracts. This is also useful in arriving at fair subcapitation packages.

## EMERGING ISSUES

The role of the CMIO as a member of the executive team is rapidly becoming that of "data compliance manager" of a healthcare organization. The CMIO, together with the other members of the executive team, is responsible for compliance with HIPAA (Health Insurance Portability and Accountability Act) and HCFA (Health Care Financing Association) with regard to the confidentiality of health information and security of all patient-identifiable data; and ORYX (the name of the JCAHO initiative to integrate performance measures into the accreditation process). "ORYX" is a term different from any other currently used in healthcare, reflecting the magnitude of the anticipated changes in the Joint Commission's accreditation process in the years ahead. The acronym itself defies interpretation, except for the fact that "oryx" is defined in the dictionary as a kind of a gazelle with sharp horns.

In addition, CMIOs are taking an active role as their respective organizations struggle with Y2K compliance issues, ranging from corporate planning and IS systems compliance, all the way to testing and replacing embedded chips in all biomedical equipment in their facilities.

## SUMMARY

In a practical sense, the state-of-the-art in health information technology is best illustrated by the fact that most healthcare organizations do not know exactly what kinds of information they already have. Among those few that do know, most do not know where it is. Some of the fortunate organizations that know what they have and where it resides do not know how to get it out in useful formats. And the lucky few that do get the information they need do not know how to use it effectively to both deliver and document quality healthcare, as well as use it for competitive advantage to protect and increase their respective market share.

Today, the ideal KBHIS does not exist. The role of the CMIO is unique in its multifaceted complexity and means different things to different people in different organizations. The main functional objective of the CMIO is to foster the unending change that is inseparable from learning. As indicated earlier, the concept of evolution does not provide a way to predict the emerging future. An ongoing diligent assessment of current and emerging trends combined with out-of-the-box thinking allows for an accurate short-term forecast and projection.

In my own position as the chief medical information officer for Superior Consultant Company, Inc., a national leader in integrated healthcare and information technology management, I offer hands-on, detailed knowledge of the issues in order to assist my counterparts, as well as other members of the executive team in provider, payer, pharmaceutical, and vendor organizations.

### References

1. Dorodny, V. S. 1999. Introducing this definition of "informatician" at the Medical Directors of Information Systems (AMDIS) Forum and Board Meeting in San Diego, CA, Feb. 16, 1999. Purpose — to define a health IT sub-specialty different from terms associated with "informatics."
2. Matthews, P. 1999. From personal communication based on unpublished work in process for the Association of Medical Directors of Information Systems (AMDIS).
3. Chin, T. L. 1998. "MCIOs, CIOs calling the doctor for clinical systems matters," *Health Data Management* 92 (Apr.): 1998.
4. Dorodny, V. S. 1998. "The piracy of privacy," *Information Security*, 46 (Aug).
5. Dorodny, V. S. 1996 (January). Sixth Annual National Managed Health Care Congress/Information Systems and Technology Solutions Forum, Palm Springs, CA.
6. Sittig, S. and Al-Daig. 1995. "The role of the information architect in medical centers," Proceedings of AMIA.
7. Bell, C. W. 1998. "A health imperative," *Modern Healthcare,* 55 (Nov 30).
8. Silverstein, S. 1998. Director of Clinical Information, Medical Center of Delaware, personal communication.

## APPENDIX: HIMSS SURVEY RETURNS

### Medical Director of Information Systems
- Seventy-five percent of time dedicated and funded by IS
- Direct report to CIO in IS role as IS medical director
- Twenty-five percent of time — practicing physician

**Role:**
- Clinical liaison between physicians, administration, and information systems
- Driver of new clinical ideas and clinical direction
- Provides strategic leadership in clinical systems projects

**Committees:**
- Chairs clinical advisory groups: groups are project specific that provide guidance and support during implementation
- Member of the technology executive committee which guides projects and funding allocation (health system executive team)

### Chief Medical Information Officer position
- Thirty percent of time dedicated and funded to IS
- Reports to CIO in IS role
- Seventy percent of time — practicing physician

**Role:**
- Provides direction and leadership with clinical community, systems users, and executive committees

**Committees:**
- Chairs clinical advisory board (multidisciplinary membership): board provides recommendations for system selections and clinical systems strategic planning efforts
- Member of the information technology governance committee: executive leadership committee responsible for approving IS projects based on the business and system strategic and budgetary plans

### Physician Liaison-Health Informatics
- Volunteer support position to clinical informatics department within IS

**Role:**
- Provides leadership for specified clinical initiatives working with both the physician community and the other IS clinical liaisons within the clinical informatics department

**Committees:**
- Participates on the executive IS steering committee
- Committee responsible for maintaining and updating the IS strategic plan annually in conjunction with the corporate strategic plan. Strategic plans serve as the drivers for the annual budgetary cycle. The committee reviews and edits the IS initiatives as required to support the corporate plan. The IS strategic plan tentatively extends out four years.
- Other volunteer physician liaisons are utilized on specified project committees
- Significant trend to formalize working relations with physicians

**Reporting Structure:**
- Sixty-nine percent reported to the CIO
- Twenty-three percent reported to the medical director
- Seven percent reported to other positions

**Funding.**
- Seventy-six percent of organization funded physician's time
- Twenty-four percent relied on volunteers

**Number.**
- Fifty-six percent IS funded time for one physician
- Twenty-two percent IS funded two physicians
- Twenty-two percent IS funding more than two physicians

## Health Informatician Trends

### Key Success Factors Identified.

- Credible and respected by peer physicians (clout)
- Communication skills
- Leadership skills
- Understanding of corporate strategies
- Visionary
- Continue practicing medicine

# Chapter 27
# Healthcare Information Services Outsourcing

*Rose Ann Laureto-Ward*

As the list of healthcare information technologies continues to grow, so too does the difficulty of implementing and managing so many systems on time and within budget. Meanwhile, training and recruiting costs continue to climb.

The rapid pace of technological evolution has changed the environment in which healthcare organizations and their information technology (IT) departments operate — instead of one or two major initiatives each year, CIOs are managing several at once. Each new project can demand a set of expertise not available internally, forcing the organization to recruit new talent that may be hard to retain in a competitive marketplace that puts a premium on IT professionals.

In recognition of these facts, organizations in several industries have adopted outsourcing strategies to control costs and share the responsibility of IS management with professionals whose core competency is providing these services. The healthcare industry is no exception to this trend, evidenced by the steady increase in demand among health systems for outsourcing partners. Sharing responsibilities for IS functions with a business partner enables healthcare organizations to focus on their core competencies: the diagnosis and treatment of patients. To meet the increased demand for IT outsourcing, several organizations — from software vendors to specialty consulting firms — have developed outsourcing programs geared specifically toward healthcare organizations.

Organizations that decide to outsource all or part of their IS departments should select a business partner that agrees to share risk. If the financial incentives of the vendor and the provider are not aligned, performance is likely to suffer, as is the strength of the partnership. The provider should expect from its outsourcing partner assured performance within specific price parameters. Outsourcing vendors must also demonstrate a solid record of success in the healthcare industry, possess the ability to deploy the right staff, offer employment opportunities to the client's IT staff, maintain vendor neutrality, and provide a solid management process based on open communication.

Before entering into any long-term outsourcing relationship, the healthcare organization should be assured that the vendor it selects will integrate disparate information systems and requirements as well as be prepared to change the operating process to optimize performance at all levels. Now that each new day brings new technologies promising to revolutionize the delivery of healthcare services, it is more important than ever to have constant access to a stockpile of the IT expertise and resources required to sort through the clutter and to develop and cultivate the most efficient, cost-effective, IS environment.

**Richard D. Helppie**
*Chairman and Chief Executive Officer,*
*Superior Consultant Company, Inc.*

Healthcare organizations are facing pressures from many directions, including consolidation, integration, and a driving need to do more in less time using rapidly evolving technologies. The organization's successful response to these pressures often springs from its ability to efficiently and effectively capture, use, share, and manipulate both data and information. And, as a result, information system initiatives and project demands are heavier than they ever have been, driven by the healthcare industry's growing trend toward mergers, acquisitions, and affiliations, managed care and case management, and the resultant need to integrate and manage disparate information systems. To compound these challenges, qualified information technology resources are scarce and the costs for both, the systems and skilled IT resources, are skyrocketing.

Outsourcing has come to the forefront as a serious strategic alternative for healthcare enterprises seeking to maximize their IT investment. It has rapidly become an accepted management and architectural resource for redefining and reengineering the delivery of information technology. It challenges today's healthcare executive to rethink the traditional vertically integrated organization in favor of a more flexible one structured around core competencies and dependable, long-term business partnerships. No longer will IT departments and their management be judged by the size and the scope of the resources they own and manage; rather, those astute enough to capitalize on outsourcing as a means of assuring a reliable source of systems knowledge and expertise will achieve levels of performance not ordinarily equaled by a traditional, vertically integrated IT organization.

Outsourcing strategies can be structured to help healthcare organizations control runaway information technology costs and stabilize labor market pressures. By choosing outsourcing, the healthcare enterprise can focus on its core competencies, that is, providing excellent quality of care, and gain benefits from a long-term partnership and business relationship with a third-party information technology specialist. The outsourcer brings its core competency and strengths — information systems solutions, best practice methodologies and expertise, knowledge and efficiencies of scale — to the healthcare provider to enable physicians and clinical staff to function as efficiently and effectively as possible, and thus reduce the cost of delivering patient care.

Outsourcing of important but non-core business functions has become a common and effective business growth strategy for many industries — among them, healthcare. Growth in outsourcing is based on specialization, expertise, and the ability to build and sustain competitive advantage. The IT function fits this mold. Its role is more essential to the healthcare delivery infrastructure than ever, when considering integrated, paperless medical records, image-based systems, and remote access to medical information, while maintaining the traditional legacy systems, and more.

Today's information technology expenditure process, however, is complex and burdened with many hidden and unrecognized costs. User departments are buying systems independent of the information technology department and, therefore, are incurring ongoing support costs. These costs include recruiting skilled IT professionals and related turnover, the full costs of consultants, the expanding costs of personal computers and local area networks, the impacts of late implementation, and the costs of poorly negotiated purchase agreements. Contributing to dissatisfaction with information technology programs are capital project overruns, the use of consultants, late starts, and business strategies that change course in mid-project. Although this is a problem throughout the healthcare provider industry — from the small to the very large — it is not isolated to this industry.

To sum it up, outsourcing is being touted as providing benefits to healthcare enterprises that may be experiencing industry pressures, which include:

- Mergers and acquisitions
- Need for rapid technology change and implementation
- Ongoing shortages of qualified information technology specialists
- High staff turnover
- Escalating hiring and retraining costs
- Exploding software costs
- Antiquated hardware platforms
- Increasing project backlogs

The purpose of this chapter is to provide a definition for outsourcing, highlight the most prevalent outsourcing models, explore the rationale or

371

justification for outsourcing, and discuss some contractual points for management consideration. This chapter will also add to the debate raging through the information technology industry: Is the increasing reliance on outsourcing an event or a trend?

## OUTSOURCING: DEFINITION AND MODELS

Outsourcing is a means of contracting with a third party to provide, usually on a long-term basis of five or more years, some service that is normally supplied by the internal resources of the organization itself. Outsourcing is a delivery and management strategy. As a strategy, outsourcing involves restructuring an organization around its own core competencies and outside relationships. Although outsourcing is not a new management concept, the practice of outsourcing is gaining in acceptance and, more importantly, in provability.

Outsourcing is not new to healthcare. A major hotel food service company has been providing dietary outsourcing to healthcare institutions for many years, as have nationally recognized laundry services and plant and facilities management organizations. It is believed that the sheer size of these companies, and their penchant for specialization of service and efficient management, allows them to provide food services or plant and laundry operation that a healthcare organization's internal staff cannot equal — in either cost or quality. Outsourcing the information technology and services functions follows that exact same logic.

Information technology outsource firms do not provide information technology and services as a sideline or as a secondary function. It is their core competency — their specialty. They are indeed experts, with techniques and methodologies that should be both proven and refined. They usually offer specialized knowledge, efficiencies of scale, and a record of successful, long-term partnerships.

### Outsourcing Models

Outsourcing models fall into two primary categories: selective or total. As described in *Outsourcing Information Technology, Systems and Services,* by Robert Klepper and Wendell O. Jones, "Total outsourcing involves contracting out 80 percent or more of the IT function to a vendor. Selective outsourcing involves outsourcing a few functions that total less than 80 percent of the whole."[1] Each option has unique considerations that should be weighed when evaluating an outsourcing decision.

**Total Outsourcing.** Total or full outsourcing, as the name implies, means that the information technology function is outsourced, in its entirety, to a single vendor. Every dimension of the IT organization, including IT management (chief information officer and director-level staff) and all of the functions provided in a typical information services department, such as applications development, technical services, and operations would be shifted to the outsourcing company.

The healthcare organization benefits from a total commitment from the vendor, wherein the vendor will:

- Supply IT professionals with the specialized skills required to complete any and all tasks as they may arise
- Make broad service-level commitments (such as 90 percent of all calls received by the help desk will be resolved within six hours)
- Provide solid planning
- Maintain reasonable levels of flexibility
- Assume the risks inherent in today's rapidly changing technological environment

Most healthcare organizations that select full outsourcing believe it will simplify management of the information services function. Full outsourcing will provide them with a single point of contact and a single solution point, because the outsourcer assumes complete responsibility for a highly results-oriented IT function.

Full-service outsourcing also offers vendor-independent software capabilities, and technology and help desk services. The full-service outsourcing vendor should also be able to provide strategic and management consulting, operational, and reengineering services for most administrative and clinical departments, and other services required to meet the demands of today's endlessly complex healthcare environment (i.e., compliance, compensation, physician relationships).

Some healthcare organizations will resist a total, or full, outsource, believing that total dependence on one vendor may be problematic. Maintaining a balance of power between the two contracting entities — the healthcare provider and the outsourcing vendor — might prove difficult. Others may fear that business will change so much that the vendor cannot keep pace, when in reality, the outsourcer, because of its keen focus on the universe of systems technologies, is often able to meet or beat any technological challenge the healthcare provider can present.

**Selective Outsourcing.** Selective outsourcing, also referred to as out-tasking or task outsourcing, is a term used to describe a business arrangement in which an outside company is hired to provide some segment or a specific functional unit of the information technology and services department. Selective outsourcing is often the model used for data center operations, systems programming, network management, and entire functional areas such as technology services, application management, and the help desk.

In a selective outsourcing arrangement, multiple organizations may be required to maintain the processing infrastructure within a healthcare organization's data center. In this example, specific choices are still available, but so are broad service providers. The choices for the contracting organization include technology firms for management and maintenance of the data center hardware, desktop devices, and network infrastructure. These firms often offer help desk services specializing in technology and office automation tools as well.

Software firms also offer outsourcing and related services, typically centered on their product or application offerings and suites. Some have expanded into more advanced technology offerings, including services to integrate their products with others or remote processing services.

Selective outsourcing has several points for consideration. In this model, perhaps several vendors provide a small set of specialized services for an organization. In the contracting organization's eagerness to adopt the best-of-breed model, the healthcare organization is forced to try to weave all of these services or options together. Each participating vendor may have a piece of the business that is too small and focused for the vendor to be made aware of the organization's overall business and IT strategies. None of the IT vendors may have a significant stake within the healthcare organization, and the opportunity to develop a partnership instead becomes more of a focused delivery relationship that ends when the job is done. Similarly, when several vendors are simultaneously employed in outsourcing endeavors, usually no single vendor has enough control or autonomy to effect any major type of organizational change.

When an organization decides to have a third party manage or provide staffing for a single area, such as desktop support, it is task sourcing. Organizations often employ task sourcing to establish a level of comfort with the outsourcing concept. If this first step meets the expectations of management, the organization will need to determine how to weave outsourcing into its short- and long-term IT strategies.

**Control.** Regardless whether a full outsource or a selective outsource model is chosen, defining the roles of management and establishing the aspect of control between the healthcare institution and the outsourcing vendor is critical. The aspect of control defines the degree of control over the information services function that the purchasing organization wishes to maintain. It comes into play because a major reason for outsourcing information systems functions and initiatives is that IT is not viewed as a core competency of healthcare institutions. Therefore, to gain management expertise, the healthcare institution must be prepared to give up a certain degree of control.

Outsourcing vendors require a degree of flexibility and control to make decisions and organizational moves to accomplish the major objectives of an engagement. In a selective outsource when partial staff and resources remain under the control of the healthcare organization, arrangements must be made regarding how to implement decisions. Other parameters regarding aspects of control that must be established from the outset include:

- Will there be a threshold for purchase decisions?
- Can the outsourcer act as an agent of the institution in personnel decisions?
- Must plans and actions be presented to the governance individual or committee for approval?
- If so, how detailed must these plans be?
- What is the reporting structure?

The importance of understanding, defining, and structuring the relationship between the two organizations cannot be underestimated, as it will demarcate critical areas of comfort or discomfort. Short of specific failure to deliver on an objective, the tone of the relationship is the largest single factor that determines success or failure of an outsourcing engagement. Therefore, the outsourcer-to-client reporting structure should be clear and free of layers of complexity that will reduce the ability of either side to react appropriately to any situation or opportunity.

## IS THE CIO PART OF THE SCOPE OF A FULL IT OUTSOURCE? THAT'S THE QUESTION

A prevailing issue with either outsourcing model centers on the IT management team. Should the healthcare organization's existing IT management team, including the vice president and chief information officer (CIO), be included or excluded in the scope of outsourced services? Paul A. Strassmann suggests, in *The Squandered Computer*, that organizations "engage in selective outsourcing, but retain most of the information management capabilities as an essential organizational competency." It is noted that perhaps high-performance companies do selective outsourcing, ranging from three to 11 percent of their budget, but that the management of the IT function, in general, be retained within the organization as a key component of their own managerial competency (p. 185).[2]

The outsourcing of IT is a long-term decision, and the purchasing organization has high expectations for improved return on the IT investment. To obtain that return on investment, the outsourced IT department must be closely aligned with the management of the institution. Should the CIO position be outsourced as part of the contract, or should the CIO remain within the organization as a key component?

Healthcare organizations selecting an outsourcing vendor want to gain the outsourcer's best thinking and strategy. This comes from the outsourcer's most senior employees — those who fill the CIO position. Most outsourcing vendors can offer a valuable resource pool — a number of experienced and proven CIOs who can be interchanged as different skill sets are required. The start-up time would be minimal, and the healthcare institution would benefit by having access to an extraordinary range of management skill sets. Outsourcer CIOs are results-oriented and are trained in best practice methodologies, which qualifies them to assume a certain level of risk and responsibility and ensure their aspect of control is maintained. In the alternative CIO staffing strategy, the CIO remains an employee of the healthcare organization. This could pose a problem for the outsourcing firm because the CIO may have an alternative strategy or agenda that may isolate or misrepresent the outsourcing vendor. The level of training, knowledge, and experience of the CIO may not be comprehensive. All of these items would potentially diminish the effectiveness of the outsourcer's IT program.

Strassmann's statement that the management of the IT function should be retained as a key component perhaps has foundation in the belief that a steady accumulation of company-specific knowledge by long-term employees is indispensable. Or perhaps it is founded in the belief that only a company's own VP/CIO/director can be trusted with the organization's secrets or confidential information. Clearly, if an outsider is in a strategic position, that person will have access to confidential information which may be shared with his or her outsourcing firm and used later for the betterment of the outsourcer rather than the betterment of the organization.

Some companies considering outsourcing as an alternative, even in the light of their own difficulties with recruiting and retaining a highly competent IT management team, struggle with issues of control and exposure. In one specific example, a healthcare organization that was part of a larger organization in which the IT management function followed a collaborative work model (i.e., a loosely affiliated organization based upon joint meetings, information sharing, selection committees) announced the organization's decision to outsource strategic applications and the CIO function. The larger organization wanted to exclude the outsourcer's CIO from all collaborative efforts because some within that organization believed that access to individuals and information was too great. They were also concerned about company loyalties. Being excluded from collaborative efforts surely would have hampered the effectiveness of the CIO within the organization. Eventually, decision makers within the healthcare organization prevailed and the outsourcer's CIO was included.

In summary, questions that the organization should address if evaluating the outsourcing models might include:

- Will it be acceptable to seek multiple partners for multiple tasks that may be outsourced?

- Will the organization seek to deal with a single vendor that can meet support, development, and other desirable goals?
- Might a single, major relationship be more desirable?
- Will a single, major relationship offer easier management and possible price advantages?
- Conversely, will the client organization lose a large degree of control and flexibility with an "all eggs in one basket" strategy?
- Will the outsourcer be in a position to supply the necessary IT management?
- Will the outsourcer's IT management offer a better solution than the organization can acquire on its own?
- How will success be measured and determined?

Some example organization structures with the full and selective models are depicted in Exhibit 1.

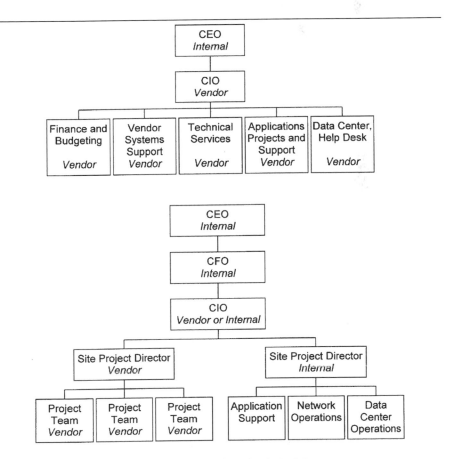

**Exhibit 1. Two Structural Models**

## OUTSOURCING: WHY WOULD HEALTHCARE ORGANIZATIONS VIEW OUTSOURCING AS A MANAGEMENT ALTERNATIVE?

Scenario: a large, multi-facility healthcare provider must implement an electronic medical record in order to meet the growing demands of its payers and physicians and to maintain its competitive position in its market. No one in the technology arm of the organization is experienced with implementing systems of the scope and magnitude of those required to support an electronic record. Management is faced with three alternatives: send its existing employees for extensive training; recruit and, hopefully, hire IT professionals with appropriate experience; or hire an outsourcing vendor to provide professionals with broad experience in the implementation of electronic medical record systems.

When outsourcing is chosen — whether selective or full — the decision is viewed as being a strategic alternative for the healthcare institution. Paul A. Strassman writes, "Perhaps the most crucial contemporary issue of information management is whether to outsource all or some of the information technologies to specialized firms. This issue is not a transient phenomenon; the shift from company-management computing to purchased services is accelerating. The decision when, how, and where to outsource is likely to be one of the few information management issues that will be coming for review at board level meetings in the future" (p. 189).[2]

The reasons, motivations, or client expectations for seriously considering, exploring, and executing an outsourcing relationship include responding to a merger or acquisition; obtaining cost savings; improving organizational finances; implementing long-term technology acquisition and implementation strategies and replacing antiquated hardware platforms; reducing project backlogs; reducing ongoing shortages of qualified information technology professionals; reducing high staff turnover and escalating costs of hiring, training, and retaining staff; minimizing exploding software costs; and even supporting a major organizational change and minimizing organization politics. The "O" word (outsourcing) has an unfounded negative reputation among IT professionals. Unfortunately, some believe that companies choose IT outsourcing as a strategy to return to organization profitability by cutting employment. The list above demonstrates that there are many reasons to contemplate outsourcing, and causing large groups of IT professionals to lose their jobs is not one of them.

Upon review of various press releases that announced healthcare organizations that had entered into an outsourcing relationship, the rationale offered was nearly always one of the following:

- The relationship with the outsourcer will allow us (the healthcare organization) to improve the quality of care.

- The relationship will allow the healthcare institution to focus on its own core competencies.
- The relationship will give the provider the skill set(s) necessary to complete the implementation of strategic applications.

### The Most Prevalent Reasons for Outsourcing

*The healthcare organization cannot consistently attract and retain talent for specialized technologies.* In light of downsizing, lean and mean organizations must ensure that an FTE (full time equivalent) is contributing fully. A manager must have a highly competent and motivated staff in place. Many managers find this to be a two-fold problem because they often do not have (1) access to a large enough pool of information systems professionals competent in the discipline that is needed, (2) at a price the organization is able and willing to afford.

**The outsourcing benefit:** Healthcare organizations will gain access to a full complement of healthcare professionals, permitting virtual resource management and an unequaled knowledge base.

*The healthcare organization's in-house IT staff does not have the skill sets necessary to implement or support a new technology* that is required to drive a competitive or strategic business strategy. If the organization must acquire additional skills and a steep learning curve exists, training costs will be incurred. More importantly, time will be required. The movement from mainframe application to client/server application represents this type of challenge. Successfully implementing this type of technology change depends largely upon the organization's ability to understand it, deploy it quickly, and support it effectively. This type of technology metamorphosis has a pervasive effect, impacting not only one personnel classification but many within the IT function, and can be very costly and require a long period of time, which may not be an acceptable proposition. Most healthcare organizations simply cannot provide the level of services necessary to successfully implement or support a sizable project.

An example of the shortcomings of many IT organizations is the help desk. Internal help desks often do not deliver the necessary levels of initial responsiveness. Phones are not answered promptly. Responses are often not provided and break/fix responsiveness is at a snail's pace. In contrast, outsourced help desks are contractually required to meet minimum response requirements dictated by the healthcare organization.

**The outsourcing benefit:** Qualified and trained IT professionals are available to the healthcare organization when and where they are required to meet project demands and organizational objectives.

*The healthcare organization needs to reduce the overall cost of the IT function.* Ordinarily, in-house IT cost control is a difficult process. The process undertaken to contract outsourcing services helps to clearly identify and understand what the organization's IT costs are. Through outsourcing, IT costs become predictable and relatively fixed — no more surprises. The vendor commits to share in the financial risk. Overruns become a thing of the past and many hidden costs go away, including recruiting, training, overhead, and temporary staff.

**The outsourcing benefit:** Outsourcing turns hard-to-control IT costs into predictable, managed fees. The outsourcer shares in the risk, provides capital, and manages the cost of delivering the right skills at the right time.

*Outsourcing allows the healthcare organization to focus its attention and scarce resources on its core competencies.* In order for healthcare systems to compete in the global economy, they can no longer afford to support services that do not add value to their current business focus. With the right information services outsourcing vendor, healthcare providers can gain access to broad applications knowledge, escape the costs of hiring, firing, and training, and benefit from the experience of other healthcare organizations while managing the costs but not the process of implementing and operating information systems.

Historically, when compared to other industries, the healthcare industry has had a low demand for information technology, a low investment in information technology, a low functionality in applications, and limited integration. Times have changed! Today, healthcare organizations exhibit an explosion of technology needs and an overwhelming need for investment. Healthcare institutions also need to achieve a strategic advantage based upon a strong information technology platform. A robust, broad-based, performance-driven, cost-effective information technology function is therefore essential. So, as healthcare organizations fight for survival, they are finding that they must focus on their areas of expertise, and recognize that acquiring, deploying, and operating information technologies are not among their core competencies. Essentially, many health systems lack the skill sets required to implement all applications and integrate information systems across the enterprise.

For years, healthcare organizations have built and invested in internal information systems functions. History has shown that even the strongest information services departments have gaps of internal knowledge and expertise. In times of intense change and knowledge transfer, consultants, vendors, or some mix of outsiders have been relied upon to fill the gaps. Vendor/consulting services have typically been purchased on a per-project basis for discrete projects that have a definite start and end date. The consultant works within the parameters of the client's information technology environment.

Outsourcing allows the organization to direct its energies toward the business it knows best — clinical care. Healthcare providers should take advantage of an outsourcing vendor's "S.W.A.T. team" approach to knowledge transfer and system implementation, wherein the outsourcer applies the entire depth of its employees' knowledge base to the client's benefit.

In summary, healthcare organizations are experiencing severe IT staff shortages, brought on by the industry's intense need for change and the need to incorporate rapidly evolving technologies. In-house IT functions, once thought to be key to the organization's strategic initiatives, are proving to no longer be a cost-effective or optimal performance driven alternative. The selection of an IT outsource firm whose core competency is IT in the healthcare industry may help the organization to focus once again on its true core competencies — providing efficient and effective patient care.

**The outsourcing benefit:** Allows the healthcare organization to draw on the expertise of experienced information professionals, and shift its focus to patient centered activities.

*Outsourcing provides consistent delivery and significant improvement of a service.* Many of the services that in-house IT departments provide really are not performed well. In fact, if the services were graded, they would receive a C. Outsourcing firms, on the other hand, have the incentive to deliver consistently outstanding levels of service. Anything less and the outsourcer's contract will not be renewed and worse, their sullied reputation will prohibit them from obtaining other contracts. Outsourcers always keep their eye on the objective and remember the old marketing adage that an unhappy customer will tell their story of frustration and disappointment to thirteen others.

**The outsourcing benefit:** The quality of the IT services that the customer receives is improved because the services are purchased, and the ongoing good reputation of the outsourcing company depends on positive word of mouth.

*Outsourcing provides access to expertise in a wide variety of operational, technological, and managerial specialties* and allows outsourcing firms to provide the necessary breadth of skills and resources to meet client needs as they arise and evolve.

As a healthcare organization's business direction and strategy change, the corresponding skill sets and systems within the IT function have been forced to change to meet the needs of the organization. In reacting to this change, very few health systems have adopted the single-vendor approach; most have pursued the strategy of choosing best-of-breed applications and have proceeded to interface those applications together. It is essential that those applications communicate with one another and ultimately share data. Currently, healthcare organizations are expressing a desire to limit the proliferation of applications, perhaps choosing logical clusters of applications or application suites; however, unique skills are still required for each application offered by any given application vendor. Therefore, supporting the application environment will offer challenges as organizations pursue the selection and implementation of new systems, such as advanced clinicals, enterprise indexing, and picture archiving. Through outsourcing, healthcare organizations will have access to flexible staffing options, and can confidently plan, knowing that competent, qualified, and experienced implementers are available when required — a radical change in applications project management and application development. The availability of outsourced resources significantly shortens the selection cycle, and virtually eliminates the training time for the IT internal support staff.

Arguments can be made that the design and testing phases of project implementation might also be significantly shortened, due to the fact that experienced staff is available when needed. CIOs may consider outsourcing some of their technical support functions but most would never consider outsourcing the application development function because it is so closely tied to strategic initiatives. Upon reflection, considering that CIOs are usually evaluated on successful progress toward strategic initiatives, it would seem appropriate that applications development may be one of the most important functions to consider outsourcing.

**The outsourcing benefit:** Healthcare organizations can be assured of having access to the skill sets required to undertake a project of any complexity, from simple break/fix service to advanced, multidisciplinary infrastructure conversions, without incurring the expense of hiring or retraining personnel.

## OUTSOURCING: STAFFING CONSIDERATIONS

Outsourcing arrangements have multiple approaches in the area of staffing:

1. The outsourcer may provide task-specific staff and management to accomplish its mandate.
2. The client may transfer its staff to outsourcer employment.
3. The outsourcer may manage the client's staff in addition to managing its own.

The first approach is straightforward and relatively easy to manage. The outsourcing company provides its own staff to carry out the agreed-upon objective; an example of this approach may be PC break/fix maintenance. Obviously, someone from the in-house IT staff performed this function before the outsourcing firm was engaged; therefore, some questions will arise that should be addressed before the outsourcing project goes into effect. Will the client personnel who previously performed this function work alongside the contractor's personnel or will they be transitioned to other duties? Might their employment be terminated? Will the outsourcer have the right to hire all or some of the client's IT personnel? What provisions will be made for those who are not selected or do not accept job offers?

The second approach states that client staff will become outsourcer personnel. The outsourcer may evaluate the staff and make offers to those who meet its requirements. Transferred staff may remain at the original site or become travelling consultants. Some will not be offered positions and others who do transition, but for some reason do not remain with the outsourcer for some minimum period of time, will participate in a job separation program. Responsibility for in-house staff does not end the day the outsourcing commences.

The last approach offers professional management of the client's staff. Here, the impact is cultural as well as organizational. The client must be prepared to accept and support the new management team as if it were its own. The issues of control here are dominant. The role and power of the new management must be clearly defined, communicated, and understood, both above and below in the organization.

If new management is the model, there will be a time for evaluation, direction setting, and plan execution to improve the skills, performance, attitude, or whatever combination of these may be required. Transitioning employees bring issues of benefit coverage and pensions as well as the natural feeling of abandonment. Extreme care must be taken by both parties to treat the transitioned employees as respectfully and compassionately as possible. The mixed model brings all these and other issues to bear. One employee working alongside another who has a different employer, different salaries, benefits, etc., can create a complex management problem. Care has to be given to work groups, treatment, and expectations.

Several major phases occur during the process of transitioning employees from the healthcare organization's employment roster to that of the outsourcer. These include the announcement to the employee base, the individual evaluation and one-on-one meetings, and the transition and start-up process.

### The Announcement to the Employee Base

The purpose of the announcement is for the outsourcing organization to inform the healthcare organization's IT employees of the business decision to outsource their department and to introduce the outsourcer. This is also the time to explain the transition process and timeline, and to hand out documentation about the company.

In many cases this is the first time employees have heard anything about the outsourcing decision or how it will impact them. From this point forward there will be a wide range of emotions — many similar to the grieving process. Initially there will be shock and denial, followed by anger and resentment. Finally, the employees will begin to understand and accept the decisions that have been made. Helping the outsourced employee move through these emotions is key to a successful hiring and transition process. The outsourcer should recognize this emotional process and let the employee know he or she is wanted and valued in the new organization.

### One-on-One Meetings and the Employee Evaluation Process

The purpose of these meetings is to allow the employees to ask questions and get answers directly, as opposed to through the rumor mill. During this time, employees can also talk about their responsibilities and accomplishments and how they would like to participate in the new organization.

This is also the time to talk to employees about the stress associated with change of this magnitude. A great deal of this stress is the result of a lack of communication. In many cases, gaps in communication are inevitable because the entire process is really an evolution. Decisions are made as the result of reactions to situations that arise during the contracting process and the transition process. Information may be withheld with the understanding that a decision today could be reversed tomorrow.

It is important for members of the outsourcing firm to be onsite and be seen. They should keep communication active by seeking out people and getting them to talk. Some employees will sit back waiting for the worst possible outcome, which increases their level of stress and reduces their productivity. Others will react to every rumor, or even start and pass on rumors. It is common to see employees gathering to talk; this is an important and acceptable step in moving through the grieving process. Encourage them to not rely on rumors. Instead, urge them to ask for answers and to seek clarification of things they do not understand. Let them know that representatives from the outsourcing firm are available and would like to be part of any discussion.

### The Transition and Start-Up Process

During the transition and start-up phase, the new employees will be oriented to the outsourcer's policies, procedures, and methodologies. Encourage them to become solutions oriented and proactive in learning new skills that will increase their value to both the client healthcare organization and their new employer. This is also the time to indoctrinate the employees in the new organizational structure and their contractual obligations to the client.

## OUTSOURCING: THE RELATIONSHIP AND CONTRACT

Regardless of the outsourcing model, when a healthcare organization enters into a relationship with an outsourcing vendor, they are establishing a long-term partnership. The outsourcing vendor will now manage the day-to-day, month-to-month, year-to-year IT functions, and will become an integral part of the healthcare organization. The cultures of the two organizations must strive for compatibility. Like a marriage, they are going to be together for a long time and need to develop guidelines for establishing priorities and for problem resolution. A contract is the most reliable vehicle for spelling out how critical this commitment is.

The supplier of outsourcing services will provide the necessary staff, commit to performance targets, and share financial risks. Their performance can be monitored and measured against identified performance targets.

Specifically, the full-service information services outsource vendor will:

- Furnish broad knowledge of the healthcare industry and applications systems
- Deliver needed services through a combination of both on-site and on-demand professionals
- Absorb the contracting organization's existing IT staff and realign the organization for increased effectiveness
- Know the industry software providers and have acute knowledge of their products
- Provide sound application selection and implementation services
- Promote predictable fees with shared financial savings and risk

By choosing the right partner for an information technology outsourcing arrangement, the healthcare organization will be able to optimize staffing, maximize information technology dollars, and most importantly, achieve the desired results. Further, the client organization should receive virtual and flexible access to the experience and abilities of a large pool of well-trained professionals and effective management of the day-to-day information technology processes.

The delivery model should ensure that the executive level, operational level, and systems consultants create a unified approach to delivered services. The outsourcing team's experience with strategy development, deployment of tactical plans, and implementation and integration of technology across the organization and a wide range of healthcare information technology vendors and products will add strength and value to the outsourcing relationship.

## THE CONTRACT AND ITS NEGOTIATION

There is an old saw that says the best contract is one that, after signing, can be put away and never looked at again. Outsourcing contracts are critical documents defining a relationship in which trust must be a major factor. These contracts also spell out specific terms of performance and management of the relationship, and outline problem resolution and contract termination procedures, metrics, and gain sharing. As the scope of the outsourced functions increases, so must the language of the contract. The process of developing a contract for outsourcing services demands that every possible permutation be anticipated and represented literally and in written contractual form to protect both organizations. This premise calls for both organizations to submit proposed contracts to qualified attorneys for careful review. It is not proposed here that the process of deal making and contract negotiation can be altered to any great extent.

Contracts for outsourcing services must contain sections that define control/management and staffing. The control/management section must describe how the client and outsourcer will relate, provide reporting structures, and list schedules. It must describe thresholds and, possibly, time-frames for decision making. The staffing section must describe the transition process, if any, and enumerate responsibilities the client retains after the transition. Issues such as the funding of pensions and other benefits, accrued benefit time funding, and benefits not available from the outsourcer may be covered in this section, along with a discussion of how employees who do not survive the probationary period will be handled.

Outsourcing contracts must contain an understandable and effective method of problem resolution, which will contribute to the partnership and trust this type of business relationship must have. Regardless whether the sense of trust was built upon a foundation laid during prior engagements or developed during the presentation and selection process, it is vitally important to the success of an outsourcing engagement. Discussing the issues that may arise and devising solutions in advance will go a long way toward protecting the common values that brought the parties together. The discussions (and resultant contract documentation) may cover such issues as how problems will be documented and discussed, and who should represent the parties during the problem resolution process.

The contract should describe how and when to escalate problems to a higher authority. In what form and to whom? What type of response is expected and how quickly?

Contract termination activities should be clearly described. The contract must anticipate the end of the contract term and a client that now feels capable of resuming ownership of the IT function. Issues that must be addressed include the return of transferred assets, ownership of developed intellectual property, and the like. Also critical here is the client's right to outsourcer personnel — those who may have come from the client initially or other personnel used on the client's engagement for a significant period of time. Both types of employees have an extensive knowledge of client tools, processes, and personnel, and may well hold positions that the client depends on for smooth performance of systems and processes.

The conditions and costs of the client regaining or retaining such staff must be spelled out.

The contract should also cover the unlikely event of contract termination or termination for failures.

Metrics and performance measurements — the factors by which the effectiveness of the services delivered will be quantitatively evaluated — should be included in the contract as an attachment completed at the time of signing or within a reasonable period thereafter. Metrics should cover performance of scheduled tasks, standards of performance in response to issues or routine requests, monitoring of capacities and throughput of equipment, and the like. Metrics need to be applied to the client as well, in areas where the performance of an automated function relies on availability, timeliness, and accuracy of input or process review. Most contracts will specify the timeframe for metric evaluations and performance measurements. In addition, some organizations also supplement the contract with separate agreements between the outsourcer and user departments. These department-specific contracts are called service level agreements and define deliverables specific to a department.

When setting the metrics for performance, ensure that consideration is given to the complete delivery of the IT function. The vendor, in a day-to-day management situation, must:

- Effectively deal with each "crisis du jour"
- Implement timely results for strategic initiatives such as system implementations
- Support the exploration of technological advances that could be exploited by the organization — perhaps through pilot projects
- Provide adequate service to the end users and fully meet their expectations for production support services, such as patient accounting, human resources, and general accounting

Gain sharing, or risk sharing, is a relationship model as well as contract language. Outsourcing is about benefits — short and long term, direct and indirect — that save dollars and make possible larger performance and information benefits in operations, planning, and decision support. While ways to measure such savings potential are complex and are continuously being refined, the identification of the more objective basic measurements such as budget performance or tangible project returns can form the basis of mutual sharing of the returns of professionally executed projects.

## SUMMATION

A healthcare organization should view outsourcing, whether full or selective, as a strategic advantage, if structured correctly. As outlined earlier, each alternative has benefits, both short and long term. If an organization evaluates outsourcing with only a short-term focus and does not consider the strategic opportunity such an arrangement can contribute, it may be seeing only a portion of the total potential of this alternative. Cost savings *are* possible in the short term, but the highest value is derived from addressing immediate cost and service issues in unison with the organization's strategic aspirations, and executing to that strategy the appropriate tactics required to reach those goals.

The short-term view looks to reduce costs, where possible, and to fill those difficult-to-staff positions required to support current projects or even to complete projects that are delayed. It may also address the measurements and metrics that leadership, the user community, and the IT function itself need for measurement and improvement of service delivery. The short term is a period of "low hanging fruit," that is, project, cost, or turnover stabilization, and building user confidence and management's trust.

With a longer-term view, the outsourcer's staff gains greater knowledge of the organization. This knowledge allows them a greater ability to initiate and implement critical projects that will expand services and competitive position, and improve data availability for medical, tactical, and strategic decision making. The long-term outsourcing relationship also provides increased opportunity to propose and implement changes in the healthcare organization's strategic or tactical course or approach. This is made possible because the outsourcer's highly skilled staff can bring to bear the correct tools in far less time than the contracting organization would require to recruit or retrain current staff.

Both short- and long-term outsourcing engagements can achieve a list of benefits, which include:

- Enhanced financial performance with the control of capital and the successful completion of major system initiatives, on budget, on schedule
- Achievement of strategic business advantages by enabling the healthcare organization to focus on its core competencies of healthcare, not information services
- Implementation of effective information services management, measurably improving customer service with greater predictability of information systems costs and performance
- Successful transition of the healthcare organization's IT professionals, providing them with solid career paths and training programs

For healthcare providers, information systems outsourcing should not be and is not a technology issue; it is a business issue. In order for U.S. healthcare systems to compete economically, they can no longer afford to support services that do not add value to their current business focus.

With the right outsourcing supplier, under the right outsourcing model, providers can gain access to broad applications knowledge, escape personnel training and turnover costs, and benefit from the experience of other healthcare organizations — while managing the costs but not the process — of implementing and operating information systems.

It is not surprising that, increasingly, outsourcing as a strategic advantage is gaining recognition as a powerful tool for business growth. That growth is based on specialization, expertise, and excellence to build and sustain competitive advantage. Outsourcing of important but non-core business functions has become a common and effective strategy for many industries — among them, the healthcare industry.

Viewed strategically, outsourcing challenges today's executive to rethink the traditional vertically integrated institution in favor of a much more flexible and nimble organization. Today, almost any organization can gain access to resources. What differentiates the leaders who have chosen a model of outsourcing is their access to intellectual capital and their access to both knowledge and expertise — not the size and the scope of the resources that they own and manage. Outsourcing should be evaluated as a proven, viable, and strategic option for the information technology function.

**References**

1. Klepper, R. and Jones, W. O. 1997. *Outsourcing Information Technology, Systems and Services.* Englewood Cliffs, NJ: Prentice Hall.
2. Strassman. P. A. 1997. *The Squandered Computer.* The Information Economics Press: New Canaan, CT.

# Chapter 28

# International Systems to Support Incremental Improvement in Healthcare

*Patrick McNees*

The primary purposes of this chapter are to address some current issues in developing, maintaining, and analyzing data and databases from more than one country and the absence of fundamental elements that allow learning to occur. While problematic in one country, such omissions exacerbate our challenges in addressing international systems. However, prior to launching into the discussion of fundamental elements and special challenges, a few points deserve mention and clarification.

One might question why the title of this chapter involves "… improvement in healthcare" rather than "data and information systems." Quite simply, the development of international healthcare data or information systems is largely irrelevant outside of the context of international healthcare itself and the conditions that govern practice. Thus, this chapter will focus on both data and practice.

Attention is also drawn to the term "incremental." Science is cumulative, with knowledge building on prior knowledge, allowing the formulation of new propositions, postulates, and theories. While this chapter will not presume to delve deeply into the philosophy of science, the chapter will stress the importance of providing information systems that allow for the incremental improvement in practice. It will be argued that this incremental improvement cannot occur in the absence of the fundamental elements that allow learning to occur. Differences in *learning systems* versus

0-8493-1498-4/03/$0.00+$1.50

*expert systems* will be discussed. Assuring the presence of these elements is among the greatest challenges that we face when attempting to develop and maintain responsive international technologies and systems.

## TOWARD A WORLDWIDE DATA REPOSITORY

Over the past several years my colleagues and I have been involved in attempts to develop and implement assessment and treatment decision-support systems in various countries. Resulting data would flow to a central repository. Analysis of the accumulating data may result in the need to alter the parameters of the assessment itself, as well as the specific treatment alternatives. Yet, the challenges that are faced when dealing with international systems go well beyond language differences and translation needs.

If I (as the author) asked you (as the reader) to speculate as to the issues that would be covered in this chapter regarding international data systems, what would be your response? Challenges implicit in the development of data standards, nomenclature issues, the need for common communication protocols, issues of platform independence and interdependence are just a few issues and challenges that would likely form the outline. By now you have probably identified several others that would likely fill out the outline of the chapter. My first draft could probably have been exchanged with your mental outline and we would discover considerable overlap. However, I just returned from a brief trip which I will describe more fully later. That trip resulted in my first draft being dragged to my laptop's trash. While the beginning of the resulting chapter is a bit unusual for a text, I beg the reader's indulgence while I attempt to development my propositions.

## AN ISLAND IN TIME

Some of you may be old enough and grew up in communities small enough where the healthcare system was described in very human and personal terms. Going to the dentist likely meant you were going to see Dr. Gibbs, since he was the only dentist in town. Going to the doctor perhaps presented more complicated choices and networks. In my community one had to decide whether to go to see Dr. Smith or Dr. Davis. Assuming a home visit was not warranted, one could delay the decision until the last minute, however, since the execution of patient choice was performed by signing one of two ruled pads (one labeled Dr. Smith and one Dr. Davis) in the reception area of the physicians' shared space. A few decades later, much has changed in these communities — or has it?

In the spirit of my focus on international issues, I am writing this from an island in French Polynesia about 4500 miles southwest of my office in Seattle and about 6000 miles from the town in which I was born. I just returned

**Exhibit 1. Writing Doesn't Have to Be All that Hard**

from a brief trip into the village (the one-hour trip I mentioned previously). I had read that the post office offered an Internet connection from which I could check my e-mail and perhaps even track down a couple of references that I need for this chapter. While the information was highly optimistic and suggestions of Internet connectivity premature, the trip was enlightening.

My driver (and healthcare informant) was born on Moorea. Max suggested that this was perhaps the most beautiful of all places and the island's inhabitants were truly blessed (see Exhibit 1). Even those who worked in Papeete (the city) on Tahiti but could return to Moorea were lucky. And healthcare ... yes, there was healthcare. Max described the system succinctly: teeth and other. However, for sea urchin stings and coral scratches I could get limes from the market or produce stands. A shaman could address certain other anomalies which are beyond the scope of this chapter. I later confirmed that even some of the written guides to the island referred to the dentist and two physicians by name. I also confirmed that lime juice does seem to help sea urchin stings.

I thought about my trip with Max in the context of our experiences and challenges during the past couple of years in such countries as Australia,

New Zealand, Germany, Canada, the United States, Sweden, England, Japan, and China. I realized that much of what I had written was not only obvious but could also be misleading. The reader might be led to presume an unquestioning devotion to a model of systematic permeability: one which simply values the reliable and predictable flow and accumulation of data and information. While not the intent, my writing built the case for a benign data system and worldwide diffusion model of healthcare which presumed the diffusion of knowledge from those who had it to those who did not.

However, rather than this benign view of the role of international data systems, the challenge in our work has been one of attempting to set in place systems that have the capacity to change practice (not simply describe practice) in an orderly, systematic way. Thus, our tasks have focused on the elements and systems necessary for an "incremental" yet empirical approach to healthcare improvement. The balance of this chapter addresses those issues and the special challenges that occur when international boundaries are crossed.

## INTERNATIONAL HEALTHCARE AS A LEARNING ORGANISM

While one may change without learning, one may not learn without changing. In other words, we only learn by changing our behavior and getting feedback regarding the effects of that change. Such is the case with all organisms.

The proposition that any system can be viewed as an organism may seem a bit odd. To view international healthcare as simply a large, complex organism may seem very odd. Yet the analogy and words have been deliberately chosen for this construct and are based on the assumption that incremental and systematic improvements in healthcare will not occur as a result of our large-scale information systems unless the primary conditions that allow learning to occur are present. Certain other assumptions deserve consideration.

The term "international" is used rather than others such as "worldwide" because we have found some of the issues faced in designing data systems vary due to political realities in various countries. Thus, if the larger worldwide healthcare system is eventually to be viewed as a single organism, the current realities draw attention to the variances that occasion consideration of important issues when international boundaries are crossed.

The term "healthcare" has been chosen rather than "medicine" or "medical care" since medicine is viewed as a subset of healthcare practice in most of the world. There are two special connotations for "healthcare" in the present context, however. The first connotation is meant to embrace what we might consider nonstandard practice or, as the United States National Institutes of Health has chosen, "alternative medicine." The second connotation is that the work described herein is focused on systems for both prevention and treatment. The importance of these distinctions should become more apparent later in this chapter.

## THE FUNDAMENTAL ELEMENTS OF LEARNING AND BEHAVIOR CHANGE

While there are various views of learning and behavior change, one paradigm divides learning (or conditioning) into respondent and operant. Respondent conditioning holds that a specific response can be elicited by the presentation of a stimulus that has been paired with another stimulus that has inherent positive or negative connotations. Think back to Pavlov pairing a bell with food for his dogs.[1] Soon the bell alone resulted in salivating dogs. While perhaps interesting, another paradigm seems to have more direct applicability to the provision of systems that allow learning.

Skinner's work[2] is representative of this other type of conditioning or learning, which suggests that an organism can learn based on the differential consequences of its behavior. It is suggested that if the behavior following a discriminative stimulus (the cues that denote when a behavior will be followed by a reinforcer) is followed by a reinforcer (a consequence that increases a behavior), the probability that the same behavior will be emitted when the same stimulus is presented again is increased. If the behavior is followed by a punisher (a consequence that decreases a behavior), the probability of the organism emitting the behavior following the same stimulus is decreased. There is a special consideration of the withdrawal of a reinforcer (extinction) that is beyond the scope of this chapter. In common terms, all animals tend to continue to do things for which they are rewarded and discontinue doing things for which they are not rewarded or are punished. In brief, organisms learn to behave differently based on the differential consequences of their behavior under specific circumstances.

By this point the reader is no doubt asking where all of this discussion is leading. What is the possible relevance to international healthcare? The relevance lies in a very simple reality: we do not have in place the most fundamental elements that will allow our data systems to result in learning. While the issue is relevant when we view one country, the effects are exacerbated when we consider international efforts. Thus, if we are to move from practice diffusion and data warehousing to systems that allow incremental improvement of healthcare practices, we must attend to the challenges associated with addressing these various elements in different countries.

## THE FUNDAMENTAL ELEMENTS OF AN INTERNATIONAL HEALTHCARE DATA SYSTEM

Most systems are premised on the assembly or arrangement of elements in a particular fashion. However, an effective system cannot exist if the fundamental elements for producing the desired outcome are not present. While this may seem an obvious and trite statement, I will attempt to illustrate that the fundamental elements necessary for employing an international healthcare system from which learning can occur are not typically present. It is the establishment of these elements in various countries that present some of our most formidable challenges.

Recall the simple elements of Skinner's operant feedback loop presented earlier. In the presence of a stimulus, behaviors that are reinforced will increase and those that are ignored or punished will decrease. In terms of feedback, the organism is getting feedback from its actions and adapting its behavior accordingly. If feedback is not tied to the stimulus and behavior, then behavior change will at best be irregular and unpredictable. While this is a simple notion, the fundamental elements that are required for such a paradigm simply do not typically exist with large-scale clinical databases and present some of the most salient challenges in attempting to implement systems across international boundaries.

There are four fundamental elements that must exist if a system is to support learning in healthcare (see also Exhibit 2):

1. Standardized assessment
2. Intervention or treatment operationally defined
3. Empirically defined outcomes are tracked
4. Capability of systematically changing both assessment and intervention based on feedback from data

While this model is about as simple and straightforward as the animal learning model presented previously, it is equally simple to see that most of our systems fall short of addressing the four straightforward elements.

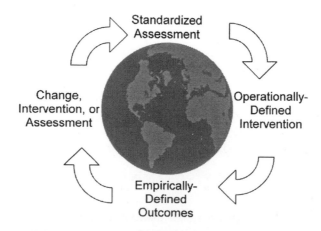

**Exhibit 2. Fundamental Elements to Support Learning**

To illustrate, it might be simpler to address a specific condition rather than generalities. Thus, for illustrative purposes, let us turn our attention to that of preventing and treating chronic wounds.

## Standardized Assessment

Standardized assessment is a fundamental element of any system that allows incremental learning. It is also perhaps the most critically important yet frequently ignored condition. This notion is premised on the fact that if we cannot operationally and reliably describe the setting phenomena which are being observed (stimuli), then we cannot determine the prevention or treatment behaviors in which we should engage to achieve desired outcomes. When necessary, we will divide our discussion regarding assessment into two areas: risk assessment (the risk of developing a wound) and wound assessment (assessment of wounds that develop). For the sake of specificity, we will also focus on one type of chronic wound: the pressure ulcer.

During our early work to develop a comprehensive system for chronic wounds, we had encountered a perplexing array of pressure ulcer risk assessment instruments. These "scales" often took their name from one of the original authors: Norton,[3] Gosnell,[4] Knoll,[5] Waterlow,[6] Braden,[7] and Douglas.[8] While the purpose of this discussion is not to delve into the various merits of the scales, the issue is raised to illustrate the challenge associated with selecting one assessment instrument and committing to it. The problem was complicated by the fact that for every formal risk assessment scale reported in the literature, there were dozens of homegrown and modified instruments devised by individual facilities. We were immediately faced with considerable pressure to adopt or include each of these instruments. This pressure was further increased when we moved beyond international boundaries. Each country or region seemed to have its own favorite. The great temptation was to simply acquiesce and include all of the scales. Had we been designing a benign data repository, perhaps we would have taken this tack. However, we were attempting to implement a comprehensive system that stood to incrementally improve practice over time. It was necessary to select and commit to one risk assessment scale (or two directly comparable) and to "sell" the use of the scale worldwide.

After having grappled with the issue of which scale to select, it is suggested that at least four criteria are important in considering a commitment to an assessment scale or instrument:

1. Which scale has the most credible science behind it?
2. Which scale is the most widely used for the target population?
3. Is there data suggesting relationships between various assessment profiles, suggested interventions, and known outcomes?
4. Can copyright, ownership, and other legal issues be resolved if the scale is to be included?

Once a commitment has been made to an assessment instrument or scale, alterations should be based on data and not individual whim or clinical intuition. The reader is warned, however, that pressures to alter the scale or use an alternative will be considerable and persistent. Each new country will likely present its own case. The cost of including a variety of assessment methodologies is considerable, with the greatest cost paid by a bankrupted learning process. We have found that the safest position for one to take is based on science and data. In other words, you will be willing to change the assessment scale just as soon as data and science suggest it should be changed. In a sense, it is similar to the adage, "In God I trust but others please bring their data."

In summary, there are a few simple issues that relate to assessment. First, standardize on one instrument or scale. Second, be prepared to fend off temptations to modify the scale or adopt others. Third, be prepared to alter the scale based on data. While relatively straightforward, the assessment issue will likely be among the most contentious issues faced as one moves from country to country.

## Operationally Defined Intervention or Treatment

If standardized assessment addresses the issue of the characteristics of the stimulus, then we must also know what was done as a result. In other words, how did we intervene? How did we treat? Drawing a parallel to our operant learning paradigm, we ask the question: how did the organism behave under the specific stimulus conditions described by the assessment?

As with assessment, this condition seems obvious and trite at first glance. However, unless one is lucky or careful (or both), one will find oneself in the midst of esoteric discussions of complete treatment/intervention taxonomies. Perhaps the most common alternative is an attempt to capture retrospectively the treatments employed. Such systems are probably very familiar to all readers and will not be elaborated here. However, we have found an alternative to be more fruitful. That alternative involves having the system serve as a clinical decision support aide. The steps in this process are described in the following.

First, we must ask ourselves what is known about treating or intervening with the target phenomenon. Is there credible evidence to suggest that certain practices are "better" than others. If so, what are the expected outcomes, and under what conditions should the intervention be employed? In the case of pressure ulcers, for example, the question is not simply whether someone is at risk. Rather, the question relates to the profile of the characteristics that place the person at risk for developing a wound and what that profile implies about the intervention(s) that should be considered. For example, if the probability of developing a pressure ulcer is increased as a result of excessive moisture, the obvious question is how that moisture might be managed to reduce the probabilities. While this observation again appears obvious, the effect on the resulting information system is direct. It means that both the decision support and data systems must be multi-leveled. To illustrate, consider our example of moisture contributing to pressure ulcer risk. Our intervention will vary, depending upon several factors. What is the source of the moisture? If the source is incontinence, is the source bowel or bladder, or both? If bladder, is the incontinence during the day or at night, or both? If bowel, are the stools loose or formed? Here the issue is not a matter simply of collecting more complete data. Our intervention will vary, depending on the answer to each of these questions. Yet, these questions are only relevant in certain circumstances. For example, the source of the moisture is only relevant if moisture is present. The time of day for urinary incontinence is only relevant if there is moisture from urine loss. Thus, the system is one that is "intelligent" enough to only ask for information that is needed to ascertain "best treatment or intervention" and captures data in that multi-leveled context.

Second, based on the literature and other sources of "knowledge," we must formulate treatment or intervention algorithms or clinical pathways. The reader probably has recognized that this is beginning to sound like an "expert system." Indeed, many of the elements thus far are the same. However, the expert system is most often devised by a consensus panel or group and the resulting algorithms are viewed as an endpoint until a similar panel reconsiders the evidence at a later time. The goal of our attempts is to provide a beginning point from which our system can learn. It might be said that "expert systems" are designed to be "smart." Learning systems are designed to improve outcomes incrementally over time.

From an international perspective, the challenge that confronts developers and managers is the variance in preferred treatment alternatives and product offerings from country to country. We have found that a single company may offer a particular product in one country but not offer or license a competitive product in another country. It is noteworthy that the most salient aspect of this discussion is not the utilization of identical interventions and products. Rather, there is a need for a precise understanding of products and procedures being used. Indeed, naturally occurring variance in practice may offer comparative data. Yet, it is only against the objective and operational specification of such interventions that effectiveness can be judged.

## Empirically Defined Outcomes Are Tracked

To this point in our discussion, I have suggested that it is essential to describe the stimulus conditions in consistent terms. Thus, we need to identify and consistently use the same assessment instrument, scale, and methodology. We have also said it is necessary to fully and operationally describe what was done. What was the intervention? What was the treatment? In simple terms, we have described the characteristics of the phenomenon that we wish to address and what was done to address it. The obvious next issue begs the question: to what end or effect?

In the case of pressure ulcers, relevant risk-prevention measures include such obvious measures as changes in prevalence and incidence rates from those that would have been expected had we not intervened. However, the data sometimes leads one to unexpected results. For example, it has been found that using systematic risk assessment and intervention paradigms not only resulted in a reduction in pressure ulcer prevalence and incidence but the wounds that did develop tended to be less severe.

One might assume that the outcome measures are obvious for most conditions. While we have that healthcare professionals do not tend to argue about "desired outcomes" in various countries, we have found a perplexing lack of agreement regarding some very fundamental definitions. Continuing with our illustration using chronic wounds as an example, many outcomes of interest involve wound healing. What proportion of the wounds healed in an expected timeframe? Did wounds heal faster when certain products were used? What is the cost-effectiveness of one intervention versus another? Yet, when the fundamental question of what is a healed wound was posed to an international panel, there was little agreement regarding the operational definition of a healed wound. For example, if there was closure and subsequently the wound reopened in one week, was the wound healed? Rather than belabor the illustration, it is used simply to highlight a challenge that is presented to designing information systems that have the capability of allowing learning to occur. We have found that the solution to the dilemma does not lie in attempting to obtain consensus. Rather, the solution lies in one of the fundamental tenets of science: operationally define one's dependent measures. If we can identify consistent differences in the results of practice A versus practice B (viz. clinical significance), the questions of clinical and societal significance can be asked. Put simply, if one operationally defines dependent measures and describes outcomes in this context, others can test and potentially replicate the findings. In the context of large-scale databases, outcomes can then be judged on their own merits.

## Change Intervention(s) or Assessment Based on Data

In the previous section I alluded to the difference in *expert systems* and *learning systems*. Just as an organism adapts its behavior based on feedback and differential consequences, a *learning system* must have the ability to adapt over time. Adaptations take three forms: (1) changes in the interventions, (2) changes in the assessment parameters, and (3) changes in conditions under which interventions are used (viz. changes in the pathways and criteria). Of course, *expert systems* may change over time. However, such changes are typically the result of "expert" reconsideration of best evidence at periodic intervals. "Best evidence" is often that derived from controlled investigations and clinical trials. I will be the first to support such controlled investigations when feasible. Indeed, controlled investigation is a cornerstone of accumulation of scientific knowledge.

Yet another cornerstone of natural science is observation and the systematic assimilation of information. Further, animals are continually testing new ways of dealing with particular situations and adapting their behavior based on the outcomes. I am suggesting that the way that we view healthcare and healthcare information systems may be quite similar. Unlike conditions that are contrived in the laboratory of a controlled investigation, there is often considerable variance in the "real world." As we cross international boundaries, the cumulative variance increases. Yet with consistent assessment, operationally defined interventions, and persistent tracking of outcomes, we have the ability to incrementally alter both assessment and practice over time.

## SUMMARY

As we move toward larger and larger information systems, our most substantial challenges in developing, managing, and analyzing international healthcare data may not come from arenas that are most often the focus of such projects. Rather, the challenges may come from attempts to assure the presence of the fundamental elements that allow learning to occur. If we cannot describe and track the conditions under which interventions occurred, the nature of the interventions that did occur, and the results of those interventions, then incremental changes in assessment, intervention, and treatment will not occur in an orderly and systematic fashion. We will not have provided adequate information technologies and the organism that we call "international healthcare" will not learn from its own experience.

### References

1. Pavlov, I. P. 1928. *Lectures on Conditioned Reflexes: Twenty-Five Years of Objective Study of the Higher Nervous Activity (Behaviour) of Animals.* Collaboration with G. Volborth. Trans. by W. Horsley Gantt. New York: International Publishers.
2. Skinner, B. F. 1953. *Science and Human Behavior.* New York: The Macmillan Company.
3. Norton, D., McLaren, R., and Exton-Smith AN. 1962. *An Investigation of Geriatric Nursing Problems in Hospitals.* London: National Cooperation for the Care of Old People.
4. Gosnell, D. J. 1973. "An assessment tool to identify pressure sores," *Nursing Research,* 22: 55–59.
5. Knoll Pharmaceutical Company. 1977. "The Knoll Scale of liability in pressure ulcers." In *A Guide to the Practice of Nursing.* McFarlane, S. and Castledine, G., Eds. St. Louis: Mosby.
6. Waterlow, J. 1985. "A risk assessment card." *Nursing Times,* 81: 49–55.

7. Bergstrom, N., Braden, B., Laguzza, A., and Holman, V. 1987. "The Braden Scale for predicting pressure ulcer risk," *Nursing Research,* 36: 205–210.
8. Pritchard, V. 1986. "Calculating the risk in the Douglas scale," *Nursing Time,* 22: 417–428.
9. Braden, B., Corriore, C., and McNees, P. 1997. "Computerized decision support systems: implications for practice." In *Nursing Informatics: The Impact of Nursing Knowledge on Healthcare Informatics,* Gerdin, U., Tallberg, M., and Wainwright, P., Eds. p. 300–304. Amsterdam: IOS Press.
10. Braden, B., Bergstrom, N., and McNees, P. 1997. "The Braden system." In *Nursing Informatics: the Impact of Nursing Knowledge on Healthcare Informatics,* Gerdin, U., Tallberg, M., and Wainwright, P., Eds. p. 562. Amsterdam: IOS Press.

# Section VIII
# Telemedicine and the Internet

# Chapter 29
# Telemedicine

*Gary C. Doolittle*
*David Cook*

The last three decades have witnessed remarkable changes in medicine. Not only have we seen advances in the field, but we have also observed an evolution (some might say revolution) in the way healthcare services are delivered and received. We are challenged to make high-quality healthcare available to all, regardless of geographic, social, and economic barriers. While there may be an adequate number of physicians in this country, there is a maldistribution of providers, with most located in urban areas. Rural areas struggle to keep primary care providers, and subspecialty care is an even greater challenge; rural communities lack the patient base and financial resources to support specialty care. It is ironic that economic barriers to medical care exist in a country that spends 13 percent of its gross national product on healthcare.[1] We strive to control healthcare costs, searching for ways to improve efficiency yet provide state-of-the-art care. Recent advances in telecommunications and information technology create opportunities to address these geographic and economic barriers to healthcare. Telemedicine provides an innovative approach to address challenges with promises of improving quality and access to healthcare, at the same time reducing costs.

Telemedicine is defined as the use of electronic information and communications technologies to provide and support healthcare when distance separates participants.[2] This may include diagnosis and treatment, or education of health providers. The goal is to move information, not people. While many consider interactive video (patient evaluations conducted by physicians at a distance) to be telemedicine, a broad definition may include the use of a telephone, fax, and computers. All providers have practiced as telemedicalists when using the telephone for brief consultation. Facsimile machines, when used to transfer medical records and reports, have become essential for the practice of medicine. More recently, computers have been used to send and deliver information concerning patient care.

The concept of telemedicine is not new. In the late 1950s, the first telepsychiatry practice was established.[3] Two-way interactive television was used to conduct group therapy consultations. In 1964, under the direction

0-8493-1498-4/03/$0.00+$1.50
© 2003 by CRC Press LLC

of Dr. Cecil Wittson, a telemedicine link between the University of Nebraska and the Norfolk State Hospital allowed speech therapy, neurological examination, and evaluation of difficult psychiatric cases. At the same time a radiologist from Montreal, Albert Jutra, reported diagnostic consultation of fluoroscopic images transmitted via coaxial cable.[4] During the 1970s and 1980s, there were 15 telemedicine sites receiving federal funding.[5] One early telemedicine project connected physicians from the Massachusetts General Hospital with nurse clinicians at Logan Airport in Boston.[6] The Space Technology Applied to Rural Papago Advanced Health Care (STARPAHC) project linked the Papago Indian Reservation in Arizona and the Massachusetts General Hospital's clinic at Logan Airport in Boston. The project utilized satellite-based communication to study telemedicine in the context of providing care to astronauts and those on the Papago Indian Reservation in Arizona.[7] While these early projects proved the feasibility of telemedicine, most were terminated when external funding ran out. The expense of equipment and telecommunications line charges was far too costly to make telemedicine practice commonplace.

During the late 1980s, significant advances in technology paved the way for the next wave of telemedicine programs of the 1990s. A shift to digital communication technologies occurred at the same time computers became affordable for personal use. Compression technologies allowed interactive video sessions to be conducted using lower bandwidth, thus reducing transmission costs. In the past decade, both hardware expenses and transmission costs decreased markedly, making telemedicine a reasonable endeavor for some applications.[8]

Telemedicine as a method of healthcare delivery is growing. In 1993, there were ten active programs in North America.[9] By the end of 1997, a survey from the Association of Telemedicine Service Providers reported that there were over 140 active programs in 46 states. Of these programs, two thirds were less than four years old, with only seven of the active programs in existence for more than six years. Clearly, the field is expanding, as evidenced by an increase in the number of consults performed using both interactive video and "store-and-forward" formats.[10]

## TELEMEDICINE TECHNOLOGY

In order to understand the delivery of telemedicine services, one must have a basic knowledge of telecommunications systems and the technology used. A general overview of telemedicine systems should include a discussion of telecommunication terminology, bandwidth options, telemedicine units, and peripheral devices used to enable electronic clinical consultative services. With the exception of peripheral devices, most of the systems used in telemedicine practice have been adapted from standard videoconferencing equipment.

## Telecommunication Terminology

For the average individual involved in healthcare, the telecommunications world is foreign. Terms such as analog, digital, and bandwidth are bantered about, which may serve only to confuse. While in the day-to-day practice of telemedicine an indepth understanding of the technology is not necessary, most clinicians will be interested and will want to understand the basics. While it is beyond the scope of this chapter to provide a detailed explanation of telecommunication terminology, it is useful to have a general understanding of the following terms.

**Digital and Analog.** Information is transmitted over telephone lines in either *analog* or *digital* signals. Analog signals move down phone lines as electromagnetic waves. With the invention of the telephone, calls were transmitted in an analog form. While this worked well for voice messages, this format is too inefficient for large volumes of information. Today, analog services are used mainly by residential customers (the so-called POTS — plain old telephone services). Gradually, much of the telephone network has evolved to a digital signal format. Digital signals are transmitted in the form of bits, as opposed to waves. This allows higher speed transmission, as digital signals are less complex to transmit. Using digital services, transmission quality is superior and there are fewer errors.

**CODEC.** The CODEC, or coder/decoder, refers to hardware and software used with interactive audio and video systems that convert an analog signal to digital and then compresses it so that lower bandwidth telecommunication lines can be used. The signal is decompressed and converted back to analog output by a compatible CODEC at the receiving end.

**Bandwidth Options.** It's all about bandwidth (see Exhibit 1). Bandwidth requirements for the practice of telemedicine may vary among the different medical disciplines, and for this reason providers will need to know the basic terminology. Bandwidth refers to the amount of information-carrying capacity of a given telecommunications connection. With a higher (or wider) bandwidth, a greater amount of information may be sent.

Bandwidth is typically described as narrow or wide. The term *narrowband* refers to slow-speed transmission, with *wideband* referring to higher speed services. Intuitively, higher bandwidth connections will provide superior audio and visual transmission (voice and picture clarity) when compared with lower bandwidth options. When starting a telemedicine practice, it is essential to include clinicians, both consulting and referring providers, in the choice of bandwidth. It is reasonable to set up a demonstration showing differences in audio and video quality at varying bandwidths. Encourage participants to keep an open mind. While most will want the higher bandwidth option, as providers are used to broadcast-quality

**Exhibit 1. A Teleconferencing Station**

video, in our experience the majority of clinical applications will require a transmission rate of no more than 384 kbps.

## Telemedicine Units

Typically, telemedicine units are described as room-based, desktop, POTS, or Web-based (see Exhibit 2). The choice of unit will depend upon the particular application. In order to assure program success, it is essential to choose a unit that fits specific needs. All too often, telemedicine project co-ordinators become enthralled with the equipment, purchasing more than is actually necessary, only to find the equipment sits idle. Room-based systems are versatile, allowing both patient evaluations as well as meetings for ad-ministrative or educational purposes. Most of these systems transmit audio and video data using fractional T1 lines, multiplexed ISDN, or ATM. The 384-kbps bandwidth provides reasonable motion handling for most clinical uses, although the precise bandwidth necessary for a particular application will vary, dependent upon the discipline and provider preference. Desktop units are PC-based and designed to transmit digitized images and data over ISDN lines. Information typically is transmitted at a rate of 128 kbps, but depen-dent upon the need may be as high as 384 kbps. POTS systems transmit via videophones, using set-top boxes that contain a camera, microphone, and CODEC, coupled with a television or personal computer. These systems run over analog phone lines, making them ideal for home-based telemedicine

- Rural Hospitals
- Community Mental Health Centers
- Jail
- Systems
- Home Health Care
- Hospice Care
- Schools

**Exhibit 2. Telemedicine Contexts**

services. Many feel the Web will emerge as the primary medicine linking patients with healthcare professionals. Now, television-quality videoconferencing is even possible over the Internet.[11]

### Peripheral Devices

For telemedicine purposes, peripheral devices may be attached to video systems, allowing the capture of information to enhance the medical evaluation. For example, an electronic stethoscope allows for auscultation of heart and breath sounds electronically. Additional peripheral devices commonly used in telemedicine practice include handheld video cameras, endoscopes, ultrasound machines, blood pressure and pulse monitors, and document stands (for the transmission of x-rays, electrocardiographs, and laboratory data online). Again, only purchase the peripherals that are necessary for the specific practice. For example, for state-of-the-art teleoncology care, peripherals commonly used include a stethoscope and document stand.[11]

### ORGANIZATIONAL ISSUES

While the enticement of new and innovative technologies often attract interest in telemedicine, a number of critical organizational strategies put these services into motion. Importantly, strategies are typically a function of situational constraints, suggesting that particular programs and even particular services within a program may be driven by distinct factors. Success is often measured by the ability of a program to balance these organizational issues. Telemedicine is a unique form of healthcare delivery that sometimes serves to bridge separate medical systems. As a result, organizational structure may extend beyond one system, causing confusion and ambiguity concerning leadership and responsibilities of the participants. For this reason, it is essential from the outset to define the mission, delineate the responsibilities of the participants, and clarify the leadership and decision-making roles for the project.[12]

### Determining a Mission

The challenge to define telemedicine creates opportunity as well as confusion for practitioners. On a basic level, "medicine at a distance" extends an encompassing definition that serves a variety of technologies and services. At the same time, it tends to undermine the efforts that utilize unique and innovative technologies to alter the face of the way healthcare may be delivered. Conference presenters frequently begin discussions of the telephone as a form of telemedicine, prior to moving toward more advanced technologies. In one sense, this discussion is useful in that it shows the technological progression of society in general; however, it also confuses the issue. Organizational mission must address the difficult task of grounding programmatic goals with technological services. This definition may distinguish solidarity or establish ties with other endeavors. Failure in this respect is typified by efforts that attempt to build a mission around one particular service, or formulate a mission that is so broad it loses its focus and appeal.

The decision-making process that leads to determining a program's mission as well as the mission itself must be flexible enough to meet the dynamic nature of the industry. Technological advances continue to discover solutions that did not exist in the recent past. One of the most significant issues to consider relates to the services provided. Does "telemedicine" encompass clinical consults, or does it include education and administrative services? Are schools and disciplines beyond medicine, such as nursing and allied health departments, to be included? For example, the term "telehealth" is frequently being used today to extend a more inclusive and perhaps more accurate label for program initiatives. Telemedicine programs are further measured by their ability to achieve certain objectives. Often these involve the ability to increase access, decrease cost, or improve quality of care. Sustainability is another practical measuring stick. Importantly, organizational mission must link services to desirable and designated outcomes. In addition, a formal ongoing evaluation process will provide feedback to all participants that will serve as a barometer for success, while providing information that will improve the service.

## Taking a Ground-Up Approach

The allure of technology has a way of overshadowing the significance of communication and "people" in program development. Unfortunately, this lesson is typically proven after the fact, as expensive technologies collect dust and practitioners struggle to find users for the system. Technology should be viewed as a mechanism in this process, but not a driving force in decision making. Instead, practitioners should begin by targeting services that already exist, rather than assuming the technology will change traditional work and referral patterns. A key to this strategy is to identify existing relationships that may be benefited when augmented by telemedicine. This "ground-up" approach will be the critical component that either makes or breaks a project.[13]

Given the premise that program success is dependent upon the referring relationship, endeavors must further recognize the salience of the distant physician or nurse as the gatekeeper in the delivery model. Intuitively, if the referring doctor feels comfortable with the consultant physician, the referrals will continue. In addition, a nurse may serve as the on-site practitioner during a telemedicine consult, as the referring physician may be tied to a busy practice.[14] Alternatively, the nurse may be the practitioner who refers to telemedicine.[15] If the nurse feels comfortable with the physician and the technology, and supported by the program, success is enhanced. Two important points explain the critical role of the presenting practitioner. First, the provider becomes the "hands" of the consultant physician. The implications of this added responsibility may or may not be welcomed. Second, the practitioner becomes the "champion" of the project. If the local (referring) provider does not support the service, no amount of prodding will enable success.

## Centralizing Services

In one sense, the idea of centralizing a service whose intention is to transcend geographic boundaries into the "virtual" community sounds counterintuitive. However, from an operational standpoint, telemedicine programs must assess the degree to which control is centrally managed.[13] Impressions by end users will significantly affect the success or failure of new innovations. In the telemedicine world, this window of opportunity is narrowed when practitioners attempt to "reinvent the wheel" for each new application. Telemedicine programmers should strategically position themselves as experts in deploying and sustaining telemedicine operations. Centralized services further position programs to champion projects to move forward. This is especially important when projects are enmeshed in bureaucratic systems that encourage entropy rather than success. Typically, this will demand the need to have a dedicated scheduler and technician to service operations. Scheduling events can be an outlandish task as appointments may balance physicians' and patients' time

411

along with telemedicine rooms that often serve many groups. What may be a scheduling nightmare internally, is simplified for end users when a centralized scheduler assumes the responsibility to ensure that a consult or event occurs. Having technicians who are dedicated to providing services proactively and on an as-needed basis supports the credibility and expertise of the telemedicine program. In addition, it will allow practitioners to take an active role in diffusing problems as they occur. Technicians from other departments or outside organizations may not share the same dedication to ensure program success.

## Marketing Services

Innovative approaches to healthcare delivery frequently face skepticism and even criticism by many in the healthcare industry. This fact is compounded as the "hype" of telemedicine often overshadows the practical benefits of a particular service. Negative attitudes are enhanced when publicity documents the "novelty" of services without regard to bottom-line expense. Practitioners face the difficult challenge of informing providers, patients, and communities, while maintaining a level of sensibility about the strengths and limitations of services. These efforts must be made based on the premise that telemedicine is an effective alternative when face-to-face consultations, for various reasons, are not readily available.

Marketing telemedicine services typically involves two avenues. First, there is an introductory message that informs entities about telemedicine. This is an ongoing process that should be repeated to target populations to continuously initiate and reinforce perceptions. Frequently, several communications will occur with a physician or patient, simply to arouse interest in what may be a novel concept. Second, energy should be expended in defining what telemedicine is and what telemedicine is not. A significant element of this will involve identifying the limitations of present technologies and their appropriate applicability. Again, the message should reinforce that telemedicine is a useful tool to augment traditional services, not replace them. The majority of telemedicine programs underestimate the importance of marketing in diffusing the application and utility of services. Furthermore, even when the significance of marketing is understood, practitioners tend to underestimate the level of resources that are needed to effectively promote and sell services.[16]

## Costs

It appears that we have a national preoccupation with the escalation of medical care expenses. Obviously the emergence of costly diagnostic and therapeutic interventions contributes to the runaway health costs in the United States. While more sophisticated advances in technology within the health field have improved our ability to treat, this has come at a high price. The search for ways to contain costs is ongoing. The reintroduction of telemedicine in the early 1990s came at the same time the concept of "managed competition" was introduced. As such, telemedicine has been studied with special attention to issues of cost. To date there are very few studies tracking expenses related to telemedicine.[17] Many are hopeful that using telemedicine may be used to contain costs. For example, home-based units may be placed to ease the transition from an acute care facility to the home. This will allow a decrease in the length of hospital stay without compromising quality of care.[18] There are a number of ways to assess the "cost-effectiveness" of telemedicine services.

Depending on the questions being asked, practitioners may inquire about the expense of technologies, delivery costs, patient expenses, societal savings, and reimbursement issues. (Importantly, reimbursement issues are outlined in the next section.) Cost studies are typically equated with financial expenditures; however, comprehensive inquiry is rarely attempted, perhaps in part because confounding variables confuse the relationship between outcomes and intervention.

**Technology Costs.** Not surprisingly, the cost of telemedicine technologies is decreasing every day. Some of the most significant declines may be found with new peripheral devices that only recently have entered the market. Arguably, despite significant developments, cost continues to be a barrier for many small hospitals in rural areas that are the very populations telemedicine promises to serve. A review of activities in Kansas helps explain these trends. When a statewide T1 infrastructure was developed in the late 1980s, dual monitor room-based systems connecting at 384 kbps cost roughly $115,000. Today, similar technologies may be purchased in the $25,000–35,000 range. To date, line charges on this network are $31.50 per hour. However, costs are expected to triple and possibly quadruple in the next year. These increases will have a significant impact on the ability of small hospitals to utilize this network. The desktop industry seems to show great promise to reduce the cost of telemedicine delivery. In a recent school-based project at the University of Kansas, one telemedicine unit cost close to $20,000 . This included a videoconferencing camera and software, a personal computer, video otoscope, analog stethoscope, and a dedicated fax machine. One year later, this same system with upgrades cost about $3000 less.

**Delivery Costs.** Assessing costs of the applications of telemedicine technologies are "central concerns of decision makers."[2] More work is being done to assess the costs of telemedicine; however, at present, much of the reported work is highly speculative and mixed concerning the ability of telemedicine to lower healthcare costs. For example, telemedicine is praised for its perceived ability to increase savings; however, definitive evidence supporting "cost-effectiveness is meager."[19] Specifically, research

413

has found telemedicine consults may be more expensive, depending upon medical application;[20] however, as Taylor explains, "one difficulty with these kinds of studies is that there may be areas where there is a genuine problem and where telemedicine is a feasible solution, but where it is not the most cost-effective solution."[21] Consequently, further research is needed assessing the ability of telemedicine to decrease costs, specifically when cost reduction is a goal of the intervention.

**Societal Costs.** Perhaps the most challenging variable to measure are the savings telemedicine services have at the community level. For example, to what extent can practitioners state with certainty that a program solidified the recruitment of a new physician or the retention of a current healthcare provider? What is the impact on the rural economy when a patient is able to stay in the community receiving services via telemedicine? What is the impact on rural communities that have access to specialists with telemedicine who would have taken a seven- or ten-hour car trip in the past? There may not be cost savings in these instances, because patients may not have had the time or resources to access care without telemedicine. Unfortunately, little research investigates the effectiveness of telemedicine at this broad level. In addition, an economic analysis of telemedicine on this level must assess care via telemedicine compared with the most reasonable alternative (i.e., the patient travels for care). While very important, these studies are difficult to carry out at best, and are years away from completion as even busy telemedicine practices do not have an adequate patient base required for these investigations.

## LEGALITY AND LIABILITY ISSUES

The state of telemedicine today is similar to many cutting-edge technologies where legal and liability issues are struggling to keep up with innovative and changing application of services. Generally, no one is an authority on telemedicine law because so few cases have been tried. At the same time, the groundwork is being laid by many in the industry to prepare providers for the "worst-case" scenario. The truth of the matter is, the answers to many legal questions concerning telemedicine are highly dependent upon who is answering the question, rather than legal precedent. Given this state, a mix of experience and speculation suggests that several issues should be privileged when designing a program.

### Informed Consent

Designing procedures for patient consent is a necessary step in program development.[23] Protocols should begin by referencing specific state statutes regarding informed consent. Next, institutional requirements need to be addressed. Importantly, final forms should be approved by legal counsel from all representative parties. Several key issues should be addressed in this process. First, informed consent should be obtained prior to consultation; however, because many programs have an emergency focus, circumstances do not always allow for this to occur. Programs must consider alternative procedures under such circumstances. Second, programmers must consider who should secure consent. This is complicated when children are the primary population base for particular services.[15] This situation warrants proactive efforts by participants to obtain parental consent. Still, programmers should consider procedures that either encourage or demand that parents be present during consultation. Third, informed consent should be obtained in verbal and written form if possible. Written forms in particular document that permission has been given. Finally, forms should be multilingual. This is increasingly important as telemedicine is serving underserved communities with significant non-English speaking populations.

## Privacy/Confidentiality

A second concern for programmers is the privacy and confidentiality of patients, clearly a challenge for the information age.[24] During a "virtual" consultation, traditional boundaries may be superseded or even eliminated. Practitioners are challenged to address these concerns for the benefit of clinicians and patients. Technological media will significantly affect the strategies used. For example, services across dedicated networks will have an increased component of security, while Internet or Web-based protocols inevitably reduce certainty. Programmers must question whether adequate precautions have been addressed in addressing concerns. For example, will materials be faxed to a confidential location? Are rooms geographically isolated? Where are medical records being stored? How are medical records being transferred? How do procedures comply with state policies and procedures? Importantly, practitioners should measure these issues in relation to how traditional services are provided. If telemedicine compromises the privacy or confidentiality of involved parties, services should not be provided.

## Licensure

The debate on licensure continues regarding the scope and definition of what constitutes "practice." Generally speaking, more questions surface than answers in regard to this issue. When a clinician in Kansas visits with a patient in Texas, in which state does the consult occur? In this event, does the clinician need to be licensed in both states? If legal matters were to ensue, in which state would they be filed? Some answers may be found in state statutes regarding the frequency of consults or the requirements for given disciplines in relation to licensure. However, the fact remains that licensure issues may be one of the cloudiest legal questions. Today the state-based licensure system in the United States discourages interstate practice of telemedicine where the physician is located in one state and the patient in another.[24] Yet, despite this, the application of telemedicine to transcend state and international boundaries continues to increase.

## Malpractice

Similar to licensure issues, speculation drives discussion relating to malpractice concerns with telemedicine applications. Some providers are concerned that telemedicine practice may increase the risk of liability. If the system fails during use, an adverse patient outcome is possible. In addition, some fear inferior diagnostic accuracy, as telemedicine does not allow hands-on examination, increasing exposure to malpractice litigation. Alternatively, it is possible that telemedicine may actually increase the standard of care for a community, making the practitioner liable for failure to use it.[25]

## REIMBURSEMENT

The first two states to pass legislation eliminating reimbursement barriers were Oklahoma and California.[21] In the past two years, however, reimbursement issues continue to cause problems for many programs. For example, a recent survey of telemedicine practitioners found reimbursement is perceived as the greatest barrier to program sustainability.[22] Blue Cross/Blue Shield of Kansas has considerable flexibility when considering payment and, in fact, was one of the first in the nation to compensate teleconsultations. In contrast, Medicare cites multiple concerns, including costs, acceptance, and quality of care, obstructing reimbursement practices. A central concern by nonadvocates is that teleconsults will increase overall costs by providing care to those whom otherwise would not travel for the services. Fortunately for teleproviders, the Balanced Budget Act of 1997 has a provision requiring Medicare reimbursement for telehealth services for rural Health Professional Shortage Areas that began in January of 1999.

Despite the challenge of reimbursement, programs can be successful if they are willing to make efforts to find alternative funding sources. In the managed care model, a fixed reimbursement is provided in exchange for medical services. In this system, care delivered via telemedicine is covered. An example of the "managed care" model would be the KUMC telehospice project in which home-based telemedicine units are used to conduct nursing and social work visits for end-of-life care. In this setting, hospice care, as covered by the Medicare Hospice Benefit, is capitated. The costs of the home telehospice units are rolled into day-to-day operational expenses.[26] Identifying "contracts for services" is another way to assure compensation for telemedical consults. The best example of this model occurs within the prison telemedicine projects. Contracts between teleproviders and correctional facilities assure that inmates will be cared for, at the same time obviating the need for travel away from the prison. A "win-win" situation is created in which the providers are compensated for their professional services while the prison saves travel expenses. Clearly, there are innovative ways to obtain reimbursement for telemedicine care. When considering professional reimbursement for teleconsultation services, we must learn to look outside of the fee-for-service box!

## TELEMEDICINE APPLICATIONS

In a sense, the application of telemedicine may be measured by the experiences of practitioners and providers. Indeed, this section outlines such endeavors, explaining the "possibility" of telemedicine applications based on the success of others. However, in another sense, this approach is inherently flawed. Program development that measures application by balancing technology and clinical or educational disciplines excludes the most significant variable in predicting program success — the people supporting the service. Having made this distinction, this section extends an overview of common telemedicine clinical and educational applications.

### Clinical Applications

An interesting footnote to discussions on clinical applications is to recognize that the most active programs in the country are situated in correctional facilities.[27] There was considerable interest among prison systems, as providing medical care necessitated expensive travel from the correctional to the medical facility. While there was strong economic incentive, there was also the issue of security. Clearly, there is less escape risk if prison inmates receive medical care via telemedicine.

Early on, clinical activity involving telemedicine included interactive video to allow patient evaluation and management. Recently there has been an increase in "store-and-forward" clinical consults in which information is collected and recorded and sent to a consultant for review at a later time. This has the advantage of providing a service that does not require the rather cumbersome task of scheduling all participants for a given time, with the obvious disadvantage of lost direct patient–physician interaction. Whether there will be general acceptance among patients and providers for store-and-forward consultation services remains to be seen.

Many telemedicine projects attempt to link rural patients and their primary care practitioners with specialists from urban tertiary care centers. Consultants provide the expertise working closely with the primary care provider in an effort to provide care in the rural setting. It is important to remember that the "medicine" is practiced in the rural setting with consultant oversight. This assumes that the rural provider is willing to take on a greater level of responsibility for specialty care than was the case previously. The system may be used for "one-time" second opinions or for ongoing patient management. In addition urban applications for telemedicine are surfacing. For example, home-based telemedicine projects are on the rise in an effort to cut expenses of home care and ease the transition from the inpatient to outpatient setting.

Telemedicine may be applied to virtually all areas of medicine. Clinical fields that are image based, such as radiology and pathology, lend themselves to telemedicine. For these disciplines, the value added from such a service may be measured considering timeliness of the service or access to clinicians. For example, a teleradiology project that provides connectivity for after-hours reading of x-rays is invaluable to a primary care provider in a small rural community. By extension, if a rural community does not have on-site radiology evaluations, teleradiology is a tremendous service. Further, for telepathology to truly add value, the timeliness of the reading of pathology slides is critical. If the service is designed to provide frozen section evaluations (reading of pathology specimens at the time of surgery), the standard of care for a rural community could actually improve. If the turn-around time for such a read is 48 hours, then there is no real advantage over sending the slides by overnight mail.

The most active areas in telemedicine to date include telepsychiatry, telecardiology (including tele-echocardiography), and teledermatology.[10] It is not surprising that psychiatry would lead the list of telemedicine applications, as it is largely a cognitive discipline, relying primarily on the patient history for assessment, with much less emphasis on the physical examination. Efficacy data are lacking, although early reports suggest that telepsychiatric outcomes are similar to those in traditional psychiatric practice.[28] Teledermatology is another application that is quite common. There is considerable debate as to whether interactive video consults are superior to store-and-forward evaluations. A randomized study has yet to be conducted. A partnership between the consultant and referring physician is key to the success of a teledermatology practice.[29] Primary care providers must be skilled in basic dermatological procedures, including biopsy techniques. Efficacy studies are ongoing, but initial reports are encouraging.[30]

## Educational Applications

The focus of programming and the technologies utilized inform insight into how telemedicine is serving educational applications. The actual topics that may be discussed are far-reaching. Program focus tends to highlight several populations. Educational courses may be designed for semester-long courses or short courses that discuss a particular topic or issue. In these instances, classes may be part of an academic curriculum. Other programs may target continuing education for medical, nursing, and allied health disciplines. These courses tend to serve anywhere from one- to five-hour credits. Focus may also involve patient and community education highlighting a variety of topics. The technologies used to educate are also quite diverse and generally transcend any topic or focal area. Interactive video at varying bandwidths may service dedicated parties and multi-point connections. Web-based technologies also provide a variety of options in delivery of educational events. In some instances, Web technology is being used as an interactive medium; however, in most cases, delivery subsumes asynchronous qualities. Modules augmented with discussion questions are frequently used to measure student activity and comprehension. Yet another approach, often overlooked by mainstream literature, is the use of the telephone conference as a medium to disseminate information. Of course, this approach does not involve a video component.

## References

1. Sulmasy D. 1995. "Managed care and managed death," *Archives of Internal Medicine* 155: 133–136.
2. Field, M. J. 1996. *Telemedicine: A Guide to Assessing Telecommunications in Health Care.* Washington, D.C.: National Academy Press.
3. Wittson, C. L., Affleck, D. C., and Johnson, V. 1961. "Two-way television in group therapy," *Mental Hospitals* 2: 22–23.
4. Jutra, A. 1959. "Teleroentgen diagnosis by means of videotape recording," *American Journal of Roentgenology* 82: 1099–1102.
5. Preston, J., Brown, F. W., and Hartley, B., "Using telemedicine to improve healthcare in distant areas," *Hospital and Community Psychiatry* 2: 25–32.
6. Bird, K. Y. 1972. "Cardiopulmonary frontiers: quality health care via interactive television," *Chest* 61: 204–205.
7. Perednia, D. A. and Allen, A. 1995. "Telemedicine technology and clinical applications," *JAMA* 273: 483–488.
8. Doolittle, G., Zaylor, C., Williams, A. et al. 1997. "Tracking and comparing costs associated with two telemedicine practices: oncology and psychiatry," *Telemedicine Journal* 3: 98.
9. Allen, A. 1994. "The top ten North American programs," *The Telemedicine Newsletter* 1: 3–4.
10. Grigsby, B. and Brown, N. 1998. Report on US Telemedicine Activity. Portland, OR Association of Telemedicine Service Providers.
11. Doolittle, G. C., Allen, A., Wittman, C. et al. 1996. "Oncology care for rural Kansans via telemedicine: establishment of a teleoncology clinic," *Proceedings of the American Society of Clinical Oncology* 15: 326.
12. Whitten, P. and Allen, A. 1995. "Analysis of telemedicine from an organizational perspective," *Telemedicine Journal* 1: 203–213.
13. Yellowlees, P. 1997. "Successful development of telemedicine systems — seven core principles," *Journal of Telemedicine and Telecare* 3: 215–226.
14. Doolittle, G. and Allen, A. 1997. "Practicing oncology via telemedicine," *Journal of Telemedicine and Telecare* 3: 63–70.
15. Whitten, P., Cook, D., Shaw, P. et al. 1999. "TeleKidcare: bringing health care into schools," *Telemedicine Journal* 4: 335–343.
16. Doolittle, G. C. and Cook, D. 1989. "Deciding on the Need for a Telemedicine Service," *Introduction to Telemedicine,* Wooton, R. and Craig, J., (Eds.), Belfast, U.K. The Royal Society of Medicine Press.
17. Allen, A. 1998. "A review of cost effectiveness research," *Telemedicine Today* 6: 10–15.
18. Goldberg, A. 1997. "Tele-home healthcare on call: trends leading to the return of the house call," *Telemedicine Today* 5: 15.

19. Doolittle, G. C., Williams, A., Harmon, A. et al. 1998. "A cost measurement study for a tele-oncology practice," *Journal of Telemedicine and Telecare* 4: 84–88.
20. Taylor, P. 1998. "A survey of research in telemedicine. I. Telemedicine systems," *Journal of Telemedicine and Telecare* 4: 1–17.
21. Lapolla, M. and Millis, B. 1997. "Is telemedicine reimbursement a real barrier or a convenient straw man?" *Telemedicine Today* 5: 32.
22. Grigsby, B. and Allen, A. 1998. "Fourth Annual Telemedicine Program Review," *Telemedicine Today* 5: 38.
23. Burton, D. and Huston, J. 1998. "Use of video in the informed consent process," *Journal of Telemedicine and Telecare* 4: 38–40.
24. Sanders, J and Bashshur, R. 1995. "Challenges to the implementation of telemedicine," *Telemedicine Journal* 1: 115–123.
25. Grigsby, J. and Sanders, J. 1998. "Telemedicine: where it is and where it is going," *Annals of Internal Medicine* 129: 123–127.
26. Doolittle, G. C., Yaezel, A., Otto, F., and Clemens, C. 1998. "Hospice care using home-based telemedicine systems," *Journal of Telemedicine and Telecare* 4: 58–59.
27. Allen, A. and Wheeler, T. 1998. "The leaders: US programs doing more than 500 interactive consults in 1997," *Telemedicine Today* 6: 36–38.
28. Zaylor, C. 1999. "Clinical outcomes in telepsychiatry," *Journal of Telemedicine and Telecare* 5: 29–33.
29. Burdick, A. and Berman, B. 1997. "Teledermatology." in *Telemedicine Theory and Practice,* Bashshur, Sanders, and Shannon, Eds. P. 225. Springfield, IL: Charles C. Thomas Publisher.
30. Loane, M., Gore, H., Bloomer, S. et al. 1998. "Preliminary results from the Northern Ireland arms of the UK Multicentre Teledermatology Trial: is clinical management by realtime teledermatology possible?" *Journal of Telemedicine and Telecare* 4: 3–5

# Chapter 30
# Netting Web Customers

*Stewart S. Miller*

The Web has grown a great deal over the past few years. It once was a medium that could deliver text and images neatly on your computer about various types of information. However, it has grown to be a much more multimedia environment that can offer a great deal of potential for business communication and offer an environment much like that of an interactive television.

The Web is a useful medium that offers full-motion video and enhanced audio capabilities. In fact, the advent of RealAudio and RealVideo has provided a new definition for the Web. The Web can provide media that is highly imitative of a multimedia environment that integrates audio and video with a degree of information that is unparalleled in normal television. You can use this interactive environment to browse a video clip on demand and enhance your online experience with supplemental information. You can retrieve supplemental information about a newscast or business presentation, then return effortlessly to your Web page.

It is important to note that a Web site that employs a multimedia background can draw a great deal more traffic because its rich content takes the HTML content from a list of information, and turns it into a graphical presentation that makes exploring the content an adventure instead of a chore.

There is a drawback, however, to rich sites with a great deal of multimedia content. When sites employ plug-ins that allow you to experience multimedia (i.e., Shockwave-enhanced Web pages), there is the problem of bandwidth. Many people are still downloading Web content at 28.8 kbps. At this rate, it takes minutes to retrieve a standard Web page, and that is just far too long for any user to wait to retrieve his Web content. This is why ISDN, cable, and satellite modems have grown to be so popular with today's Internet users.

0-8493-1498-4/03/$0.00+$1.50
© 2003 by CRC Press LLC

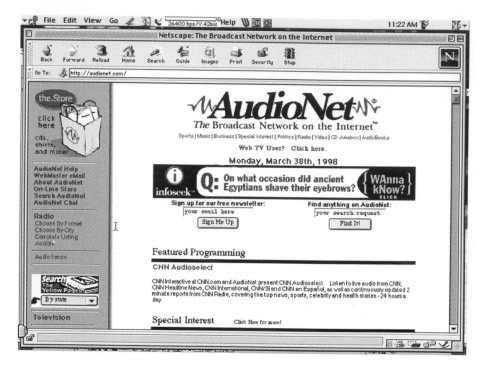

**Exhibit 1. AudioNet Web Site**

## GETTING ATTENTION

A well-placed video clip or audio presentation can significantly increase the interest generated in online content. This is why sites such as http://audionet.com (see Exhibit 1) has met with so much interest. People often miss the radio station from their hometown after they move. However, with Audionet, users have the ability to look up a radio stations from anywhere in the country. This is possible because many radio station simulcast their audio in RealAudio format over the Internet as well as in their home area. This site has an even greater potential by allowing users to listen to live concerts as they are offered in various locations. The nicest part of this Web site is that location is not a factor. You can use the audio capabilities of your computer, sound board, and Internet connection to listen to signals all over the world.

The cost for you to enable your computer to listen to audio transmitted over the Internet has decreased significantly over the past few years. The type of hardware you need is often standard on many new computers. The standard hard drive has increased significantly to accommodate at least 23 gigabytes on a typical desktop computer. More than two thirds of machines in operation are Pentiums (and that number is rising with the decrease in market prices). Sound cards of 16 bits are also standard in many machines, as are integrated microphones.

In addition, once you get really hooked into this environment, you will find that you will also want to expand your multimedia on the Internet with a digital camera hooked up to your computer. The advent of videoconferencing brings the Web into another dimension by allowing for an inexpensive form of communication that links offices from diverse locations around the globe.

You will find that this endeavor requires that you gather better hardware, increased storage space, better-quality microphones and speakers, the ability to record your own multimedia CDs, and you will also need to purchase a computer to act as a server that can broadcast live audio as a streaming audio server.

## CONTROLLING YOUR DIGITAL AUDIO FILE

You will note that your sound card and original source directly affect the quality of your digital audio. You have the power of controlling both the size and quality of your digital audio file simply by altering the properties of your file. These properties include:

*Sampling Rate*: This quality determines the per-second rate (kHz) that the incoming audio signal is sampled (measured) and then converted to digital sample channels. This is best illustrated by the fact than an eight-bit sample records 256 levels of sound, while a 16-bit sample records at 65,536 levels.

A mono recording employs one channel, while a stereo channel needs two. Analogously, a stereo recording is twice the size of a mono recording. However, in all of these events you will note that an increased size of the file indicates a proportional increase in the quality of the recording. This can indicate that the digital audio from a computer consumes disk space at the rate of approximately 10 MB per recorded minute. Therefore, audio that is recorded at a lower quality sounds like an old monaural radio. However, this indicates a far smaller requirement for space at approximately 1 MB per minute.

Now this can have significant effects on your audio requirements. Lower sized files are far easier to work with when editing or mixing audio files. In addition, you will find that you can visit a Web site that has two versions. One is rich with multimedia content; the other is optimized for connections at lower bandwidth. You may have seen such examples with Web sites for high-profile movies. The site is there to promote the new motion picture, but the author realizes that most users will not wait an hour or more to download rich graphics and sounds because the enjoyment is lost on the time it takes to retrieve the multimedia content. Therefore, you may wish to use audio quality that has somewhat less quality, but can be heard in one tenth the time it takes to download its rich equivalent. In this way, the resources of the Web are split between two classes of Internet users — those with and those without a high-speed Internet connection.

It is possible to stream large audio files for hours over the Internet, this is why it is possible to broadcast live audio events such as the case of AudioNet. However, streaming audio is very complex and often needs a dedicated audio server that has a great deal of available bandwidth.

RealNetwork's RealAudio is the most popular company that is working in streaming audio. You will find the company offers two versions of its RealPlayer application that works with your Web browser. One version is for pay, while the other is a free download. You do get benefits from the pay option that allows you to personalize the product with various site information that reflects your needs.

There are several audio-editing packages that have the ability of exporting RealAudio format. In addition, RealNetwork also offers a RealAudio encoder. One of the benefits of this application is that you produce audio that has the same quality as a good FM transmission over a 28.8-kbps connection. Again, the audio quality is proportional to your connection. A faster connection means an even higher quality of audio that allows you to benefit from streaming RealAudio files from a regular Web server. In addition, performance is usually not sufficient for larger files or for numerous people connecting to the same RealAudio server.

The reason for this performance degradation is because RealAudio servers are dedicated and licensed for only a specific number of simultaneous connection streams for either or both audio and video. The server software costs several thousand dollars and often require dedicated T1 connections.

You will find that both RealAudio and RealVideo server and client software are components of both Internet Explorer 4.0 as well as the NetShow multimedia streaming server software.

## COMPRESSION

Compression is a very important tool for any resource or bit of information you find on the Internet. Just as with any connection, users will find the most enjoyment when multimedia content flows much quicker through their connection and into their computer. Furthermore, the Web has also grown to encompass a great deal of FTP capabilities that allow users to download extensive multimedia files from the Internet. Compression can reduce a typical file to about half its size and make downloading less difficult.

Shockwave provides some very useful compression radios that are as high as 176:1. This means that ten seconds of 16-bit audio that is sampled at 22 MHz would measure at 440 kB in the AIFF format. Shockwave audio can compress that same sound as far down to 20 kB without any apparent quality loss. However, TrueSpeech is optimized for exceedingly low bandwidth speech reproduction without the requirement of a dedicated server. In addition, Liquid Audio is finding success with a MusicPlayer that plays songs using Dolby digital audio while it displays the matching album art and lyrics. Liquifier Pro and Liquid MusicServer offer content creation tools, audio streaming, and electronic commerce services.

While the majority of sound cards come bundled with editing tools, you will note that preparing audio for the Internet usually necessitates features present only in sophisticated commercial editing programs. You should try to acquire a program that is able to handle multi-megabyte files, reduce noise, increase recording levels, minimize distortion, and adjust the recorded frequencies of various files. There are also capabilities that allow you to gain the ability to mix multiple files, insert silence or computer-generated tones, reduce or enhance a file to match a specific time period, and apply DSP effects that include echo, reverb, and flange.

## WEB BROWSER DIFFERENCES

Internet Explorer and Netscape Navigator work with round sound playback in different ways. Prior to Internet Explorer version 4 and Navigator, the best method of utilizing cross-browser background sound files on a Web page was to add one line of code for Internet Explorer and one for Netscape Navigator. Each browser played the sound with respect to the tag it recognized, and it then ignored the tag it did not. However, when the Internet Explorer migrated to version 4, it added support for background sound through the EMBED tag. This was problematic because it now included both the BGSOUND and EMBED methods in the HTML; therefore Internet Explorer recognized both tags and played the sound twice. Because the Web browser loads the sounds at different times, the user would hear a clash of the same sound overlapping.

If instead you choose to just use the EMBED method that both browsers support, you end up losing all the Internet Explorer users who do not have the Internet Explorer version 4.0. It seemed as though the best answer was to add a browser detect to your site on either the client or server side that uses some ActiveX and ASP (Active Server Page) programming or JavaScript method. At this point you can create the EMBED or BGSOUND source dynamically with respect to the specific browser that has been detected

## WEB VIDEO

Web video is a growing aspect of multimedia; however, in many ways it is still not appropriate for the majority of users. Downloading a sizable video clip can cost you a great deal of time unless you have a very fast connection. Besides, very few viewers have the patience to wait as long as an hour to receive a video clip that lasts only a minute.

Streaming video offers a solution to the problem by condensing several files through the Internet's limited bandwidth. Much like its audio component, it offers immediate response to a request for multimedia content. The video starts to play the moment you click on a link. Analogous to the audio component, bandwidth is still a very important problem. Competing video formats and disparate playback requirements for each can only act to distort your reception.

It should be pointed out, however, that while Web video is very enticing, it is still very important to work around its restrictions through the continuous evolution of the Internet's bandwidth. Ultimately, the Web will act as a replacement medium for the television. However, that day will only come once the limited bandwidth of the Internet has increased to encompass the amount of traffic needed to accomplish reliable delivery of Web video and other multimedia content.

It is important to make certain that your video adds a great deal of value to your Web browsing. Furthermore, the bandwidth condition is only further illustrated by the fact that streaming Web video must have a very limited frame rate that would make fast action look sloppy. You may find that there is more benefit in downloading simple scenes with a type of slide show format that would allow a given frame for each ten seconds of audio. Otherwise, if you were to have something on the order of several frames per second (to compete with television), you would lose all of the fine details necessary for enjoying the video. You would achieve only a very low-resolution video through a standard modem connection.

In addition, your frame-rate selection is dependent on the type of video you are viewing. Action videos require a faster frame rate, while news clips of announcers are less demanding of a high frame-per-second count. In the majority of cases, a frame count of seven to eight frames per second (fps) is adequate for videos with only moderate action. Additionally, while compression does lower the size of the file, it also reduces the clarity of your video file.

It is possible to include the video file as a download from an HTML page so long as your video is not too large. Video files are saved in one of three formats: AVI, QuickTime, or MPEG. AVI and QuickTime are the most common. However, each of these formats has its own problems. QuickTime videos began on the Macintosh operating system, but will play back on either Macintosh or Windows systems as long as you have installed the correct browser plug-in. Playback support for AVI is a Windows format.

MPEG video format offers excellent clarity that is as good as or better than VHS tapes. It offers the best compression of the three formats listed above. MPEG playback capability is integrated into most newer PCs and Macs. In addition, all of the current versions of both Internet Explorer and

Netscape Navigator, most free MPEG players do not support synchronized MPEG sound. Depending on the encoding or editing software you utilize, QuickTime and AVI files are simpler to build than MPEG files.

There are two primary factors that should dictate your decision in creating digital video for the Web:

1. Frame rate
2. Resolution

Should you wish to reach a broad audience and you do not require quality that is as good as the standard television videos, you need to save your files in the QuickTime format. An average file size is 5 MB per minute of video, while the ideal rate is 10 to 15 fps. In addition, the best resolution is 160 × 120 pixels.

The MPEG target frame rate is comparable to that of television, which measures at 30 fps. This allows you to achieve a resolution of 320 × 240 pixels. However, the files are almost twice the size, measuring at 9 MB per minute of video.

Video streaming resolves the downloading problem by providing nearly instantaneous playback. It functions by using specific algorithms that are used to compress the video file into a proprietary format; after that, it sends the file out in data packets. The only problem with this format is that streaming can actually reduce access time with respect to your entire Web site. Streaming delivers data to users as fast as it can; however, this may require consuming all of your available bandwidth to that end.

## VIDEO STREAMING

Several vendors offer video streaming; the only problem is that each product offers its own video format. The most popular products include:

- RealNetwork's RealVideo (part of RealSystem 5.0)
- VDOnet's VDOLive
- Vivo Software's VivoActive
- Microsoft's VXtreme's Web Theater

RealVideo, VDOLive, and Web Theater function best with a dedicated video server. Conceptually, streaming-video systems can operate on your existing Web server; however, in order for you to take advantage of these products' enhanced functionality, you will need an individual server. VivoActive does not need its own server. Furthermore, this product embeds the video as part of an HTML page in both Netscape and Internet Explorer. Web sites producing streaming video often pay on a per-stream basis.

Real System 5.0 pricing begins at $5995 for 100 video streams using an Internet server, while pricing for 200 streams starts at $11,995. VDOLive 3.0

offers 25 concurrent streams at no charge; however, licenses begin at $2500 and can cost as much as $7500 for unlimited streams. The pricing for Web Theater starts at $1495 for the server and unlimited streams. This product offers the advantage of a dedicated server because of its ability to control packet throughput dynamically. You can also optimize a dedicated server so that you can deliver video instead of having a general-purpose Web server that sends out a variety of file types.

## SCALABILITY

Scalability is a very important factor with the server method because it is simpler to manage the amount of concurrent streams. In this setup, you can add streams as the size of your audience increases. If your site's video files are accessed sporadically with about 100 hits a day, then scalability is not a problem. However, if you are receiving tens of thousands of daily Web hits, scalability is crucial to the effective distribution of your Web resources. Vivo's serverless approach means you will not need to pay a great deal of money for more expensive hardware. In addition, it does not function on a per-stream basis; this allows you to avoid extraneous costs too. It does have the potential to deliver information to as many users as your Web server's bandwidth permits.

Vivo is also very simple to use because it includes video and some simple code in your HTML pages. However, you do not have a great deal of control over the transmission process through the Internet, and your scalability options are somewhat limited. If you have a good ISP, you can deploy Vivo streaming video from a Web site on the ISP server. However, the ISP must terminate access to your site if it consumes too much bandwidth. Video delivery is good for very large images; however, videos with some degree of motion can prove less than perfect.

Each of these video products required the installation of a browser plug-in. Different products offer different capabilities that allow you to zoom the picture to a larger, but less focused size. Since each streaming-video vendor uses a proprietary format, it is hard to decide the best one. However, if a dedicated video server is not an option, Vivo is the economical choice. For improving control and scalability, it is therefore important to save up for a video server, server management software, and per-stream charges.

## TRENDS

Because Web video is still somewhat new, today's format could be lost to another version. Should you change video-delivery systems, you will still be able to use your server. The next trend is to watch how video takes over for static graphics and animated GIFs. The Web is evolving to take advantage of algorithms for compressing the video and increase the speed at which multimedia is delivered. The Internet is growing to use the Web as the preferred medium for multimedia distribution.

## WEB INTERFACE

As much as this chapter has focused on the evolution of the Web into a medium that will ultimately replace television for multimedia distribution, we should also point out how it has evolved recently to take advantage of many different mediums that are common to many people.

The Web became the marketing tool of the 1990s. It offers you the ability to replace ordering through the telephone. The Web gives customers an interactive catalog that can be used to instantly view products of interest. In addition, encryption technology has evolved to the point where consumers are starting to gain confidence in ordering products on the Web.

In addition, money matters are now commonplace on the Web. One of the factors that has made ATMs so popular is that they are open 24 hours a day. What a terrific marketing tool the Web is — it offers a 24-hour interactive ability for customers to order products, view financial statements, pay bills, buy or sell stocks, or anything else involving credit card transactions.

## EVOLVING INTERFACE

At one point in time it was necessary to have separate applications for e-mail, FTP, Gopher, Archie, viewing Usenet newsgroups, and browsing the Web. However, all of these features have combined into the latest incarnations of both the Netscape Navigator and Internet Explorer browsers. People just use their Web browser to download files, search for news, find programs of interest, or even read newsgroups right through the hierarchy of their browser.

Mail is an important mode of communication; and while most browsers offer an integrated mail program, it is often difficult for users to access their e-mail from co-workers' computers. Instead of having to type in your settings and going through a great deal of aggravation to access e-mail, some companies offer Web sites that have e-mail capabilities right through the Web browser.

The idea is very sound because you need only call up a Web page to access your e-mail and respond to it right online. This is very useful when you travel or if you are working on different computers all the time. This gives you a certain level of freedom that was not possible before.

## WEBTV

Because this discussion is about all of the powerful resources that the Web offers, it is important to point out a product that has evolved quite a bit over the past several years. The concept of a small black box that could

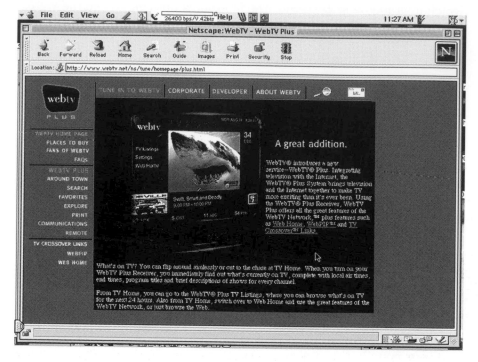

**Exhibit 2. WebTV Web Site**

turn your television into a Web browser (see Exhibit 2) was introduced into the market just as the Web became the predominant mode of communication for the large majority of people who use the Internet.

It originally was intended for people who did not want the complexity of learning a computer, but the product has evolved past that stage. Its latest incarnation is WebTV Plus that integrates features of television into that of the Web. Users can build the bridge from the television channel to its associated Web site. In addition, you will also note it has the capability of using wireless transmissions to gather news and information even when the unit is offline.

The system offers decent speed and functionality, but is restrictive because you cannot deal with attachments to e-mail. However, for all Web browsing activities, it is ideal. In fact, that may be the primary reason why WebTV is so useful. Because users cannot deal with downloads or e-mail attachments, the bandwidth is relatively uncongested from the WebTV network.

If you consider that the Web deals with a great deal of multimedia content that does slow down transmission, you need to consider that on your normal ISP many uses are downloading files that are several megabytes in length. Downloading files consumes the majority of your bandwidth and has the most potential of slowing down your network.

## STATE OF THE WEB

The Web is becoming a useful tool that allows users to conduct many business transactions, read the daily news, and many other features. We live in an information age that is highly dependent on the speed at which we receive information. The newspaper has always been a great source of information; but with the rate that information changes each day, it is just not quick enough to inform us about current events.

The Web offers a continuously updated source of information that is more often than not free. Even the sites that make you pay for access do not charge an exorbitant fee and offer content that is changed constantly.

Internet Explorer can even "push" content directly to your desktop by using channels. These channels are streams of news or information that you are interested in that is sent directly to your desktop through a component of your Web browser and Windows operating system. The idea of push technology is quite simple in that you choose what information you like and that content is effortlessly delivered to your active desktop without you so much as pushing anything. In fact, even the connection to your dial-up Internet provider can be programmed to occur automatically throughout the day.

## CONCLUSION

The Web has fostered a medium that replaces the telephone, television, newspaper, and bank. You can use this medium to accomplish things 24 hours a day. The way in which it offers dynamic multimedia content is unparalleled because it is an instantaneous medium.

Multimedia is an important step for the Web to offer information in a direct, aesthetically pleasing environment. Yes, it does offer a great deal but does have an enormous potential of doing a lot more. In the years to come it will ultimately replace the telephone and the television. Who would want to talk on the telephone when the Web offers videoconferencing at a fraction of the price? Global communications can be achieved at a price that is equivalent to the monthly fee you pay your ISP. Office communication bills will decrease substantially to take advantage of the potential that the Web offers.

There is only one problem with the evolution of the Web and that is that of limited bandwidth. In the years to come you will see that ISDN, cable, and satellite modems will become very popular. However, none of these items will matter unless the bandwidth across the Internet is increased exponentially to provide for all of the multimedia content being sent across the network.

431

When the congestion of the Internet is alleviated, you will find that this network of computers known as the Internet will perform exceedingly well in a number of current and future applications.

The ability to use a low-cost medium for audio, video, and information connects people in a way that has never been done before. When people are more informed about current events, they can make more informed decisions about their business, money matters, and have more developed opinions on the state of technology.

The Web offers several resources and seems to be the epitome of all that the Internet stands for. Its versatility and capabilities makes the Web a desired medium for anything involving information, business, and communication.

As a messaging platform, its diversity is unparalleled and will only serve to grow even more to provide even more functionality in many, many more applications that will serve to enhance business productivity and communications.

# Chapter 31
# Handheld Technologies in Healthcare

*Andres Llana, Jr.*

The personal digital assistant (PDA) first made a brief appearance in 1993 when John Scully, CEO of Apple Computer, Inc., introduced the Newton. He envisioned a way simple mobile devices could be used to connect mobile users. Now, nine years after the unveiling and four years after its demise, PDA manufacturers are fulfilling Scully's vision. The Apple Computer device did not last very long. Perhaps it was the timing of this device, which lacked the capabilities that were yet to come along. PDAs did not take on their current appearance until much later when first beginning as a simple device to keep track of phone numbers and to-do lists. However, smart handheld devices are predicted to exceed 63 million units by 2004, with more than 60 percent of office workers carrying one or more mobile computers. With this, it is expected that the demand for remote systems management solutions will expand to nearly $630 million by 2005.

E-mail, perhaps, provided the impetus to expand the application of a mobile device from a basic electronic handheld address book to a capability that could independently access a distant server for personal e-mail. From this we arrived at the capability to send and receive e-mail in any number of settings. A good example would be Research In Motion and their Black-Berry software, which provides a means for private companies to establish their own wireless e-mail. Another example of software that supports e-mail in the enterprise environment would be Infowave's Wireless Business Engine. This software works with many devices, including WAP phones, handheld computers, laptops, and PDAs. It also will work in several network environments such as Cellular Digital Packet Data, GSM, General Packet Radio, TDMA, CDMA, and Mobitex, to name a few. An example of a wireless e-mail service would be SumaCom. SumaCom provides wireless e-mail service support that allows an end user to access their e-mail via a

0-8493-1498-4/03/$0.00+$1.50
© 2003 by CRC Press LLC

Web browser on their wireless device. This capability can also include WAP-enabled phones.

There are even software packages that allow mobile users to have access to Microsoft Exchange or Lotus Domino based information. The software provides access support for Palm operating systems (OS) based devices, Windows CE devices, Pocket PC devices, laptops, and RIM wireless and handheld devices. However, until recently, access to e-mail was limited to selected geographical areas, with little or no access in remote locations. This has changed as the result of the introduction of newer e-mail packages and off-Net service providers.

## PDAS TO DATE

At present, those PDAs that utilize the Palm operating system (approximately 95.8 percent) dominate the PDA market. The rest of the PDA market (approximately 4.2 percent) is shared by the remaining vendors (Compaq's H3600, HP's Jornada, and Casio's Cassiopeia). Microsoft has introduced Windows CE OS version 3.0, which supports the Pocket PC and is a contender for PDA market share. However, the attempt at imitating a desktop on a handheld has still not caught on.

The Palm OS market is shared by Palm, Inc., and Handspring, Inc., the latter being headed by developers of the original Palm product lines. It is estimated that for every five Palms sold there are two Handspring Visor PDAs sold.

## PDA CONTRIBUTIONS

PDAs have made a very strong impact in a number of application areas, not the least of which is in the medical field, where more than 85 percent of physicians use PDAs today. Palm, IBM, Handspring, and Symbol are the most popular, while Psion PDAs are popular in Europe. In a recent study by AvantGo, it was determined that 92 percent of physicians with PDAs are using their devices for multiple activities including calendars, access to drug reference guides, and reference medical journals. The study also found that 48 percent of those surveyed would like to be able to access medical reference Web sites, while 33 percent would like to write and transmit prescriptions. Another 28 percent would like to access pharmaceutical Web sites. A smaller group (27 percent) would like to be able to keep records of clinical trials. Fully 93 percent of the physicians feel that this additional information would make them more productive and allow them to provide a better level of patient care. The survey also indicated that doctors felt pharmaceutical companies would be more productive if their representatives had more immediate access to information on new drugs and clinical trial results. Coupled with ongoing technology innovations, the manufacturers of PDAs and related software products continue to make announcements of new product offerings to the medical practitioners. On the Microsoft side, the WinCE devices from Compaq/Hewlett Packard and Casio come in a PDA format. The current Pocket PC Windows CE OS is still undergoing development and does not have the level of application that the Palm PDAs have.

As a recent patient, experiencing a triple bypass operation, I was amazed at the number of doctors and physician assistants equipped with PDAs. All were very comfortable with the daily real-time use of these devices as a very important accessory as they moved between patients, operations, patient recovery reviews, and office follow-ups. There are any number of attachments to assist in extending the application of the PDA, including interface devices for measuring heart rate, EKG, and respiration.

There are more than 50 companies, with more coming into the marketplace developing mobile computing, hardware, and software for the physician end user. Of course, some of these companies are getting help from large, established companies such as IBM, Siemens, Johnson & Johnson, Eli Lilly, GlaxoSmithKline, and Bristol-Myers Squibb, to name a few. At present, a very large and growing segment of doctors have downloaded a version of ePocrates, a popular drug reference software program for handheld devices. This program allows doctors to check up on drug interactions, side effects, etc. The program is updated on a regular basis as new drugs appear or others being tested become approved. Several companies have introduced software that allows the doctor to prepare a prescription for a patient in real-time and then transmit it by fax, the Internet, or other network arrangements to an appropriate pharmacy. This makes the product a very successful tool in personal efficiency because the doctor can make the best use of available time. Doctors are now being migrated to the new handheld applications for all of their needs in a number of instances.

## CREATING THE MOBILE ENTERPRISE

Cedars-Sinai Health System is the largest nonprofit hospital in the western United States. It occupies a campus close to Beverly Hills in Los Angeles, California. The biggest business unit is the medical center's 850-bed hospital. To date, the medical center has completed four different wireless projects and is still ongoing with their applications. There is wireless access in the accident and emergency area and communal business areas. There is access from outside the hospital through the use of Palm handheld computers. Medical staff in the pediatric department use clamshell computers to access clinical systems. Much of the new medical center building will be set for wireless access, with cable being used for high bandwidth applications. Many of the patients are treated by doctors with offices outside the hospital's immediate area. This requires remote access, with the use of handheld computers being the most viable. Deploying Palm

435

VII PDAs automatically connected via BellSouth's Mobitex network provided an immediate solution for the medical center's remote users. After making a few changes to the Web-based applications, the Palm VIIs and Palm Vs worked well with the clinical applications.

At present, about 200 physicians use Palm machines to give them complete mobility with Web-based access to clinical information at any time. While they also have access to e-mail and schedules, the main clinical use is to obtain clinical information such as lab results, surgical reports, and intensive care unit and emergency room visits. Some specialists have little need for remote access while physicians taking care of very complex or very sick patients such as intensive care, cardiologists, and anesthesiologists can use their Palm PDAs to closely monitor their patients when they are away from the hospital. In another area, handheld computers in the form of the HP Jornada running the Microsoft Windows CE operating system are used and prove to be quite popular for application in the pediatric ward and clinics. They have a complete keyboard and fold into a single device that fits neatly into the pocket of a lab coat. The keyboard allows the resident to enter information about a patient, as well as look up information. At present there are over 16 machines, which are passed along to the next resident as he or she comes on duty. The trials held at Cedars-Sinai proved to be a success, with both staff and faculty enthusiastic. The clinicians love the capabilities of the new technology and want more functionality. The key is that every application tried bore positive results, making it possible to get funding to expand the application of wireless technology.

## OTHER APPLICATIONS

### ePocrates

ePocrates, is one of the largest handheld physician networks, with over 500,000 users. The network supports the ePocrates Rx clinical drug database and the ePocrates Rx Formulary. At present, there are any number of health organizations using this capability. For example, CalOptima will soon allow the physicians in their practice to download Medi-Cal drug formulary information, which can be combined with the ePocrates Rx Formulary and the ePocrates Rx clinical data. This will allow physicians point-of-care access to current drug information. This includes indication-specific dosing, adverse effects, and other drug interactions. This combination of real-time information makes it easier for physicians to check out formulary and allow for the most economical medication for a patient. Studies have shown that this type of capability reduces the amount of time physicians and pharmacies spend on the phone resolving formulary issues. Physicians using this capability have access to formulary drugs covered at lower patient co-pays, prior authorization requirements, and quantity limits. The advantage of the ePocrates Rx system is

| New ▼ ☒ | Chart | C ? OK | |
|---|---|---|---|
| Easily remember a patient, touch any section and zoom into more detail | A. Llana<br>79 yr Old Cau<br>Univ/East/<br>06:04:HospCare | 189-22-4879<br>01-09-30dob<br>05:07:01<br>Medica Yes | Customize every menu in program |
| Procedures: No lost charges | 1 Cough 786.2<br>Hypertension | ornoxi 500<br>ibupro 600 | Track admissions, chief complaint, insurance information available |
| Problems: Track patient problems Create relational reports | 06/05 H&P<br>06/06 Proced<br>06/07 Progres | 06/06 Hgb 14<br>06/07 Hct 08<br>06/07 MCV 05 | Medical information available Lab information available Access to lab results |
| Capture notes at point of thought Rapid capture of to do lists | Lab Chem Bat<br>Call Pl | Phy/Rd  Wife<br>Phy/Att Flemin<br>Rel/Spo Wife | Critical contact information available |

**Exhibit 1. Raphael PC Screen (LAN shareable with Access 97)**

that the entire system can be updated every time the physician performs an auto-update. Studies have found that physicians using the ePocrates Rx can avoid one to two adverse events per week while saving time in patient practice.

## Raphael 99

PDA Medical has been a provider of medical productivity software since 1993. Its new Raphael 99 for the Palm Organizer from 3Com offers unprecedented improvements in personnel effectiveness for medical professionals (see Exhibit 1). In 1993, PDA Medical started with a contract from a midwestern clinic in Minnesota. The first PDA application helped physicians to capture chargeable consultations. From this application came a range of applications, culminating in the now popular Raphael, which is used in over 450 major medical institutions across the United States In 1998, PDA Medical developed the Raphael, a medical productivity tool that specifically used the Palm Organizer and Microsoft's Access and SQL databases. Using synchronicity to the desktop PC and searchable outcomes with customizable reporting using a standard database, the Raphael soon became a leader in palm-sized medical software.

## WardWatch

WardWatch is a package of software designed specifically for the Palm Organizer to aid medical staff involved in ward rounds. It is designed to record investigations, medications, consultations, or other work requested by the treating physician. The results of these investigations can then be recorded on a desktop PC. The software is developed by Torlesse Systems, a small software developer in Australia. At present, WardWatch claims a worldwide user group of about 1000 users. The system begins with three basic screens: a Patients screen, a Patient View screen, and an Event Detail screen. From these screens there may be access to an Update Patient screen. The Patient View screen allows the user to go to a specific event and get more details from a related screen. The user can also tap on individual note icons for each event, from which one obtains access to additional information as may be required. The Update Patient screen allows the user to go to an unstructured notes screen for the patient to add information or transfer the patient to another Palm Organizer. WardWatch is a very powerful program and provides a basic system for tracking patients in the hospital or those who may only be outside patients. The system is easy to install and lends it self to smaller institutions.

## ONGOING DEVELOPMENT

To improve point-of-care services, numerous medical, educational, and industry developers have created an array of services aimed at servicing end users. A large array of applications, content, and electronic books has been developed for the handheld computer. More are still being developed with the aim of improving those that already exist and are in use. Electronic databases (e.g., Ovid@Hand and ePocrates) and electronic books (e.g., Griffith's Five-Minute Clinical Consult) are just a few examples of ongoing developments.

At present, university and medical centers are teaming to provide unabridged access to handheld computers, software, and related support. Many of these institutions are supported by grants that allow these institutions to supply equipment and software to members of the medical community. For example, the University of Illinois' Library of Health Sciences in Peoria provides a complete sub-library of PDA applications. They support a complete array of applications covering every aspect of medical practice. From a master list, the end user can seek specific information regarding an area of interest. For example, in the internal medicine area there are over 20 areas offering downloadable software ranging in price from $12 to $80. All of the application software is aimed at running under the Palm OS environment with reference to one or more readers or other requirements. Assuming the end user is properly configured from the point of the required operating software, he or she can download the desired software for immediate use.

## REAL-TIME SIMULATION

Medical schools are increasing the actual experience level of their students in dealing with real-life emergencies. For example, at the UCLA Medical Center, three medical students were challenged when visiting a patient who was awaiting gallbladder surgery. A patient in the adjoining area connected to a heart monitor and IV lines suddenly stopped breathing. The medical students had to figure out what to do to save the second patient. They proceeded by administering a sedative and ran a tube down the patient's throat to aid breathing. They then gave the patient fluids and epinephrine to increase blood pressure and shocked him twice with a defibrillator to restore normal heart rhythm. The patient finally regained a normal heart rate and vital signs were back to normal. The application of a simulator — a life-size, computer-controlled human patient — proved to be a valuable aid in creating a real-life situation for the medical students to gain exposure.

Medicine is information overload and PDAs are one way of dealing with this problem. Today, students are being challenged with information overload every day and are learning how to deal with the problem. The simulators enable the students to gain hands-on clinical experience sooner and without any risk to patients. The PDAs, CD-ROMs, and Web-based curriculum help the students manage and absorb an enormous amount of expanding information.

## ONGOING DEVELOPMENTS AND NEW PRODUCTS

Recently, Verizon Wireless announced the availability of Audiovox Thera. This is the first Pocket PC Phone to enter the marketplace. Basically, this device is a PDA with a phone — not the other way around. The included software is everything that is required to run a Pocket PC PDA. The phone is simple because the Thera does not come with the Pocket PC 2002 Phone Edition. A third-party dialer called Watcher is used instead. This copies phone numbers into its own directory. The end user selects a number in the directory and Watcher dials it. The phone works on CDMA 800/1900 MHz networks and can be used in hands-free mode. This device can be purchased with a two-year service contract for $800. Plus, a Micro Innovations Keyboard and JS Landscape software bring the investment to approximately $1000.

## PAYOFF IDEA

There are no longer any problems with getting started in the application of a PDA and its related software used to assist the medical practitioner. The issue is the kind of application and initial level of difficulty that the end user wishes to take on. In actual practice, there are a number of PDAs that a user may wish to consider. The price revolves around the configuration of the PDA. Initially, there are PDAs that range in price from $350 on up to $550 that would be quite adequate for a first-time user. For a more compressive PDA with telephone capability, there is the Audiovox Thera (discussed above).

Simple Palm applications can be downloaded from numerous locations across the Internet. For example, MedsPDA.com offers several PDA packages, including a DrugGuide for nurses at $49.95. This guide contains detailed, up-to-date, and practical information for 4000 trade and generic drugs. There are nearly 50 drug classifications, over 1500 drug monographs, and 475 commonly used combination drugs. This is one of the most comprehensive nursing drug guides available.

The PDA Headquarters online directory and reference service of the Library of Health Science at the University of Illinois is another source of inexpensive software for medical applications, including internal medicine, obstetrics, pediatrics, psychiatry, patient management, medical reference, and calculators. There are separate references to other related areas as well. For example, the PDA applications under medicine reference over 20 different references and guides, all of which will work on a Palm OS or Pocket PC. Some packages require special software, such as the iSilo Reader or Franklin Reader. However, all of the packages are reasonable and range in price from $12.00 to $99.00. These can be downloaded from the Internet but the end user who does not have the proper equipment or software and ISP support may elect to have the software sent via express mail. The bottom line is that PDAs are available at modest cost, as are the various software packages. End users must decide the system and software configuration that will best support their initial requirements.

## THE WAY AHEAD

The development of technology for the support of the medical field is growing by leaps and bounds. This discussion of the growth of PDAs and handheld devices is just the beginning of a continued development of technology that expands the effectiveness of medical practitioners. Since the late 1990s, we have grown from a small select group of experimenters to an almost universal application of specialized tools like the PDA to assist the medical practitioner in the delivery of a reliable practice. As we move ahead in this new century, we can expect to see an ongoing trend in the application of PDAs and similar devices to aid in the practice of medicine.

# Section IX
# Emerging Technologies

# Chapter 32

# Speech Technologies

*Gregory W. Pierce*

On January 27, 1999, Bill Gates presented the keynote address at an advanced technology symposium at Stanford University, Palo Alto, California. In that presentation, Mr. Gates stated, "Speech recognition will become a standard part of the interface to a computer system, creating an entirely new paradigm." This is indeed an impressive statement coming from the person who significantly influences the direction of the computer industry. This chapter examines the broad spectrum of speech technology as applied to medical systems.

The phrase "speech technologies" describes a broad category including multiple distinct technologies. Although speech recognition is the most commonly understood of these technologies, there are several companion technologies. This chapter provides a brief definition and clinical example of speech recognition, text-to-speech, speaker verification, and natural language processing.

## DEFINITIONS AND EXAMPLES

Speech recognition systems accept human voice as input, interpret the speech into words through complex algorithms, and generate text output, usually into a word-processing package. The classic example of speech recognition in a clinical environment is a radiologist dictating into a microcomputer-based speech recognition system that automatically generates textual reports, eliminating the need for medical transcriptionists. Speech recognition is the most dominant of the various speech technologies and occupies the majority of this chapter.

Text-to-speech systems have the ability to convert coded information from a computer system into pseudo-human speech. A typical text-to-speech application in an HMO call center could verify insurance coverage. The physician's office manager could call into the system, enter a patient member number, and hear the system speak the types of coverage, deductibles, and required co-payments. This eliminates the necessity of a customer service representative.

Speaker verification systems provide security and access control. They match the unique voiceprint of a particular individual against a predetermined database of voiceprints for all individuals authorized to access the particular computer system. In this regard they operate like fingerprints; however, the system can operate automatically over a telephone connection and does not require messy fingerprint impressions. The accuracy of these systems can reach 99.75 percent and they can be structured to overcome such common problems as a bad cold or an attempt to tamper through the use of a recording. Speaker verification in hospitals could control access to sensitive clinical information systems without requiring the use of either a physical key mechanism or a password. As the popularity of speech recognition systems grows and more microcomputers include sound cards and microphones, speaker verification systems become very attractive.

Natural language processing is one of the most exciting of the speech technologies. If the essence of speech recognition is to determine "What did I say?" then the essence of natural language processing is to determine "What did I mean?" This is an entirely different proposition! The current state-of-the-art in natural language processing requires that it be used in a very narrowly constrained information domain. The domains defined so far are areas that support the use of speech recognition. This includes the command and control of microcomputer applications, navigation through documents, and editing documents generated by speech recognition. In the context of navigating within a document the phrases "move to next paragraph," "go to next paragraph," and "jump to next paragraph" might represent three ways that people would express the same idea. All three phrases would perform equally in a well-designed natural language processing system.

## MODES OF DELIVERY

Speech technologies are also differentiated according to four modes of delivery or the context in which they occur. Direct dictation indicates that a speaker is speaking directly into a microphone connected to a computer system. Recorded speech implies the speaker is using a handheld device that records the voice onto a tape or memory chip to transfer to another computer system for interpretation later. The telephony mode requires speaking into a normal telephone handset to a distant computer for interpretation. The quality of both microphone and transmission medium varies considerably between direct dictation, recorded speech, and telephony. Direct dictation into a high-quality microphone usually yields the highest quality speech recognition. Recorded speech is somewhat less accurate and more troublesome because of the additional gadgetry and lack of immediate feedback to the user. The telephony mode produces the least accurate speech recognition because of limitations in the bandwidth of the phone system and the presence of static.

It is interesting that vendors specialize in one particular mode of delivery. IBM, Dragon Systems, and ScanSoft all originally focused on direct dictation and added recorded speech later. An entirely different set of vendors, including ALtech, Nuance, and Lucent Technologies, focused on the problem of telephony. The telephony vendors dealt with limitations of the telephone system but also typically operate within the constraints of a narrowly defined application, such as banking by phone. Telephony systems are characterized as speaker independent because they must service the entire population without requiring any training. Telephony systems require a small vocabulary as they focus on a narrowly defined business context.

The fourth and completely different mode of delivery is embedded speech systems. This mode does not even require a computer system but rather has a highly specialized microprocessor chip embedded within a consumer product. The voice dialing capabilities of many car phones are a good example of embedded speech systems. In the future we may expect to see more highly customized embedded speech systems appearing in a clinical setting. Imagine a complex surgical device that today requires the physician to use both hands for the primary usage and to tap a foot pedal to provide secondary control of the device. If the secondary control function were provided with an embedded speech system, the physician could merely speak to the device. The embedded speech system could both respond to spoken commands and speak back recorded phrases to the physician. The potential for embedded speech systems in areas requiring hands-free operation, such as the operating room, intensive care unit, or laboratory, appears great.

This completes our quick overview of the various forms of speech technologies and the modes in which those technologies operate. We will now focus on the timing of corrections, hardware and software components, and operation of speech recognition systems.

## REAL-TIME VERSUS BATCH

There are two entirely different ways to structure the processing and correction of speech recognition: real-time and batch. Real-time systems require the dictator to speak into a microphone connected to a powerful microcomputer containing the speech recognition system. The system interprets speech files and displays results on that microcomputer for correction. The dictator can either correct in the middle of the dictating or defer correction until the entire document is completed. The essence of real-time is that the dictator is the person doing the final correction. In a clinical setting, the intention of a real-time system is to eliminate the cost of a centralized medical transcription service. This makes the clinical documents available for signature and distribution more quickly and reduces costs.

Batch processing is similar to the traditional cycle of using dictation equipment to route input to a pool of centralized medical transcriptionists to be typed, proofed, and returned to the physician for signature. Batch systems route the voice files to a central processor for interpretation. The system displays results on the screen of the medical transcriptionists while replaying the voice files into their headsets so they can correct any errors. This structure is highly satisfying to the physicians because it isolates them from the vagaries and nuances of speech recognition and error correction. However, cost savings now depend on the tenuous proposition that transcriptionists or proofers can correct the results of the speech recognition much more efficiently than they can type dictation. This assumption depends on the efficiency of the transcriptionists in typing, the accuracy of the physician in using the system, and the efficiency of error correction within the system by the transcriptionists.

Vendors have taken different approaches to the question of real-time versus batch operation. Dragon Systems, IBM, and ScanSoft now support either real-time or batch operation. The Philips Speech Systems engine only operates in batch mode, although a real-time version is rumored. The vendors using the Philips MedSpeak (Philips Speech Processing, Atlanta, Georgia) engine, Dictaphone and Voice Input Technology, are strongly tied to the architecture of distributed dictation into a centralized system with medical transcriptionists. Real cost-savings seemed more difficult to achieve in the batch structure.

The best possible system will provide both real-time and batch capabilities. The batch structure may be preferable for radiologists generating high volumes of dictation or for very lengthy dictation such as history and physical reports. However, real-time capabilities are clearly indicated for the clinic notes of a primary care physician. Organizations considering speech recognition must carefully balance this question of real-time versus batch and their attendant strengths and drawbacks. Next we address the hardware and software components of speech recognition.

## COMPONENTS OF A SPEECH RECOGNITION SYSTEM

### Hardware

Effective speech recognition requires four hardware components: a powerful microcomputer, a significant amount of memory, a quality microphone to capture the input, and a sound card to convert analog signals into digital form. The newest model of the Intel Pentium IV is an excellent hardware choice because of its speed (up to 2.53 GHz), large onboard cache, and an instruction set specifically designed for speech recognition. However, as usual, software lags behind hardware and the speech recognition vendors must rewrite their software to completely optimize for the latest technology.

Laptop computers pose special problems for speech recognition because of memory limitations, fan noise, questionable integrated sound cards, limited battery power, and susceptibility to electrical noise based on the compact design. Some laptops work well; the author dictated this chapter on a Dell Latitude CPi P-II with 128 MB RAM. Users considering laptops should consult their speech recognition vendor for current recommendations.

## Memory

Memory is the second component. Although 128 MB of RAM may be sufficient, doubling the RAM will provide faster processing and better recognition accuracy. Users should also consider the memory requirements of their other office automation, clinical systems, and Internet software.

Speech recognition vendors provide the third hardware component, a headset microphone that provides basic adequate performance. Serious users will want to upgrade to a more expensive (roughly $100) microphone including features such as (1) active noise cancellation, (2) an on–off switch, (3) more rugged construction, (4) a quick disconnect cord for easy mobility, and possibly (5) stereo earphones. Users frustrated by the use of a headset microphone have several options: lapel microphones, desk-mounted microphones, handheld units, and, soon, a near-field microphone. Lapel microphones usually do not produce results equal to a headset because of their position. Desk-mounted microphones, such as the Sennheiser MD 431, produce excellent results but are relatively expensive (roughly $500). The handheld Philips SpeechMike Pro (Philips Speech Processing) resembles a standard Dictaphone mike but has the added functionality of being a trackball mouse and providing programmable function keys. However, some users have reported stress to their hands. Near-field or array microphones contain several microphone elements and are designed for placement on the keyboard or computer system. These elements accept input coming from within an arc of about 30 degrees. Eventually, vendors could include this type of microphone in all keyboards, eliminating the hassles of headsets and wires.

Two entirely different classes of microphones can meet users' requirements for mobility. The first class is a wireless microphone, available in both infrared and radio frequency versions. A knowledgeable and experienced reseller should assist you in the selection and implementations of a

447

wireless microphone system as there are many functional, security, and environmental considerations, particularly in a hospital setting. The second class of mobile solutions is digital recorders. There are many makes available, varying greatly in their design, functionality, recording time limits, file formats, and method of connection to the computer. Representative examples include the Dragon Naturally Mobile Voice-It, Olympus D1000, and other units from Sharp, Sony, and Norcom. There are serious issues of ergonomics, recognition accuracy, training, and lack of feedback to the user that require the assistance of a knowledgeable reseller. In any event, master the basics of speech recognition using a headset microphone before venturing into either of these mobile arenas.

The sound card within the microcomputer is the final hardware component necessary for speech recognition. The popular Creative Labs Sound Blaster Gold 64 works very well for speech recognition, but avoid the low-end Sound Blaster value models. Users configuring or upgrading a system might consider the low-cost Creative Labs Ensoniq AudioPCI card or the highly rated, but more expensive, Turtle Beach Montego Bay series.

## COMPONENTS OF THE SPEECH RECOGNITION SYSTEM

### Software

The various hardware components interact with the software in a complex manner. The input phase begins when the microphone passes analog speech signals to the sound card. The sound card converts analog signals to a digital form, filters both echoes and noise, and compresses the resulting signals. Next, the compressed signals are subdivided into small samples and passed to the recognition engine.

The speech recognition engine accepts the sampled speech as input and converts it into output of either text or computer commands, depending on the mode of operation. The user should understand generally how the recognition engine operates so he or she can achieve maximum efficiency. The recognition engine uses three basic files: the vocabulary, speaker profile, and language model. We will examine these components in some detail (see Exhibit 1).

Most current continuous speech recognition systems support an active vocabulary of about 60,000 words. Consumers purchase the language and version unique to their needs (i.e., American English, U.K. English, German, French, etc.). Although these consumer language models work well for the general user, they will prove severely frustrating to a physician doing clinical dictation. This is because the general vocabularies lack the precise terminology for diagnoses, procedures, clinical equipment, and medications. Replacing the consumer vocabulary with a broad medical vocabulary may satisfy the needs of a primary care physician. However,

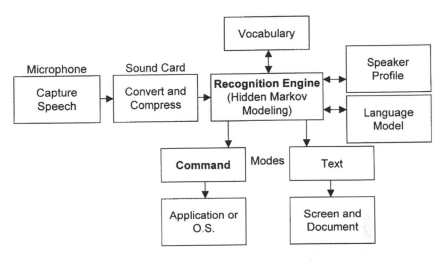

**Exhibit 1. Components Needed for Speech Recognition**

radiologists, pathologists, and many other clinical areas require more highly specialized vocabularies. The vocabulary presents a collection of phonemes, the 40 basic unique sounds in English, representing all words known to the speech recognition engine.

The speaker profile describes how a particular user pronounces specific words. The process of initial registration creates the individual speaker profile. The system prompts the speaker to read about 30 minutes of text to develop his or her unique profile. Later, the system refines the profile as the user trains the system for new words. Training involves typing and then speaking new words, such as referring physician names, into the speaker profile. Most vendor licenses allow several users to create speaker profiles on one computer. Various users may share the machine by activating their appropriate speaker profile.

The language model, sometimes called a context, is the final component used by the recognition engine. The language model contains information about the various forms of words, their pronunciation, and a statistical profile of the sequence in which various words are likely to occur. Language models boost recognition rates and increase accuracy by providing much more information than is available in just the vocabulary and speaker profile.

Creating an accurate clinical language model is a long and difficult process. The vendor must accumulate many thousands of clinical reports for the particular clinical specialty. Then they must meticulously correct any misspellings to avoid building errors and ambiguity into the language model. A sophisticated program then processes all of the cleaned files to generate the tables of word combination statistical probabilities. Vendors carefully design the vocabulary, speaker profile, and language model to work together. General medical language models are available from the major continuous speech recognition vendors: Dragon Systems, IBM, and Lernout & Hauspie. Specialty language models are also available from Voice Input Technologies, Voice Automated, and Zydoc Technologies, in addition to the major vendors. Check with the vendors for current availability and purchase the best fit for your specialty. Never attempt clinical speech recognition without an appropriate clinical language model.

The recognition engine compares strings of the sampled speech snippets against the combinations of phonemes comprising the vocabulary, searching for the best match against a particular word. Consider the phrase "blood count" broken into a string of eight snippets that sound like "b l uh duh kuh oiu n t." The recognition finds a word matching "blood" and one matching "count." It does not find a word "bloodcow" nor "ent." As the recognition engine determines multiple candidate words it compares them with both the language model and the speaker profile to determine the highest probability sequence of words. The language model reveals "blood count" as a common phrase with high probability. Hidden Markov modeling procedures perform this statistical analysis to determine the correct words.

The recognition engine operates in two separate modes: text and command. In text mode, the recognition engine converts the words into text for display on the screen, as when a physician dictates a discharge summary. In command mode, the recognition engine interprets the spoken command and passes that command to the application or the operating system, such as "FILE SAVE" or "CAPS ON." Vendors vary in their mechanisms in switching between these two modes. This simplified and generalized example shows how the major components of the system interact and their importance.

Speech recognition systems are very dynamic, having the ability to learn new words and adjust the speaker profile through the correction facility. Users must review the output of the system against their expectations and correct mistakes by highlighting the error and invoking the correction command. This displays a list of possible options in a pop-up box. Two situations result. If the correct option is listed, the user says something like "select 3" to select the third option in the list. This corrects the word and strengthens the link of word and pronunciation in the vocabulary and speaker profile. In the second situation, the correct word does not appear in the option list. For example, if using a consumer vocabulary and speaking the word nephrology, the system may suggest (1) and frolic in, (2) in a frolic in, and (3) and frolic the. The user would type the correct word and later speak the pronunciation into the training function to build this word into both the vocabulary and speaker profile.

It is extremely important for users to diligently correct mistakes so that the speaker profile does not become corrupted. With continued use and careful correction, the system will gain accuracy, becoming both more useful and less frustrating to use.

## CLINICAL DOCUMENTATION SYSTEM

The speech recognition engine is the core of the automated clinical documentation system we desire. But this system requires other technical components and architectural decisions. We will start by examining some of the basic decisions, then look at broader integration issues and conclude by reviewing workflow questions.

The central decision is whether to use the text editor capability included with the speech recognition system or to use speech recognition within a word-processing package, such as Microsoft Word or Corel WordPerfect. The major speech recognition vendors include with their program a text editor that provides most basic functions and fast performance. Unfortunately, this editor usually has limited capabilities for templates, macros, and integration with other systems. Using the speech recognition product within a word-processing package yields more powerful template and macro capabilities. Additionally, many organizations have expended considerable effort developing templates and macros using their preferred word processor. However, this approach does require more system resources and results in greater complexity.

Templates provide a set structure for a particular type of report. A history and physical report may have the organization name at the top of the page, all of the patient demographic information structured in a block in the top left, and the referring, attending, and consulting physician information in the top right corner. Macros can expand small commands into large blocks of predetermined text. The speech recognition program may have a fill-in option that allows the dictator to input patient variables. Vendors can combine these capabilities in creative ways to minimize the physician's effort and ensure comprehensive reports. Organizations should insist that their most knowledgeable and technical medical transcriptionist, the person currently developing templates and macros, receive thorough training on the speech recognition system capabilities. This person should then work closely with the vendor implementation team.

To ensure accuracy and maximize efficiency, an interface should import patient demographics and certain clinical information into the documentation system. In an inpatient setting, the interface is from the hospital information system and scheduling system; in an outpatient clinic, the interface is from the practice management system. The objective is to move information accurately and quickly into the templates and clinical reports, mini-

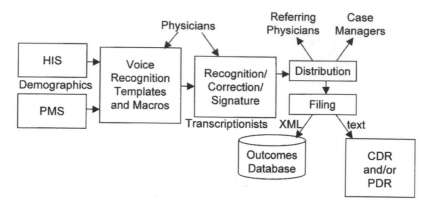

**Exhibit 2. Voice Technology Clinical Documentation System**

mizing dictation and the hassles of surnames. Refer to Exhibit 2 for the interfaces and workflows that follow.

The automated clinical documentation system also needs a database to manage the documents and track their flow. Regardless of whether we are following the real-time or batch structure, the system must manage various versions of the document: initial dictation, corrections, and the final report signed by the physician. The database manages these versions and enforces security, allowing access only to qualified individuals. In the real-time model, physicians make their own corrections at their microcomputer. In the batch model, voice files are routed to a centralized server for interpretation. Then medical transcriptionists or editors review the resulting reports and make corrections while listening to the original voice files. It is critical to the ongoing accuracy of the speech recognition system that both physicians and medical transcriptionists correct errors using the prescribed mechanism of the speech recognition system. If either party merely types in the corrections, the user profile degrades and future recognition accuracy will decline. Corrected reports return to the physician for review, signature, and distribution. An electronic signature mechanism is ideal.

Now the completed and signed report is ready for filing and distribution. The completed document may be filed in multiple systems. The word-processing document is locked down and stored within the database of the speech recognition system. Another copy is routed to the text component of the clinical data repository or computerized patient record. These outbound interfaces may follow HL-7 standards and use an interface engine. The original voice files reside on the speech recognition system for only a short time because of their size. Some vendors provide optional telephone access to the voice files similar to the first impression access provided by a digital dictation system.

Distribution of finalized reports adds significant value to the system. The ideal system would use electronic mail to reach attending physicians, consulting physicians, medical records, and QA/UR personnel, the Internet to reach case managers, and fax to reach nonconnected referring physicians. It is not obvious where this distribution capability should reside, within the speech recognition system or as a document management component of the clinical data repository or computerized patient record.

Speech recognition vendors committed to the healthcare industry quickly recognized that text reports are only part of the value of the process. Embedded within that text are discrete data fields useful to secondary processes if the system can identify, codify, and store the elements in a variety of formats. Discrete data may include diagnosis, procedures, vital signs, medications, reports of pain and mobility, and many other elements. Vendors able to extract this information will provide significant increased functionality, value, and product differentiation.

ScanSoft uses an integrated combination of clinical knowledge bases, HL-7 standards, XML, and Internet standards to provide enhanced query and reporting capabilities. Physicians can query reports across fields such as presenting illness and primary diagnosis. The system creates HL-7 transactions from extracted data fields and exports records to an outcomes database or clinical trial database. These secondary extensions to the speech recognition system provide enormous value and potential. Users should expect other vendors to add similar capabilities and should carefully examine the added value from these secondary processes. It will be interesting to observe how the marketplace rewards one additional percentage point of recognition accuracy versus the significant power of capturing coded data.

## BENEFITS

The benefits of a well-designed clinical documentation system include faster completion of clinical documentation speeds results to referring physicians. Such a system also jump-starts the coding and billing cycle and may reduce hospital stays in certain circumstances. Oliver Escher, M.D., Director, Laboratory Research, Department of Radiology, University of Texas Medical Branch, Galveston, reported a 79 percent reduction in mean turn-around time (completion of exam to availability of finalized report) for general radiology reports and a 93 percent reduction for residents in the emergency room using IBM MedSpeak (IBM Corporation, Armonk, New York).

Another benefit is reduced costs for medical transcription and the associated dictation services. Well-designed templates and macros ensure quality reports with higher accuracy because of the imported data elements. Reporting timeliness and completeness are increasingly important

453

to CMS, the Joint Commission on Accreditation of Healthcare Organizations (JCAHO), and numerous payers.

Perfectly legible documentation saves significant time for secondary caregivers referring to the record and may reduce misinterpretation and associated errors. A well-designed system provides this level of clarity.

A maximized system supports the computer-based patient record by capturing the majority of documents, eliminating a significant source of paper. It also ameliorates the impact of repetitive stress injuries and allows skilled workers to return to full productivity or partial productivity performing data entry for clinical trials, etc.

## MAXIMIZING PROJECT SUCCESS AND RECOGNITION ACCURACY

Those who have successfully implemented large technical projects in a medical environment recognize the importance of a strong clinical champion and a multidisciplinary implementation team. The strategic plan of the organization determines the clinical and information system goals and specific architecture it uses. The speech recognition project must complement those goals and architecture. The implementation team is composed of a vendor project manager, vendor support, and education personnel, and internal staff from administration, the clinical department, information systems, medical records, and transcription.

Before investing in new technology, most organizations develop a cost justification considering the costs and benefits of the project, both direct and indirect. Input from the legal department and the risk manager will clarify the benefits of legible and timely documentation. Human resources personnel can establish the current cost of workers' compensation for repetitive stress injury cases and project possible savings. Improved turnaround time is easy to quantify but more difficult to evaluate. Consider both the increasing documentation requirements of CMS and various payer organizations and the intangible but surely strategic value of moving closer to the computer-based patient record.

Reasonable and clear expectations are crucial to a successful implementation. Speech recognition technology is still evolving toward maturity and remains as much art as science. Not every physician is a good candidate for this technology, but organizations can receive significant benefits from a 90 percent implementation with ten percent outliers. Organizations should expect to provide optimized hardware and microphones, not the minimum requirements suggested in vendor literature. Even more important is an understanding of the level of effort required of users. This technology absolutely requires a considerable start-up effort, continuing diligence during its use, dedicated support staff, and continuing equipment upgrades. There are also environmental issues of noise and privacy.

Before the system is ready for use, programmers must build the inbound interfaces from the hospital information system, practice management system, and scheduling system. There are architectural questions such as whether to use the fax capability of the speech recognition system or the fax capability of existing document management or office automation systems. Questions arise concerning both document management and workflow. Programmers must build the outbound interfaces to the clinical data repository or computerized patient record and test all the interfaces.

Getting a new user started with speech recognition requires a period of registration, vocabulary building, and user training. An experienced microcomputer user can master the basics and advanced capabilities in about six to eight hours of training spread over several sessions. Your vendor or reseller will train users to dictate text, use punctuation, dictate numbers, dates and time, edit text, make corrections, and save files. Advanced topics include creating macros, creating templates, and dictating into templates. Users must learn the proper placement of the microphone and the correct enunciation of words. Although the speech recognition system adapts to the dictator, the dictator also learns the system's nuances and adjusts his or her dictation accordingly.

Ongoing support and customization begins when the system is live. It seems like an endless process of developing new templates and macros, educating new physicians and residents, troubleshooting problems, and performing required upgrades of software and hardware. The use of either handheld or wireless input devices further complicates the required training and support. The contract with the speech vendor should clearly specify the vendor's responsibility versus that of the organization. Solid support personnel should be specified in the cost justification, identified prior to implementation, and trained by the vendor during implementation.

## SELECTING VENDORS AND PILOT TESTS

We recognize speech recognition as an evolving and somewhat immature technology. The transition from discrete speech systems to continuous speech has occurred only over the past two years. So who are the players, and what are the key considerations that should guide your selection of a vendor?

In evaluating the speech recognition marketplace, it is helpful to consider four categories of vendors: top-tier, second-tier, resellers, and clinical system vendors. The four top-tier vendors, Dragon Systems, IBM, ScanSoft, and Philips Speech Systems, each produce their own recognition engine. Interestingly, only ScanSoft currently develops and markets a comprehensive speech recognition application into a hospital or large clinic environment. The other three vendors prefer to develop core technology and are represented in the application marketplace through key development and distribution partnerships. Fonix recently became Dragon Systems' premier clinical integrator by purchasing both Articulate Systems and the speech recognition division of the MRC Group. In the fall of 1998, IBM repositioned themselves in the clinical speech recognition application marketplace by transitioning their installed users of MedSpeak products over to the privately held Talk Technology, Inc. TalkStation (Talk Technology, Inc., New York City) product. Dictaphone uses the Philips recognition engine in its batch model Enterprise Express CSR (Continuous Speech Recognition) (Dictaphone Corporation, Stratford, Connecticut) product, which is strong in workflow and particularly attractive to users of Dictaphone digital dictation systems.

Many hundreds of individual resellers recognize the importance of the medical marketplace. Only a few of these have the expertise and technical depth to develop language models and full clinical applications. 21st Century Eloquence is a physician-led organization selling the Eloquent Physician (21st Century Eloquence, Palm Beach, Florida) documentation system, using either the IBM or Dragon engine and including a comprehensive database and many templates. Voice Automated develops clinical language models, sells a series of CMS-compliant templates called MedFlow (developed by Gary Flashner, M.D., Wapwallopen, Pennsylvania) and sells the Medical Desktop (Voice Automated, Huntington Beach, California) database product, based on the MedFlow templates. ZyDoc Technologies is another physician-led organization that has developed language models in 11 clinical specialties based upon the IBM ViaVoice recognition engine.

The clinical systems vendors, represented by Cerner, McKesson-HBOC, IDX, Siemens, and many others, are generally expected to offer speech recognition embedded within their product suites. A variety of small vendors of electronic medical records and practice management systems also incorporate speech recognition. Infor*Med Corporation is a physician-led organization offering the Praxis (Infor-Med Corporation, Van Nuys, California) speech recognition enabled electronic medical record. Praxis uses a unique and flexible Concept Processor instead of structured templates. The Medical Manager is also evaluating several third-party speech recognition extensions to its suite of products, which incorporate the clinical knowledge bases and templates of ScanSoft.

Obviously there is no one-size-fits-all solution to the selection of a speech recognition vendor. A reseller may be perfectly adequate for a small pilot. Second-tier players may satisfy the requirements of a small group practice or clinic. Hospitals and integrated delivery systems face an interesting choice between the first-tier players and their traditional clinical systems vendors, the usual suspects. You will want to carefully consider the following questions.

- What is the financial viability of the vendor you are considering? Are they publicly held, profitable, well-financed, etc.? How long have they been in business? These questions may be particularly acute for those moving from giant IBM to privately held Talk Technologies or those evaluating the amalgamation of Fonix.
- What is the balance of the vendor's depth in a particular clinical area versus their breadth across multiple clinical specialties? You must consider progressing from the initial pilot department across your enterprise. Has the vendor demonstrated scalability across your size of organization?
- How do the vendor's plans and architecture match your strategy for the electronic medical record?
- What are the products and plans of your existing clinical systems vendors? Do they have a speech recognition strategy? Are they open to integrating a third-party product?
- What are your existing in-house capabilities for dictation and transcription? Does this suggest a possible vendor? What are the cost and operational implications?
- Do you require real-time mode or batch mode, or must you have both options available?
- Does the proposed solution generalize to other applications? That is, can you use the speech recognition component to dictate into other applications? Is there a software development kit available to facilitate this integration? Of course, references, site visits, and all the other usual vendor selection questions impact this decision.

Selecting a department for the pilot project may involve the following considerations.

- Does the clinical specialty have a body of literature documenting effective uses of this technology?
- Does the department have clinical leadership with a track record of successfully implementing new technologies and a sincere interest in this specific technology?
- Are there strong economic or strategic benefits to implementing the technology in this department? How does this particular department fit in the clinical systems strategic plan?

## HOT ON THE HORIZON

Now we can project four exciting extensions of speech technology in clinical applications. Some of these applications are in prototype today, but others may be several years into the future.

### Item 1

Available in prototype today are several fascinating applications geared to meeting the requirements of CMS for physician documentation of evaluation and management services. CMS currently has a draft proposal that would require considerably more documentation for these common clinical services. Physician compensation depends upon which of four levels of service (problem focused, expanded problem focused, detailed, or comprehensive) they provide. The levels depend on various components in the areas of history, examination, and medical decision making. Each of the components consists of various subcomponents and the overall scoring algorithms are quite complex. The physician must provide more documentation to meet the guidelines. How can a speech recognition system help the physician?

First, the vendor structures the templates for the various evaluation and management documents to satisfy the general CMS requirements. Then they develop a real-time application to provide feedback to the physician. This application would provide a running score on the various components within the CMS grading scheme, displayed within a small window superimposed on the main dictation window. The application may track how many systems the physician has mentioned for the review of system component. It may also provide prompts for the appropriate components of the 11 separate organ system examinations. The system may provide a running score as to the level of the examination and even make suggestions regarding additional requirements.

Similar functions could operate in batch mode but are more effective in real-time. Fonix demonstrates a real-time CMS application and ScanSoft has a hybrid application with both batch and real-time components.

### Item 2

Natural language processing determines the intent of the speaker. Unfortunately, this powerful concept has been limited to very narrowly constrained domains of information such as command and control, navigation, and editing functions within a word processor. In the future, vendors will extend natural language processing to many additional domains. Consider the confusion that exists today in the names of pharmaceuticals. How might natural language processing assist in assuring the correct interpretation of drug names? Hydroxyzine is an antihistamine, while hydralizine is a similar sounding cardiac drug. If cardiac patients received hydroxyzine, they may become sleepy and breathe clearly, but their heart problem would certainly not benefit! A natural language processing system with drug awareness might compare the interpreted drug name against either the chief complaint or the diagnosis to verify the interpretation. Developers could eventually extend this concept into a complex drug order verification system by including drug–drug interaction tables, age, sex, weight, allergies, and other pieces of information.

## Item 3

Experts in speech recognition frequently emphasize that today's systems support continuous speech but not conversational speech, an important distinction. Future implementations of speech technology will achieve conversational status by incorporating speech recognition, natural language processing, and text-to-speech. Such a system would compare the results of the recognition engine against both English grammars and domain-specific natural language processing knowledge bases. If the system discovered an error or possible misinterpretation, it would formulate a clarifying question to speak back to the dictator via text-to-speech. "Did you mean hydralizine the cardiac drug, given the diagnosis of congestive heart failure?" in our previous example. Thus, man and machine enter into a natural dialogue or conversational interchange approximating that between two people. This would have a profound impact on the way in which we interact with our microcomputer!

## Item 4

Medical record coding is an intriguing application with great potential benefit but a distant horizon. Incorporating the entire ICD-9 coding table is only the beginning of the medical record coding application. An extremely powerful natural language processor is also required. Dictaphone has identified that there are 110 specific ways to express hypertension. All of the various phrases and representations must link back to hypertension and be carefully differentiated from other diagnoses. We can expect that the first medical record coding systems to appear will focus closely on a specific area, such as a radiological mammography study. We should also expect this type of system to act only as a preprocessor, augmented with knowledgeable human review, before completing the reports. Even given the limitations, the possible benefits could be enormous.

## CONCLUSION

This chapter provides a broad overview of the current and future applications of speech technologies to clinical systems. The opportunity to replace the keyboard and mouse with the spoken word as the primary computer interface presents a new opportunity for collecting clinical information. Speech technologies are poised to play an indispensable role in both capturing clinical documentation and facilitating the computer-based patient record.

# Chapter 33
# The Future of Automated Patient Identification, Bar Coding, and Smart Cards

*Chris Kavanaugh*

The average healthcare transaction is very complex. Handling payment for a simple medical procedure, for example, is quite different from the average retail transaction. The healthcare payment may be split among as many as six different entities: the guarantor, the primary insurer, the secondary insurer, in some cases the tertiary insurer, the patient, and perhaps even the state or federal government. In cases not involving payment, medical charting for example, the accuracy of the data in the transaction might be of life and death importance. This poses many unique challenges to those that seek to apply automated identification technologies to the healthcare industry. The most well-known and successful technologies to come out of the automated identification industry are bar coding and swipe cards. They have been so successful in payment applications for so long, that it is difficult to imagine improving them. But where healthcare is concerned, these technologies have only recently evolved to a point where they can offer meaningful solutions.

## BAR CODING IN THE MEDICAL LABORATORY

Nowhere is this more apparent than in the medical laboratory. Laboratories must process large volumes of tests on tissue and fluid samples, and they must accurately track each test tube, jar, cup, tissue cassette, and microscope slide. Any inaccuracy could mean a wrong diagnosis, which could lead to the death of the patient. In 1996, I was involved in a project that sought to reengineer the processes of a large cancer-testing laboratory. The extraordinary demands of this application challenged engineers in bar coding, laser marking, label printing, and adhesives.

At issue was the tracking of microscope slides and tissue cassettes. The laboratory performs hundreds of thousands of tests per year on prostate and bladder tissue. The tissue arrives at the laboratory in a cylindrical plastic container prelabeled with a patient identification number. Lab technicians take the tissue samples and place them in tiny plastic baskets called tissue cassettes. These cassettes are soaked for hours in very harsh chemicals. From the tissue cassette, the sample is very thinly sliced and placed on microscope slides that are further processed in harsh chemicals before being given to pathologists to render a diagnosis.

One of the chemicals used is xylene solvent. Xylene is a petrochemical that can also be used as a fuel for high-performance jet engines. Prior to my company's involvement, the laboratory had performed extensive tests on labels made from exotic polymers and having special adhesives, but nothing they tested was able to stand up to prolonged exposure to xylene. So lab technicians were hand-marking over 200,000 tissue cassettes and over 1,000,000 microscope slides per year with indelible ink pens. Imagine getting a degree as a lab technician only to end up writing patient identification numbers on microscope slides all day long, because you have good penmanship.

Several ideas were ruled out because of expense. The answer had to be very cheap — pennies per slide or cassette. It eventually became apparent that direct marking of bar codes with a laser was a viable solution. Currently, the best marking laser for high-resolution and high-volume marking is the neodymium-doped yttrium aluminum garnet laser (commonly abbreviated Nd-YAG and pronounced "en dee yag"). We found that using the Nd-YAG, we could mark bar codes on both slides and tissue cassettes that were consistently legible by certain very sophisticated models of bar code scanners. The method for marking these objects is far from obvious. Since clear glass is invisible to Nd-YAG light, the bar code is placed on the microscope slide by burning through an epoxy-resin-coated portion of the slide. To mark tissue cassettes, a special colorant must be added to the plastic during manufacture for the laser mark to have enough contrast for current bar code scanners to "see" it.

How these new technologies will ultimately transform the medical laboratory is subject to debate. Perhaps the cost of Nd-YAG marking lasers will drop to a level that every lab will want one of their own. Perhaps all slides and tissue cassettes will one day be premarked with unique bar codes, which laboratory systems will anticipate. Perhaps a better solution will emerge. Regardless, this illustrates how the rigorous demands of the healthcare industry make it difficult to find and integrate automated identification products from other industries. Innovation is required. In this example, one U.S. patent was issued and two others are currently pending.

## MEDICAL CARDS

Just as innovation is required to automate the medical laboratory, so it is with the basic doctor/patient encounter. As a patient moves through the U.S. healthcare system, he or she meets absurd redundancy. Each time a patient sees a new care provider, he or she must hand-write his or her basic medical history and demographic data on paper, then it is keyed into the provider's database. Insurance data is usually keyed in as well by visually copying it from the patient's insurance cards, which are usually plastic or paper and have no machine-readable features of any kind. The cost of delivering healthcare in America includes paying for clerical personnel to key in the exact same patient data dozens of times. It would be tough to create a more inefficient system. Undoubtedly the automated identification industry in 1999 can provide the tools to improve it. Why haven't they?

Much of the problem is almost certainly due to the financial disincentive that punishes medical insurers for streamlining their claims processes. Who can blame them? Why would anyone want to pay their bills more quickly than necessary when they can earn interest on the funds until they have cleared? Even if they want to, the competitive environment will not allow health insurers to take any actions that would erode their profit margin. This explains why insurance companies have not implemented the same techniques that credit card companies use for payment on a large scale. There are a few exceptions, however, where the financial disincentive does not appear to exist either because the government is the insurer or the insurer is also the care provider. In 1994, the Clinton Administration attempted to pass a Health Care Reform Act, which included a provision for a national health card. If passed, the government would have been in a position to force insurers to streamline the payment process. The measure failed, but nonetheless the desire on the part of health insurers to automate their payment processes has been rising ever since because of the increase in managed care programs.

But why stop with payment? Why not alleviate all of the redundancy? Why not have an easily accessible data file that includes insurance, medical history, emergency contacts, medications; in other words, all of the information that each one of us has to provide in every healthcare encounter? Why not put all that on a card that can be read by a PC?

The benefits of such a move might be obvious to the reader, but I cannot resist stating them anyway. By making a record accessible at every point of care, providers will no longer have to worry about patients intentionally or unintentionally withholding information relevant to their treatment. Insurers will see common costly claims mistakes like double billing, as well as most forms of insurance fraud, disappear because they will become apparent to everyone with access to the health record.

Each time the card is read into the computer, the record will be automatically reviewed with algorithms derived from disease models and treatment protocols. The PC will be able to point care providers in the direction of the most likely diagnosis for documented complaints, as well as the most proven treatment method for any disease, in seconds.

The system would also be available for writing prescriptions. It would check the medications in the record for possible dangerous interactions and allergy conflicts. It would also serve to note that prescriptions were filled. This would virtually eliminate two of the most frequent causes of health crises for the elderly.

Governments will be able to perform statistical analysis on the health records of entire populations without violating patient privacy. Databases can be built from backed up card data omitting only each patient's identity. This will enable early detection of pockets of disease. Environmental causes will be found, fostering a deeper understanding of many diseases, and doubtlessly leading to some cures. Also, the effectiveness of alternative treatment protocols can be evaluated with indisputable accuracy using information derived from the experience of the total patient population.

## SMART CARDS

The technology to do this exists and it is being used today. The *smart card* is a device that is the same size and thickness as a credit card, but it is embedded with a microcontroller chip that is capable of storing up to 32 kilobytes of reprogrammable data in an extremely secure manner.[1] They can be read and reprogrammed through devices called terminals or reader/writers, which come in an amazing variety of configurations. For the PC, there are terminals available that are built directly into a drive bay, or into a keyboard. There are some that plug into a serial port, and others that work like a 3.5-inch diskette. For laptops, there are readers/writers that work in a standard PCMCIA slot.

In Europe, the technology is a necessary part of everyday life. Cards with embedded computer chips are used in all types of payment applications, from pay phones to vending machines. You even have to use smart cards to buy concessions at many public events. In the United States, you probably do not have a smart card unless you have a GSM cellular phone or a satellite dish.

The idea of storing medical information on a smart card has been around since the late 1980s and several countries, including Germany, France, Italy, Belgium, the Czech Republic, and Slovenia, have already adopted national health smart card programs. In many other countries, in particular Ireland, Spain, the Netherlands, Norway, Finland, Sweden, Portugal, Austria, Greece, Taiwan, Korea, Hong Kong, and Japan, major projects are underway and smart cards have become central to the national strategies for the implementations of healthcare information solutions.

Most of the countries mentioned above have government-run, single-payor healthcare. A relatively small group of people has decided on behalf of the entire nation that smart cards make sense in their system. The failure of Clinton's Health Care Reform Act makes it less likely that will happen in the United States. If smart cards are going to be adopted here, it will be by one provider network at a time. Even though this eliminates much of the privacy concern that exists when the government is the card issuer (because we already trust provider networks with our medical records), it still means that adoption of medical smart cards in the United States will be a much greater challenge.

Countries that have the ability to force their healthcare industry to adopt smart cards can simply tell their populace to make them work, and not worry with the details. In the United States, however, we must develop new processes for implementing the technology so that participants are willing to undergo the change, and the financial burden of the smart card system is distributed fairly to those who benefit.

**Criticisms**

This idea has faced plenty of criticism in the United States. Critics most often focus on the expense of the smart cards themselves. They say that healthcare computing dollars are better spent on online networking than on offline smart card technology. In an offline system, if a patient loses his smart card, he has lost a vital record that must be manually reconstructed. If an online network is built to remedy this problem, or perhaps the Internet is used, so their logic goes, then the smart card becomes an unnecessary redundancy in that network.

This objection overlooks the fact that smart cards bring vital data to care providers in circumstances where there is simply no way it can be obtained from a remote database. This is certainly the case in ambulances where two-way wireless data communication is either unavailable or impractical. It is also the case in natural disasters, like earthquakes or hurricanes, where telecommunications usually fail. This means that a system that relies on retrieving patient data from a remote server will not work during the time it is needed the most. During a disaster, no one will think of smart cards as unnecessary redundancies.

Also, putting the medical record on a card gives the patient a sense of control over the information and its distribution that does not exist in alternative architectures. The patient will be present when information is added to his or her medical record. Consider a friend of mine who has a family history of colon cancer. In the past few years, research indicated that there is a genetic predisposition for colon cancer, which can be determined by DNA testing. He had the test done, but paid for it out of his pocket and did not report it to his insurance company. He did not want a positive result to be used as the basis for a denial of future coverage. Genetic testing technology has advanced so rapidly that most insurance companies still do not have a coherent policy for dealing with results. Until they do, my friend may be justified in his decision to keep them to himself. Without the sense of control that is inherent in a card-based system, my friend and the many like him would object to any effort to create a broadly accessible electronic patient record (EPR).

Furthermore, if a broadly accessible EPR system is to be of maximum benefit, it must be updated by care providers in a timely manner. This is a significant procedural change to the way that healthcare is documented today. Smart cards provide the means for patients to ensure that this is done. Without a card-based solution, this would be very awkward.

Perhaps more importantly, critics ignore the radically different requirements placed on a network whose job is to provide online access to patient records with reasonable response times versus a network whose job is to be a backup for offline patient smart cards. For example, if one wishes to back up smart card transactions from a physician's computer to a remote system, it can be done at midnight, and it is likely that no one will care if the doctor's main office phone line is tied up in the process. But if the physician's computer must be connected to a remote server during every transaction, instead of the smart card, at the very least a dedicated phone line is needed. This is bound to be a significant extra expense.

Just how compelling are the savings in communications expenses from using smart cards? Each healthcare organization will have to determine that themselves. A 1990 study conducted by Andersen Consulting in Wyoming predicted substantial long-term savings for the state, primarily from telecommunications costs, if their public health system was smart card-based. This study eventually led the government to conduct the Western Governors' Health Passport Project, a smart card pilot that is currently being rolled out to 20,000 mothers and children in public health programs in Wyoming, Nevada, and North Dakota. Since 1990, however, the available options and costs of both smart card technology and telecommunications have changed so dramatically that a new study is sorely needed.

### Smart Cards as Network Security Devices

Probably the most compelling single reason the critics of smart cards are wrong is only just becoming apparent to the computer industry. The problem is open network security. A consensus is quickly building among security experts that smart cards offer the very best combination of features for user authentication on the Internet and other open networks. Already some of the most powerful and influential hardware and software companies in the world are touting smart card technology as the key system component that will allow maximum security in the Internet applications of the next century. They have gone so far as to state that smart card readers will soon become a standard peripheral device in PCs, like the mouse or CD-ROM.

**Threats to Patient Privacy.** Few applications have the security demands of electronic medical records. Each individual's health file must be kept private from people who are not directly involved in patient care. Individuals must be confident that their medical records will not be used against them in any way. In the world of paper medical records, a security breach is limited to all the records that a person can carry. In electronic medical records, a breach could involve hundreds of thousands of records and go undetected. There are many reasons that people would go to extraordinary lengths to steal or alter medical records, and healthcare technologists must be confident that none of them have been ignored.

**Smart Cards for Strong Authentication.** Correctly applied, smart card technology can control all of these threats by serving as *security tokens*. A token is any device you possess that authenticates your identity to a network. To understand why this is necessary, one must recognize the current limitations of Internet security. With cryptography alone, users can be assured that the communications they are having over the Internet are private. However, users cannot be confident that they are communicating with the right entity. Using smart cards for this purpose is more desirable than alternative methods because it gives the user mobility. A physician using a smart card, for example, will be able to work just as securely on the healthcare network from his or her home computer, as from the office.

## STANDARDS

Healthcare organizations in the United States that are considering smart cards as part of their long-term strategy, like anyone who is first to adopt a new technology, will be very concerned about standards. No one wants to buy a smart card system that will ultimately be the Betamax of the card industry. This very problem happened to many of the first healthcare organizations that bought optical disk systems for document storage before the CD-ROM became the standard format. They were punished for being pioneers because the companies that made the optical platters went out of business and there was no one to support their systems. Ultimately, they had to pay someone to convert to standard CD-ROM, an expensive fiasco that many have not forgotten.

Hardware standards are no longer a serious risk with smart cards. The kind of smart cards used all over the world in healthcare applications are covered under International Standards Organization (ISO) 7816. ISO 7816 ensures that the chips are in the same location on the cards, and they have compatible voltage. There are two standards that ensure that smart card readers/writers are interchangeable in any healthcare application. Smart card terminals should be PC/SC compliant. PC/SC, for Personal Computer/Smart Card, is the industry-accepted standard interface for 32-bit (Windows) applications.

Any application that adheres to ISO 7816 will be able to power up and communicate with any ISO 7816 standard smart cards. Any application using PC/SC device drivers will be able to replace its terminals with any other terminal with compliant device drivers.

The one area in which standards have not emerged is in the operating system for the smart card chip. During the manufacture of a smart card chip, the instructions that tell it how to operate and allocate security and memory resources is burned in the chip using something called a ROM mask. There are probably over a hundred ROM masks in the smart card industry today. It is not likely the industry will ever agree on a single ROM mask because of the widely varying security needs that exist across applications. So the early entrant in the medical smart card arena risks having to change its code to accommodate a card with a different ROM mask, in the future, while supporting the cards they have used in the past. This is a minor software issue, which should be addressed by guaranteeing that this type of software support will always be available. Healthcare organizations need not be concerned that an early commitment to smart cards will force them to replace hardware prematurely.

Finally, healthcare organizations that are planning to integrate smart cards into their existing systems in the future (or for that matter any form of integration) will be well advised to purchase computer systems which already have the ability to import and export data using a standard interface. The standard interface for exchanging clinical data in healthcare computing is Health Level 7 (HL-7), and they can be found on the Internet at http://www.hl7.org.

**Notes**

1. This definition is woefully inadequate for any discussion of smart card technology that is not limited to the healthcare industry. The technical distinction that would be necessary in a broader discussion is that these are "micro-controller chip smart cards." I chose to avoid having to explain the distinction between these types of smart cards and others that are used in nonmedical applications because this would be unnecessarily distracting. I am confident this is the right approach because at the Health Card '97 conference in Amsterdam, with only one exception, all of the projects represented — from dozens of countries — had chosen this basic platform for developing health card systems.
2. *Washington Post*, August 16, 1997.

# Chapter 34
# Electronic Messaging in the Healthcare Industry

*Rhonda Delmater*

Healthcare reform is imminent due to a number of factors: government issues, dramatically increasing costs to employers, etc. The common objective of healthcare providers, payers, and patients is timely access to quality care in a cost-effective manner.

As is true of most American industries, such as electronic messaging, the healthcare industry has been undergoing dramatic change. The traditional focus of the messaging industry has evolved from interpersonal electronic mail to a much broader scope encompassing electronic messaging applications such as electronic commerce and workflow.

Changes in the healthcare industry may be considered even more dramatic with emphasis shifting reactive treatment of patients to proactive "wellness" programs, and payment for services changing from "fee-for-service" to "managed care" or even "capitation." Under "fee-for-service," healthcare providers submit claim forms for services rendered, and are reimbursed up to the amount considered "reasonable and customary" for the location where the service is rendered. Under "managed care," rate schedules are prenegotiated. The providers accept a smaller fee in exchange for access to the patient population covered by an employer or healthcare administrator. Under "capitation," a provider organization agrees to provide healthcare services for a monthly fee per member. In other words, if the members are healthy, the providers get to keep the fees while providing little service, but if the members are less healthy than the providers expect, they can be in a losing proposition.

Information systems in healthcare have historically been focused on the financial business of obtaining reimbursement for services rendered. Under the new paradigm, there will be increased emphasis on measuring the effectiveness of treatments, or what is commonly referred to as "outcomes measurement." This will require increased collection and dissemination of clinical information. The number of medical specialists will decrease due to cost restructuring, so it will be important to provide appropriate clinical information to caregivers, and to make the specialists as accessible as possible through the application of information technologies, such as telemedicine.

Telemedicine simply means practicing medicine across a distance. In practical application, it is often used to supplement the capabilities of the local care provider, such as a rural physician, or to provide specialty or even subspecialty consultation regarding a case. In the future, it may even be used to practice remote surgery utilizing robotics. Current telemedicine is almost exclusively based on point-to-point or dedicated network connections such as video teleconferencing, file transfer, or direct file access, and can utilize nearly any network topology. Many telemedicine applications utilize video-teleconferencing technology, while others utilize file transfer technologies, such as in teleradiology, where large binary files of diagnostic images are transmitted.

In the future, as networking capabilities continue to advance and electronic messaging networks evolve from a textual medium to an object-oriented one supporting multimedia, telemedicine may take advantage of electronic messaging to provide worldwide access to medical specialists for consultations. The referring physician could send a multimedia message including transcribed documents, video clips, portions of the patient record, dictation (audio), and so on, to whatever expert was needed for a particular case. As telemedicine becomes more commonplace, e-mail is likely to become, not only viable, but also the preferred transport vehicle for telemedicine consultations.

The current point-to-point connections support consultations by a limited, predetermined set of specialists. E-mail-based telemedicine could make a much broader field of specialists available for consultation for unusual or dramatic cases. Multimedia electronic messaging will dramatically impact healthcare delivery by transforming telemedicine from real-time point-to-point video teleconferencing, to "store-and-forward" video referrals composed of a full range of clinical information (such as diagnostic images, EKGs, voice, and video for telemedical consultations, etc.). At the same time, electronic messaging will support "administrative" requirements such as electronic commerce.

Workflow applications are also receiving increased emphasis in healthcare, for both administrative and clinical applications.

Today, most healthcare institutions provide some form of interpersonal messaging, or e-mail, for internal staff use. Many hospitals have central host-based systems based on legacy e-mail applications such as IBM PRofessional

**Exhibit 1. Administrative Transaction Set**

| | |
|---|---|
| 257 | Healthcare Eligibility/Benefit Inquiry |
| 258 | Healthcare Eligibility/Benefit Information Immediate Response |
| 270 | Healthcare Eligibility/Benefit Inquiry |
| 271 | Healthcare Eligibility/Benefit Information |
| 276 | Healthcare Claim Status Request |
| 277 | Healthcare Claim Status Notification |
| 278 | Healthcare Services Review Request |
| 279 | Healthcare Services Review Information |
| 834 | Benefits Enrollment and Maintenance |
| 835 | Healthcare Claim Payment/Advice |
| 837 | Healthcare Claim |

OFfice System (PROFS). PROFS is one of the early mainframe electronic mail systems. Most university hospitals and large provider organizations have more robust messaging capabilities with interconnection among two or more e-mail systems along with Internet access (SMTP).

The current use of Electronic Data Interchange (EDI) in healthcare is primarily to verify eligibility for benefits and to submit medical claims. However, the Workgroup for Electronic Data Interchange (WEDI) was established in November 1991 to promote the expansion of EDI in healthcare. The WEDI Board of Directors has approximately 31 members, including several large insurance companies, such as Blue Cross/Blue Shield and Kaiser Permanente; several prominent industry associations, including the American Hospital Association, the Medical Group Management Association, and the American Medical Association. Medicaid and ANSI X12 are also represented. The WEDI charter pertains exclusively to healthcare. They assert that from $8 to $20 billion could be saved in the United States by implementing only "four core" transactions, and up to $26 billion could be saved by implementing the first 11 business transactions. There are three types of healthcare transaction sets: administrative, materials management, and patient care (see Exhibits 1 through 3).

## SPECIFIC CASE

St. John Medical Center (SJMC) of Tulsa, Oklahoma, is a 750-bed acute care facility. It is comprised of multiple entities, including the Regional Medical Lab, Cardiovascular Institute, and Physicians Support Services. It a partner in an HMO with St. Francis Hospital, St. Anthony's and Mercy Hospital in Oklahoma City, and a member of the Community Care Alliance. SJMC is part of the Sisters of the Sorrowful Mothers (SSM) Ministry that has hospitals in several locations, within and outside of the United States. SJMC has earned a reputation for high-quality healthcare.

SJMC recognizes information technology as a strategic investment. Its business requires the processing of a vast amount of data and the availabil-

**Exhibit 2. Materials Management Transaction Set**

| | |
|---|---|
| 810 | Invoice |
| 812 | Credit/Debit |
| 820 | Payment Order/Remittance Advice |
| 832 | Price Sales Catalog |
| 836 | Contract Award |
| 840 | Request for Quotation |
| 843 | Response to Request for Quotation |
| 844 | Request for Rebate |
| 845 | Price Authorization (Contract Charges/Award Confirmation) |
| 846 | Inventory Inquiry/Advice |
| 849 | Response to Request for Rebate |
| 850 | Purchase Order |
| 855 | Purchase Order Acknowledgment |
| 856 | Ship Notice |
| 867 | Product Transfer/Sales Report |
| 867 | Product Transfer/Sales Report |

ity of meaningful information to support patient-care processes. It has recently completed a large project to upgrade its network infrastructure in preparation for implementing new distributed applications. As are other healthcare organizations, they are looking forward to implementing a Computer-based Patient Record (CPR); SJMC has recently implemented to provide a clinical information resource regarding its patients. SJMC is the alpha site for the MasterChart CPR.

A CPR is an information system that collects and disseminates patient data across multiple episodes of patient care, often comprised of a clinical workstation (user interface), a clinical data repository (data warehouse), a master patient index (table of patient identifiers), and an interface engine (gateway to ancillary information systems, such as admissions, laboratory, radiology, pharmacy, dictation/transcription).

SJMC has approximately 3400 employees with nearly 70 percent having electronic mail accounts. Their first-generation messaging system was a mainframe CICS-based system called Wizard Mail. CICS (Command Information Control System) is an IBM teleprocessing monitor that is widely utilized for mainframe transactions. The system has also provided e-mail accounts for affiliated organizations — Jane Phillips Hospital, Omni Medical Group, and Regional Medical Lab — from a single host.

**Exhibit 3. Patient Care Transaction Set**

| | |
|---|---|
| 274 | Request for Patient Information |
| 275 | Patient Information |

SJMC has made very effective use of e-mail as a communication medium among multiple sites within the organization. However, their information technology management recognized the gap between the capability of their mainframe-based e-mail system and what will be needed as the healthcare industry continues to experience increasing competitive pressures and the emphasis shifts from administrative to clinical information systems. It is clear that a robust electronic messaging capability, with unlimited connectivity options, will be essential for St. John Medical Center.

SJMC purchased Wizard Mail in the mid-1980s for a very small sum. The vendor is H&W Computer Systems, Inc., of Boise, Idaho. Integration products offered by the vendor include Wizard Mail Gateways for Message Handling Service (MHS) from Novell; IBM Mail Exchange, PROFS, and Office Vision from IBM; and SYSM, another e-mail system offered by H&W.

Wizard Mail is a host-based system with a character user interface that supports the following features and functions: sending mail, reading mail, directory of messages, mailing lists, filing messages, user lists, bulletin boards, calendars/scheduling, online help, ticklers, and common messages (i.e., structured "forms").

Although enterprisewide scheduling is available through Wizard Mail, utilization was predominantly at the workgroup level, with information technology (IT) making the most use of the system.

SJMC developed its own interface to accept incoming messages from both batch and online application systems for distribution to Wizard Mail users. These are primarily for notification and report distribution. There are currently more than 200 types of messages routed in this manner. Some examples are dirty room notification, error messages to computer programmers, and patient transfer. These types of notifications can continue to be routed to other e-mail systems from the Wizard Mail interface, as long as Wizard Mail and the related interfaces continue to be used.

SJMC has also been the premier site (installation number 001) for the Cerner PathNet system, which is one of the leading laboratory information systems. As such, SJMC desires the capability to send lab results and reports automatically through the e-mail network. The computing environment at SJMC includes an IBM mainframe, AS400s, RS6000s, Suns, and DEC Vaxes and Microvaxes as host computers, along with various LAN servers. Users access these hosts (or servers) through various types of terminals and both DOS and MS/Windows PCs.

Even though SJMC has a diverse computing environment, until it began its electronic messaging migration project in 1995, described below, it had a homogeneous e-mail network. SJMC skipped the generation of e-mail systems based on LAN file sharing almost entirely and went directly to client/server e-mail based on Microsoft Exchange. The driving forces behind

473

migration to the new system were file attachments in connection to Internet mail. Any of the leading LAN e-mail applications would offer similar benefits over the current mainframe e-mail system, including a graphical user interface featuring windows, icons, menus, and pointers, and the ability to attach binary objects (e.g., documents, spreadsheets, pictures, graphics) and collaborative features including shared folders.

Even though there was no connectivity to other e-mail systems implemented within SJMC or to external e-mail networks, SJMC made a significant investment in enhancing its networking infrastructure to support these and other information systems enhancements. An electronic messaging plan was developed that identified both tactical and strategic implementation activities, as described below. The planning methodology included a site survey of the medical center, a technical survey of current and announced messaging products, a survey of messaging applications in the healthcare industry, and development of a vision of future messaging applications for healthcare delivery systems.

SJMC selected Microsoft Exchange as its LAN e-mail system, based on earlier standardization on Microsoft Office. SJMC found interconnection between Wizard Mail and MS Exchange to be an essential element in supporting the migration. SJMC planned to phase out Wizard Mail entirely by the year 2000.

Another element in the SJMC messaging architecture plan was implementing external e-mail connectivity via SMTP.

The SJMC Printing Services organization currently has a limited implementation of an electronic forms package, Formflow from Delrina. SJMC has had the software for four years and has licensing for 20 "filler" users. The proposed LAN messaging implementation must support transport of the Formflow electronic forms. It is desirable for the messaging system as a whole to support e-mail routing of forms created using Formflow. Printing Services has identified four phases of electronic forms evolution:

1. Print on demand
2. Typewriter replacement
3. Intelligent forms (includes calculations)
4. Data collection (includes DBMS interface)

Of the 2800 forms used at SJMC, about 125 have been converted to electronic format using the Formflow developer package, with some forms at all phases of the evolution path. There is also interest in routing forms to physician offices and to Jane Phillips Hospital, and in support of electronic signatures.

The vision for the SJMC Messaging System is to take full advantage of the emerging technologies that will support multimedia clients. This is likely to become important in support of telemedicine as the capability emerges to support store-and-forward of video transmissions for expert consultation.

SJMC has identified the following system-level goals for e-mail:

- E-mail should be available on the users' native platform.
- Each user should be able to originate (and receive) mail from his local work platform to be routed to (from) the standard SJMC e-mail systems and to external users (via SMTP).
- Message addressing should be easy.
- Users should be able to access an accurate directory from their platform.

As the healthcare industry continues to increase emphasis on clinical applications, the electronic messaging network will be required to provide the electronic transport for many types of objects, including audio, video, graphical representations (such as EKGs), and diagnostic images. It is unknown whether a single multimedia client will emerge, but it is probable since the APIs will support a "best-of-breed" approach on a single messaging server, that there will be many special-purpose clients as well as some general-purpose client applications.

## SUMMARY

The messaging technologies and products that are rapidly becoming available, can have an exciting impact on patient care. Multimedia messaging servers and client software can support electronic delivery of a full range of clinical information (such as clinical graphics, diagnostic images, EKGs, voice, and video for telemedical consultations, etc.), as well as supporting "administrative" requirements including electronic commerce. Electronic messaging also supports "workflow" that can improve administrative and clinical processes when combined with process engineering.

The vision for healthcare is to take full advantage of the emerging technologies that will support multimedia clients. This could change the face of telemedicine from real-time point-to-point video teleconferencing consultations, to "store-and-forward" video referrals addressed to virtually any specialist for a specific consultation. The specialist may receive a compound message that includes any or all of the following types of "body parts": text, audio, video, graphical representations (such as EKGs), and diagnostic images.

The healthcare organizations that have such capability available early may well have a competitive advantage.

# Chapter 35
# Improving Information Management with Imaging

*Robert G. Gehling*
*Michael E. Whitman*
*Michael L. Gibson*

Information is the lifeblood of any organization, and timely access to this information can provide an organization with competitive advantages. Imaging technology provides not only timely access to information, but also cost savings resulting from reduced physical space and staff.

## DOCUMENT SHARING

Information technology is no longer just a means of achieving organizational strength, it now empowers individual workers within the organization to become knowledge workers. Advances in end-user computing and related application interfaces, coupled with the continuing decrease in the cost of desktop and portable computing, provide end users with access to a growing wealth of organizational information and computing power. Information technology also enables document-based information systems to become more widely distributed throughout organizations. Document processing has therefore evolved from being an isolated task to a function that has the potential of cutting across all organizational dimensions.

## WHAT IS IMAGE PROCESSING?

Image processing refers to two types of imaging technology. The oldest and still dominant form is micrographics. Micrographics uses analog photographic processes to create microfiche under computer control.

0-8493-1498-4/03/$0.00+$1.50
© 2003 by CRC Press LLC

Although this is still the most economical form of computer image processing, it does have drawbacks. Processing micrographics is slow, inflexible, difficult to integrate into a conventional data processing system, and ecologically unsound because the processing of film involves the use of toxic chemicals.

The second type of imaging technology, electronic image processing, is slowly displacing micrographics in business. Electronic image processing relies on an all-digital process to scan an image into a digitized form to be stored and manipulated electronically. Electronic image processing is more expensive than micrographics, but as the technology matures, costs related to this technology decrease. Electronic image processing is geared to applications requiring frequent online access to documents for processing transactions, updating document content, or sharing information with multiple users. In these areas, electronic image processing provides greater flexibility, better productivity, and more compact storage than either micrographics or paper files. This chapter focuses on electronic image processing.

### The Storage of Information

Whereas computer hardware has a typical life cycle of three to four years before it is changed or upgraded, and software has a life cycle of only two to three years, information or data generated or collected by most organizations tends to be retained indefinitely. The number of paper documents organizations have to store and retrieve therefore grows as time goes on. One way to control the amount of physical space needed to store paper documents is to convert them to an image-based document storage system. The advantages of converting existing paper-based document storage and retrieval systems to an image-based system include:

- The cost of the physical storage file space required for an image-based system is significantly less than the amount of space needed for a paper-based system.
- The chances of documents getting misfiled or lost in an image-based system are significantly reduced.
- The time required to refile documents in an image-based system is virtually eliminated.
- The overall integrity of the file is significantly improved. Once the documents are scanned into the image-based system, they are also entered into the system database file for future reference and retrieval.
- Documents that are recorded as images can be retrieved more easily and quickly than those from paper-based filing systems.
- Paper copies of the document images, when needed, are relatively inexpensive to generate.
- Paper copies of the document images are generally accepted as legal documents in court.

To achieve the benefits of converting from a paper-based document management system to image-based technology the organization should fully understand and plan for imaging's impact on its operation.

Without proper long-term planning, the problems that plague paper-based record-management systems also affect electronic document storage systems. These problems include inadequate storage space; cumbersome, unenforceable filing and retrieval procedures; and data indexing schemes that do not meet the needs of the organization or its end users. If the organization does not address these problems in the design and implementation processes, an improperly electronically filed document will have the same fate as an improperly filed paper document: it will become lost in the system.

## IMPLEMENTATION

Exhibit 1 lists eight questions organizations should consider before implementing an imaging system. Related technology and management issues, including the organization's communications networking capabilities, the overall impact on the end users, and changes that may occur in the overall structure of the organization, should also be addressed in planning for an imaging system process.

---

**Exhibit 1. Questions Organizations Should Ask about Imaging Technology**

1. How many fewer people will the organization need, and can the leftover staff handle new tasks (e.g., scanning and indexing of documents)?
2. What is the value of the space freed up by eliminating files? Do all the existing documents need to be converted immediately to images? Will imaging help meet the organization's record retention needs?
3. How critical to the organization's performance is the absolute reliability of document filing and retrieval?
4. Measured over the past five years, what additional investment in more staff, space, and related equipment would be needed by the organization to maintain its existing paper-based system? How do those costs compare with the cost of installing and operating an imaging system?
5. In relation to the organization's size, nature, location, and business, will an imaging system improve the organization's market position?
6. Is workflow seriously impeded because it depends on serial-based paper processes, with which only one person at a time can view a physical document? Would productivity substantially increase if several people could work simultaneously with the same electronic document?
7. Will the organization's imaging applications deliver a large return in relation to the amount spent? Is rapid processing of documents vital? Does the process involve high-volume, high-value transactions? Is the process repetitive?
8. What challenges will be faced by integrating an imaging system into the organization's existing hardware and software?

*Source:* R. Osterman, "The Investment: A $64,000-plus Question," *Imaging Magazine,* June 1992, p. 72.

Once managers decide to integrate imaging into an existing information system or to develop a new information system based on imaging technologies, they must follow a series of steps similar to a systems development life cycle. Most life cycles follow an established methodology with specific steps and the methods, tools, and techniques to be used to complete those steps. Although methodologies vary in the number of steps, most share common characteristics. A typical analysis and design methodology might contain the following steps:

- Problem definition and feasibility analysis
- Systems analysis
- Systems design and construction
- Systems implementation, conversion, and training
- Maintenance and change

### The Analysis Team

To support an imaging strategy, the analysis team must first examine existing manual or automated information processes to determine how to use the information to be imaged. This examination helps obtain a detailed understanding of how to handle, process, and store the information, and helps determine what manual or existing automated systems to supplement or replace.

A knowledgeable individual must examine the compatibility of the imaging system with current systems to determine what additional technological support will be needed. Integrating such a system involves much more than purchasing additional hardware and connecting a few cables. The capabilities of the new technology must also be studied to allow intelligent decisions on quantities and types of materials purchased. Consideration must also be given to projected expansion of the business to allow for growth. Analysis and design teams should develop a blueprint of the desired system deliverables, incorporating technical specifications on physical layout, software development, integration requirements, and overall operating parameters. This blueprint guides the transition from existing systems to the end product.

The resources necessary to make the transition from the existing system to the new system and to operate and maintain the new system must be clearly delineated, focusing on operations, maintenance, personnel, and financial resources requirements. A critical analysis of existing versus new personnel requirements can be projected and necessary steps taken to help gain or retain qualified personnel.

### Staffing

In evaluating personnel issues, the team is likely to find that the skills necessary to operate the information collection and entry facets of the new system can be easily taught to existing employees familiar with current business operations. Technologists must become familiar with the systems operations and maintenance of the new imaging technologies, however, and current IS personnel may not possess the technical skills or the aptitude to learn them, which would require hiring new employees. Employers must determine whether existing employees can be retrained or whether new employees should be hired.

One of the largest obstacles faced by organizations in planning to reengineer information and document management is how it may affect the existing organizational culture. Changes in workflow can mean changes in organizational structure, loss of some organizational loopholes, availability of more information, and changes in the proprietary nature of information.

Many organizations are either investigating the possibility of or actually downsizing their systems operations. Workflow management can aid in more effectively restructuring the organization and in maintaining an existing market share and business volume with a reduced staff. Existing loopholes and inefficiencies become evident as current processes are analyzed and eliminated during the development of integrated information systems structured around automated workflow rules. If this flatter organizational structure is too rigid and tightly structured, however, it may inhibit the ability of workers to participate and contribute to dynamic and spontaneous communications.

The amount of information available to workers continually increases, often causing information overload. Therefore, the information system must be managed with the worker in mind. Improperly managed access to information causes workers to lose their proprietary interest in the processes they use and the information they can provide.

## Physical Space

Organizations are always concerned with containing operating expenses. Extra physical space to support additional staff and storage needs may be unavailable or cost-prohibitive, so organizations may acquire additional space by converting existing space used for filing cabinets into office space or by converting existing files or processes to an image-based filing system.

One $5\frac{1}{4}$-inch optical disk can store 650M bytes of information, equivalent to 12 filing cabinets filled with paper documents, which would take up 18 square feet of floor space. Of course, the imaging equipment occupies a certain amount of floor space, but the potential exists for a significant savings in floor space needed for operations. Optical disk systems with capacities of more than 940M bytes are beginning to be put into use. As this storage technology matures, the storage capacity of each disk will continue to increase, providing additional savings in floor space.

As the number of document files retained by an organization continues to grow, the savings in floor space and costs could be significant. For example, the United Services Automobile Association (USAA), one of the leaders in the use of imaging technology, previously used 39,000 square feet of floor space for filing paper documents. After those documents were scanned and the images were stored on optical disks, only 100 square feet were needed for physical storage. According to USAA, the savings resulting from electronic filing and eliminating paper forms more than paid for the electronic imaging system.

As part of the planning process to move to document imaging, the organization must address what files need to be converted (e.g., how many years of documents) and how to perform the conversion. Document retention requirements are dictated by both internal and external forces, including federal and state reporting and retention requirements, auditor needs, legal requirements, and internal rules or practices of the organization itself. These requirements should be addressed by the organization before implementing an imaging system and, if possible, be modified or eliminated, depending on the current and projected needs of the organization.

The conversion of existing historical files to optical storage can be a long and expensive process. Simply scanning documents into a new system does not improve the overall workflow process because access to existing files are usually still structured around the old process. For extensive scanning of historical files into the imaging system, managers must determine who will be doing the actual work. Is the existing staff able to handle the work without a significant impact on its existing workload, or is it more cost-effective, and faster, to contract out the scanning to a consulting firm? This entire conversion process is not an easy task, and time should be taken to evaluate the impact of each method.

## Performance

Many organizations (e.g., banks, insurance companies, and government agencies) are inherently paper intensive. An image processing system can provide time savings through changes in workflow processes. Through image processing, workers can have faster access to documents and other information on file. Image processing also eliminates the need for document refiling because once a document is filed in an image processing system, it remains in place. This in turn significantly reduces time lost searching for misfiled documents.

As in the case of USAA, imaging potentially reduces the length of time it takes to provide information to organizational customers. Faster customer responses provide better customer relations and possible increases to business.

In some situations, it may be beneficial for more than one staff member to look at the same file at the same time. With a paper-based system — in which people are at different locations — files would have to be copied and sent. Even with fax technology, file processing takes time. For the same data stored on an imaging system, additional copies and the time needed to generate them are significantly reduced. In an imaging-based filing system, all authorized users within the organization can access the same files and documents at the same time. The only limitation is access to the equipment and the imaging system itself.

An imaging-based document storage system also reduces the potential for damaging or destroying stored documents. Once scanned, the document is permanently recorded on CD-ROM. If personnel follow proper system backup procedures, the chances of the accidental loss or destruction of the documents is virtually eliminated.

Organizations also need to evaluate the competitive advantages an imaging system provides. If competitors use such a system, have they gained advantages in the market? Is faster access to information likely to result in better services to organizational customers?

## IMAGING'S EFFECT ON BUSINESS MANAGEMENT

It should not be assumed that any one technological solution, whether a detailed change intervention or a quick-fix system, can single-handedly improve an organization's competitive position. American Airline's Sabre system, the USAA imaging system, and Citicorp's Asynchronous Transfer Mode machines, however, were all simple information transaction-processing systems that, once implemented and fully integrated, became strategic information systems.

Although the technology itself cannot entirely change the competitive strategy of an organization, an innovative perspective plus competitive determination on the part of the planning authorities can help an organization realize the potential advantages of the technology and successfully integrate it into the organization's overall strategy. Competitive advantage occurs when a firm is able to create a value for its buyers (e.g., by implementing a new technology), and the benefits of the value exceed the cost of creating it. More important than a simple competitive advantage, however, is a sustainable one — that is, if the sources of a firm's cost advantages are difficult for competitors to replicate.

Should the business decide that a new imaging system is the basis for a competitive thrust, the ground for the growth of the strategic information system vision and awareness must first be prepared. As such, senior management should affirm its belief in three principles:

1. The general purpose of the firm is to organize the use of the resources at its disposal so that it can achieve its long-term profitability and growth goals.
2. The range of possible uses of the resources at the firm's disposal is limited only by the experiences, knowledge, and imagination of its employees.
3. Entrepreneurs are responsible for identifying new productive uses of the resources at the firm's disposal.

Once ideas for such systems strategies as imaging have been generated, matching the strategy to an information systems plan is required.

As far as changes in the organization's size, nature, location, and business, imaging applications are really just complex data entry techniques, albeit powerful ones. Except for the inevitable reduction in physical storage requirements as the company moves from paper to image and the minor changes in staff requirements, impacts on organizational architecture are determined by sound internal managerial decisions.

### Changes in Document Workflow

Everyone is familiar with the old in-basket to out-basket method of document processing. As one individual reviews key materials, anyone else who needs to do likewise must either wait for the information or manufacture copies, creating an additional waste of resources. By allowing individuals to simultaneously review documents, an information-intensive organization could significantly improve workflow through imaging technology. Workflows that are slowed because of delays in document routing may be a symptom of a more serious problem and more drastic measures, such as business reengineering, may be necessary.

The primary theory behind imaging is to initially address the 20 percent of the documents that represent exceptions to the typical information flow within an organization and cause 80 percent of the work for the staff. Storing these documents as images could significantly reduce the staff time spent on this exception processing.

### Imaging's Return on Investment

Imaging's return on investment is affected by factors internal and external to the organization, the types of documents and information to be accessed, as well as direct and indirect costs and benefits. For organizational processes with paper-file intensity, imaging may be a workable solution. USAA was able to save time and money by converting its existing paper files to images.

The time required to access documents is also an important factor in considering the storage media, especially where it affects customer service.

For example, in the healthcare industry, patient files may need to be accessed quickly by different hospital departments, allowing healthcare professionals to provide better care to the patients. In addition to patient demographic data, other important information can also be maintained in each patient's imaged documents, including EKGs, x-ray images, CAT scans, and other diagnostic test results. Imaging in this environment may not only be well worth the cost, but also perhaps critical to the organization.

Calculating the break-even point and projected return on investment expected from imaging is usually done for a five-year period. Although it can be factored by many variables, users of imaging technology generally agree that a break-even point should be somewhere between the second and third year.

The overall cost of imaging technology continues to decrease, and one of the most expensive factors involved in imaging technology may be not the hardware, but the specialized database software needed to store, track, and retrieve the images scanned into the system.

Some payback calculations for implementing imaging technology may be easy to compute. Organizations that maintain certain historical information for a specific period of time should be able to determine the total number of documents and the potential growth of those files over the next few years. They should also be able to compute the costs to store the paper documents (floor space, filing cabinets or boxes, and file room staff) and then determine the cost savings of image-based document storage relative to physical paper documents.

Other factors, such as the impact on the organization's communications network, employee training, and programming development and support should also be considered, depending on the size of the implemented imaging system and the organization's existing information technology infrastructure.

### The Organization's IT Infrastructure

Before integrating an imaging system into the organization, the organization must evaluate its existing technical environment to determine whether it can support new image-based applications. A small, stand-alone imaging system used by a limited number of users may not significantly affect the organization's communications network. Imaging applications used by a wider group of people, however, may have a large impact on the organization's telecommunications network. Images are usually transmitted through networks in a compressed mode to reduce the impact of individual image transmissions on the transmission media. As the number of images flowing through the data network increases, response time experienced by end users may be reduced.

485

If more than one document image is requested at the same time by an end user, display of the first one will be delayed. While the first image is being displayed, however, the others requested will be in the process of being transmitted, which significantly reduces any perceived transmission delays. Organizational management must be aware of any potential problems such transmission delays may cause and their impact on the overall functional capabilities of the system.

**Hardware Costs.** The organization must examine how and where to scan the documents that are to be entered into the system. This is a critical point in changing the document workflow. Scanners range in price from $2000 to $10,000. The prices vary with the processing speed and image quality of the scanner. These factors, along with placement in the workflow process, must be considered carefully.

Another hardware constraint that should be addressed is end-user equipment. Most imaging applications require graphics monitors to view the images online. These monitors also range in price from $2000 to nearly $10,000. Using these monitors may require replacing some of the system access devices (e.g., terminals and microcomputers) used by the end user with equipment capable of handling image-based graphics applications.

**Security.** Organizations should also be concerned with user access to and the security of the information and documents stored in an image-based filing system. In a paper-based system, access is controlled by who has the keys to the filing cabinet or file room. It is also limited, by the very nature of the paper-based system itself, to who has actual physical possession of the paper file. In an image-based system, access security changes dramatically. End users no longer need to have physical control of the document to view it; they just need to electronically request that the system present them with an electronic image of the document or file. This situation makes it necessary to address such access security issues as:

- Who in the organization needs access to what documents?
- Do they need access to all the documents in a file?
- Will individuals outside the organization have access to the communications network that handles the transmission of the document images?

Information has value to an organization, and proper safeguards should therefore be put in place to guard against its improper use.

As the use of document imaging applications spreads throughout an organization, the potential exists for different departments or areas of the organization to implement their own imaging systems. To avoid any potential cross-system access conflicts, an organizationwide planning committee should to be established to formulate certain imaging system standards. The following basic system standards ensure that future end users needing cross-system access to image-based information do not experience compatibility problems:

- Operating system of the image server
- Graphic user interface of the image server
- Operating system of the workstation
- Graphic user interface of the workstations
- Image index file database
- Image file formats

Smaller, less mission-critical applications should be converted to imaging first to determine the best ways to convert existing files, the impact on the organization's communications network and computer hardware, modifications to the organization's workflow, and the acceptance of the system by the organization's staff. By using less mission-critical applications, any problems with the system's implementation will not have as significant an impact on the overall operation of the organization.

## A SUCCESSFUL TRANSITION TO IMAGING

### Know the Organization

To successfully replace paper-based systems with imaging technology, the selected conversion team must first gain a thorough understanding of its own internal needs and capabilities. The team can do this through first examining the information needs of the organization. This reveals where the imaging intervention is most needed, if at all. Once the team has a better feel for what information is most critical and who its users are, it must study the current information systems (IS) environment and analyze its capabilities and restrictions. This information becomes vital once technological implementation considerations are studied. Key members of the organization's IS staff can provide useful components for this analysis.

Next, the team must focus on the integration capabilities of the overall organization — that is, the technological, behavioral, and economic considerations of implementing a new technology into the corporate culture.

### Know the Technology

The best way to gain an understanding of the technology is to research it thoroughly. A detailed review of published materials on various systems and technologies enables the management team to better understand the information presented by technology vendors and manufacturers and allows them to make more intelligent choices. The team should query numerous vendors, searching for different architectures and technologies as well as prices. An examination of established systems standards provides a benchmark for comparison of the various

487

products on the market as well as those just entering the market. It is also important to find out how reliable the sales, service, and technical support aspects of the vendor are before selecting the final product. The conversion team should also take the opportunity to interview other customers of similar technologies and find out what they like and dislike about their purchases.

## DEVELOP AN IMAGING-ORIENTED METHODOLOGY

An established methodology enables the imaging conversion team to better cover all the bases in selecting the appropriate solution to the information problem. It might determine that imaging is not the perfect solution. Taking the following simple steps allows the team to better understand the situation and the desired solution:

- *Clearly define the problem and evaluate the feasibility of the proposed imaging solution.* Team members must ensure that the problem is not a symptom of a deeper problem. They should also make sure the organization has the financial ability, information technology, and corporate willingness to accept the recommendation.
- *Thoroughly analyze the information needs of the organization.* This is a useful exercise in and of itself. By better understanding the information flow, the team is better equipped to address solutions to problems in the organization.
- *Select the best imaging system based on the organization's information needs.* Once all other preceding factors have been considered, it is time to select the best candidate for the job. The least expensive or the most technically complex may not be the best for the desired operations. The team must select the system that best suits the needs of the business.
- *Pay specific attention to imaging system integration.* Technology aside, it will be difficult for the organization to move from a space-and-paper-intensive environment to digital media without some resistance from die-hard paper pushers. In addition, unless a natural disaster occurs, there will be a virtual mountain of archival materials to be sorted, destroyed, scanned, and even in an imaging environment, refiled. Some training and retraining is required as old and new personnel alike learn how to effectively operate the new system.
- *Provide an organized structure for ongoing maintenance and change.* The organization will continue to grow and change. Information technology must be capable of growing and changing with it, or old problems will resurface. An important consideration in selecting the technology is its ability to expand. As the business environment evolves, the needs of customers and suppliers change. The successful business will be one that can keep up with this evolution.

## A Role in Reengineering

Proven information management in an organization has two primary benefits. First, information management allows an organization to fulfill its organizational goals by providing timely access to appropriate information. Better information access leads to better, more timely, and more profitable business decisions. Second, information management makes information accessible to those who need it and keeps the information under control. This information is essential to the smooth operation of the organization.

As the need for information increases, the need for newer technologies becomes essential to the very survival of most information-intensive organizations. Quick and accurate access to information by workers is essential to providing higher levels of service and support to organizational customers.

Increasing costs of doing business are also a major factor in improving organizational management of documents. With proper short- and long-term planning, organizations can benefit both functionally and financially by moving to imaging-based technologies. However, if the organization acquires imaging technology for the sake of the technology and does not adequately plan for how it will affect the structure and workflow of the organization, it may not work.

Planning is the key to reengineering organizational processes using imaging technology. The executive questions listed in this chapter should be used only as a basic framework for an overall reengineering of organizational workflow processes using imaging technology. Other factors unique to the organization or industry, if they are known up front, should also be taken into consideration. Imaging can provide a strong, supportive weapon with which modern business can fight and emerge victorious in the next generation of competitive arenas.

## ACKNOWLEDGMENT

Funding for this research was partially supported by a grant from First Interstate Bank of Nevada and the Center for Business and Economics, University of Nevada, Las Vegas.

# About the Editor

Kevin Beaver is Founder and President of Principle Logic, LLC, an Atlanta, GA based information security consulting firm. He has over 14 years of experience in information technology and has spent the last eight years specializing in information security. He has served in various information technology and information security roles for several healthcare, e-commerce, financial, and educational institutions. Kevin currently specializes in HIPAA security readiness consulting and training. He is Technical Editor of the book "Network Security for Dummies" by Wiley Publishing. He is also a regular columnist for the information security portal SearchSecurity.com, and offers his information security and HIPAA advice in the "Ask the Expert" portion of their website. In addition, his work has been published on SecurityFocus.com, Computerworld.com, and in the *HIMSS Journal of Healthcare Information Management*. He also frequently teaches and speaks on information security and HIPAA security compliance at various workshops and conferences around the nation.

Kevin is Founder and Chair of the Technology Association of Georgia's Information Security Special Interest Group as well as Secretary of InfraGard Atlanta. He is active in the Southern HIPAA Administrative Regional Process (SHARP) Workgroup and Georgia Strategic Local Implementation Process (GSLIP) on HIPAA compliance. He also serves as an advisory committee member for several Georgia based university engineering and management schools. Kevin is a Certified Information Systems Security Professional (CISSP) and earned his bachelor's degree in Computer Engineering Technology from Southern Polytechnic State University and his master's degree in Management of Technology from Georgia Tech. Kevin can be reached at kbeaver@principlelogic.com.

# Index